ABOUT THE AUTHOR

Morse Peckham is Distinguished Professor of English and Comparative Literature at the University of South Carolina. Among his other books are *The Triumph of Romanticism, Beyond the Tragic Vision, Man's Rage for Chaos, Art and Pornography,* and *Victorian Revolutionaries.*

ROMANTICISM AND
BEHAVIOR

*Published in Columbia, South Carolina, during the one
hundred and seventy-fifth anniversary of the
establishment of the University of South Carolina
and the two hundredth anniversary of the
establishment of the United States of America.*

Published in Columbia, South Carolina, during the one hundred and seventy-fifth anniversary of the establishment of the University of South Carolina and the two hundredth anniversary of the establishment of the United States of America.

ROMANTICISM
AND BEHAVIOR

Collected Essays II
by MORSE PECKHAM

UNIVERSITY OF SOUTH CAROLINA PRESS
Columbia, South Carolina

Copyright © UNIVERSITY OF SOUTH CAROLINA 1976

FIRST EDITION

Published by the University of South Carolina Press,
Columbia, S.C., 1976

Manufactured in the United States of America

Library of Congress Cataloging in Publication Data

Peckham, Morse.
Romanticism and behavior.
Companion volume to the author's The triumph of
romanticism, published in 1970.
Includes index.
1. Romanticism—Addresses, essays, lectures.
2. Civilization, Modern—Addresses, essays, lectures. I. Title.
PN603.P39   809'.91'4   76-29623
ISBN 0-87249-328-8

Preface

This second collection consists of most of the papers, essays, and addresses I have written since its predecessor, *The Triumph of Romanticism* (1970). "Romanticism" and "behavior" may seem strangely associated, but they indicate my two principal interests. Many years ago I concluded that I could not comprehend Romanticism unless I had theories of language, art, cultural history, and epistemology on which I could rest some weight. My investigations into these problems led me to the conclusion that they could not be understood without a theory of behavior. With few exceptions the present essays are addressed to comprehending the character of those problems somewhat more adequately. Judging, however, by various responses to my previous collection and to several of my other books, it would perhaps be wise to point out that by "behavior" I do not mean what the academic behaviorist means. I find academic behaviorism seriously deficient in its theory. As I said in an essay on art and disorder, "The irresistible advantage and appeal of all forms of behaviorism is that the behaviorist insists that all conclusions be based on, and only on, phenomenally observable behavior. 'What is the organism doing?' the behaviorist asks, and that is the rock on which he builds his house. It is a very firm rock, though we have yet to see very much in the way of a house." (*The Triumph of Romanticism*, p. 267.) My objection to academic behaviorism is that it is not nearly behaviorist enough.

I have included after each title the year the essay was written and in a footnote, when appropriate, the occasion for which it was prepared. Thus again I express my gratitude for those who have persuaded me to speak out. Since, like all my writings, these essays are interim reports, I have made no effort to eliminate thematic repetitions and inconsistencies.

Columbia, S.C.
May 1, 1975

Contents

I THE
ROMANTIC
TRADITION

1

ROMANTICISM

AND BEHAVIOR

[1974*]

In discussing Romanticism it is still wise, I think, to begin by
making as clear as I can what I propose to talk about. The
word "Romanticism," as Lovejoy long ago pointed out, more
than most terms used in cultural history, is particularly subject
to polysemy. It is no longer very necessary to worry about the
antithesis, once so common, between Romanticism and Classicism. Some people still worry about that, and it is still not uncommon to see the two terms thus juxtaposed. But on the whole it is
now reasonably clear to most historians and other scholars that
when one uses Romanticism in an historical sense, it is quite
unnecessary to bring in classicism. This is not to say that late-
eighteenth-century Neoclassicism can be pushed out of the pic-

* Reprinted by permission from *Philosophical Exchange: The Annual
Proceedings of the Center for Philosophical Exchange*, 1, no. 5 (Summer
1974): pp. 65–83. Copyright © 1974 by the Center for Philosophical Exchange, by the State University of New York, College at Brockport, New
York.

ture when one is discussing the beginnings of Romanticism. Among literary historians, at least on this side of the Atlantic, and I think generally on the Continent, Romanticism is thought of as a more or less clearly identifiable widespread cultural redirection that begins to become observable in the course of the 1790s, though not in the sense of a self-conscious movement, such as Futurism, for example. Among art historians, however, and social and political historians and musicologists, the term continues to include historical phenomena which most literary historians no longer think of as Romantic. Social and political historians apparently continue to think of late-eighteenth-century sentimentalism, utopianism, libertarianism, and anarchism as Romantic phenomena, but to the literary historians—I think this is now generally the case—such attitudes are quite typically Enlightenment and can be traced to Enlightenment assumptions, against which Romanticism was a reaction, or, to put it more carefully, to the failure of which Romanticism was a response. Many art historians look at the matter much as do these historians, a way that to literary historians is very old-fashioned. Art historians still tend to decide the issue on fairly simple iconographic grounds. Since there are storm pictures in the last couple of decades of the eighteenth century, and since they continue to be common well into the nineteenth century, they judge both periods to be Romantic. But there are storms and storms; the significant matter is not the subject but the way it is handled and the rest of the iconographic data to be found in the picture. Architectural historians have traditionally identified Romanticism with the revival of the Gothic; thus they trace Romanticism in architecture halfway back or more into the eighteenth century. But there is a great deal of difference between building a folly or villa or fake ruin in the Gothic style and building Gothic cathedrals and railway stations. The one is private, an amusement; the other is public, central to social life. Literary historians no longer think of Gothicism or Medievalism as a defining attribute of Romanticism, the Gothic novel itself being judged as Enlightenment not Romantic. Their position is reasonably close to that of historians of philosophy, and that branch of philosophical history known as the history of ideas has, of course, been of great importance in the development of the literary notion of Romanticism. But musicologists, who for reasons I cannot fathom seem to think that cultural redirections in music occur thirty years after they occur in the other fields of art and also thought, tend to put the beginning of Romanticism about 1830. To the literary historian this is very odd. To be sure, he can grasp the early Beethoven as a typically late Enlightenment or late Neoclassic composer, but he also sees the kind of profound change overcoming Beethoven's music in the first decade of the century as the same kind of change as that which literature shows and also painting, for to him Ingres and Delacroix are equally Romantic. Indeed, Mozart's intense interest in baroque music, particularly in Bach, in the last couple of years of his life, suggests to one with the literary sense of Romanticism that had he lived he would have moved in the direction that Beethoven took—would have become a Romantic composer—so common in all the arts is the revival of the baroque in the early nineteenth century.

In the present paper I shall be using the point of view developed in the last quarter of a century by literary historians, namely, that if one examines the production of a certain few European writers—and this includes English writers as well—who were born in the years around 1770, one can discern a common pattern of cultural redirection; that that redirection was repeated and continued by more and more writers born in subsequent years; and that cultural changes since then have been, in spite of a great many changes and varieties, a continuation of that innovative culture which began to emerge in the 1790s and by 1800 is clearly identifiable. In asserting that high-level emergent culture is still Romantic I am in disagreement with a good many of my colleagues, who prefer to see Romanticism ending in the course of the 1820s. For my part I feel that the identification of certain early Romantic cultural patterns makes it impossible not to see that these same patterns still obtain, and that the problems of the early Romantics can be explained in a language which is equally appropriate today. Before identifying that pattern, however, and before relating it to a more general explanation of human behavior, it will be necessary to bring forth certain assumptions and make them as clear as I can.

I

The first of these has to do with history itself. What are we doing when we compose an historical discourse? Can it be said that we are writing about events? Historians certainly act as if they think so, and frequently they say so. But if we take the trouble to watch what they are actually doing, to observe their behavior, it is apparent that they are doing nothing of the sort. They are writing about documents and artifacts, and only if this is grasped can it be seen that historiography has in any sense a scientific character. A great deal has been written about order in history, but such efforts always remain unresolved, and for a very simple reason. The regularity and the causal relationships said to be found in history are not a feature of history itself but of historical discourses. The regularity and the causality are attributes of the verbal behavior of historians, not of historical events, which are obviously inaccessible. Though it seems reasonable enough to say that there has been what we call history, at least reasonable enough to justify historical effort, nevertheless historical events cannot be observed. All that can be observed is documents and artifacts.

This puts the historian in an awkward position and seems to deprive him of all claim to a scientific justification for his enterprise. But the picture, though gloomy enough, is not so gloomy as that. There are sufficient similarities between the behavior of the historian and the behavior of the physical scientist to give the historian at least some respectability, assuming, of course, that the activity of the physical scientist is the best model for the acquisition of what we call knowledge. I believe this to be the case, for the behavior of the physical scientist, in its pattern and its results, is the behavior of all men in their dealings with the observable and nonverbal world. The behavior of an Indian propelling his canoe through the rapids is not fundamentally different from that of the atomic physicist in his laboratory. To be sure, the behavior of the physicist is an enormous elaboration of that basic behavior of a man dealing with the world, and the most striking difference is verbal, the immensely complex verbal responses or explanations of what he has observed. But even that is but an elaboration of the simple sentence, "If you do so-and-so, such-and-such will be the consequence—probably." And such simple sentences are the verbal foundation of both canoeing and atomics. They are at what, a little carelessly, I call the empirical frontier of language.

Like the scientist, the historian is also engaged in the construction of elaborate verbal explanations. In this they are alike, but what is the historian's verbal frontier? Does he, indeed, have any? From one point of view, yes, he does. In the "If . . . then . . ." sentence above, the inclusion of "probably" is of the greatest possible importance. Only that can be explained which exhibits regularity and recurrence. The totally random is beyond explanation. Hence, for example, it is scientific doctrine that an experiment must be repeatable before anything can be done with it. Redundancy of information is the condition of scientific behavior. I myself think there is something a little dubious about this doctrine and this notion of scientific condition, but at least it does seem to be the case that any behavior can be stabilized only by repetition of that activity, and that the condition of that stabilization is redundancy of information, or, more precisely, comprehensible instructions for response. In short, though I believe it to be the case that the foundation of scientific behavior is the repeatability of experiment and observation, I would put the emphasis not on the repetition of either but on the repetition of the scientist's behavior. He accepts the reliability of an observation because he can repeat his response to the observed when he *judges* that he has encountered another instance of it. This is why innumerable repetitions of what are judged to be the same observations or the same experiments never produce absolute certainty. Hence, it is always wise to include "probably" in "If . . . then . . ." sentences, for "probability" introduces statistics, and statistics is a behavioral strategy for extracting regularity from the random. When the carpenter says to his apprentice, "You have to be careful in sawing this kind of wood, because knots can turn up at any point, and most unexpectedly," he is saying that the occurrence of knots is not random but only approximately predictable. In the same way my own guess is that the Rhine experiments in ESP reveal the limitations of contemporary statistics, a possibility that seems to me to have been insufficiently explored. For that reason we are not yet in a position to say that there is such a phenomenon as extrasensory perception, though there very well may be. I merely wish to emphasize that statistics is, after all, something that human beings do; it does not necessarily reveal the laws of the universe.

Regularity or the occurrence of the nonrandom, then, is the basis for the enterprise of scientific behavior, of which the construction of explanation is a part. In what sense can it be said that the historian is also engaged in nonrandom behavior and thus is engaged in scientific behavior? The patterned recurrence to be found in his explanatory constructs means nothing, because that is the characteristic of all explanatory constructs, including those of the wildest occultism. The question is, What kind of "If . . . then . . ." sentence can lead him beyond the empirical frontier of his explanations? It is only there that any recurrence and regularity, any nonrandomness, of scientific significance is to be found. If we pay attention to what the historian responds to, the answer is easy enough. The nonrandomness which is the occasion for the recurrence of similarity of response in the historian is the distribution on the face of the earth of documents and artifacts. Documents pertaining to English history are more probably to be found in England than in Tibet, and the probability is increased if the documents antedate the English penetration of Tibet. Or, one might say, "If you go to such-and-such a place, then you will find instances of such-and-such categories of documents and artifacts, probably." If history had never been written, this possibility of statistical control would make it possible to write it.

Does the physicist do anything more? There is at least an apparent difference. The physicist, it is affirmed, can, after he has located phenomena which he judges to be recurrent, perform experiments which verify his explanations. The historian, after all, is limited by the interpretation of the content, or meaning, of his documents and artifacts. He is involved in the hermeneutic problem. How can an interpretation be verified, except by other documents and artifacts, which, however, also are subject to exactly the same kind of hermeneutic limitation? The historian is confined to the interpretation of verbal and nonverbal man-made semiotic configurations. This, it seems, is not the limitation of the physicist. But is this actually the case? What does the physicist do? What is his behavior? Briefly, his observation, like all observation, such being the nature of perception, is selective; further, his judgment of recurrence depends upon categorization, and categorization is a human activity. He judges that two phenomenal configurations are sufficiently similar to be placed, for his purposes, in the same category. His behavior is thus conventionalized, and he too is engaged in hermeneutics, for his activity is based upon interpretation of what he has observed. His act of verification by experiment is, moreover, just as bound up with interpretation as is the historian's verification of interpretation by turning to other documents and artifacts. From this point of view, then, the historian is on as sound a footing as the physical scientist. Neither can arrive at certainty.

Nevertheless, there is a difference, one that increases greatly the degree of uncertainty as we move from the physical sciences to historiography. It is not that the scientist is involved with the present and the historian with the past, for the historian is not involved with the past. He is engaged in hermeneutic response to documents and artifacts. His chronological ordering of those documents and artifacts is itself a construct and filled with uncertainty, even though chronology is the closest the historian can ever come to certainty. Chronology is the precondition of all his activities. Furthermore, the making of artifacts is itself under verbal control. Directly or indirectly the historian is responding to verbal behavior, and moreover to verbal behavior abstracted from the situation in which it came into existence. The very survival of documents and artifacts evinces a randomness which is impenetrable, and this is a kind of randomness with which the physical scientist is not faced. Among scientists only the evolutionary theorist is exposed to the same impenetrable randomness in the survival of his observables that is the condition of the historian. For other scientists the selection of the observables is susceptible to innovation, but for the historian that selection has already taken place, and there is nothing he can do about it. This necessarily increases his uncertainty over that of the scientist.

But even this is not the gravest distinction between the two.

The scientist can modify his explanations by negative feedback. Not verification but falsification is what keeps the scientist going. The occasion of that falsification is the manipulation of the nonverbal. Such manipulation results in recategorization, reinterpretation, and innovative explanation. The historian, on the other hand, confined to the verbal or to that which is controlled by the verbal, has no such recourse. His reinterpretation of his observables does not arise from negative feedback but from modification of his explanation. Thus historiography proceeds by the discovery of new documents, by a hermeneutic which makes judgments of incoherence, and by developing new explanatory modes. But above all it proceeds by a hermeneutic assertion of the recurrence of statements or groups of statements sufficiently similar to each other to justify categorizing them as modes of the same statement, that is, by subsuming these documentary statements under a statement which, controlled by his explanation, he has generated. Thus the difference between the physical scientist and the historian is that the latter spends most of his efforts in verbal behavior, while the former is constantly engaged in a behavioral interaction with the nonartifactual world, an interaction, moreover, that, unlike that of the historian, involves a modification of his own manipulative behavior. Hence the scientist is constantly engaged in an activity like that of crossing the street in heavy traffic, while the historian rarely if ever has the occasion to modify his physical behavior. Thus the instrumental or directional character of scientific theory is fairly obvious, but the corresponding verbal constructs of the historian are far more easily hypostatized, and the normative and fictive character of those constructs far more easily ignored.

The traditional, straightforward historian is principally engaged in the construction of a narrative made up of event statements. As we have seen, his first problem is chronological; and this is certainly the basis of the cultural historian as well, but the latter asserts that he is engaged in constructing a narrative of mental events, or ideas, or the manifestation of those ideas in works of art and similar artifacts, such as, for example, instances of historical discourse. But mental events, even if there are such things, are not accessible, even at the present moment, let alone in the past. What he means by mental events are in fact statements found in documents and exemplified in nonverbal artifacts, though to be sure he often has a difficult problem in finding a statement to go with, or explain, an artifactual exemplification, a statement, moreover, which must be close enough chronologically to justify the assertion that the statement and the exemplification properly go together. For my immediate purposes I shall restrict myself to statements found in documents.

The cultural historian proceeds, then, by observing the recurrence of certain key terms and statements of an abstract or high explanatory character, and also by categorizing differing terms and statements as exemplifications of various explanatory terms and statements. The latter behavior increases the frequency of the recurrence that depends upon, and thus facilitates enormously, his activity. However, there is a difficulty here, and it is the difficulty found in the usual practice of the history of ideas. The recurrence of a term or statement, or the recurrence of his own explanatory terms which subsume somewhat different terms and statements, does not necessarily mean that the historian is justified in his procedure. The recurrence of even identical terms or statements is a consequence of the historian's act of categorial judgment, an act which is carried out by verbal behavior. How does he know that the individual who made a particular utterance—a statement or a term—would make the same judgment of categorial subsumption about his utterance that the historian makes? The fact is that the historian can be reasonably sure that the individual in question would not have made the same subsumptive judgment, and the explanation of why he would not is indeed the subject of cultural history. However, the fact that at different times different explanations are given of the same recurrent explanatory terms does not necessarily mean that the differing regressive explanations are necessarily dissimilar, though they might be. The question is whether or not such differing explanations belong to the same family of explanations. To be sure, this involves further and more regressive explanatory subsumption, and so on, in what promises to be an infinite explanatory regress. The problem, then, is to stop that regress at what, following this line of reasoning, might be called the family level. Thus, if the family is epistemological, the question is whether or not the statement or term in question properly is subsumed by an epistemological statement and if this statement can appropriately be subsumed by one of the various styles of epistemological theories available to the historian.

Even so, however, the question of family is more complex than that, for such a solution makes available only those epistemological theories available in the historian's own cultural situation, but his problem is to determine whether or not, for example, the statements and terms in question are properly subsumed under an epistemological theory no longer available. My assumption is rather that a more adequate circumscription of a family of explanations is best determined, not by the recurrence of single statements or individual terms, but by the recurrence of families of terms and statements. Yet at this point the metaphor of families begins to lose its value, because the relationship of the terms is by no means immediately apparent. "Family" must be used in a very loose sense so that the observation of the recurrence of such terms or statements must be prior to the effort to show the family relationship. On the other hand, the attempt to establish a family relationship has a dialectical relationship to the observation of the recurrence. Moreover, as I shall attempt subsequently to show in the notion of Romanticism, one can assume quarrels within the family, or even familial adoption—the effort to yoke together terms and statements which in the course of time are revealed to be incompatible. This last notion is particularly useful, for the dynamics of explanation emerges from the judgment of an incoherence and the effort to restructure the explanation so that the incoherent factor is either made coherent or is eliminated. An example may be found in the very history of the effort to define or circumscribe the notion of Romanticism, that is, by the coherent subsumption of various terms and statements under a single term, "Romanticism," or under a set of familial terms and statements themselves subsumed by the term "Romanticism." The term I have in mind is "nature." For a long time an approving attitude toward the natural world was held to be a mark of Romanticism. There was much talk about the Romantic "return to nature." Thus it came about that any pre-nineteenth-century approving attitude toward nature was judged to be Romantic. Even a great scholar, Marjorie Nicholson, was misled into thinking that since Anglo-Saxon poets indicate that there is a positive value in an approving attitude toward nature, Romanticism is peculiarly English. Gradually, however, it was judged that the eighteenth-century attitude toward nature was somehow different from the nineteenth; thus the term "pre-Romanticism" came into use. The next step was to decide, as I believe most students have now decided, that there is a striking difference between the eighteenth-century-Enlightenment attitude and nineteenth-century-Romantic attitude, although as the continued popularity of *The Seasons* indicates, the Enlightenment attitude certainly persisted, and indeed continues to persist at the present time, side by side with the very different Romantic attitude. To use the present terminology, it was concluded that the two uses of "nature" belong to quite different families of terms or statements. With this instrument of analysis it is possible to observe in Wordsworth the effort to disentangle the two ways of responding to nature and of responding to the word "nature" itself, a shift from judging that nature and the word are univalent to judging them to be ambivalent. Considering the richness of European explanatory culture by the end of the eighteenth century and the semantic shifts the terms and statements central to the culture underwent in the course of the nineteenth century, it is not surprising that the writings of people we call Romantics show considerable internal incoherence, nor that historians of Romanticism are perplexed and get strikingly different results when they attempt to construct a coherent explanation of Romanticism.

From these considerations I propose several further assumptions from which to proceed. First is that the perception or judgment of an incoherence in what has been held to be a coherent explanation is the result of some traumatic event, such as Kant's reading of Hume or the development of the French Revolution (in the judgment of at least a few of its contemporaries) into an increasingly brutalized military dictatorship. Or, to take a case from my own experience, I was so traumatized by what seemed to me the hopeless incoherence of Romantic theory in the 1920s and 1930s that I have been unable to free myself of the problem.

A second assumption is the nature of cultural stratification. Thus, at the present time a small minority of individuals in the European culture area construct explanations of some phenomena in what I judge to be the Romantic tradition. A far greater number construct explanations in the Enlightenment tradition. The youthful rebels of the 1960s made observations and explanations in the tradition of the late Enlightenment; almost all regressive justifications of their judgments and of their observations can be found in Schiller's *Kabale und Liebe*, but virtually nothing in the conclusions of Senancour's *Obermann*. Bible-belt Baptists, however, explain in a style which long antedates the Enlightenment. In any given document, moreover, various strata may appear side by side, or even in the same sentence. This is the explanation for cultural incoherence and lies behind the dynamics of the efforts to resolve that incoherence.

A third assumption is that of cultural transcendence, the recognition of an innovative style of explanation. No member of a family is necessarily innovative; rather, the family as a family, or pattern, or syndrome, is innovative. Here the cultural historian runs into further difficulties, for a cultural innovation of several hundred years ago may appear to him to be platitudinous, since he is much later in the same cultural tradition and since by his time so many of the incoherences have been eliminated. Further, with this instrument of analysis the problem of periodization can be greatly simplified. A fourth assumption is that of cultural convergence, which depends upon the observation that various individuals may arrive at a similar or virtually identical cultural transcendence without any knowledge of each other, without cultural contamination or influence or dependency.

Finally, for me none of this can be convincing unless it can be explained and justified by an explanatory system which has nothing to do with cultural history, that is, by a theory of human behavior which, though itself necessarily a part of cultural history, is not derived from cultural history, even though it may be demonstrated that it derives from the explanatory style the emergence of which and the character of which it purports to explain. I can scarcely here present a full theory of behavior, a theory which I am currently engaged in writing, but something of it will emerge in what follows. At any rate, though its ultimate explanatory regress I myself judge to be in the Romantic tradition, nevertheless it is derived not from that—at least not directly—but indirectly, at best, from an observation of human behavior controlled by certain explanatory sentences which I see as having been led to by what I call Romanticism but which are, nevertheless, very different from the Romantic beginnings.

II

I suggested above that possible alternatives to the notion of family are pattern and syndrome, and the last is particularly appealing to most intellectuals because of its Freudian associations, Freud himself being very directly in the Romantic tradition; the syndrome of his own explanations is a pseudopsychologization of much of Romantic German Idealism. However, this Freudian association does not make it appealing to me, for I find Freudian theory as intellectually unacceptable as I find contemporary academic professional behaviorism. Further, the notion of syndrome, like that of pattern, is excessively static, and both terms seem to imply an immanent or inherent coherence, a coherence far from the notion of family. For a family is always changing; a family is still a family even if some members of it are absent or have not yet appeared; and, as I suggested above, a family can include by adoption or illegitimacy members which are subsequently discovered to be alien to it, just as a family can reject various of its members—delegitimatize them, as it were, or disinherit them, assert that they do not belong and never have. Now the Romantic family, the terms which to me can subsume with considerable success most of the term- and statement-members of the family to be found in those writers and artists we call Romantic, is made up of the following, not necessarily coherent, terms (though most of them are): "explanatory collapse," "alienation," "isolation," "the antithesis of role and self," "cultural transcendence," "redemption," "anti-redemption," and "epistemological tension." To these terms I shall attempt to give a behavioral explanation.

Explanatory collapse was the traumatic experience to which over and over again Romanticism has been the emergent response, not merely around 1800 but ever since. Cultural stratification can explain how this can have been so, for an individual can move from a more historically regressive stratum of explanation to a more recent emergent stratum at any time after the newer stratum has become culturally available. Assuming that Romanticism was a break with a collapsing explanatory system, it is obvious that in the beginning the collapse affected only a tiny number of individuals in the European cultural area. By 1800 there were only a couple of dozen that we can be reasonably sure of, if that many, though judging by bits of evidence here and there, there were many more who left no record, who were neither artists nor philosophers nor theologians. The number of individuals who have had that experience has grown steadily since, a growth aided by the inroads of Romanticism into the general culture. Thus, in the course of time, the collapse has come to be precipitated in two ways; both (like the collapse of the first Romantics) autonomously and from exposure to Romantic documents and nonverbal works of art—that is, from exposure to Romantic propaganda, my position being that all art is ideologically controlled and might as well be called ideological propaganda.

Explanatory collapse is by no means an uncommon experience. Psychiatrists encounter it quite often. It can be the collapse of a fairly simple explanatory mode, one that affects only a small but crucial area of the individual's behavior and leaves other areas intact. Thus the quite common sudden appearance of sexual adventurism in an individual's life, or of heavy drinking, or the sudden and emergent pursuit of a hobby like target-shooting, or hunting, or building model railways, is often preceded by an unanticipated and unexplained or, to the individual concerned, unjustified defeat in the social hierarchy in which he earns his living—a dismissal from his job or a failure to be promoted or a transfer to a position of lesser status with his economic institution. Such an experience can be traumatic, even though on Sundays and when asked by poll takers the individual continues to be a believing Methodist. His explanatory grasp of his economic life is not perceived or judged to be in any way connected with his social trauma. If such a connection is seen, the explanatory collapse may well involve and bring down his Christian beliefs.

A similar trauma can be the collapse of erotic life, and by

eroticism I mean, not sexual behavior, but that peculiar cognition of a woman, a man, or an old shoe that invests that object with the power to elicit from the individual a total resolution of tensions, a paradisiacal state of being. Now explanation itself is a resolution of judgmental incoherence, and of the tension that judgmental incoherence elicits. I do not mean that explanation and eroticization of experience are identical, but that they are similar in their tension-resolving capacity. Explanation resolves incoherence, but eroticization eliminates it. Certainly, however, if one wishes to use such a word as "cognitive," a word I do not particularly care for, both are cognitive modes. Eroticism is thus remarkably similar to religious experience, and indeed whether we call eroticism a mode of religious apprehension, or religious apprehension a mode of eroticism, makes, so far as I am concerned, little difference. It is merely a question of which mode one prefers to use to explain the other. In any case both erotic and religious conversion, by avoiding or circumventing explanatory incoherence, are invariably described as granting to the converted an extraordinary sense of the value of their own existence, while, of course, the object of the apprehension is said to be the cause of that experience of value, and the converted describe themselves, that is, their experience of their own value, as dependent upon the object. Explanation works much the same way; the resolution of verbal incoherence, whether by what is claimed to be a logical process, or by a leap of faith (not that there is much difference), is so often described in language appropriate to religious or erotic conversion that it seems reasonable to describe it also as a mode of conversion. And like conversion, the result is the sense of the explainer's value and the ascription of value to the world, though more accurately it is an ascription of value to the hypostatized explanatory language, accompanied by the same dependence upon that language. Thus Tennyson could describe himself as having abandoned belief in all theological utterances except the proposition that the soul is immortal. Without that, he said, he could not continue to live. In the same way in popular songs the whining lover sings to a music of whines that without his beloved life is impossible. Furthermore, the more metaphysical the explanation—the more removed it is from the observable world by successive explanatory regressions—the greater the dependence upon it, for the more remote it is, the greater the number of sentences it is capable of subsuming, and the greater number of lower-level explanations it is capable of organizing. Men will die for faith, explanations, and love, including that eroticization of self known as honor. It is curious how interchangeable is the language of each of these modes of conversion; the lover feels himself redeemed by his love, the insulted man redeems his honor in a duel; a metaphysic is seen as capable of redeeming the world, though actually it can only redeem verbal behavior, and faith redeems the soul. A verbal statement of any kind of conversion, then, I shall call the redemptive mode, or more simply the redemptive, while a rejection of the validity of any kind of conversion I shall call the antiredemptive.

From this point of view explanatory collapse can be understood as a mode of deconversion, the effect of which is quite the contrary to explanatory conversion, for it is the judgment of incoherence in an explanation once seen as coherent, and the consequent loss of the power of explanations to resolve tensions and therefore the loss of value both to the verbal construct and to the deconverted himself. Religious and erotic deconversion, however, tends to have consequences strikingly different from those of explanatory deconversion. In the redemptive state of the former the attention and the interest are directed to states of being, to internal conditions, and this attention and interest are concomitants of the circumvention of explanatory incoherence. But in the explanatory deconversion the effect is to turn the interest of the deconverted outside of the state of being, and beyond language to the nonverbal world. The explanation for this is that language, like all culture, is, when considered from a behavioral point of view, directions for performance. The language of religion and of eroticism, circumventing as they do explanatory incoherence, are directions for manipulating states of being, that is, for manipulating what is inside the skin, to produce a tension-free or paradisiacal internal weather. The language of explanation, however, arises initially from the judgment of incoherence in the world outside the skin or in the world inside the skin when what is inside the skin is judged to be neither quantitatively nor qualitatively different from what lies outside of it. Explanatory language consists of directions for dealing with the world. The collapse of explanation, therefore, tends to lead to an explanation-free exploration of the nonverbal. Thus the man who has lost his job turns to sexual adventurism, Wordsworth turns to an examination of the dimensions of ponds, and the scientist whose theory has failed him turns to the random manipulation of his instruments. Erotic and religious deconversion, to be distinguished from the collapse of an explanation couched in the terms of theological rhetoric, leads to a quasi-psychotic inability to act, while explanatory deconversion leads to naïvely empirical exploration of some segment or category of the nonverbal, which can be either natural or man-made. The initial effect of Wordsworth's explanatory collapse or deconversion was a lengthy concentration upon mathematics, something he judged to be metaphysically neutral, a nonverbal set of signs free from verbal explanation.

The explanatory collapse to which Romanticism was a response was the collapse of an epistemology, though, to be sure, it was not always presented in that mode. Rather, since epistemological rhetoric is the explanatory mode most regressive from the nonverbal and nonartifactual, it can be used to subsume other manifestations, and of course virtually all of the principal Romantic figures were directly interested in epistemology. At the end of the eighteenth century two epistemological modes were culturally available, idealism and empiricism, though of course these were available in a great variety of epistemological rhetorics. Using an old-fashioned terminology, the idealistic position, the older one, the explanatory stratum first laid down, was that the categories of the subject can exhaust the attributes of the object, while the more recent one, which had gradually been emerging for several centuries, was that the categories of the object can exhaust the attributes of the subject. Preferring as I do a behavioral rhetoric, I would put the epistemological problem thus: What happens between the input of sensory data and the output of semiotic behavior, or the production of nonverbal and verbal signs? Is semiosis isomorphic with the sensory data to which it is a response? or is it not? And if it is not, how can we know whether it is or not? Or is this the wrong question? And if so, what is the right one? We do seem to be able to cross a heavily-trafficked street in the middle of a block, but then on the other hand we sometimes get run over. We can be reasonably certain, to be sure, that perception itself, of any kind, selects, simplifies, organizes, and constructs, but then on the other hand we can be equally certain that that activity is modified by perceptual experience itself. The question is, then, can the disparity or tension between sensory input and semiosis be resolved by an explanation, or not?

In these terms the older epistemology, the Platonistic-Christian tradition, asserts that the disparity can be resolved by an explanation which ascribes ultimate validity to semiosis, or the subject, while the newer empirical-Enlightenment tradition asserts that it can be resolved by an explanation which ascribes ultimate validity to the sensory input, or the object. In the course of the eighteenth century, most strikingly in Hume, skepticism reemerged, a more powerful skepticism than the ancient variety, for the issues had become much clearer. It amounted to an explanatory demonstration that empiricism, the judgment that the object determines the subject, is, after all, a judgment of the subject. It is we who say that the world determines us, not, after all, the world that says so. This was devastating, not in itself, but because the newer epistemology had emerged in response to a judgment of incoherence in the older. The new skepticism thus asserted that the newer epistemology, far from being an antithesis or correction of the old, was merely another form of it, just as the collapse of the values of the French Revolution led to perception that Revolutionary Utopianism, the illusion of Absolute Freedom, as Hegel called it, was no more than a secularization of the Christian heaven. This meant that the failure of the French Revolution, its degeneration into a brutal and militaristic dictatorship, was not merely a political failure but an epistemological failure. It was a failure of the ultimate explanatory modes of European culture. Nor was skepticism a possibility, though a good many Romantics tried it, for, as Kant and others came to realize, skepticism is itself a judgment of the subject, and in the way of skepticism lay, as once again Kant and others realized, the already impressive accomplishments of the physical sciences, or natural philosophy. Of the vast array of efforts to get out of this dilemma, to restructure one's relation to the world in response to this trauma of explanatory collapse—made crucial though not initiated by the failure of the French Revolution—it is impossible to speak here. To do so would involve, indeed, a history of nineteenth- and twentieth-century explanatory culture and its exemplification in art and science. Nevertheless, the thrust of these efforts can, I believe, be subsumed in small compass. But first it is necessary to speak of both the consequences and the great significance of that trauma of explanatory collapse.

Romantic literature is filled with wanderers. They are alienated from their society and they are isolated from contact with their fellow human beings. How can this be explained? The first important factor is what the wanderers are actually engaged in doing. Their wandering is search behavior, and this is indicated by what is judged to be a successful outcome, the consummation of the search, the arrival at a new integration, an innovative mode of redemption, though the nature of that redemption is currently the central problem of the theory of Romanticism, and to it I must return. This search character of their wandering is particularly salient in *Alastor*, for in that work there is no consummation, no goal is reached. To use what I have already presented, this wandering is the common response of explanatory collapse, and indeed sexual adventurism—as in *Don Juan*, and in Byron's and Shelley's own lives, and in the lives of a great many Continental Romantics—was commonplace enough in Romanticism, just as it is today in the lives of middle-class suburbanites who lose their jobs or suffer hierarchical humiliation, or who, having achieved the goals of their youth, are without goals. The values by which they live are no longer effective, but for the greater Romantics those values were the values of epistemological rhetoric, which explained and justified and validated all other values. Only a wandering search over the face of the earth, all of Europe, or much of Asia and America—only this search could adequately symbolize the devastation of the trauma they had experienced. Indeed, when you start counting up, it is instructive to observe how many of them were exiles from the lands of their own origin.

The explanation for this searching is that for individuals who are accustomed to having their goals determined for them by a highly regressive explanatory rhetoric—ontological and epistemological—an explanatory collapse leaves them with no resources for goal-setting and decision-making, leaves them without verbal directions for behavioral performance. Although I can scarcely justify my next step here, it is my position that the principal output of human energy goes into the limitation of the range of behavior. A goal, an interest, a purpose in life, a hobby, a faith, a drug, a scholarly problem, falling in love are all strategies for limiting the range of behavior, for placing within as narrow limits as possible the activity of decision-making, that is, freedom. Further, the more regressive the explanatory collapse, the more extensive the range of the search behavior. The ordinary sexual wanderer has the range of his wandering limited by the value-belief that sexual prowess is the perfect symbolization of aggressive adequacy, but for the Romantic—for whom explanatory collapse involved the inability to control his behavior by any of the ultimately regressive European values—the search behavior approached and sometimes arrived at a randomization of behavior, symbolized by the enormous geographical area covered by so many of the Romantic literary wanderers. The consequence is large-scale alienation. The humiliated suburbanite is scarcely able to alienate himself from his income-producing institution, but he can, with a little effort, alienate himself from his marriage. But the large-scale alien is alienated from all values, that is, from all behavior-limiting, decision-making cultural directions, or at least from those that are dependent upon high-level explanatory regression. But often enough, as the Romantic documents show, even eating and sleeping are seriously disturbed.

This leads to a complex of Romantic motives, a sub-family—to carry out the metaphor I have been using—of Romantic factors: alienation, cultural vandalism, and selfhood, or the distinction between self and role. I have been talking about the Romantic "self" for a great many years, but I have always wondered what it is that I have been talking about. If language, as I believe, is instructions for performance, and one of the performances it instructs us to do is to look for something, what does the word "self" instruct us to look for? Many years ago I judged that there

was a connection between the negative or wandering stage of
Romantic emergence and the self, but what that connection was I
could not grasp. Now I believe it to be the case that what we look
for when we judge "self" to be instructions for observation is
negational behavior, and this conclusion also explains the phenomena of alienation and cultural vandalism.

I do not use "vandalism" idly. This stage of Romanticism may
be examined today in apparently pointless vandalism by young
men and women who have been well brought up in middle-class
homes. Such vandalism, including occasionally murder, is by
no means pointless. If all behavior is adaptational, then all behavior is an attempt to control the environment for what is
judged to be the benefit of the individual. Thus all acts are aggressive. Even perception, since it is selective and structuring,
is an act of aggression, while what we call submission is concealed aggression or seduction. If you cannot control another
human being directly, you can trap him, you can disarm him by
submission. It is the standard and universal strategy at all but
the top level in any hierarchy, even in the constantly shifting
hierarchy of marriage. The consequence of this aggressiveness is
that the most explosive condition for the individual is the feeling
of helplessness, the feeling that he has no aggressive control over
his environmental situation. Of the strategies open to him—
psychotic collapse into inactivity, suicide, or symbolic aggression
—all may be found in the history of Romanticism. Symbolic
vandalism is no less real for being symbolic. I call it symbolic
because the vandalism is performed under circumstances from
which the possibilities of retaliation by others is absent. Empty
houses are splendid targets for adolescent vandalism. What vandalism produces in the individual is a powerful sense of selfhood,
of being a man, and his own man; it is that sense of sudden glory
which Hobbes called the result of the aggressive act of laughter.
"I" is opposed to "they," and not the "I" but the "they" are the
victims.

Now the typical adolescent vandal, whether he is caught or not,
ordinarily grows up to be a respectable citizen, not at all alienated.
With the Romantics it was different, for they were not vandalizing empty houses but rather the behavior-validating and -in-

structing rhetorical modes of European high culture, and the Romantics were cultural vandals, without exception. The explanatory collapse they had experienced was, after all, confined to them as—initially—individuals isolated from each other, but of course the explanation collapsed only for them, and continued in the bulk of the population to this day. That cultural vandalism, that all-encompassing negation of available high-level explanations and validations, is the behavior subsumed by the term "self" as distinguished from "role." When Julien Sorel shoots Madame de Rênal, Stendhal gives us one of the most powerful exemplifications of Romantic cultural vandalism. With this act Julien at last established his selfhood. The values and behavior of the "others" are judged to be those of individuals who have no self-consciousness, who have suffered no explanatory collapse because of their mindless inability to grasp the incoherence of their culture. They are not autonomous individuals, but players of social roles. Autonomy, therefore, is to be established by attacking those values and behaviors, by negation of their explanatory and validatory sufficiency, that is, by alienation and cultural vandalism, the strategies by which selfhood is experienced. This tension between self and role, this continuous alienation and vandalism, is of course utterly anti-erotic, and in this stage of Romantic emergence, which I long ago called Negative Romanticism, the Romantic hero is most often presented as incapable of love, incapable of resolving those tensions. Thus Julien Sorel's shooting of Madame de Rênal is an anti-erotic act, as well as an antireligious act, taking place as it does in a church. Further, his subsequent symbolic isolation in prison leads to the next member of the Romantic family.

The usual pattern of the modern humiliated individual who turns to sexual adventurism and to the cultural vandalism of his marriage is, once he has re-established the sense of selfhood by means of aggressive sexuality, to return to his marriage and his family or to begin a new one. That is, he returns, like the adolescent vandal, to the socially validated behavioral patterns of his culture, to his role. But the Romantic had dismantled European explanatory culture. Once his selfhood had been established by alienation and vandalism, it was impossible for him to redeem himself by returning to the culture; even if, like Coleridge, he returned to Christianity, it was a new Christianity that he invented himself. The truly Romantic alien could only innovate a new mode of escaping the tension of negation, autonomy, and vandalism, a tension increased by the continuous searching for a strategy to limit behavior and control decision-making. His goal thus became necessarily a culturally transcendent redemption, which was given various names—the infinite, the blue flower, and so on. Thus it became necessary to sustain and if possible to increase his wandering and searching behavior. The solution for this problem lay in isolation. Here again I must make a step which I cannot explain here but can give only the behavioral principle itself. Culturally transmitted behavior is the overwhelming mass of human behavior, but any behavior pattern, such is the character of the brain, spreads into a delta-like pattern of deviation unless it is not only transmitted but continuously maintained by the repetition of cultural instructions. This process I call semiotic redundancy, the sociocultural mechanism which sustains limitations on the range of behavior and thus channels it through time. It is not sufficient to learn a behavioral pattern; we must be told constantly to repeat it and how to repeat it. Further, the degree to which redundancy is effective depends upon the rate of interaction of the individual with other individuals. The higher the interaction rate, the better behavior is limited and channeled, and the lower the interaction rate, the greater the randomization of behavior, the effect of the delta-like spread into deviancy. However, the greater the randomization of behavior, the greater the statistical probability for the innovation of a new and fruitful mode or pattern of behavior. The scientist whose theory fails him randomizes his behavior until he strikes on something which he judges to be capable of fruitful development, and the higher the cultural level, the more frequent are social spaces for the randomization of behavior. Thus an extremely important member of the Romantic family is isolation, the steady reduction of the individual's interaction rate, the lowering of his rate of exposure to redundant cultural instructions, and the statistical increase of the probability of an innovative response to even familiar utterances and artifacts. Thus the reinterpretation of age-old utterances and artifactual signs is a constant in the Romantic tradition, a factor indeed that makes the enterprise of the cultural historian of Romanticism so perplexing and the objects of his study filled with ambiguities. Hence social isolation is extraordinarily common in Romantic documents, both imaginary and biographical. Furthermore, so long as the alienated and culturally vandalizing autonomous individual maintains a high interaction rate, his condition continues to be one of behavioral limitation. What he encounters in his wanderings consists of negative redundancy. Hence as the Romantic seeks to resolve the tension of alienation, he turns to nature, not because of the presence of nature but because of the absence of man, and Romantic documents become increasingly full of instructions to reject familiar responses to stimulus configurations and to continue rejecting them until a fresh response occurs. The point is that a fresh, or completely deviant, response may possibly be exploited to produce a culturally transcendent mode of redemption from the tension of alienation and vandalism.

Before proceeding to the final members of the Romantic family it is worth pausing to emphasize the historical importance of what I have called Romanticism's negative phase. The preconditions of adaptationally and culturally fruitful innovation are explanatory collapse, alienation, autonomy, vandalism, low rate of interaction, and randomization of behavior. The cultural establishment of this discovery and its cultural preservation through literary and other documentary redundancy, as well as artifactual redundancy, was possibly the most important innovation for which Romanticism was responsible. Its importance lies in the fact that any society, any large-scale complex of interrelated behavioral patterns maintained by redundancy and high interaction, is adaptationally inadequate to the degree its energy is chiefly expended on limiting the range of behavior to validated modes and patterns of behavior. This is the price of its survival. Nevertheless its survival also depends upon adaptationally appropriate innovative modifications of such patterns, that is, upon cultural transcendence. Until Romanticism only the socially stabilizing mode of survival had been socioculturally organized and established in explanation and experientially. Romanticism, as the consequence of a uniquely severe explanatory trauma, discovered the second principle of social survival, which has always been in existence of course, but which, before Romanticism, had not been socioculturally organized and established. This is one of the two reasons I have for judging that we still live in the Romantic period, or rather, that a small but highly important segment of explanatory culture and its exemplification in art is Romantic and has not been transcended, though it has appeared in innumerable forms and in an enormous variety of metamorphoses. The second reason for this judgment is the character of the redemptive modes the Romantic tradition has innovated, and above all the internal incoherence of those modes, which has given the Romantic tradition its extraordinary dynamism, its high rate of cultural change.

For the Romantic, then, whose explanatory collapse was severe and traumatic, there was no return. Radical explanatory innovation was the only possibility, and even though he might reject explanation and turn to an experiential or nonverbal mode of fusion of subject and object—a mode that, following the model of Kant, became known as the aesthetic mode of apprehension—still even that was explained and justified in language, in verbal behavior. As I have suggested, nonverbal redemptive response is not significantly different from verbal. Both are modes of reducing or eliminating the tension between subject and object, between sensory input and semiotic response. Further, this kind of aesthetic response can be culturally maintained either by language or by observation and imitation of behavioral paradigms, as in Oriental religious institutions and traditions. For Romanticism, however, lacking such institutions, the establishment and propagation of this aesthetic ideology depended upon verbal redundancy. Though it was not a response to verbal explanation, nevertheless it was a response to verbal explanation as instructions for a particular mode of behavior. Hence throughout the history of Romanticism to the present there has been considerable confusion and difficulty, since it is exceedingly difficult, for all but a few temperaments, to experience such a response with the help of only verbal directions and to be certain one has indeed had the experience the language has directed one to have. Further, once the ineffable and indescribable experience has been attained, the temptation to explain it and justify it verbally is so powerful it becomes or is judged to be a necessity, since it was a negation of non-Romantic explanatory traditions, still omnipresent in the culture. As a response to an explanatory collapse, it required an explanatory justification. Otherwise it could not negate those non-Romantic traditions. Thus it is reasonable to put the principal emphasis on emergent or innovative Romantic explanations, the explanatory cultural transcendence of Romanticism.

In Blake's remark that he must create his own system or be subject to another man's and in his mythological poems, it is apparent that innovative explanation maintains the sense of selfhood, a perpetuation necessary for cultural transcendence and to sustain the sense of selfhood in the face of what it negates in the culture, which is almost everything of an explanatory character. Yet Blake's effort is a very primitive example of such transcendence, for his elaborate mythology was little more than the exemplification of a neo-Platonic and Hermetic redemptive explanation, regressive to the sixteenth century. It was a mythologically concealed return to an already existent and available mode of verbal redemption. Consequently the tendency in the study of Romanticism in the past few decades to take Blake as a model Romantic has been responsible for a serious distortion of Romanticism and for an emphasis upon the Romantic innovation of redemptive explanations. One group of Romantics, right up to the present, has responded to explanatory collapse by generating innovative explanations. But another group and another tradition has done something quite different. The two traditions, the incoherence between which has been the source of the extraordinary innovative dynamism of the Romantic tradition, can be presented in the form of two questions: one, "Redemptive explanations having failed, what new redemptive explanation can I create?"; the other, "Redemptive explanations having failed, how can I create an antiredemptive explanation, an anti-explanatory explanation?" One asks, "What new explanation will suffice?" The other, "Why do men create explanations?"

The first question and the answers to it were controlled by the overwhelmingly powerful European, and indeed human, tradition, emerging at least since the beginning of the Neolithic and probably before, that the human goal is properly redemption and that its highest verbal goal is properly a redemptive explanation: in short, Paradise. This resulted in what is often called the apocalyptic Romantic tradition, and the identification of Romanticism with the search for the apocalyptic, a search which is after all quite easily satisfied, has given us only one part, and that the more historically regressive part, of Romanticism. After all, the overwhelming part of human culture is aimed at the reduction of tension, and in particular the reduction (such is the nature of language and the rest of semiotic behavior) of epistemological and ontological tension—its reduction and ideally its elimination. Thus it is not surprising that redemptive or apocalyptic Romanticism should have occurred, nor is it any more surprising that scholars, subject to the enormous cultural innovations and disturbances of the twentieth century, should respond by an interest in it. The scholarly and critical interest in apocalyptic Romanticism, especially during the sociocultural disturbances of the 1960s, is itself a redemptive response, a repetition, since the dominating high culture of the United States is almost pure Enlightenment, of what the apocalyptic Romantics themselves underwent. But this repetition also explains the intense interest in the mythological modes of Romantic apocalypticism. In early human history— so far as we can understand it at all on the basis of pitifully few records, themselves involving dreadful hermeneutic problems— mythology was most likely the first stage of an explanatory regress from the observable. I think Comte was probably right in that. However, modern mythology, aware that it is mythology, is an effort to resolve the inadequacy of abstract explanation by masking it in exemplary language. This accounts I think for the notes of hysteria and sentimentality so often found in the writing of those scholars who insist that the heart of Romanticism is a mythology of apocalyptic redemption. For the real issue of the explanatory collapse of Platonistic-Christian idealism, of Baconian-Enlightenment empiricism, and of skepticism itself at the end of the eighteenth century is that explanation itself collapsed. Hence the question, Why do men create explanations?

The first great answer was Hegel's, although Senancour anticipated much of what was to come, as did Schiller in his last period. To Hegel the category of Being is empty. An explanation of Being is not derived from Being but is the Geist's, that is, culture's response to Being. The validity of that response must rest upon the Absolute; but when, at the end of the *Phenomenology*, the Absolute is achieved, it turns out to be as empty a category as Being. The only thing to do is to go back to Being and start all over again, though this time with the Spirit's conscious awareness of what it is doing. Men create explanations because explanation is the condition of their existence, but even so it is only an instrument for sustaining that existence. An explanation is to be found only in the acceptance of the impossibility of redemption. There is no resolution of the tension of subject and object, of the tension between sensory stimulus and semiotic response. A splendid modern example of this position is to be found in Wallace Stevens' "The Well-Dressed Man with a Beard." After a marvelous evocation of tension resolution, of Paradise, of affirmation following upon negation, he suddenly breaks off and writes, "It can never be satisfied, the mind, never." An explanation is a supreme fiction. When we weary of the imagination, we turn to the *necessary* angel, reality.

I would not deny that apocalyptic Romanticism, redemptive Romanticism, explanatory Romanticism, was indeed Romanticism, but rather I would assert that it was the historically regressive mode of Romanticism, responding to explanatory collapse by innovating culturally transcendent explanations. And I would also assert that compared with antiredemptive, anti-explanatory Romanticism it was relatively superficial, for in contrast this subtler Romanticism recognized that the explanatory collapse which was the cultural trauma that precipitated Romanticism was the collapse of explanation itself. It was the fundamental incoherence of these two modes of Romantic response to cultural trauma that has been responsible for the astonishing culturally innovative dynamism of high explanatory culture and its artistic exemplification for the past 180 years. For nearly two centuries various modes of redemption have been innovated, most of which still remain with us: social redemption, as with the various forms of socialism as well as Marxism; erotic redemption; scientific redemption; redemption by means of art; redemption by means of sex, the most widespread mode today, since it has the greatest potential for popular appeal and even has sacred texts, the monthly issues of *Playboy*; redemption through Oriental mysticism; redemption by means of drugs; even redemption by means of radical reinterpretations of the rhetoric of Christian theology, as with Coleridge and many others. However, avant-garde artists today are busily engaged in a self-conscious destruction of art, but art can scarcely be destroyed, since it is an adaptational strategy. Rather, what they are engaged in destroying is what remains the most potent redemptive mode for the redemptively inclined members of high culture, the redemptive notion of art. Art having been used as a fortress from which to negate the adequacy both of the traditional mode of redemption and of the nineteenth- and twentieth-century innovative modes of redemption, that fortress can itself be destroyed. As this happens, I think we will see in the scholarship of Romanticism a turning away from the still fashionable limitation of Romanticism to its relatively superficial apocalyptic or redemptive mode, and a turning toward its more penetrating tradition, the anti-explanatory, the antiredemptive, the refusal to accept any consolation for the irresolvable tension of human existence.

2

THE FUNCTION OF

HISTORY IN NINETEENTH-CENTURY

EUROPEAN CULTURE

[1971*]

Early in Eça de Queiroz's comic and satirical novel *The Illustrious House of Ramirez* is a passage which illuminates brightly the function of history in nineteenth-century Europe:

A colleague of his . . . had founded a magazine called *The Fatherland*, "with the lofty intention" (the prospectus sonorously affirmed) "of reawakening, not only among the academic youth but throughout the country, from Cape Sileiro to Cape Santa Maria, the dying love of the beauty and grandeur and glories of Portugal!" Devoured by this idea, "his Idea," and feeling that here lay his career, almost his mission, Castanheiro incessantly and with the stubborn ardour of an apostle, proclaimed throughout the taverns in Sofia Street, through the cloisters of the University, in his friends' rooms amid cigarette smoke, "the necessity, *caramba!* of reviving tradition! of clearing Portugal, *caramba!* of the deluge of foreign matter inundating it! . . . [His aim was to] reawaken a consciousness of our heroism in this disheartened nation."

* Prepared for an international seminar on history, held in Venice in April 1971. Reprinted by permission from *Survey* 17, no. 3 (Summer 1971): 31–36. Copyright © 1971 by the Oxford University Press.

Writing in the 1890s, Eça de Queiroz clearly regards such am-
bitions as absurd and, as he later indicates, old-fashioned, something properly belonging to the 1840s.

Inspired by Castanheiro, the novel's hero sets out to write an
historical novel, and Eça de Queiroz shows very well who was
the most popular disseminator of historicism in the nineteenth
century, and who more than anyone else was responsible for
that dissemination—Sir Walter Scott—just as in the passage
quoted above the capitalization of "Idea" suggests the great
philosophical historicizer, Hegel. The link between nationalism
and historicism is perfectly obvious in both Scott and Hegel,
and that link certainly is to be found in *The Illustrious House of
Ramirez*, in which the author is particularly concerned with the
transition from historicism to parliamentarianism by way of a
self-seeking political corruption. That theme is suggested in the
phrase "here lay his career, almost his mission." Nevertheless,
nationalism and historicism are not necessarily linked. Indeed,
the link may have been something of an accident. It is not with
the nationalistic use of historicism that I am concerned here, but
with something quite different. A hint may be found in the
phrase, "the necessity of reviving tradition, of clearing Portugal
of the deluge of foreign matter inundating it."

There is no denying the nationalistic emphasis here, nor would
I suggest that that emphasis is other than the most reasonable
primary interpretation of the passage. If, however, we put
aside the nationalism and examine the passage at a more remote
level of explanation, an interesting pattern emerges. The phrases
to be abstracted for a nonnationalistic interpretation are "reviving tradition" and "clearing X of foreign matter." At a still
more remote level of explanation, the two ideas here are "the
restoration of X's true character" and, connected with that, "the
purification of X of alien attributes." Applying these formulas
to historicism divorced from nationalism, one can interpret the
function of nineteenth-century historicism as redeeming by restoration and purification whatever is subjected to historical
explanation. The pattern that now emerges is "redemption by history" or, more properly, "redemption by historicizing."

Whenever a pattern of redemption is encountered in secularized European culture, the reasonable assumption is that a secular pattern has emerged from a Christian pattern. The temptation to reduce the secular pattern to the Christian pattern may very well be a wise temptation to succumb to. It is not quite enough to cry "Reductionism!" If no new factor has been added in the pattern, it may very well be that the innovative pattern is indeed nothing but the original pattern in which the terms have been changed but the structure remains unaltered. I believe this can be said, for example, of Marx in the 1840s and probably throughout his intellectual career. For "God created Man, who sinned, and as a necessary consequence of that sin, given the nature of God, God sent His Son to redeem Man from sin," it is no perversion to substitute, "History created Society, which sinned in producing Capitalism, and as a necessary consequence of sinful Capitalism, History will send the Proletariat to redeem Man from Capitalism." The identity of the two patterns is made more probable by pointing out that both Christianity and Marxism promised an ideal world after redemption—the one in heaven, the other on earth—the State or Satan (the instrument of man's sin) or Capitalism having withered away. In the sect of Universalism, even Satan is to be redeemed. In the same way, Marxist rhetoric is not merely an analytic rhetoric—whether of historiography or economics—but a rhetoric which ascribes evil, even intentional evil, to its object.

However, the mere presence of redemptionism in a secular pattern that has succeeded a Christian pattern is not necessarily sufficient to justify a reduction of the innovative secularism to a traditional Christianity. "Redemption" is certainly a concept of considerable vagueness, but, however vague, it is not exclusively Christian. Though it is doubtful if it can be said with sureness that it is a human universal—to be found in all cultures —it is common enough outside of Christianity to make it possible to assert that in secularized Western culture a pattern that includes redemption may exclude Christianity. The basic pattern of Marxism, however, appears to me to be such that it adds nothing to the patterns of Christianity, its departure from which involved little more than substitution of terms. (I would not deny that that pattern enabled Marx to make a great many acute and valuable propositions.) On the other hand, the pattern of "redemption by historicizing" can conceivably be so far from the patterns of Christianity that reductionism to Christianity is a temptation properly to be resisted.

Christianity is, of course, a religion of history, in that it hinges on two unique historical events, the Revelation and the Incarnation, but it is by no means to be identified with "redemption by historicizing." In Christianity the historical process is immanent in history itself, in this also being identifiable with Marxism. Redemption by historicizing is quite a different matter. In Christianity the historical process is revealed to the individual—initially through biblical inspiration; subsequently (after the Incarnation) through the Church, or through a church, or through Grace. Similarly, in Marxism the immanent historical process is discovered by the inquirer; it is something to be found in the object by the subject. On the other hand, in redemption by historicizing the emphasis is not on a process immanent in history, in the object, but rather on the activity of historicizing; the emphasis is on the experience of the subject, on the subjective consequences of historicizing to the subject, not on the objective determination of immanent structure or teleology in history.

I believe that this, or something very like it, is the point of the final pages of Hegel's *Phenomenology*. History, to put it in non-Hegelian terms, consists of a series of interpretations of the world. Each interpretation is partially adequate and partially inadequate. As each interpretation is put to use and tested against actual situations, its internal incoherences are revealed. As they become increasingly intolerable, the next step is to preserve what was adequate in an innovated pattern of interpretation. Yet this development of a new interpretation is not in itself as important as the conscious realization of the structure of that process of development. That realization—not the structure of the process— is the distinctively Hegelian contribution. Just as Hegel anticipated that he would be superseded, so the importance of the realization is that it prepares whoever grasps it to realize, in time, its not-yet-apparent incoherences and to transcend it. Thus, to the sympathetic, the *Phenomenology* marks a period of peculiar importance in history, for a realization of the structure of the historical process makes it possible to transcend the historical process and to move into a larger freedom. From this point of view, Marx did not, as he claimed, turn Hegel right side up after all; he merely poured him into an already existing Christian mold.

Now I am not concerned with whether Hegel was right or not. For my personal taste, he is far too optimistic. Rather, I am concerned with the pattern he appears to exemplify: that which historicizing of explanation does, or is felt to do, for the individual who engages in it. The very rhetoric, if nothing else—and there is a great deal else—of the final paragraph on history in the *Phenomenology* indicates that redemptionist interests are at work. Further, it is possible to apply at this point the formula given above: The function of nineteenth-century historicism is to redeem by restoration and purification whatever is subjected to historical explanation. In Hegel the "whatever" is the historicizing subject. To use a word commonly found throughout the nineteenth and twentieth centuries, it is the "self" that is restored and purified. Hegel disintegrates what today we would call culture, personality, and role. Only the pure self, or the Absolute, free from all attributes, is left. Thus stripped naked, it has nothing to do but to be engaged with concrete situations and to re-create the world, that is, to reinterpret the world from this point of view. To be aware that we live in a world interpreted by our own interests grants us a freedom to innovate and to manipulate interpretations that is not granted by the commitment to any particular interpretation. It is the freedom to maintain an irresolvable tension between subject and object. Be that as it may, the pattern to be observed is the transcendence of the current conceptions of society, personality, and culture. (For convenience, this pattern may be abbreviated as "cultural transcendence," a term henceforth to be taken as including personality and society [or role] as well.)

This makes it possible to propose a few formula for the function of nineteenth-century historicism. The redemptive power of historicizing enables the historicizing individual to transcend his necessarily inadequate and even destructive culture. However—and this is particularly important for the comprehension of nineteenth-century redemptive historicizing—the transcendence does not precipitate the individual into a new cultural stability; rather it condemns him, or frees him—the choice is a matter of taste— to a permanent cultural instability. To put it another way, cultural transcendence, rather than cultural commitment, becomes the mode of existence. Cultural transcendence as a mode of existence is another way of expressing the formula suggested above, the acceptance of an irresolvable tension between subject and object (old-fashioned as those terms may be). Very abstractly, the process involves several stages: recognition of cultural incoherence, alienation, historical explanation, and cultural transcendence.

The basic pattern of nineteenth-century—i.e., Romantic—alienation was analyzed by Hegel himself, though the grandiose scale on which he worked tends to conceal it. That pattern is, of course, the recognition of a cultural incoherence and the transcendence of the culture, discussed above. From this point of view, his explanation of history is a projection upon history of his own self-alienation from his own culture, observing that pattern to have happened over and over again in the course of history. This is not to suggest that his insight into the processes by which various interpretations of the world have become culturally established is necessarily invalid. Quite the contrary. Like any theory of history, however, his is necessarily selective and incomplete. Indeed, it may even be asserted that he did not write a theory of history so much as a theory of the relationship among a few books, arranged in chronological order. The important point is that he perceived the process of alienation and cultural transcendence because he had experienced it himself. More precisely, he had experienced the alienation. The *Phenomenology* is his effort—his voyage of discovery, as he called it—to transcend that alienation. Since he had experienced the incoherence of his own culture, it was, of course, impossible for him to transcend that incoherence by returning to commitment to his own culture. So what at first appears to be an explanation of culture by historicizing that culture, turns out, more profoundly, to be Hegel's explanation of himself by historicizing himself.

In the early decades of the nineteenth century, the solution of the problem of alienation by historicizing the personality is a phenomenon frequently to be found among the advanced thinkers of the time. Wordsworth is an excellent example. Goethe, in *Faust*, used a middle strategy of displacing the personality into history, thus combining—in a single strategy—alienation, historicizing the personality, and historicizing the culture. Scott moved from alienation to historicizing the culture, simultaneously presenting, with great incoherence, a pre-nineteenth-century ideology. Historicization was to become a popular strategy. The subsequent realistic novels apply historicizing to the present, as the Goncourts were fully aware. It is as if it were first necessary to historicize the past—as opposed to moralizing it in the pre-nineteenth-century manner—before the same strategy could be applied to the present. In the work of Flaubert all modes can be discerned. From this point of view, both the character and the tradition of Freud are quite obvious, as are his conclusions. Experiencing his own internal incoherence, and his consequent alienation both from himself and from his culture—it amounts to the same thing—Freud subjected himself to a rather novel kind of historicizing; he found his explanatory mode for self-historicizing in family relations. Subsequently he accused his culture of sexual incoherence, and thereafter devoted himself to historicizing his patients. The result was consistent with the pattern: The patient is not cured but is inured to a permanent mode of cultural transcendence. To be cured would mean to return to the culture as functional within that culture. And to be sure, that sort of cure was the best Freud expected for the great majority of his patients. A few, however, entered what Philip Rieff has aptly named a "covert culture." That is, as others had discovered before Freud (Browning and Tennyson, for example), the culturally transcendent individual is both alienated from his culture and socially functional within it.

The emergent cultural problem of the nineteenth century, then, was alienation. The solution was cultural transcendence by historicizing, a strategy no doubt derived from Christianity but by no means to be reduced to it. In philosophy, in historiography, in the emerging social sciences, and in the arts, the advanced and advancing thought of the nineteenth century can be understood as lying along a continuum between two poles—one being historicizing the culture and the other historicizing the personality. Each instance on the continuum has its roots in the perception of incoherence within the individual's own culture, or within a special instance of his culture, his own personality. The perception of that incoherence is the source of alienation.

Alienation in this sense, however, is not to be confused with the term "alienation" as it is commonly used today—for example, in discussing alienated youth. (At least the term is commonly used in this sense in the United States.) Such alienation should more correctly be called polarization by negation. One set of cultural values is perceived as incoherent and is judged as unacceptable, and another set is perceived as coherent and judged as acceptable. This is mere moralizing, as both Hegel and Nietzsche were aware, for the perception of polar opposites or the juxtaposition of affirmation and negation is not the perception of incoherence but rather of reflective or mirror coherence. Polarization obeys the norms of logic, but the perception of incoherence emerges when the norms of logic are judged to be failing or, at best, inapplicable. This is the source of the perception of the uncrossable gap between language and the world—so common in the nineteenth century, in Browning and Hegel, as well as in Nietzsche; prefigured in the eighteenth century in Hamann; and strongly realized in the first decade of this century in the recently recovered work of Fritz Mauthner. Hence, moralizing is seen as a linguistic process, and as something to be transcended by historicizing. It is not surprising, then, that the polarized of today, the miscalled alienated, are profoundly and even violently antihistorical, for they have not reached the stage of alienation, the precondition to historicizing and cultural transcendence.

Perhaps—because of the weakening and disappearance for many of Christianity, and the weakening and disappearance of the historical component within Christianity—historicizing has become increasingly unavailable as a strategy, particularly within the popular culture, from which, more and more, members of high culture must be recruited. Whatever the reasons for the current antipathy to historicizing, the results are unfortunate, for my studies have shown me no mode of cultural transcendence yet available other than that offered by historicizing.

3

REFLECTIONS ON

HISTORICAL MODES IN THE

NINETEENTH CENTURY

[1971*]

When Sir Walter Scott died, Carlyle wrote in his journal, "He understood what *history* meant; that was his chief intellectual merit. . . . He has played his part, and left *none like* or second to him."[1] Did Carlyle mean that in making others understand the significance of history, whatever it might be, Scott was playing his part? If this seems not too unreasonable an interpretation of Carlyle's remarks, the explanation is that probably no one had a greater responsibility than did Scott for one of the most important transformations in the nineteenth century—the historicization of European culture. Certainly Scott was not alone. Hegel contributed mightily, but Hegel's contribution was confined to high-level culture. Scott worked at a considerably lower

* Reprinted by permission from *Victorian Poetry*, Stratford-upon-Avon Studies 15 (London: Edward Arnold, 1972), pp. 277–300. Copyright © 1972 by Edward Arnold (Publishers) Ltd.

[1] 30 September 1832, in J. A. Fronde, *Carlyle: The First Forty Years* (Longmans, Green, & Co., 1882), 2:310–11.

cultural level, so much so that it was not until his death that
Carlyle could find a good word to say for him or could recognize
the importance of the part he played. Furthermore, Scott's mode
of writing historical novels could easily be applied at a considerably lower culture level than that at which he normally worked.
Ainsworth and Dumas modeled themselves upon Scott but were
even less intellectually and culturally demanding. Hugo, on the
other hand, could use the Scott tradition at a higher level in
Notre-Dame de Paris and did the same thing in his historical
plays. *Les Burgraves* is more demanding than a Waverley novel.
Moreover, Manzoni performed at a cultural level which Scott
never attempted to reach, though without Scott it is doubtful
if there could have been an *I Promessi Sposi*. Scott made history
accessible; he made it familiar; he made it comfortable. Macaulay
recognized this when he set out to write a history that would be
as appealing as Scott's novels, and he seems to have felt that the
audience he wished to reach would not have existed had it not
been for Scott.

On the other hand, it is not true that European culture was
without historical consciousness before the nineteenth century.
On the contrary, it may reasonably be said that the Renaissance
began when certain Florentine humanists undertook to think
about Cicero, not in universal categories, but rather in relation to
the circumstances of the culture in which he grew up and lived.
History and the development of a discipline of historical discourse were important elements in the four centuries before 1800
—a period ushered in by a culture crisis and terminated by a culture crisis more severe and fundamental than any of the minor
crises during that period. Yet in these four Renaissance centuries,
as they may perhaps be called, historicized culture was very different from the historicizing culture of the nineteenth century.
Historical discourse, as distinguished from mere chronology, was
dominated by an interest in models, positive or negative. To our
taste, formed by the nineteenth century, even the incomparable
and delicious Gibbon, unrivaled for intellectual entertainment, is
abstract. His figures, fascinating as they are, are self-subsistent
monads; there is little or no feeling of social depth, and environ-

mental detail is quite lacking. He offers us a vast and endlessly amusing comedy of manners presented on a stage virtually without scenery.

He is best understood if one visualizes his events as if they were historical paintings by Tiepolo, or as if they were to be found in Metastasio's libretti for historical operas. Handel's *Rodelinda* takes place during the rule in Italy by the Lombards, as does Davenant's *Gondibert,* but in neither is the historical setting of the slightest importance. They could happen anywhere. So in Tiepolo's classical paintings the scenery and the architecture are universalized. Both are virtually identical with the scenery and architecture for paintings from Tasso. To be sure, in the Villa Valmarana in Vicenza there is some suggestion of classical costume, but there are also Renaissance, Roman, and Moorish costume details. In the Palazzo Labia in Venice and in other paintings of Antony and Cleopatra, she invariably appears in a sixteenth-century dress, but Antony is just as invariably in Roman armor, though not armor that any Roman ever wore.

In what I have called the Renaissance centuries, the past functioned as did the country life in the pastoral poetry of the same period. It was a backdrop used to isolate an interactional problem, morally conceived, from its social situation. The interest of that isolation was to detach the problem from its social and environmental ramifications. Even in *Robinson Crusoe* we learn very little about life on a tropical island. Defoe was not interested in how an individual relates himself to, and establishes himself in, an unfamiliar environment—though that *was* the interest at work in *Swiss Family Robinson* and Jules Verne's *The Mysterious Island.* Defoe was interested in isolating the moral problem of the individual as individual, that is, of the individual in moral interaction with himself. Just as the portrait of Friday is not a contribution to cultural anthropology, the island is merely an isolating backdrop. Clearly these works are not critiques of social management, nor of validation, nor of explanation (metaphysics). They are studies of how these fundamental modes of human action are manifest in moral problems and conflicts. So in the plays of Racine and Voltaire, as in Addison's *Cato,* the past is not conceived as an atmosphere that made people different from the people in the audience, but, as in Shakespeare, is a way of isolating and selecting moral attributes of the people in the audience. In Gibbon and other historians there is little or no sense of the pastness of the past, of the otherness of the past, but rather of the sameness. Consequently in pre-nineteenth-century historical discourse both the visual appearance of the past and the total social environment were equally neglected. But the otherness of the past, its pastness, the difference of its visual appearance, the strangeness of past modes of interaction—these were precisely what the nineteenth century *was* interested in. These were precisely the factors which gave the novels of Scott their strength and an appeal that is still attractive.

I

The first notable appearance in English literature of this sense of the otherness of the past is in a work we normally would not consider an historical work at all, Wordsworth's "Tintern Abbey." "I cannot paint / What then I was." To be sure, he proceeds to do so in considerable detail, but the important cultural break which led to *The Prelude* had been made. In his *Confessions* Rousseau is a monad on which the world impinges and which impinges on the world; it maintains, however, its monadic stability. In *The Prelude* Wordsworth historicizes the personality. If we jump forward a hundred years, we find Freud, whose aim was to make Wordsworths out of his patients. Not only, as in *The Prelude*, does Freud explain a present condition of the personality genetically, not only does he account for it by its past history, he goes even further. He defines the neurotic as one who has remained a monad, as one who has *not* transcended the past. The technique of psychoanalysis involves, first, the historicization of the personality and, second, a transcendence of the historical forces responsible for that personality. But here, as in Wordsworth, the peculiar character of Romanticism emerges. In transcending its own past, the successfully psychoanalyzed personality (such personalities are extremely rare; even Freud was never absolutely sure that he was one himself) transcends a very recent sociocultural past—so recent that it is continuous with the sociocultural present in which the transcending process takes place.

Such a personality, then, transcends its own culture. A critique of oneself (as opposed to a moral judgment of oneself) necessarily involves a critique of those forces responsible for oneself. The proper effect of psychoanalysis, as Freud was perfectly aware, is an alienation from one's culture and society. As Philip Rieff has pointed out, the rare individual who is successfully psychoanalyzed enters a covert culture, a concealed subculture, just as William and Dorothy Wordsworth and Coleridge, in their alienation, established and entered a concealed covert culture, complete with spy. Freud, in short, was brought up in the tradition of German Idealism and nineteenth-century German Romantic culture. Faust is the model for his patients, for Faust, reaching the limits of his culture, and seeking to escape those limits, first had to explore that culture, including—as in the Classical Walpurgisnacht—the past of that culture. He had to resist the temptation of the hypostatized moment, the temptation to be a monadic personality. He had to reach the point of accepting the eternal feminine, the eternal not-I, the eternal otherness which draws us forever onward.

It may be hazarded, then, that, from the first emergence of nineteenth-century culture, the interest in the otherness of the past was rooted in the perception of the otherness of a former state of the personality, a state which, as in "Tintern Abbey," is judged to have been transcended. That sense of self-transcendence was, therefore, something to be maintained, since the new state was judged to be superior to the former state, for the new state was founded on the resolution of problems encountered in the old. Thus the discontinuity of personality, its fluidity, and its permanent potentiality for self-transcendence became attributes to be maintained. As in Hegel's *Phenomenology*, self-estrangement was perceived as desirable, since it and it alone offered the possibility of freedom. The personality, therefore, came to be conceived historically and also progressively, not—as before the nineteenth century—in reference to cultural improvements but rather in reference to terms of freedom. Since, however, there was almost no cultural support for such a position—since, indeed, the weight of culture, particularly its religious aspect, was all on the side of the monadic continuity of the personality—it was necessary to devise strategies for the maintenance of the sense of otherness. This is the resolution of the apparent incoherence in "Tintern Abbey," the fact that the statement of the inability to reconstruct a former state is followed by a detailed reconstruction of that very state. It is as if Wordsworth were saying: "I cannot describe my former state; but to maintain my present state it is necessary to do so; therefore I create an imaginative construct of that state." Thus the construction of otherness became a central ingredient in innovative nineteenth-century culture, which was, it must always be remembered, quantitatively only a very small part of the century's total cultural repertoire. To put it in Fichtean (not Hegelian) terms, in order to maintain a thesis, it is necessary to construct an antithesis. Indeed, this is a basic strategy of that very puzzling kind of verbal behavior we call logic. In Hegelian terms, there are no negatives, only alternatives; a concept can be said to exist only when there are alternatives to it. It is instructive that Coleridge interpreted the second person of the trinity as otherness—identity, alterity, and community being to him the fundamental aspects of existence.

From this point of view it can be suggested that the interest of emergent nineteenth-century culture in the imaginative construction of historical situations—whether in literature, the visual arts, the dramatic arts (including some nontheater music)—and in disciplined historical discourse based on research was the need to maintain the sense of otherness and also to authenticate that sense. This makes it possible to develop an explanation for historical realism—the inclusion in historical constructs of details of the visual environment, whether natural or man-made, of modes of interaction, and of personality attributes which were derived from historical research. Since what was needed was, not sufficient historically authentic detail to make the construct convincing, but rather a continuing opportunity to experience otherness, there was no built-in limit to the amount and authenticity of the historical detail. It was impossible to know or offer enough, since as authentic detail became familiar it lost its attribute of otherness. The test of successful historical detail became, in only apparent paradox, its novelty. Thus what was good enough for Scott was not good enough for Manzoni, whose reconstructions of early-seventeenth-century Italian life, customs, personalities, scenery, country houses, and city-scapes were much more authentic than Scott's, just as the nonfictive historical personalities were more carefully researched than any similar personalities in the Waverley novels. Later in the century Charles Reade was even more thorough in his research for *The Cloister and the Hearth*.

This process of including more and more authentic historical detail can be seen very clearly in the course of nineteenth-century architecture. Architectural design shows a very marked shift in the first decades of the century, the indicator of that shift being a striking increase in archeological correctness and authenticity. The designs of Robert Adam, to be sure, often used details from Pompeii and Herculaneum, but they were incorporated in a design scheme clearly in the Renaissance tradition, just as Strawberry Hill was a rococo fantasy on Gothic themes. Classical Edinburgh, however, was a very different matter. An effort was made not only to use authentic Greek details—not vaguely classical details transformed by the Renaissance tradition—but also to combine them in a Greek fashion. In the same way, the furniture designs of Thomas Hope were based on Greek vase paintings and stelae. The Greek revival spread throughout Europe, among its major sources being the eighteenth-century clearing of Paestum and the publication of Piranesi's magnificent renditions of the Paestum temples. The well-preserved temples at Agrigento in Sicily were also becoming known; Goethe went to see them in his Italian journey. Eighteenth-century experiments in both Gothicism and archeological Classicism were follies, fantasies, garden-pieces. In the new century, however, Gothic and Greek styles alike were used for buildings of great importance—churches, town halls, mansions which were virtually palaces, and important schools, such as the magnificent Edinburgh High School and the never-finished National Monument, planned to be a replica of the Parthenon. St. George's Hall in Liverpool was a similar experiment in the style of Roman Imperialism. It is scarcely necessary to mention the masterpiece of Pugin, the decorative detail of the Houses of Parliament.

To our eyes, nevertheless, both the Greek and the Gothic buildings of this period look more nineteenth-century than they do

Greek or Gothic. To us Pugin himself could not design a convincingly Gothic church. On the other hand there were in the 1830s and 1840s a number of small houses which do have the flavor of authenticity. The casual glance suggests that they are centuries older than they actually are. The explanation is that such buildings had little detail and the masses were relatively simple; native cottage architecture in stone had remained relatively unchanged for perhaps a thousand years. Large, complex buildings rich with detail, however, presented different problems of authenticity in both detail and mass. From the testimony of contemporaries, as well as from the self-satisfaction of the architects, it seems to be reasonably clear that at first these buildings were convincing. The relentless demand, however, for further authentic detail—at work alike in architecture, formal history, and the historical novel and drama, including stage design—rapidly revealed their inability to meet the ever-rising expectancies for convincing authenticity. As suggested above, familiarity converts the historically authentic into the historically inauthentic.

Through the century, therefore, activities of architects were governed by constantly more stringent demands for historical authenticity, and at the same time the means for satisfying those demands became available through the rapid development of architectural history and archeology. *The Stones of Venice* was an effort to go beyond even the archeologically correct to what were conceived to be the values responsible for the various Gothic styles, both the functional values and the semantic values. In the next generation Morris mounted his attacks on restoration, because it could not be authentic enough, while simultaneously architecture was mastering authenticity in all of the pre-nineteenth-century styles, including, in time, the styles of the eighteenth century. By the end of the nineteenth century it was possible to design buildings of which it could be said with accuracy that they were neither replicas nor nineteenth-century versions of an historical style—particularly if the scale was the same—but were truly authentic. Even today, some of these buildings—the Morgan library, for example—almost seem in truth the past recaptured. This achievement coincided in the late nineteenth and early twentieth centuries with an intense and widespread cultural concern with the very nature of time, as in Bergson.

In spite of this development, nineteenth-century architecture shows a peculiar and instructive split, one which comes out very clearly in the fact that Barry did the floor plans and general layout of the Houses of Parliament, while Pugin did the Gothic detail. The superb and strikingly original character of Barry's planning has long been recognized, so much so that Pugin's contribution was for a considerable time comparatively neglected. This division of the task between two men is typical of the general character of the relation between the floor plans of nineteenth-century historical architecture and the historically derived and increasingly authentic detail. A study of nineteenth-century architectural planning throughout Europe and America and throughout the century shows the effort architects were making to abandon Renaissance and Gothic planning and to create new types of room relations, whether in domestic, religious, or public buildings. This planning effort was aimed at founding planning on the actual character of interaction in both private and public social situations. Barry's plan for the Houses of Parliament was a kind of visualization of the social and interactional structure of Parliament itself, including its relation to the monarch and to the people, expressed in the way Westminster Hall was integrated into the new building. And this same kind of thinking can be found in innumerable country homes, villas, and town houses of the time. It was literally an historical realism, a new sense of social reality in the plan coupled with historical authenticity in the external and internal decoration. Thus the envelope of historical detail became a costume for a freshly conceptualized segment of society, and this odd symbiosis was a symbiosis of otherness and social reality.

This peculiar combination is also to be found in the figure of the Dandy—not so much Beau Brummell, who is best perceived as an Enlightenment Dandy, interested in egalitarianism, but rather in the Dandy of the 1830s and 1840s, inspired by a reinterpretation of Brummell. This is the Dandy of Bulwer Lytton and D'Orsay, and of Baudelaire. The connection between historical realism and the Dandy lies in the perception that if historical

architecture has a costume relation to a social reality, and makes
that reality into an otherness, then a formalization of clothes into
costume makes a contemporary social reality into an otherness.
The Dandy revealed the identity of self-estrangement and social
estrangement, and at the same time turned contemporary social
reality into an historical situation by turning clothes into costume.
It is hardly necessary to point out that this is what *Sartor Resartus*
is all about—the perception of the contemporary world in terms
of historical process, the turning of that contemporary world
into an otherness by means of what Carlyle called "The Centre
of Indifference," the realization that this alienation is accomplished by perceiving clothes as costume, that is, as symbol, and
by perceiving clothes and costume historically.

From this point of view it is possible to explain the importance
at the time of the organic conception of society. The organic
metaphor for society was an Enlightenment notion—superseding
the mechanical metaphor—but the emergent culture of the nineteenth century used the metaphor in a different way. The eighteenth-century use was a validational use, a justification for not
reorganizing society from its foundations, or a justification for
reform controlled by a metaphor of growth. The new nineteenth-
century use was explanatory. The interest was in a metaphor that
would have the attribute of history and at the same time would
serve to make a society cognitively comprehensible from the
outside. The organic metaphor thus serves the interest of social
estrangement, of perceiving one's own society as an otherness,
though of course it does not necessarily do that. The metaphor
prepares society to be perceived as an otherness, while the otherness itself is accomplished and maintained by the discovery and
presentation—both in the various arts and in formal historical
discourse—of social detail, the counterpart of historical detail.
It seems to be a matter of cultural convergence that at this very
time, the 1820s and 1830s, sociology was established as an intellectual discipline, and thus sociology can be seen as the counterpart of historical discourse. Sociology is historical discourse about
the present, and Mayhew's research into the life of the London
poor was the equivalent of, and probably modeled in part on,
historical research.

With this in mind, it is now useful to return to the problem of historical fiction. In the early decades the main consciously innovative effort in fiction was in the historical novel, and also the historical play, the historical opera, and the historical ballet. It is insufficient to consider historical poetry without considering the historical novel, and it is insufficient to neglect the theatrical historical modes of drama, opera, and ballet; similarly, in considering any or all of these, one must constantly be aware of the simultaneous development of historical architecture and historical painting, and likewise the equally simultaneous developments in historical research—the opening of hitherto closed archives, the publication of hitherto unpublished material, and the composition and publication of formal historical discourse. Thus the emergence of historical fiction as a dominating genre is best explained, at the first level, by pointing out the simultaneous emergence of historicism in the arts and intellectual disciplines in which it could possibly be introduced—including, in time, anthropology and biology, and eventually, with Freud, the formal study of personality, as differentiable from the informal or intuitive studies of personality to be found in literature (as in Browning's development of a soul), the theater, and historical discourse. Nevertheless, the fate of historical fiction was rather special and is highly instructive.

In England and on the Continent historical fiction was the dominant genre for the first half of the century, beginning with *Heinrich von Ofterdingen.* There were, to be sure, two great exceptions to this, Dickens and Balzac. The first of Balzac's works to be included in *The Human Comedy* was an historical novel, *Les Chouans.* The *Comedy* came to include a number of other historical works, but they were shorter and minor works which served as an introduction to the *Comedy* proper. Nevertheless, they establish the convergence between history and what was Balzac's principal thrust, sociology. The titles of the subdivisions of the *Comedy* indicate Balzac's interest in constructing an exemplary sociology. Dickens, the other great exception, wrote an historical novel, *Barnaby Rudge,* early in his career, but the true character of his thrust—like Balzac's, a critique of society, a sociological thrust—begins to emerge in *The Old Curiosity Shop,* in which the wanderings of Nell and her grandfather are in Dickens's intellectual career very much the same sort of things as the wanderings of Teufelsdröckh during the "Centre of Indifference" are in Carlyle's intellectual development. (The point is given even greater significance if the real "old curiosity shop" is English society itself; there may be some justification for this interpretation.) But even in *Pickwick Papers*, the exploratory character of Dickens's works, as opposed to the judgmental character, is already emerging. Thus, though certainly *Barnaby Rudge* is not a novel one cares to reread repeatedly, it served for Dickens the function of social estrangement and displacement provided at the time by historicism. Dickens was always torn between the relative claims of explanation and validation; their incoherence marked him as a man of the emergent culture of the nineteenth century. As he grew in intellectual and imaginative power the validation, or judgmental, or critical, interest was gradually subordinated, in the late novels, to the explanatory interest. A critique of society became more important to him than a criticism of society. In this development, the self-estrangement of Pip, the underlying theme of *Great Expectations*, probably played a part of considerable weight.

With those two important exceptions, then, the dominating fictional mode at the higher cultural level before the middle of the century was historical fiction. In the 1850s, however, something we call realistic fiction emerged. Somehow or other we do not feel that Balzac and Dickens quite wrote realistic fiction. For one thing, of course, they have the extravagance of the arts and of the cultural style of the 1830s and 1840s, an extravagance which Dickens never transcended, though he was to push it to extraordinary developments. The new realism lacked that extravagance, but a judgment by the Goncourt brothers provides a better explanation for the difference between the sociological fiction of Dickens and Balzac and the sociological fiction of Thackeray, Flaubert, and the Goncourt brothers themselves. The Goncourts claimed to have invented the realistic novel, and they defined it as an historical novel about the present. As the figure of the Dandy has already suggested, the sense of otherness learned from the social estrangement provided by historicism can be applied to one's contemporary world. What marks Dickens and Balzac off from realistic fiction proper is that they never fully learned from writing historical fiction that sense of otherness, though this statement is somewhat less appropriate to Balzac than to Dickens. Hence the conflict in both writers between critique and criticism. This I think is also true of Dostoevsky, who began writing in the 1840s but did not continue until the 1860s. Tolstoy, on the other hand, eventually moved from the historical realism of *War and Peace* to the contemporary otherness of *Anna Karenina*. The realistic fiction which emerged in the 1850s seems to be usefully described as the result of applying the techniques for maintaining the sense of otherness developed in the historical novel to contemporary material. Thackeray, for example, was able to include himself in that otherness; and in novels which begin as historical novels but end in the contemporary world of the novel's author and readers, he was able to combine the themes of self-estrangement and social estrangement—in *Vanity Fair* as intermittent narrator and in *Pendennis* and *The Newcomes* as protagonist. The strategy was identical with that of architects. An historical style made possible a fresh and disengaged critique of a segment of the total complex of interaction —that is, of society. Consequently, it is congruent with this transformation of the historical novel into the realistic novel that in the late 1850s Ruskin—even today identified with architectural historicism—was able to assert that the only point of designing in the Gothic style was to learn how to design architecture appropriate to the modern world. The theme of social estrangement continues, however, in his further assertion that such an effort would be fruitless, since the organization of nineteenth-century society was not of a validity that would make an appropriate architecture possible: What architects could not do, Ruskin thought—and for a long time he was right and perhaps still is—novelists could do.

The character of realistic fiction was capable of extraordinarily rich development in the same way that historical fiction had been, though it must be remembered that historical fiction continued—and continued with increasing historical authenticity—alongside realistic fiction; Thackeray could turn from his own world to the historical world of *Henry Esmond* and *The Virginians*. Even so, historical fiction soon began to sink to lower cultural levels. Just as historical fiction was maintained by an insatiable demand for innovative historical detail, so innovative social detail maintained and still maintains—though no longer so brilliantly—realistic fiction. Further, the processes of preparing to write were taken over from historical fiction and were applied to the new realistic fiction. Even the most primitive historical fiction requires a certain amount of research from the author. Swinburne, who applied the techniques of research to writing poetry—even footnoting his allusions in an ode to Victor Hugo—wrote wonderfully funny parodies of two novelists who had neglected their homework, Dumas and Hugo. Mark Twain made much the same point about Cooper. The historical authenticity of *Scottish Chiefs* is not very convincing; Scott, however, was an assiduous researcher of both primary and secondary documents. Subsequent writers, as suggested above, raised the standards of research even higher. The research for *Westward Ho!* (1855) was careful and extensive, though before 1861 probably no historical novel had been so carefully researched as *The Cloister and the Hearth*. It was quickly matched, however, by Eliot's *Romola*. The cases of Reade and Eliot are instructive. Each wrote both historical novels and realistic novels. Reade is particularly instructive, for his major effort before *The Cloister and the Hearth* was *It Is Never Too Late to Mend*, and that book is based on the kind of research that may be called journalistic research—which is, however, very hard to distinguish from sociological research. The intuitive sociological novel is to be distinguished from the realistic novel precisely on the grounds that the author of the latter sets up the social categories which he wishes to explore and to exemplify in the novel and performs his preliminary research in terms of those categories. Balzac certainly did research, but it was organized not so much in explanatory categories as in geographical. It remained, on the whole, intuitive. The change in Dickens's later novels seems, from this point of view, to be closely connected with his editing of *Household Words* and *All the Year Round*. There flowed across his desk a steady river of the results of journalistic research. In addition, he himself did a considerable amount of research, too often of a kind which today has been assigned to the professional sociologist.

As every researcher knows, the very activity of research produces a sense of self-estrangement and of social estrangement, even a sense of one's own unreality. At least that is the complaint one often hears from those whose professions require constant research activity. The unworldly scholar is a figure that long antedates the nineteenth century. In this connection it is instructive to think of those nineteenth-century novelists who were permanent tourists—Turgenev and James, for example—continuously engaged in exploring societies other than their own. Tourism, particularly as conducted in the nineteenth century, is also a form of research, carried on in a foreign country; the tourist situation has a basic character of social estrangement, and in the nineteenth century the sense of social estrangement, or otherness, was often the value hoped to be gained from tourism. The transfer of research from the historical novel to the new, nonintuitive realistic novel meant both a technique for maintaining a sense of the otherness of the contemporary world and also a technique for discovering endless amounts of realistic detail to feed the insatiable demands for the sense of otherness. In time, Zola set up a vast fictional program, requiring and dependent upon all the kinds of research mentioned: historical, journalistic, sociological, touristic (*Lourdes, Rome,* and *Paris*). Perez y Galdos set for himself similar programs, and even Hardy seems to have been governed by some self-imposed directive, a research design, at least, for covering in his fiction the entire nineteenth century.

In summary, recalling the symbiosis in architecture of historical style and fresh social analysis, it appears to be the case that the central drive of nineteenth-century fiction throughout Europe was the drive to construct a critique of society; that this drive first found satisfaction in nineteenth-century historicism; that the realistic novel is a special case of historicism, as was sociology; and that the self-conscious exploitation of the techniques of research made it possible to solve the problem of the intuitive sociological novel by fusing it with the historical novel. Further, behind the drive to construct a critique of society was the drive to maintain and authenticate the sense of otherness of social estrangement and self-estrangement, of alienation, of (to use Coleridge's term) alterity. To explore the phenomenon of historicism more fully, it is therefore necessary to explore its relation to the opposite of otherness, to explore the concepts of identity and selfhood, concepts barely mentioned so far. To put it somewhat differently, why was it necessary to maintain the sense of otherness? Why was it vital to validate that sense? A hint comes from Coleridge. Alterity and identity he experienced. The third member of his trinity, community, he could only long for; he never experienced it. Nor has any man of that century or this whose trinity begins with identity and alterity yet proceeded to the Pentecost, to the descent of the Holy Spirit, to community, except when he has managed to forget about the first two members. At any rate, from Coleridge we can take the link between Father and Son, between identity and alterity—the interdependence of self and other, of selfhood and otherness.

II

Long ago George Herbert Mead said that the mark of Romanticism was the distinction it made between self and role. This notion has been both revived and rediscovered and is now fairly common. It remains, however, an extremely slippery, and even a very puzzling, notion. The notion of role is fairly clear, although its metaphorical character is frequently ignored. The notion of self, however, is anything but lucid. A role can be understood as a persistence of behavioral attributes through time, attributes which are sufficiently stable to enable their recurrence to be predicted with some success. The sense of estrangement from self is marked by a judgment that one's behavior does not emanate from oneself, but from culture, or society, or values, or beliefs: in short, from the not-self, from the other; behavior seems to consist of roles played for sociocultural interests which are judged not to be identical with the interest of the self. This kind of estrangement of one's behavior from oneself is fairly frequent, and its occasions are of very wide range. It appears to be a constant in human existence. However, at certain times the estrangement emerges not so much from a social or interactional matrix, which can be called with some reason the normal estrangement situation, but from a cognitive matrix at a high cultural level. When that happens there is a major cultural crisis—initially for a very few individuals, but marked by a more or less simultaneous and independent appearance. If the crisis is severe, this high-culture estrangement spreads through personal contact and through literature, the arts, philosophy, theology, and so on. Simultaneous with that spread, such estrangement continues to emerge independently, as other individuals experience the same estrangement without influence from their predecessors. There is both synchronistic and asynchronistic culture convergence. In time, a network of this kind of estranged individual establishes itself throughout a culture by means of various kinds of contact and communication, everything from personal conversations to performances of music. The cognitive situation that brings this about is the perception by individuals that the modes of explanation, validation, and social management current in the cultural situation are no longer coherent with each other or internally coherent. The metaphysics, the values, and the patterns of social interaction are no longer acceptable as valid or—to use a more recent and fashionable term—authentic. Normal estrangement, which is individual and is interactionally limited, does not question these factors of sociocultural coherence. It is not a matter of high culture, and the various kinds of therapy employed to aid the individual to recover, whether he is his own therapist or turns to another—parent, friend, psychiatrist, priest—consist of charismatic assertions, in propositional or other semiotic form, of the culturally current modes of explanation, validation, and social management. To the cognitively estranged, of course, such therapeutic devices are ineffective. What he sees as authentic and valid is the continued assertion of the invalidity and inauthenticity of the cultural modes. To maintain his position, however, requires powerful resistance to immense cultural pressure emanating from himself as much as from society, since all kinds of situations elicit behavior modes in himself that he finds unacceptable.

Various strategies are developed to deal with this problem. The simplest is avoidance of such situations—that is, of most social situations. Social isolation, retreat, turning to nature are employed; in the nineteenth century the value of nature lies in the absence of man, not in the presence of nature. Another strategy is the development and acting out in situations of antiroles—Bohemian, Artist-Redeemer, Dandy, Historian, Virtuoso were the most common nineteenth-century antiroles and still, of course, persist, an indication that the cultural crisis of the early nineteenth century is still with us, is still our cultural crisis. A third strategy is the metaphysical postulation of a self. Now each of these has its disadvantages. Social isolation deprives the individual of the social support of others of like mind and also of occasions for social resistance. Turning to nature poses the risk of eliciting eighteenth-century Enlightenment notions of nature and opens the way to a return to the culturally standardized modes of explanation. This appears to be what happened to Wordsworth. Playing an antirole is, after all, playing a role. To sustain it one must associate with others who are playing the same or a similar antirole. The result is the emergence of a subculture and a subsociety, with consequent loss of the sense of otherness and the sense of self. Thus, though the antirole of Bohemianism, for example, is useful, it is useful only temporarily; this is the problem Murger explored with great penetration in *Scènes de la vie de Bohème*. The postulation of a self presents the greatest difficulty of all, because it involves the hypostatization of a metaphysical entity. There is a definite empirical basis for social isolation; there is some empirical basis for the concept of role; there is no empirical basis for the self.

A brief discussion of Hegel's *Phenomenology* will perhaps clarify this. When Hegel set out to write that masterpiece, he had no notion of what goal he would arrive at. It was, he later said, a voyage of discovery. The whole immense effort and the work itself can be seen, I believe correctly, as a stripping away of culture. This is what he means by history's becoming self-conscious. Whatever we do, whatever we believe, has its origin in unique historical situations. To discover what we really are, it is necessary to peel off the layers of historical deposit. And that is what happens in the *Phenomenology*. What is left after this extraordinary estrangement from everything we have imagined ourselves to be? The Absolute is left, the true Self. But what is the Absolute? It turns out to be nothing at all. It is an empty category with neither range nor attributes. It is a mere metaphysical construct, a notion that does no more than terminate the process of estrangement. The self has no empirical existence. In short, the self is not self-maintaining. It can be maintained only by maintaining the sense of estrangement, by continuously experiencing the sense of otherness. (As Hegel says, once the Absolute has been arrived at, there is nothing to do but to turn back to the empirical world and begin all over again—but this time without innocence, this time estranged.) This, then, is the source of the insatiability of the demand for historical and social realism, and of the steadily increasing reliance upon research techniques to discover and organize authentic historical and social detail.

III

There remains a problem of considerable severity. If this explanation for nineteenth-century historicism and sociologism is at all valid, it is clear that it is valid only for the estranged who created in the historical and sociological modes and for those members of their audience who were likewise estranged. But this last group was obviously only a very, very small part of the audience. The bulk of that audience and the bulk of the imitators of the new modes of historical and sociological realism were neither socially estranged nor self-estranged. Indeed it seems paradoxical that so many estranged writers and artists commanded mass audiences of a wholly novel size. Obviously there were innumerable artistic and cultural values, quite independent of estrangement, that could account for that appeal, but the problem is that historicism—to confine the problem for the moment to that phenomenon—in itself was enormously attractive, in spite of the fact that the source of nineteenth-century historicism lay in estrangement. Thus, there must have been two factors at work in the great public success of art in the historical mode: the historically local factor of estrangement and the historically constant factor of interest in history. To deal with the great success of nineteenth-century historicism it is desirable to locate that constant factor. And to do so, one must begin with the dreadful question: "What is history?"

The first stage of analysis is to distinguish between two quite different semantic functions for the word "history." One is "historical discourse"; the other is "historical events." "Historical discourse" is said to refer to "historical events." But the word "refer" is filled with difficulties. If I am told that there is a drugstore at the corner, I can go and look; but if I am told there was a battle in Silesia in the eighteenth century, I can do no such thing. If "drugstore at the corner" refers to a drugstore at the corner, then "a battle in Silesia in the eighteenth century" cannot refer to a battle in Silesia in the eighteenth century. The drugstore is empirically accessible; the battle is not. My response to the word "drugstore" can be extended to include a response to the drugstore itself, but my response to "eighteenth-century Silesian battle" cannot be extended to include the battle itself. If the latter response is extended, it can only be extended to include other statements, statements to be found in what we call primary and secondary historical documents. In short, historical events are inaccessible; their existence is only linguistic. We cannot study or respond to historical events; we can only study or respond to historical discourse. History is not the persistence through time of historical events, nor the persistence of memory; it is the persistence of statements, as well as the innovative derivation of statements in response to existent statements, that we judge to be persistent statements. What we call historical evidence consists of statements which we judge to have come into existence before the derived statements. That is why historical forgery is possible. The forger provides no more and no less than what authentic documents provide—statements. The mark of an historical statement is the past tense. However, what we call authentic primary historical documents frequently use the present tense. In the same way, if there are sufficient indicators that the historical discourse is derived from authentic historical statements, it is possible to use without confusion the present tense, that is, the historical present. The historical present is a recognized rhetorical device, but its use makes it evident that the use of the past tense in historical discourse is also a rhetorical device. Keeping in mind the notion that history is the persistence of statements, it seems reasonable to assert that history is a rhetorical mode, that is, a linguistic overdetermination. The reason for the common semantic confusion between history-as-past-events and history-as-discourse is that there is, in fact, no difference between the two. The confusion is a tacit recognition of their identity.

The professional historian, then, is one who spends much of his life in composing statements in a particular rhetorical mode. In doing so, however, he has simply specialized in a rhetorical activity we all engage in, uttering statements in which the verbs are in the past tense. Moreover, in many languages, verbs are capable of several levels of pastness, just as adverbs and other indicators perform the same function. It must not be imagined, however, that such indicators place an event in time; on the contrary, they merely establish a sequential order among persistent and innovated statements. The rhetorical mode of history is not just a matter of the tense of verbs; for all that, however, it remains a rhetorical mode. On the other hand, the mere use of a linguistic indicator for the past does not make history. History is a matter of overdetermination, that is, it is a matter of a sustained mode of rhetoric; it is not a sentence but a discourse. Why do we engage in the utterance of this kind of discourse?

A good place to begin is to consider the basic form of historical rhetoric—gossip. The fundamental appeal of history is identical with the appeal of gossip. But the appeal of gossip is also the appeal of fiction. Basically, the rhetorics of history, fiction, and gossip are identical, and of these three the fundamental mode is gossip itself. The appeal of gossip certainly seems to be relief from various kinds of tension. The feeling of enjoyment of a good gossip changes radically if the gossip takes such a turn that action is required of us; tension enters a situation from which tension has been absent. There is also a change of feeling tone when explanation of the gossip events (that is, the gossip statements) is introduced or seems to be required or appropriate. Once again tension enters the situation. The appeal of gossip, then, is the relief from the tensions of action and explanation—the latter being, indeed, a form of action, verbal action. The simplest form of gossip is made up of statements connected only by a presented or an implied copulative. It is the simplest structure of cognitively comprehensible hypostatizations of empirically inaccessible events. I believe with Fritz Mauthner—happily we are not absolutely alone in this—that ultimately all that language can do is to give directions for performance. It cannot construct the world. However, it can give us directions for locating the empirically accessible. Since, moreover, it is a necessary assumption for action directed by language that any utterance does give us such directions, the universal linguistic assumption is that all language gives us directions for locating the empirically accessible. Linguistic hypostatization is the prerequisite for action. Even a heuristic epistemology requires linguistic hypostatization as preparation for scientific experimentation. Gossip, then, is a relief because it frees us from testing the empirical validity of linguistic hypostatizations. Pastness indicators in gossip are instructions that such testing is inappropriate. Research and explanation indicators cancel or negate pastness indicators and introduce once again the tension of action—that is, of testing the validity of linguistic hypostatization. Further, testing the validity of linguistic hypostatization creates a continuity between language and the world and also raises the possibility of discontinuity. It comprises and weakens cognition and comprehensibility. The field of cognition and the limits of the structure of comprehensibility become uncertain, vague, indeterminate. The rhetoric of gossip, on the other hand, since it allows no testing by either action or explanation, has boundaries and limits for both cognition and comprehension. Linguistic hypostatization is the foundation of our understanding of the world. Gossip in the past tense is its simplest mode, the mode most pervasive in human behavior, and probably the most important mode. Such gossip is the simplest form of history and constitutes the basic appeal of history. That is why history can draw an old man from a chimney corner. It offers an alternative chimney corner.

For practical purposes, however, we do make a distinction between history and gossip, but the source of that distinction is the accumulation of additional indicators of pastness, such as "in 1792" or "during the reign of Louis XIV." When the simple past becomes an historical past depends upon the individual's sense of the sequential scale on which he places statements. The greater the number of indicators and the more frequently they are encountered, the greater the sense of pastness and the more precise the sense of which particular past is in question. Such indicators—historically authentic details—are not only symptoms of the rhetorical overdetermination of history. They can also become ends in themselves, just as Hollywood steadily eliminated anachronisms from its historical movies in response to the pressure of history buffs, eventually reaching an extraordinarily high standard of research, for which it paid professional historians and paid them well. It is a superficial judgment, however, to define historical indicators as ends in themselves. On the contrary, they serve the interests of cognition, comprehension and hypostatization. By increasing, as it were, the density of the pastness and by defining more rigorously the temporal boundaries of that pastness, historical indicators increase the hypostatization and provide greater insurance against the tensions of action and testing.

These considerations help to explain the apparent paradox of the wide appeal, for a nonestranged audience, of literary and other works of art created by estranged artists. I have suggested that the demand for the sense of otherness was responsible for the insatiable demand for historical detail. It can now be added that the historically constant demand for historical indicators is equally insatiable, since hypostatized inaccessible events can easily show a resemblance to linguistically hypostatized accessible events and to apprehended accessible events. One of the most common uses for the past tense is, after all, to construct an inaccessible event with an analogical similarity to an accessible and current event, the purpose being to make the current event analogically comprehensible and to determine a course of action which promises success because that course of action was successfully used when the now inaccessible event was, allegedly, accessible. This analogical threat to the inaccessibility of history is responsible for the insatiable demand for historical indicators. Thus, both the estranged artist and the nonestranged audience shared a constant factor of interest in historical rhetoric and its accompanying insatiable demand for historical detail. This dual interest in historicism—an historically local interest and an historically constant interest—provides an explanation for the astonishing vitality and productivity of nineteenth-century historicism.

There remains the possibility that an historically constant factor was also present in the conversion of the historical novel into the realistic novel, and also in the conversion of the intuitively sociological novel into the controlled sociology of the realistic novel. For the first of these, the fact that realistic novels continued to be narrated in the past tense certainly served to facilitate the conversion by providing some protection against the threat of analogical similarity. Nevertheless, the indicators of contemporaneity worked powerfully against that protection. Such indicators made it difficult to maintain the sense of otherness. As we have seen, however, the historical novel offered a model for maintaining that sense, and cultural support was provided by the other instances of historicism; not the least important for the realistic novelist was the rapid development of professional historical discourse. As for the second conversion, since the interest of the intuitively sociological novelists was in establishing the sense of otherness, the processes of writing the realistic novel on the model of the historical novel provided a strategy for increasing the sense of otherness. These, however, are historically local factors. It is the constant factors that need to be explored.

It is instructive to listen to historians and sociologists argue about their respective disciplines: The historians insist that the sociologists become more historical, and the sociologists that the historians become more sociological. To the observer the only real difference between the two is that the historians use the past tense and the sociologists the present. Now if there is any justice or adequacy in claiming that gossip is the primitive form of history, and the primitive form of fiction, there is equal justice in claiming that gossip is also the primitive form of sociology. In discussing with friends, for example, the contents of the semipopular sociological magazine *Trans-Action*, I observe that what is usually discussed is the empirical data offered, not the explanations. In fact, the latter are either ignored or dismissed with a certain contempt, even by sociologists, though admittedly the sociologists I am intimate with are extremely atypical. What is of interest is clearly the material that is good for gossip—or is, in fact, social gossip, not differing much from the primitive sociology found in the currently popular newspaper advice columns of Dear Abby and Ann Landers, columns which everyone appears to read, no matter what his intellectual sophistication. Again, the advice or validational language of those columnists is usually dismissed. It is the fantastic things people actually do that are endlessly amusing.

It was suggested above that sociology in the nineteenth century emerged from historicism, or at least emerged in a cultural atmosphere permeated with historicism. Since the difference between the two is principally a matter of tense and character of indicators, sociology as well as history can best be understood as a rhetorical mode. What they have in common, of course, is research, and their modes of research are virtually identical, though with a difference in emphasis. The historian depends upon primary and secondary documents, but he also depends when he can upon interviewing people who were alive at the time of the historical events of which he is engaged in composing a construct. This does not change anything, for he depends upon statements and discourses, whether they are written or not. The sociologist too depends upon statements and discourses. Now it is true that he also makes use of direct observations of behavior as reported by himself or others; such direct observations, however, do not form the substance of his rhetorical mode but are only statements and sets of statements to which he is responding in constructing his discourse. The historian likewise depends upon primary documents and inclines to put greatest credence in the written reports of individuals who are believed to have observed the events he is concerned with. Nevertheless, there is a great difference between "This is the way things were" and "This is the way things are." The sociologist is apparently not protected by inaccessibility; consequently, it is the general character of sociologists to feel impelled to recommend action on the basis of their explanations. But this lack of protection by inaccessibility is only apparent. In fact, in constructing his discourse, he, like the historian, is constructing cognitively comprehensible hypostatizations of empirically inaccessible events, because all of his data have in fact ceased to exist. The threat to the gossip interest of sociology comes not from accessibility but from analogy.

If any two configurations or constructed configurations are judged to be analogically similar, that similarity is always based upon the elimination from consideration of various details in both. Likewise, analogies can be invalidated by paying attention to details. I do not think it to be true that what we call analogical thinking is bad; on the contrary, I am convinced, analogical thinking is the only kind of thinking we have. If this is the case, it is all the more pertinent that, if an analogy appears to be leading us to an action we do not wish to engage in, we invalidate the analogy by drawing attention to details which were ignored in the construction of the analogy. The present tense and the contemporaneity of his rhetorically overdetermined indicators tempt the sociologist to action, action which he often feels (and his colleagues of even slightly different ideology usually feel) is at best precipitate and at worst a bad mistake. Further, to the degree he takes action, he ceases to be a scientific sociologist. He has only two defenses: one is the permutation and innovation of explanation, the other is the accumulation of analogically invalidating detail. Since sociological explanation is like historical explanation, intellectually quite feeble, he has no recourse but to concentrate on the gathering of data. Thus sociology, both at present and since its inception, has concentrated upon the accumulation of massive detail as the only way of protecting the source of its vitality—its fundamental function as gossip.

Those novelists, such as Dickens and Balzac, whom I have called intuitive sociologists were faced with precisely the same problem. The use of rhetorical indicators of contemporaneity tempted them constantly in the direction of action, if only in the form of recommendations. Like so many sociologists, who imagine they are or ought to be social reformers, Dickens saw himself as a social reformer. It was necessary for the intuitive sociologists, in order to be novelists and to maintain their estrangement, to accumulate and even to invent social detail, and this necessity was, from the nature of the case, insatiable, just as in gossip the drive to contemporaneous detail is insatiable. Lacking, however, the techniques of research and the estrangement made possible by research as it had been developed in the various manifestations of historicism, those novelists had only one way to fill that gap—uncontrolled invention. This is the source of the exaggeration and caricature of which both Dickens and Balzac have so often been accused, exaggeration and caricature given further power by the extravagance of all the cultural modes of estrangement in the 1830s and 1840s. Thus, on the one hand, the constant of the insatiable thirst for social detail which protects everyone from the tension of action by breaking down analogies between the accessible and the constructed inaccessible provided them with a widespread audience, and, on the other, a similar factor with a different source was at work in their estranged effort to maintain the sense of otherness. It is not surprising, then, that intuitive sociological fiction fused with historically founded realistic fiction. Research could take the place of the enormous demands upon invention that resulted in exaggeration and caricature.

To consider the historicism of the nineteenth century, it is necessary also to consider its sociologism, and both must be considered in terms of the historically constant and the historically local insatiable drive for historical and sociological detail. Constant historicism and sociologism have their roots in gossip; and nineteenth-century historically local historicism and sociologism had their roots in post-Enlightenment estrangement. My title promised some mention of poetry, a promise which I have quite deliberately broken, since I wished only that the reader should always have poetry at the back of his mind. The reason I have broken that promise without any sense of shame is that I do not believe that poetry, just because it is poetry, offers any special problem of historicism which is not subsumed by the general phenomenon of nineteenth-century historicism. Finally, should anyone wonder, I am perfectly aware that this chapter is itself an instance of history as a rhetorical mode.

4

REBELLION

AND DEVIANCE

[1973*]

The word "rebel" is so rich and slippery a notion, one with so many aspects, a category with so many attributes, a grandiose palace of meaning with so many entrances (and, once one is inside, with so many trapdoors that suddenly precipitate one quite outside again), that it seems best to begin with reasonably safe platitudes. Since we spend the balance of our lives unlearning half the platitudes we were taught when we were young—platitudes we had to learn in order to enter into social existence—and, unhappily, confirming the validity of the other half, it is not necessarily either unwise or unsafe to rest one's weight on a platitude. Certainly I find it difficult to think of any proposition of literary history more resoundingly and flatly platitudinous than the one that asserts that Milton's Satan is the arch-exemplar of the rebel. And equally platitudinous is the notion that the early

* Presented at a comparative literature conference on "the outsider" held at Florida State University, Tallahassee, Florida, in January 1973.

nineteenth century saw, among the tiny handful of Europeans we call the first Romantics, the conversion of this same Satan from a villain into a hero. And matching these platitudes is the one that asserts that Byron, above all writers and above all men, in his works and in his life exemplified most purely the Romantic Rebel. The result of the Romantic enterprise has been the establishment of the rebel as an heroic figure, and the word I would emphasize is not "heroic" but "establishment." From that cultural event in the early nineteenth century to the present, there is a direct and unbroken line. We are engaged in considering a well-established social role, a role moreover for which there is an equally unbroken historical line of approval. I daresay there is hardly an academic, especially an academic humanist, who does not covertly or overtly ascribe to himself certain attributes of this heroic figure, and who does not feel, at least at times, that only insofar as he can identify himself as something of a rebel is there much possibility that within his disciplinary specialty he can hope to do something innovative, original, and creative.

Why the valuation of the rebel was changed from negative to positive is of course the great central question of the cultural problem of Romanticism. Any theory of Romanticism hinges upon that. I shall not, however, be concerned with proposing an explanation of why that should be so, but rather with related questions. The first is the puzzling question of why Satan was chosen when there were so many recent possible models of the rebel. Certainly the Romantics emerged from and within an age of revolutions, though I do not believe they can be identified with that revolutionary enterprise. If the revolutionary is identified with the rebel, the fifty years or so after the outbreak of the American Revolution provided plenty of political revolutionaries, many still alive in the early nineteenth century, whom the Romantics could have used for purposes of self-identification and for establishing the social role of the rebel. Now it is true that many of the Romantics admired and even worshipped certain of the late eighteenth-century political revolutionaries, but it is equally true that just as many Romantics were antirevolutionary. Indeed, among those individuals who are generally agreed to have been Romantics, there was a full spectrum of political attitudes, from the extreme right to the extreme left, and—a fact which is more helpful—a number who were politically indifferent. Indeed, I have long obscurely felt that Byron's going to the aid of insurgent Greece was somehow or other not a Romantic act at all, that it was like the decisions of certain members of the European nobility and military class to go to the aid of the American revolutionaries, and that it was an act more congruent with his avowed sympathies with such an eighteenth-century figure as Pope than with the general tenor of the Romantic enterprise. When one recalls, moreover, those members of the French nobility who quite sincerely sided with the radical revolutionaries of France, one is inclined to think that Byron's self-identification as a noble led to his Grecian adventure and that his decision, to a considerable degree, was governed by *noblesse oblige*.

A mythological figure, found in a seventeenth-century poem, then, was the model for the Romantic role of rebel. Surely one explanation for this is that the ideology of the eighteenth-century revolutionaries was an Enlightenment ideology. For those who have come to believe that Romanticism was not (as was once widely accepted and still is in some disciplines, such as art history and political history) a fulfillment of Enlightenment thinking but a rejection of it, the Romantic choice of Satan rather than an eighteenth-century revolutionary as the archetypical rebel is readily comprehensible. Equally easy to understand is the choice of a mythological figure rather than an historical figure. The attributes of mythological figures are both clear and coherent; an historical figure can be made into an ideal type only if he is purified of attributional trivialities and incoherencies. The United States, still by far the most consistently Enlightenment culture within the European culture area, thus turned Washington into an heroic figure. There is possible, however, a further explanation, which will perhaps serve to clarify the difference between the revolutionary and the rebel. I believe making such a distinction is justified on historical grounds; that is, the revolutionary as hero is clearly a bequest of the Enlightenment, and the rebel as hero, a bequest of Romanticism. Although it is true enough that some Romantic rebels were intensely interested in revolution, and that this tendency has continued to the present day, it is at least possible that such phenomena were the result of a crossing or a confusion of two quite separate categories of quite distinct historical origins. Thus Marx began with a Romantic philosophy, Hegelianism, mixed it with Christian-Enlightenment redemptionism, and ended with an Enlightenment vision of a future society, a secularization of the Christian heaven. All efforts to create a Romantic politics have much the same character. The central Romantic tradition has yet to develop a Romantic politics and perhaps is incapable of doing so.

A little examination of Milton's Satan may clarify all this. His initial activities consist of two quite different stages. In the second stage he was certainly a political revolutionary. He subverted and organized a third of the hosts of heaven, fled with them to the north, and there raised the standard of revolt. As a revolutionary he was seeking to displace the existing authority. But it was not this political act which seems to have interested the Romantics, and it was certainly not this which led them to make Satan into a model. It was the first stage, and that, from the point of human behavior—which Milton knew something about, though he knew nothing whatever about archangelic behavior—was a cultural act. It may, not too unfairly, be put thus. For aeons Satan and the other heavenly beings had been thronged in serried hierarchical order around the Heavenly Throne, worshipping the Divine Being. One fine day, however, Satan said to himself, "Really, there must be *something* else to do." What happened can be put, I think, quite simply. He had been engaged in a socioculturally validated pattern of behavior—a pattern validated, moreover, by the highest possible authority; a pattern, worse still, which he had been created to perform. His sin was simply that he innovated and performed an alternative pattern of behavior. On the other hand, in the second stage he did nothing of the sort. His object was to displace and to take the place of a power which he believed to have been illegitimately usurped. This, of course, is the classic rationale of the revolutionary; one is almost tempted to say, the classic rationalization. In this second stage there was no rejection of an existing social pattern; there was merely an attempt to replace one of its elements with another of the same sort. In conceiving of an alternative, Satan was a rebel; in seeking to displace the ultimate social power, he was a revolutionary.

Now it was this second stage that was characteristic of the eighteenth-century revolutionaries. Any culture is characterized by an incoherence of values, but when the culture is stable there is an almost irresistible tendency to perceive those incoherencies as coherent. Yet a little more refinement of this notion is essential. Rather, the individual—and this is perhaps what we mean by individuality—selects a certain package of the cultural patterns for himself and perceives them, in himself, as a coherent structure. A careful attention to the verbal behavior of individuals reveals with depressing clarity what an enormous and continuous effort goes into reconciling into a coherency the incoherent elements of this package. Further, this metapattern of creating coherency out of incoherency is itself guided by models selected from among the individuals—phenomenal, literary, or whatever —which the individual becomes aware of. This notion, of course, is still crude and purposive, and I shall attempt later to refine it, but for the moment it will serve. Currently the elements in the package and what I have called the metapattern are dignified and sanctioned by the name "values." What Satan did was to move from the perception of a cultural coherency to the perception of an incoherency. But in restoring his lost coherency, he merely selected one element of the dissolved coherency and used that as the pattern for a new coherency. His first stage, conceiving the possibility of an alternative mode of behavior, was the act of a rebel; his second stage, selecting a mode of behavior already available within his culture, was the act of a revolutionary.

If this distinction can be accepted, an explanation becomes possible of why the Romantics chose Satan rather than an Enlightenment political revolutionary as their ideal type and chose to reverse the valuation of the rebel rather than that of the revolutionary. The eighteenth-century revolutionaries saw the interests of ultimate power and the interests of the individual as incoherent, although they had always been seen as coherent, even by Satan. Thus the American revolutionaries eventually created a constitution which sundered ultimate power into three separate but equal powers, a solution which is constantly threatened with instability, as at the present time, at least if we are to believe the publicists of the Northeastern Liberal Establishment. Whether this threat exists or not, I confess I do not know, but given the inherent instability of the Constitution, I suspect it is so. Like Milton's God, President Nixon seemed to become increasingly dark with excessive bright, a phrase I never understood until now. However, the important matter is that the values the eighteenth-century activists forged into a coherent ideology were by no means novel. They had been available within the culture for a considerable period of time and had been widely discussed and extensively and constantly publicized. In rejecting the new ideology made out of old values, the Romantics were engaged in rebellion, not in revolution. Hence the eighteenth-century revolutionary could not serve them as a model or ideal type. However, a relatively pure mythological figure could so serve, since useless attributes could so easily be neglected and ignored, an activity much more difficult when dealing with an historical figure, particularly if he is recent and perhaps still alive. Even the mythological deification of Napoleon, in spite of the propagandistic efforts of his artists and publicists, did not get fully under way until after his death. Mythology is enormously valuable in organizing coherence, precisely because the attributes of mythological figures are so easily added and subtracted. And this is as true of terms that have a mythological function in more sophisticated constructions of cultural and individual coherence—terms such as the State, the Family, Society, the Individual, and Liberty, Equality, and Fraternity.

Moreover the Romantics had a particular difficulty with historical figures, a difficulty that made it necessary to turn to literary and mythological figures. The act of rebellion—that is, the act of conceiving the possibility of an alternative without, however, formulating a particular alternative—gives one, if not a powerful sense of actuality, at least a terrible lust for an actuality different from and opposed to the decent veils of mythology and mythologically functional terminology which cover the rather repulsive facts of human behavior, facts which can elicit compassion as well as disgust and cynicism. This was the lust, for example, that gave Balzac's thrust at the heart of French life its terrible power and energy. To misquote myself from an essay I wrote many years ago, to the Romantic no bone is so sweet to gnaw on as the white bone of a fact. Consequently, historical figures were relatively useless as models. The Romantic was in no position to ignore the facts of the matter, and for every historical figure, no matter how glorious, there are always embarrassing and compromising facts.

At this point it would perhaps be wise to introduce a note of clarification and caution. I am not saying that "rebel" *really* means one who has conceived the possibility of an alternative mode of behavior, a mode not socioculturally validated, or that "revolutionary" *really* means one who takes political action by selecting an ideology from values available within his culture. For one thing, it is clear that, before the Romantics, either "rebel" and "revolutionary" were interchangeable or, if a distinction existed, it probably was a distinction between one who refused to obey authority and who perhaps set up his own independent authority and one who attempted to overthrow authority and to displace it with his own. Rather, I am proposing a distinction which seems to apply to the present conference, and as evidence I offer the title of this conference. "Outsider" is, I take it, to be conceived as subsuming "rebel" and "exile." Judging by the association of these three terms and by the papers to be given, the terms appear to be meant in a cultural sense, not a political sense. I have assumed therefore that my task is to clarify, if I can, the notion of cultural rebellion. I believe that it is correct to state that such a notion was an innovation of the Romantics. It was an innovated category of behavior, and the only way to innovate a category, except by nonce words, is by metaphor. Indeed, a metaphor is, I believe, a culturally emergent category. The political term "rebel" was used as a metaphor for nonpolitical cultural behavior. Again, the line extending from the Romantics to this conference is quite clear. We are dealing with a phenomenon of Romanticism.

But not just with a phenomenon of Romanticism in the historically restricted sense, that is, with only the first couple of generations of nineteenth-century artists and philosophers. It is my conviction that high culture today is a continuation of Romanticism in so thoroughgoing a way that the term can properly be extended to include the high cultural events of the twentieth century. What is emergent today at the level of high culture is part of the Romantic tradition, and one of the best evidences of this is what I have already suggested, the establishment of the cultural rebel as a well-defined and well-established social role. But this creates a curious paradox. If a rebel is one who conceives of the possibility of an alternative mode of behavior, that is, alternative to any mode of behavior culturally available, then one mode of behavior now culturally available is to conceive of the possibility of a mode of behavior alternative to any mode culturally available. Or, to be a rebel is not to be a rebel.

This paradox accounts, in part, I think for the extraordinary cultural dynamism of the Romantic tradition. It has been justly called the Tradition of the New. This has meant that in the arts the Romantic tradition has created no style, as previous cultural traditions have, such as the Gothic, the Renaissance, the Baroque —. Each stylistic period of Romanticism has been, not a stylistic period in the traditional sense, but a group of individual styles sufficiently similar to be grouped together as a family of styles. Nevertheless, they have been sufficiently dissimilar so that the similarity is best accounted for by the cultural forces that controlled the artists' decisions rather than by any configurational similarity. What the various stylistic periods had in common was the discovery of some strategy of behavior; this process culminated in the curious and instructive episode of late-nineteenth-century and early-twentieth-century Art Nouveau, rediscovered in recent years and popularized. It is the only stylistic episode in the Romantic tradition which had the character of the styles before Romanticism. Nevertheless, it was quite different in origin, because the strategy of behavior discovered was the phenomenon of style itself as a universal of behavior. Consequently, for the first and last time groups of artists banded together to create a style—deliberately and self-consciously.

That effort was necessarily brief, like all Romantic efforts of rebellion. Its effect was to be one of the factors that released the artist to strike out entirely on his own. Thus, since 1908 or so it has been necessary to speak of the modern *styles* of art. The very concept of style has become pluralized.

The current state of the arts is even more curious and instructive. For reasons it is not necessary to go into here—it is sufficient to take note of the fact—in the Romantic tradition the primary vehicle for rebellion has been the arts. Sooner or later it was bound to happen that the rebellious act should be turned against art itself. The consequence of every artist's striking out for himself, so that his art was judged to be successful to the degree it symbolized self-conscious cultural rebellion, required that, as behavioral strategies were discovered in the creation of works of art, there would sooner or later be an exhaustion of possible strategies. The bottom of the barrel was reached by Abstract Expressionism. At least, the last strategy was discovered that, it appears, art is capable of discovering: the presentation in the work of art of those feeling states which underlie and are a concomitant of all behavioral strategies. Pop Art was the first stage of the rebellion against art itself. The result has been that the tradition of high art has spread out into a delta of culturally unrestricted deviance. One effect has been that the avant-garde artist is no longer interested in creating works that will last. His art is disposable. It may be that the tradition of high art is gone for good within European culture, which is fast becoming the dominant world culture. Happily, we still have lots of high art left, though, to be sure, it is not going to last forever.

An examination of another strain of the Romantic tradition will, I think, give us another clue to understanding what the Romantic tradition of cultural rebellion actually involved, or at least how it is profitably understood, for so far I have attempted only to isolate it as a category of behavior. The strain I am referring to is the tradition of Symbolism. Although it reached a climax in the late nineteenth century, it was there from the beginning, as such works as *The Ancient Mariner* and the paintings of Turner indicate. Romantic symbolism is best understood by looking at what the arts did before Romanticism. It was put—at least in English—most clearly by Sir Philip Sidney. The task of the arts was to exemplify a validated explanation of the world.

Sidney, of course, called such explanations "truths," as they are always called. Sidney's truths were part of Christian mythology. Our mythological truths today consist of such terms as Society and Individual. The proper response of the reader or observer was to think of these truths. The exemplifications of art and the explanations that they implied are by no means something that identifies the arts as art. On the contrary, the complete structure of explanation involves examples, for examples lead us from explanation to the phenomenal world. Examples tell us in what areas of phenomenal experience the explanation is to be appropriately applied. An explanation without examples is useless to anyone who is not so familiar with that particular explanatory mode that he can supply his own examples as the explanatory discourse unfolds. Further, since there is no necessary connection between explanation and exemplification, we have all had the experience of providing what turn out to be inappropriate or wrong examples for someone else's explanation which has insufficient examples, or even none. One of the difficulties of the history of philosophy is that so much philosophical explanation is entirely without examples. The result is that misinterpretation is common; or even worse, interpretation by exemplification leading us to the phenomenal world is in fact impossible.

Against this structure of explanation and exemplification, the Romantic tradition of symbolism becomes clearer. It is just the opposite of metaphysical discourse without examples. In poetry this led to such poems as those of Mallarmé—in one of which the subject of the poem is a word Mallarmé made up, a word to which there was, therefore, no possible explanatory response. Some of the results of this anti-explanatory or symbolist strain in the Romantic tradition are instructive. It led, very early, to the worship of Shakespeare, for the explanatory system which governed Shakespeare's exemplificatory decisions in writing his plays had been lost. Now that scholarship has recovered that system, the plays of Shakespeare tend, to me at least, to be somewhat less interesting. To the Romantic of the nineteenth century, Shakespeare was great because, as Arnold put it, he does not abide our question, that is, he resists explanation. Similarly, the cryptic conclusion to Goethe's *Faust* with its "The eternal feminine draws us onward" is particularly baffling to the explainer, because it includes the kind of words normally found in explanatory discourse, but not enough of them to give adequate clues as to what the explanation ought to be.

This anti-explanatory tendency is also to be found in another Romantic literary phenomenon, the rise of the novel to the level of high art. Narrative fiction had in the past been mostly at the cultural level of entertainment art: only slightly above, and very closely allied to, pure gossip, the appeal of which is that it offers us relief from the effort to explain the world and to experience interactions with it. Here, then, was a form ready to hand for an art of anti-explanatory exemplification. It is not surprising that the first great Romantic novelist was the historical novelist Sir Walter Scott, for history consists of masses of verbal statements which are taken to be true statements about a past, and hence unchangeable, actuality and which are peculiarly resistant to explanation. Although there were other reasons for the historicization of culture by the Romantic tradition, one reason can be derived from the fact that the previous mode of historical discourse, exemplary history, was rejected in favor of what came to be called "scientific" history—that is, history which purported only to discover and record the facts, with explanation reduced to the very minimal (though still mythological) causal explanation, or, in the hands of some historians, to no explanatory dimension at all. Thus Macaulay could write history modeled on Scott's fiction, and could reach an audience such as no historian had ever reached before, simply because he reduced history to almost pure exemplification, something extraordinarily close to gossip.

Another consequence of this anti-explanatory or symbolist strain in the Romantic tradition was the rise of music from the status of being a subordinate art—that is, one governed by the situations for which it is written—first, to the status of an independent or nonsituational art, then to an art equal to the great or major arts, and then to the status of the ideal or model art, so that in the second decade of this century various abstract painters explained their work by calling it visual music. Now I do not believe that music is, as is so often maintained, meaningless, in the simple and ordinary sense of "meaning." The fact that it is not is well indicated by the way verbal responses, or explanatory identifications of musical meaning, tend to fall into families of similar responses. The conclusion of Beethoven's Fifth Symphony has been called triumphant, heroic, martial, and so on, but I do not believe it has ever been called sad or melancholy or neurotic or grief-laden. However, music certainly does not contain within it an explanatory dimension, for explanation is a property of verbal behavior and of no other kind of behavior. Nor is there any agreement or established convention as to how music ought to be explained. On the other hand, the phenomenon of family resemblance is true not only of verbal explanations but of verbal explanations of every sign system, including words themselves, particularly verbal exemplifications. Coleridge's "Kubla Khan" has been explained in as many ways as a popular piece of music has been; in the same way, since there is no necessary connection between explanation and exemplification, the same example can be used for virtually any explanation. In philosophy the sentence, "The moon is made of green cheese," has been used to exemplify an endless variety of philosophical explanations, but they all fall at least in the admittedly large family of sentences of the rhetoric of philosophy. Music, then, fulfilled admirably the demands of the anti-explanatory strain of Romanticism. Indeed, the nineteenth century has been called the century of music, and of the various nineteenth-century arts, its music has survived at the high cultural level when so much else has been abandoned.

The same phenomenon can also be observed in painting. Modern painting emerged from the landscape tradition. Literary painting, painting that exemplified some set of verbal statements, was increasingly abandoned and in time was actively rejected, so that within a hundred years it was asserted that painting should not have a subject but only a motif. This amounted to the assertion that when one sees a painting of a mountain it is inappropriate to dwell upon the fact that it is indeed a mountain that is represented. One should not engage in the identification of the word which the particular configuration exemplifies. One should only respond to the purely painterly characteristic of the work, or at least what were thought to be such characteristics. The necessary result was the emergence of abstract painting.

For the same reason the poetic doctrine of semantic autonomy emerged—as in the famous statement of Archibald MacLeish, "A poem should not mean but be," a statement found, of all places, in a poem. This doctrine asserts that there is such a thing as poetic truth, and that its defining attribute is that such a truth cannot be uttered in language other than the language of that particular poem. In effect, this means that the poem cannot be explained. It is the most radical and explicit form of the anti-explanatory or symbolist tradition. As a statement of what is supposed to be a universal truth about poetry, it is a prime example of cultural ethnocentricity, the universalization of a culturally local phenomenon. But this need not surprise us. I know of no instances of literary and artistic critical doctrine that are not culturally ethnocentric. In saying "This is what is," they are all covertly saying, "This is what ought to be." But then, it is more than likely that all "is" statements are covertly "ought" statements.

Be that as it may, the anti-explanatory strain of Romanticism can tell us a great deal about the cultural rebel and cultural rebellion. Before it is anything else, an explanation is verbal behavior. If a rebel is one who conceives of the possibility of an alternative mode of behavior, then one kind of behavior to which he can conceive an alternative is verbal behavior. When the rebellious child says, "I won't do it," we usually explain it by saying that he is rebelling against his parent, but this explanation misses an important step. He is in fact rebelling against words which convey instructions for his behavior. Thus he is refusing to control his nonverbal behavior by a pattern of verbal behavior. He is rejecting directions for behavior. The cultural rebel does the same thing, though with an important difference. The rebellious child may very well say, or rather whine—like adults, children usually whine when they ask for an explanation—"Why?" Thus he is demanding an explanation for the instructions; he is demanding that the instructions be regarded as an exemplification of an explanation. The difference in the behavior of the adult cultural rebel is that he is rejecting not merely the exemplificatory instructions but the explanation as well. But this is of the highest importance, for, as the example of the child shows, explanations organize our behavior. We ordinarily short-circuit this process by saying that explanations explain the world, but it is far more accurate and complete to say that explanations organize our transactions with the world. Hence when an explanation fails, a segment of our behavior collapses, and a segment or area of the world is left without explanation. We cannot conduct transactions with that explanation. It is not sufficient, then, to define the cultural rebel as one who conceives the possibility of an alternative mode of behavior. Prior to that conception has occurred the rejection of an explanation. If it is the rejection of a rich and overriding explanation, the kind of explanation that may be called a meta-explanation, one that subsumes and thus explains other explanations (explanations closer to exemplifications, or instructions for transactions with the world), if it is the rejection of such explanations as Christianity or the Enlightenment explanatory modes, which purported to explain everything, then the consequences can be widespread and devastating. The individual can be reduced to only the most minimal transactions, those necessary to keep him alive, but not much more than that. And this is indeed the crisis which most Romantics have gone through, from the early nineteenth century to the present.

It follows, however, that if transactions are to be renewed with that area of the world where old explanations have failed, then alternative explanations must be accepted or developed. From this point of view the various apparently quite dissimilar strands of the Romantic tradition and of our own high culture, current Romanticism, can themselves be explained. It is a matter of the strategies adopted to meet the crisis of failed explanations. The first strategy is the search for existing but alternative explanations. One strand in the Romantic tradition is the search for new general explanations of the world from outside the European tradition or—as with the regressive Blake and in such phenomena as Catholic Revivalism and Satanism—for explanations once current in European culture but long since abandoned by high culture. The nineteenth and the twentieth centuries have experienced a culturally minor but continuous experimentation with explanations taken from Oriental culture.

A second strategy is the generation of novel explanations. There have been a good many of these and they continue to emerge. Many are quite bizarre and idiosyncratic, but even these are often useful for the creation of works of art. After all, since the task of art is to exemplify explanations, it does not matter a great deal what explanations are exemplified. This is why we can enjoy works controlled by an explanation which is no longer acceptable—such as *Paradise Lost*. In the English-speaking world quite the most famous of recent explanations in the literary tradition is Yeats' *A Vision*, about which he quite frankly stated that virtually its only real value lay in providing metaphors for poetry. Thus, in this tradition, the tendency is always toward a position in which the art justifies the explanation, not the other way around, as was the case before the nineteenth century.

The third strategy I have already discussed in somewhat limited manifestations: the anti-explanatory strategy. In this tradition meta-explanations are subsumed under the general notion of explanation, and explanation itself is rejected. It is for this reason that Kant is often considered to be the beginning of Romantic thinking, and Hegel is his great continuator. For Kant, since we cannot know the thing-in-itself, we cannot know the world, and consequently any explanation of the world cannot correspond to the world. For Hegel, freedom is the absolute self-consciousness of explanatory behavior, though he scarcely expressed it in such terms. For Hegel, Kant had not arrived at this self-consciousness and thus was ultimately victimized by his own explanatory impulse. To Hegel, we must explain the world in order to maintain a transactional relation with it, but freedom is knowing this and knowing also that any explanation can only be a means to accomplish such transactions.

This rejection of the authenticity of any explanation is clearly the most complete act of cultural rebellion it was possible to make. Two forces have kept the social role of cultural rebel alive and expanding: One is a behavioral pattern such that—if an emergent behavioral pattern is established, or even gains a mere toehold— it will be continued simply because it is now among the possibilities for organizing behavior. The second is precisely this anti-explanatory strategy at the heart of the Romantic tradition. That such a judgment is not exaggerated is shown, I think, by the fact that the anti-explanatory tradition has been responsible for the creation of those works of art and also of philosophy which have survived best from the nineteenth century and which are most powerful and successful in the twentieth. Thus one factor, I believe, in the current rebellion against and rejection of the tradition of high art is the fact that the explanations of art and the explanations of the historical development of Romantic art—though not to my mind at all adequate by any stringent intellectual standard—were nevertheless too complete. Thus, what is happening today is as much a rejection of the explanation of high art as it is the rejection of that tradition itself.

Of these three strategies, the first two have added little or nothing to the resources of human culture and of the human condition. But I do not believe that statement applies to the third strategy, the anti-explanatory tradition. Belief in the eternal and absolute truth of any explanation appears to be the primary source of the kind of suffering that man imposes upon himself, the suffering of violence and of war. But an explanation is only a kind of verbal behavior that enables us to organize our transactions with the world. I have pointed out the devastating effects the loss of meta-explanations can have upon individuals. When a culture is dominated by a meta-explanation—or even, as with ours, by a bundle of more or less unrelated meta-explanations—the threat of losing a meta-explanation is terrifying. It threatens, of course, the total disorganization of behavior. But since no meta-explanation can be true, or can be more than a way of organizing by subsumption less general explanations, meta-explanations are constantly threatened by dissolution. Much of the cultural history of man can be understood from this point of view, the attempt to shore up meta-explanations which from their very nature are inadequate and constantly threatened with failure. They are frequently divorced from exemplification and they are constantly being applied to the organization of modes of transaction called into existence by our very transactions with the world. From this point of view, cultural rebellion was by no means discovered by Romanticism; but it was socioculturally established. War, which is the ultimate effort to shore up a meta-explanation, is the most metaphysical, the intellectually most abstract of human activities. This applies even to the

Marxian doctrine that modern war is the result of economic conflict. That is simple-minded. Rather, assuming that economic conflict does play a part in the generation of wars, they arise from economic explanations of man's transactions with the human and nonhuman world. Yet, as any modern economist will tell you, we have no real understanding of economic forces, though we have a number of very elegant theories. A war fought for an economic explanation of the world does not differ from a war fought for a religious explanation.

Any explanation of the world hardly seems worth fighting for, though perhaps any explanation of the world is worth fighting against, when it strives to shore itself up by violence and by war. Any explanation, and above all any meta-explanation, is inadequate because it limits the range of our transactions with the world, and indeed it can be maintained only by that continual threat and application of violence or force which we call policing. Although there is little hope in the foreseeable future that enough people will be weaned from a reliance upon illusory explanatory truths to make very much of a difference in the conduct of human affairs, nevertheless the continuance of the anti-explanatory tradition of cultural rebellion as one mode of the cultural rebel is at least a continual reminder to a few people of the dangers of reliance upon the absolute truth of explanatory verbal behavior.

A second contribution of this anti-explanatory tradition has been its revelation, even discovery, of the process by which new explanations are brought into existence. This can be shown by the symbolist tradition, for its effect has been to elicit from interpreters of symbolist art tremendous efforts to explain it. Some of these efforts have been successful, at least in the sense that they have become culturally established. But those efforts show that a new explanation of some usefulness is brought into existence by purely exemplary behavior, divorced from explanation. Further, as I have suggested above, the cultural rebellion of the first Romantics gave them a powerful thrust toward actuality. The equivalent of actuality in the arts, and in science as well, is exemplary material. The two are by no means the same, in spite of the almost universal tendency to think so. The symbolic tradition consists of instructions to engage in transactions with the phenomenal world. I do not mean specific transactions, but rather a continuous reminder of the value of dealing with actuality, of seeing things as much as possible as they are. Gossip relieves us from the strain of explanation, but it also relieves us from the strain of doing something. We can never, of course, see things as they really are, but we can always see more than we have seen and can always see everything better. That is the second way the symbolic tradition has been valuable. A third way comes out strongly when we consider the history of nineteenth- and twentieth-century fiction from this point of view. To make way for both the rejection of an explanation and the generation of a more adequate one, the validated explanation must be broken down. One of the best ways to do this is to overload it with more and richer exemplary material than it can handle. As I have suggested above, the very nature of the fictional tradition makes it a superb vehicle for bringing together into a single narrative vast amounts of exemplary statements. Both Balzac and Zola are cases in point. Both attempted to organize their sequences of novels by explanatory modes which are in fact hopelessly inadequate to subsume as exemplifications the vast material which they deployed, and both gave rise in themselves and in their interpreters to new modes of explanation.

The third contribution to culture made by the Romantic tradition of the cultural rebel has been the uncovering of the behavioral processes by which such rebellion comes into existence. To grasp this it is necessary to have some notion of deviance and deviant behavior, because, simply enough, the rebel, if not identifiable with the deviant, is certainly subsumed by the deviant. Indeed, throughout the history of the social role of the Romantic cultural rebel he has constantly been identified with the deviant, and in the late nineteenth century, during that period inadequately called the Decadence, a good many cultural rebels deliberately adopted the role of the deviant or wore the deviant's mask. So the first question is, How does the deviant come into existence? But this question is necessarily subsumed by a more general explanatory question, How does any personality become what it is? What is the etiology of personality? That is, what are the causes of particular and individual personalities? Why is a personality what it is? I must confess that I believe these to be unanswerable questions. Apart from the fact that the term "cause" is a mythological term, or, a little more mildly, a purely explanatory term, a term that connects sentences on the same level and also is used to subsume one sentence or term under another, it seems clear to me that all the etiologies of personality have failed. Anna Freud herself has confessed that her father's theories of personality formation have no predictive power, and prediction is the best test of explanation. If an explanation cannot yield predictive sentences which can be interpreted as having been confirmed, then that explanation is best discarded. Rather, I think that the only possible model for constructing an explanation for personality is a statistical model. To be sure, it is not possible at the present time, and perhaps never can be, to go beyond this to a determination of personality variables and the statistical calculation of possibilities of combinations of those variables. The variables are too many for our present statistical resources, too uncontrollable, and too difficult to define. A question about personality amounts to a question about what behavioral patterns that particular organism evinces. Now, aside from the fact that many behavioral patterns are covert and inaccessible to observation, there is also the fact that the notion of behavioral pattern is itself a construct, that is, an explanatory, not an exemplary, term. When we speak of a behavioral pattern we are saying that we have observed sequences of behavior sufficiently alike to be subsumed under one category, but the observational process itself is a matter of selective perception.

There is a further difficulty. The individual organism is autonomous, that is, self-directed. That at least is the contention of humanistic psychology, which is opposed to behaviorism. I confess the term "autonomous" means little more to me than the term "free will," which is merely another way of saying the same thing. I can give it content only by pointing to the fact that the human brain is so constructed that we cannot learn any behavioral pattern perfectly. The consequence is that innovation is the norm of human behavior, and innovational drift, to be comprehended only from a statistical point of view, is the principal dynamism of cultural change. Human culture has developed, however, a counteragent to this drift, an agent I call channeling. Channeling works against the spread of deviance. To the degree any behavioral pattern is badly transmitted to the young of each generation, that behavioral pattern shows the delta effect: the spread into a wide range of deviance from the pattern. Channeling—of which the principal instrument is policing, the direct and indirect use of physical force—is the cultural means by which a cultural pattern is kept within a tolerable range of deviance during the individual's lifetime and from generation to generation.

In the emergence of a personality, which is a package of behavioral patterns always marked by a certain degree of drift, there are two immensely complex sets of factors: the genetic variability of the staggering complexity of brain activity and the immense complexity of behavioral patterns. From the interaction of these two sets of factors emerges that package of behavior we call personality and which, as I suggested above, we strive manfully to grasp, both in ourselves and in others, as an organized structure, a task which always and necessarily eludes us. Now in human behavior the connection between stimulus and response, with a few exceptions, is not genetic; it is a matter of convention. That is what we mean, in the widest sense, by human culture. The establishment of conventions is channeling, carried on by policing. If policing were not part of cultural behavior, culture itself could not possibly have emerged, nor could human beings be human beings. That is why freedom always means the channeling of our behavior in ways that are, for whatever reason, satisfying to us.

From this point of view explanatory behavior is a mode of channeling, carried on by policing. That is why in education punitive measures of various sorts are used to teach the young that particular explanations of the world are true. The question "Is this explanation a true explanation?" is a mode of saying "Should this explanation be channeled by policing?" The cultural rebel, I have suggested, is one who rejects a mode of explanation. But the rebel, like all personality types, is produced by a random process, which means here by a process which is beyond our comprehension, but for which only a statistical type of explanation is conceivably appropriate. Just as the policing process which prevents most people from stealing or committing sexual crimes is always ineffective for some, so the policing process by which explanation is culturally channeled through time and history fails with some individuals. Cultural rebellion, then, is a form of deviance. What the Romantics did was to convert some kinds of cultural rebellion from a negative to a positive valuation. They did it by using the word "creative" to designate certain types of deviance.

However, we need not leave the problem here, for something more can be said. Some years ago two psychologists, MacKinnon and Barron, conducted a study of creativity. The study itself is somewhat suspect, because creativity is a Romantic concept. To define some modes of deviancy as creative is a result of the Romantic tradition of granting to some modes of cultural rebellion a positive valuation. That is, in the very study of creativity there is a cultural ethnocentricity of which, it appears, the psychologists who carried out the study were unaware. They had not grasped that creativity is validated deviancy. And the study is made more suspect by the fact that increasingly—it is one of the unhappy results of the Romantic tradition—almost any mode of behavior sufficiently deviant to be noticed is called creative and self-expressive, the Self being one of the central terms of Romantic mythology. Nevertheless, there is much of interest in their investigations, once this cautionary note has been introduced.

As part of their study they made a composite of the most common childhood and adolescent experiences of those architects whom other architects had designated as creative. Within the fascinating constellation of experiences, many of which the subjects had in common, one of the most interesting is that when they were children their families moved frequently within a community, or from community to community, and that as children they were usually lonely, shy, and withdrawn. That is, they were never integrated, as we say, for long periods of time into a single community, and in fact were never really integrated into a community for even short periods.

I am aware of the dangers of ethology and of deriving human behavior from animal behavior, yet one observation of John C. Calhoun, the famous student of rat populations, is, I think, highly instructive here. When he undertook his studies he divided his rats quite arbitrarily into high-, medium-, and low-interaction groups, tagging each rat accordingly. He was then astonished to discover that such a division actually corresponded to different types of behavior. The high-interaction rats were fat and sleek and competent, and they did everything well. The medium-interaction group did practically everything badly. Female rats built sleazy nests and, when they moved them, invariably managed to misplace one or two of the litter. Low-interaction rats, however, were quite different. These were the rats who innovated novel behavioral patterns, some of which were then adopted by the high-interaction rats and imitated, though incompetently, by the medium-interaction rats. He has observed the same phenomena in rats living in a natural environment. The similarity to the childhood experiences of the creative architects is striking and irresistible.

Romantic literature from its very inception is full of individuals, both adults and children, who are characterized by low interaction and by shyness, loneliness, and withdrawal. Senancour's great work, *Obermann*, is about an individual who withdraws from the world and begins to reject on an astonishing scale the explanatory modes of his culture and to arrive at notions which no one else that I know of arrived at before the twentieth century, although *Obermann* was published in 1804. The explanation is really quite simple, I think. Channeling by policing is not done merely by authorities and superiors. It is also done by peers and inferiors. Thus, the greater the integration of the individual into a community, the more successfully his behavior is channeled by policing strategies which come at him from all sides. Now it is evident from biographies, autobiographies, and literature that the rejection of a culturally dominant explanatory mode immediately results in a reduction of the individual's interaction rate. The result was a stance, a mode of existence, of which we have heard much in recent years—though, I think, for the most part the word has been incorrectly used—alienation. Or, if not used incorrectly, at least the word has been used for individuals who in fact increase their interaction with either politically revolutionary groups of an Enlightenment type or with dropout groups.

Romantic alienation is just opposite. It is the consequence of cultural rebellion, as I have defined it. Two things may be said of it.

First, Romantic alienation increases the probability, as with Obermann, that the individual will move on to further rejection of available and dominant explanatory modes, and, as with the creative architects as well as with Obermann and the low-interaction rats, it increases the probability that he will innovate significantly in his area of competence. In identifying and establishing alienation the Romantic tradition discovered the path to the transcendence of one's culture and its limitations.

Second, I think we may say that the Romantic tradition established a way of making sociocultural use of those individuals, the accidents of whose personality formation make them susceptible to the role of cultural rebel, to creative deviance. By changing the valuation of the cultural rebel, whom we may call the explanatory heretic, from negative to positive—if only within a very small subculture at the level of high culture, which in itself involves only a very small proportion of any population—the Romantic tradition rescued the talents of those susceptible to the role of cultural rebel from cultural waste and transformed them to cultural productivity and valuable innovation. I do not say that before Romanticism all such individuals were wasted. Obviously, that is not and could not be the case. Rather, Romanticism increased enormously the probability that susceptible individuals of talent could achieve cultural transcendence. It established, as a social role, the kind of individual who could play that role effectively and created the mechanism that makes that effective role-playing possible. To return once again to our paradox, by establishing the social role of cultural rebel, the Romantic tradition channels and polices susceptible individuals into breaking the limits of explanatory and exemplificatory channeling and policing; it channels and polices them into cultural transcendence. One of the neglected, degraded, and misunderstood resources of humanity has been recognized, validated, understood, and put to use.

5

ICONOGRAPHY AND ICONOLOGY

IN THE ARTS OF THE

NINETEENTH AND TWENTIETH CENTURIES

[1973*]

In recent years art historians have begun to realize that the paintings of the nineteenth century are appropriately interpreted in other than purely painterly and representational language. To be sure, genre, anecdotal, and historical paintings have always been so interpreted; they have been called "literary." And of course that tradition of nineteenth-century painting has for many years been denigrated. The history of nineteenth-century painting has been judged from the point of view of avant-garde twentieth-century painting. What led to Cézanne and Matisse and Picasso was important. What did not lead to modern painting was not. As I shall try to show, there is considerable justice in this interpretation, although it has led to the neglect of a good many very attractive works, which only in the last few years— and then by a very limited number of art historians and lovers of painting—have begun to be re-examined at least with equa-

* Reprinted by permission from *The Structurist*, University of Saskatchewan, Saskatoon, in which it appeared in abridged form in issue no. 12 (1972–73), pp. 26–31.

nimity and occasionally with real pleasure. Recent interest in Art Nouveau styles and such events as last summer's "French Symbolist Painters" exhibition in London have raised puzzling questions about a kind of painting which is not exactly "literary" and yet is "symbolical"; that is, some kind of verbal interpretation seems to be appropriate, although what kind is rather uncertain.

The study of the line of painting that led to modern art has both assumed and confirmed that it developed out of the landscape tradition. To be sure, there were certain exceptions. The contribution of Delacroix to the tradition was not in landscape, nor was that of Manet. Nevertheless, it is generally felt that the prime interest of those men was not in the subject but in, so to speak, the rendering, in that aspect of painting which could not be subsumed under some "literary" interest nor was controlled and directed by it. Delacroix, it is generally assumed, was less interested in painting, let us say, Hamlet, than he was in the place of the representational configuration "Hamlet" in the set of formal interactions that *was* the painting, really the *painting*. Consequently it was crucial that in the course of time the notion of subject was abandoned for the notion of motif. As in music, the formal manipulation of the motif was far more important than what motif was chosen. One can say that such men as Delacroix and Manet looked at human figures and artifacts as if they were no more than elements, not in a landscape, but of a landscape.

However, in recent years there has been a growing tendency to assume that the main line of nineteenth-century painting presents not only an iconographical problem but also an iconological problem. Briefly, the iconography of the main line leading to modern art is the landscape, although the nude—the prime element in the academic tradition—played an important part in the emergence of modern painting in the first decade of this century (but again, it was the nude as landscape, as motif). The nude presented formal possibilities that the landscape did not, and Cézanne, of course, synthesized the two in his "Bathers" series, reducing the nude to an element in the landscape. Following him, both Matisse and Picasso used the nude in their struggles to break through to a new conception of painting, the kind of painting we call modern. The iconological problem, however, raises the question of why so much nineteenth-century painting was landscape and why the landscape was the primary path to the modern. Or it raises the problem of why musical instruments were such an important element in the iconography of cubism, or why the Impressionists chose particular categories of landscape motifs. It asks the question as to whether the reduction of subject to motif is at all an adequate explanation of why painters selected the particular motifs they did select. Do Cézanne's numerous pictures with Mont Sainte-Victoire as motif or the great Fontainebleau forest scenes of his late period raise the possibility that iconological explanation is as appropriate as iconographical identification?

There have been efforts, of course, along these lines. Most interestingly, as I shall attempt to show, some of them—for example, some explanations of Van Gogh and Cézanne—have been efforts to locate an iconological system in psychoanalytical explanation. Other efforts, such as John W. McCoubrey's *American Tradition in Painting* (1963) or my own *Beyond the Tragic Vision* (1962), have tried different lines of inquiry. A more recent effort of great interest, though by no means fully satisfactory, is the essay by William Vaughan in the catalog of the Caspar David Friedrich exhibition held in the Tate Gallery in London in September and October of 1972. My goal in this essay will be to put these efforts in a larger historical frame and at the same time to point out certain relationships among the various arts. To do so, however, it will first be necessary to clarify, at least for my purposes, certain perplexing terms: not only "iconography" and "iconology," but also "meaning," "symbol," "mythology," and "redemption."

To begin with, "iconography" is itself used rather loosely. For example, the iconography of a still life may be said to consist of a pipe, playing cards, a glass of wine, and so on; or the pipe, the playing cards, the glass of wine, and the rest may be said to be an iconography of relaxation, pleasure, and amusement. This can be clarified by saying that the configurations in the painting mean "pipe," "playing cards," etc., and that the pipe, playing cards, etc., mean "relaxation," "pleasure," and "amusement." A statement of meaning, then, is the verbalization of an act of interpretation, and the verbalization may be either subsequent to the act or simultaneous with the act. In behavioral language—a language which attempts to restrict itself to the phenomenally observable—both the act of interpretation and the stating of meaning are responses. Thus the response to the configuration is the interpretational perception of it as a pipe, and the verbalization may be either a response to the configuration or a response to the interpretational perception. Further, stating that the assemblage of configurations of pipe, playing cards, glass of wine, etc., is an iconography of relaxation and pleasure and amusement is stating the meaning of the assemblage and can be simultaneous with the interpretational perception, or with the verbalization of the meaning of the various configurations, or subsequent to both. Once more, the statement of the meaning of the assemblage is a response either to the interpretational perception of the members of the assemblage or to a verbalization. These stages of regression from the initial perception of a configuration prior to its interpretational perception (as, for example, when one sees the painting from a distance and cannot yet make an interpretational perception but can only perceive that there are configurations distinguishable from their ground) are stages of subsumption. The initially unidentifiable configuration is, in the act of interpretational perception, subsumed under the configurational category "pipe." If this is verbalized, it is categorized with the other categorially identified configurations (playing cards, glass of wine, etc.) under the more general categories "relaxation," "pleasure," "amusement." If we should now ask why the artist painted such a picture, we may respond to these verbal categories by such statements as "He painted many such pictures," and if we should ask further why he did so, we may respond by such statements as, "Other biographical data indicate his hedonistic personality" or "At the time there was a ready market for such pictures, as evidenced by the fact that a great many artists were painting pictures of this sort." Each of these stages of interpretation of the preceding stage may be termed verbal explanation, and the whole series may be regarded as an explanatory regress from the initially unidentifiable configuration. And this is the structure of all explanation.

But we may also turn in another direction. Let us assume that this particular still life, without intervening verbalization, induces a feeling of hedonistic relaxation. Such a feeling state is a response to the picture. It is perfectly within the conventional limits for the usage of the word "meaning" to state that the meaning of the picture is that particular feeling state. At the present time it is more than likely that the form that statement would take is "The picture symbolizes hedonistic relaxation," or less likely but more precisely, "symbolizes a feeling of hedonistic relaxation." And for such a statement to be made it is not necessary that the speaker actually experience the feeling state in question. Further, it would be equally correct, linguistically, to say that the picture symbolizes relaxation, pleasure, and amusement, or, skipping over the intervening stages of explanatory regress, that it symbolizes the interest of the artist's society in hedonism. What is at issue here is brought out if the statement is made that the picture symbolizes relaxation, pleasure, and amusement, and also the interest of the artist's society in hedonism. That is, we use the word "symbol" and its various forms when we are indicating that two or more responses are appropriate to a given configuration, whether it is visual or verbal. Further, a statement that a painting symbolizes a feeling state is also an instance of explanatory regress.

All this can be understood if a radical conventionalism is adopted as a theory of meaning. Thus, the meaning of any configuration is the response to that configuration. It follows that any configuration can elicit all possible responses (which are theoretically infinite) and that all configurations (likewise theoretically infinite) can elicit but a single response. Obviously, successful interaction either with ourselves or with others depends upon limiting the meaning responses to configurations. Consequently, when we used the word "mean" or any of its derivatives, we are generally making a normative assertion that the verbal or nonverbal response to a configuration, whether verbal or nonverbal, ought to be a particular response or category of response. Nonnormatively—or rather, self-conscious of the normative character of the statement—we are in fact asserting that, given the particular situation, some particular response is the appropriate response. We are doing the same thing when we say that a configuration is a sign of something or that it refers to something. On the other hand, when we say that the configuration is a symbol or symbolizes, we are asserting that two or more responses are equally appropriate, or that one of them is additionally appropriate.

All this is perfectly usable in discussing nineteenth-century painting of the main tradition that leads to the modern, but when we seek to make use of "iconology" we run into difficulties. The examples of its use in discussing nineteenth and twentieth century painting given above do not in fact conform to the established use of "iconology." Is an answer to the question, "Why does cubism so often make use of an iconography of musical instruments?" in fact an instance of iconological study? As iconology is practiced, it is not such an instance, nor are psychoanalytical interpretations. Iconology was founded by Émile Mâle and Aby Warburg, though there were isolated predecessors. In 1933 the Warburg Library was moved from Hamburg to London and became the Warburg Institute in the University of London. In 1931 Erwin Panofsky brought the Warburg tradition to the United States, first to New York University and then to Princeton University. Aby Warburg's goal was to relate the study of art to the rest of culture, and his achievements and those of his followers, particularly Panofsky, have been as impressive as they have been fascinating. Some twenty years ago D. W. Robertson led the way to applying the tradition to the study of literature, though, to be sure, he was not the pioneer. It cannot be said, however, that Warburg's goal has been completely realized. Iconological study has remained, on the whole, within the limits that he and Panofsky set, Medieval and Renaissance art, though since World War II it has been extended into the seventeenth and eighteenth centuries, but not beyond.

The reason is that iconology is concerned with traditionally established meanings. For example, in many fifteenth-century paintings the Romanesque style was an iconography of the dispensation before Christ and the Gothic style, of the dispensation after—that is the Synagogue and the Church. This could scarcely be deduced from the paintings themselves, and in fact was not deduced until that interpretation was established from written sources. What this means is that iconological study makes statements parallel to such statements as, "Other biographical data indicate his hedonistic personality," but not of precisely the same sort. That is, they are statements of a more regressive stage than iconographic statements but are concerned with rediscovering and determining the conventions of explanatory regress which controlled the iconography in the painting under study.

This can be best understood by examining such a typical example of religious iconography as a picture of St. Christopher. The first stage of iconographic identification judges the configuration to be that of a human being, but certain iconographical attributes—his gigantic size, the infant Christ on his shoulders, the ford he is carrying the Child across, and the palm tree he used as a staff when he carried travelers across the ford—make possible the second regressive stage of iconographic identification. The Child of course has certain attributes, such as halo and orb, that serve as iconographic identifications for him. Iconology comes into play when the history of these iconographic attributes is studied. But of course they cannot be studied apart from the tradition of Christian culture in general. It is that tradition which establishes the iconographic conventions, which controls the decisions of the painter, and which—above all—provides the explanation for the attributes. Thus legends of St. Christopher also make use of the same iconographic attributes and in addition explain why St. Christopher came to carry the Christ child. For example, the saint was searching to serve the greatest ruler in the world, and the orb or world icon which the child carries indicates that he has found him. And that is why the saint is presented, in spite of his great size and strength, as bowed under the weight of the world-ruler. Thus an iconological explanation of a painting subsumes the iconographical attributes in the painting. In the same way, the ball which is one of the gifts the shepherds give the Child in the *Second Shepherds' Play* is likewise an icon of the verbal phrase "world orb" and the action is iconologically explained as the submission of human souls to the governance of Christ. And the governance of Christ means the possibility of redemption.

Thus the system of iconological explanation which explains the iconographical attributes of St. Christopher and establishes the human figure as St. Christopher is the same system that explains and establishes the iconography of all the other saints from Agatha to Zenobius, and of the Trinity, the Madonna, the nine orders of heavenly beings from Angels up to Cherubim, and of the three members of the Trinity—Father, Son, and Holy Spirit—and ultimately of the Trinity as a Unity. Thus a painting of St. Christopher is a visual exemplification of an elaborate and wide-ranging system of explanation, which regresses from the visual sign through a hierarchical series of stages of explanatory regress, from the picture of the saint to the ultimate "cause" or explanatory termination "God," which subsumes explanatory stages explaining not only St. Christopher but everything else. Hence everything in the world is an exemplification, through various stages of explanatory regress, of the single terminal explanatory term "God." Traditionally iconography establishes the icon (or, in literature, the image) as exemplifying that explanatory system, while iconology studies the history of the icon and its attributes, its place in the system, the system as a whole, and—such was Aby Warburg's goal—the place of that Christian explanatory system in Western, and ultimately human, culture. Yet iconological study has done little with exemplifications of other explanatory systems and just as little with Warburg's ultimate goal.

Furthermore, the Christian explanatory system is not only an explanatory system, it is a mythology. All mythologies are explanatory systems, but the reverse does not hold. Explanation subsumes mythology, and mythology thus may be said to exemplify the more general explanatory regress, "explanation." But how can one tell the difference? The simplest and most general mark of a mythology is that it includes verbal icons—such as the ball in the *Second Shepherds' Play* or the word "Christ"—which can also be presented as visual icons. Indeed, aural icons are also possible: for example, the ancient bull-roarer was an icon for the voice of a god. Whether in human history visual icons preceded verbal icons or whether the reverse was the case or whether either or both preceded explanatory statements which included verbal icons is something we can scarcely know; but as we shall see, it was frequently assumed in the nineteenth century, especially in its later decades, that icon creation must precede the explanatory statements which subsume icons. The second and more subtle mark of a mythology is the reification or hypostatization of explanatory terms, that is, the unanalyzed assumption that such terms must necessarily refer to entities in the natural or supernatural worlds. Words, however, do not refer. What is commonly known as a referential or empirical statement is a set of directions to locate a particular configuration. One appropriate response is to locate it. Reification, or hypostatization, on the other hand, assumes that something can be located without, however, taking the trouble to do so, and thus conceals the behavioral aspect of reference and the direction-giving character of the statement in question. In the eighteenth-century Enlightenment mythology, which is still very much with us, such terms are Man, Nature, and Society. These terms were so manipulated as to yield by subsumption such notions as "Human Rights" and "Human Dignity," which were in turn subsumed into such terms as "Freedom" and "Equality." The famous exhibition of photographs of Man at the New York Museum of Modern Art was a collection of icons of the reification Human Dignity, as has been recently pointed out, and so are the statues of the Races of Man by Malvina Hoffman. To judge by the latter, human beings are all quite astonishingly beautiful, graceful, and noble. The notions of Human Rights and Human Dignity clearly mark the Enlightenment mythology, still the dominating mythology of Western Europe and increasingly of the world, as a redemptive mythology. The explanation is that the third mark of a mythology is that in human behavior it has a redemptive function.

To understand this it is useful to return to St. Christopher, who is still very much with us in the form of statuettes on the dashboards of automobiles and medals which are displayed in the same way and worn on chains around the neck. St. Christopher is the patron saint of travelers. He protects them. If we look at the automobile driver's behavior from a point of view outside of the mythological system it is not difficult to comprehend that the effect of the display of the statuette on the dashboard is to control the behavior of the driver so that his performance is dangerous neither to himself nor to others. This statement can be subsumed by the more regressive explanatory statement (of the kind commonly called "scientific laws") that culture consists of directions for performance, directions presented in the form of signs—verbal, nonverbal, visual, tactile, and so on. As the driver rolls down the highway he is continuously responding to a wide range of signs, from the road-curve on the horizon to the sound of the engine. To these signs, singly and in combination, an indefinably large range of responses is possible. What the statuette of St. Christopher does is to limit the range of those sign-responses so that the driver performs within a socially validated range of driving behavior, within limits constantly policed by highway patrolmen. Now the statuette is a visual icon of the verbal icon "St. Christopher"; the mythological explanation is that he is an embodiment of divine grace, emanating from God. The saints, so to speak, split up that divine grace so that it may be functional in particular classes of situations or for individuals through naming a child after a saint. In short, God as One— through the mediation of Christ as a member of God as Trinity and through the further mediation of St. Christopher—redeems our driver from deviant driving behavior. Or if he is hypnotized by the interstate and nearly has an accident, St. Christopher saves or redeems him from death. Or if he engages in deviant behavior by making a forbidden U-turn across the median (tempted by Satan, of course) he may be arrested and redeemed back to validated driving behavior by punishment—a jail sentence, a fine, points on his license, or temporary loss of his license. Even in our predominantly Enlightenment culture, the police are the avatars of the government, and the government's authority is explained by the Constitution, which places the state and its citizens under the protection of God. The mythology is attenuated from its medieval and Catholic richness and plentitude, but it is still there and it is still effective.

From within the mythological system, however, the interpretation of these events is quite different. To the believing driver the statuette is the immediate cause of his safe driving. Of course he will protest that the statuette is only an immediate cause, and that the mediating cause is St. Christopher himself, and that the ultimate or final cause is God. But however he constructs his explanatory regress, the important word is "cause." Whether he says that St. Christopher helps him drive well or protects him or whatever, the underlying notion is a causal explanation of the relation between the statuette and the driving performance. Now the word "cause" is one that, for two hundred years, philosophy has become increasingly suspicious of. If we say, "Brake failure causes accidents," the only way to find out if the statement is reliable or not is to put it in the form, "If I disconnect the brakes on my car and take to the road, the probability is that I will have an accident," and then to follow the directions in that statement and see what happens. The fact that you reach your destination safely does not disprove the statement. Only if just before an accident you apply your brakes and do have an accident can you say that the statement has some reliability. To be tested, then, a causal statement must be recast as a direction-giving statement in an "If . . . then . . ." form, that is, in the form of a prediction which can be responded to by some behavioral performance. In such recasting the word "cause" is eliminated. "Cause," then, is a word that subsumes two other words by implying a relation between them. It is a word in an explanatory regress. Consequently, it is a word easily absorbed by reification into a mythological system, as in "God is the final cause of all being." A mythological explanation is redemptive and an essential ingredient in such explanation is the word "cause" and its various derivatives and concealments, such as "aid," "inspire," "encourage," and so on.

Of redemption, two forms have already been identified: staying within socially validated and policed limits of behavior and returning to them after deviation (or sin). There are two other forms pertinent to these speculations. The first is the subjective or psychological aspect of redemption. Visions of heaven tell us all we need to know. In any heaven any sign elicits only one response: there are no alternatives. In the Christian heaven there is but one mode of response, the worship of God, or in more refined versions, the absorption of the individual soul into the being of God. The subjective aspect of redemption is the feeling of relief from all the tension that comes from facing alternative responses to signs. It is the sense that the individual and the universe are aligned or even fused. It is the sense of being absolutely "with it." A common word for it is "love," and in Christian and other mythologies God is frequently said to be love. It is the sense of absolute congruence of mind and world, of individual and nature, of subject and object. It is the feeling that the forces of the universe are entirely on your side. In extreme forms, it is the mystical experience.

A further form of redemption perhaps exhausts the category. It is intellectual redemption or, more properly, verbal redemption. It is the verbal construction of an explanatory regress, of a "true" explanation of some phenomenon or set of phenomena (and often enough the phenomena explained are words). Of the alternative explanatory regresses available, all have been rejected but one. The mind is satisfied. Any explanation or explanatory construct is, then, redemptive. It is mythological to the degree that the terms of the explanation are reified. Thus when the sociologist asserts that the forces of Society are responsible for the deviant behavior of Individuals, he is engaging in mythological thought. And the same thing holds for any scientist who reifies explanatory statements into Laws of Nature, something a few scientists are now aware of. On the other hand, it seems impossible to construct any explanation without at least temporarily reifying its terms. Even the explanation offered here, though it is as demythologized as I can make it, has a mythological aspect or tendency. It is even redemptive, since my goal is to redeem myself and my readers from error (i.e., intellectual sin) in using such terms as "iconology" and "iconography." Perhaps only the awareness that the best explanation possible is only an explanation, only verbal behavior, can redeem one from being caught in one's own redemptive mythology. An explanation is a redemptive intellectual satisfaction. Nevertheless, as Wallace Stevens wrote in "The Well-Dressed Man with a Beard," "It can never be satisfied, the mind, never." At any rate, such attenuated mythologies as this are very distant from rich mythologies with a plenitudinous store of icons, and from a tradition which presents those icons in works of art.

The presentation of an icon, however, does not make a work

of art. It is merely one of the possible ingredients of the semantic aspect of art—that is, of its sign or meaning functions—and there is no sign or meaning presentable in a work of art which cannot be presented outside of a work of art. Briefly, my position is that the defining aspect of art is that it offers the occasion for experiencing the violation or frustration of various kinds of expectancy. The semantic aspect of art offers order and orientation, as all signs do, providing one has learned the conventional responses to them. But the formal aspect of art offers disorientation and disorder.[1] This is important not only for what has been said so far but for what is to follow. Iconography and iconology are explanations of only some of the semantic aspects of art, and they are best understood if they are restricted to icons that can be related to a plenitudinous mythological system of explanation. However, it is at exactly this point that the problem of iconological study of nineteenth-century art arises, whether it be painting, sculpture, architecture, literature, ballet, opera, drama, or whatever, including the decorative arts. For it is evident that there was no pervasive mythology for what we like to consider the important art of the nineteenth century, the art of the avant-garde tradition, beginning with such men as Constable, Friedrich, Wordsworth, Shelley, Runge, and the rest.

The explanation for this disappearance of an ancient iconographic tradition is that in the eighteenth century the Christian explanatory mythology was attenuated and to a great extent abandoned, and most of what was kept was secularized. As an example of the latter, the notion of heaven was secularized into an allegedly realizable perfection of human life on earth. As I proposed above, it was an explanatory mythology that offered redemption through the perfect alignment of Man, Society, and Nature. That mythology has done immense damage, as well as good. To create that alignment, one must grasp the Laws of Nature and must put the forces of Nature to Human use. It was on this redemptive rationale that industrialization and the concept of the self-regulating market were founded. The immense damage that resulted we are

---

[1] For further discussion see my book, *Man's Rage for Chaos: Biology, Behavior, and the Arts* (Chilton: Philadelphia, 1965; paperback, Schocken: New York, 1967).

now becoming very aware of.[2] However, two events were responsible for the fact that a few Europeans—and in time a few
Americans—rejected not only the Christian mythology but its
Enlightenment secularization. These events were the philosophical efforts of Kant and his followers, and of a few others whose
thinking was convergent with Kant's, and the conversion of the
French Revolution into a bellicose and bloody dictatorship. The
second meant that Enlightenment mythology was a failure, and
the first meant that redemption is an illusion. Kant said that we
cannot know the thing-in-itself. In behavioral terms, this means
that the link between sign and meaning, or stimulus and response,
is a matter of human convention, not of cosmic necessity. And
his distinction between the reason and the understanding meant
(again behaviorally) that behavior is constantly innovative, so
that it automatically spreads into a deviance from any norm.
But even Kant could not resist a moral redemption which behaviorally involves a constant human effort to work against the
spread into deviance by channeling human behavior, that is, by
policing it. In effect, these few Europeans and Americans were
stranded without a mythology. Since the traditional task of art
had been to exemplify an explanatory mythology by presenting
conventional icons, the artists among them were faced with the
problem of abandoning art, or of devoting themselves to trivial
subjects—portraits and genre scenes.

There was, however, a third possibility, creating a new mythology. And this is the direction in which the major artists
moved. After an initial period of disorientation and floundering,
an explanatory causal term was arrived at by most artists in all
fields, and by those in philosophy and in what was left of Christianity as well. In place of the Christian Soul and the Social Individual of the Enlightenment there emerged the desocialized or
alienated Self. The Self became the termination of the mythological explanatory regress of the Romantic tradition, and on the
whole it still is. The source of mythological causality became
the Self. Initially, on the whole, behind the Self was the more
regressive term "God." In this regress the Self replaced the Saint,

[2] See, among innumerable other essays, Alfred Caldwell, "Lost Cities of
America," *The Structurist*, no. 10 (1970), pp. 67–75.

or, more frequently, Christ, as in Feuerbach's assertion that every man is his own Christ. To discover the true Self became, therefore, the redemptive act, at first as the path of God, but later as the termination of the redemptive quest. Late in the century Nietzsche said that "you must become what you are," that is, you must discover your true Self and that Self must control your behavior. But the Self was, on the whole, the only ingredient in common to Romantic mythologies, which are frequently very difficult to recognize for what they are. Everything was tried— history, anthropology, and non-Christian religions were given a Western interpretation, Christianity was given a new interpretation. Every important artist was engaged in creating a new iconography, whether verbal or visual. At first glance this situation seems to rule out the possibility of iconological study, and it has been the barrier. However, iconology studies the history of the explanatory systems that govern iconography and the development of iconographic conventions. Now a semantic convention is a convention whether it is unique to an individual or common to an entire culture. If an individual responds repeatedly to a sign in a given way, his response may be idiosyncratic as far as the rest of his social milieu is concerned, but it is nevertheless a convention within his own behavior. The task of iconological study of a culture's iconography and of an individual's iconography shows therefore no logical difference.

Perhaps the most grandiose effort to establish a new mythology was Ruskin's in *Modern Painters,* and it is a valuable clue to the development of mythology during this period. In the first volumes, Ruskin asserted that landscape painting takes its iconography from nature because nature consists of icons of the attributes of deity. But in the later volumes he moves in the direction of nature as presenting icons of feeling states. This is virtually identical with Zola's famous statement of Naturalism as a corner of nature illuminated by a temperament, which, however, should be more correctly stated as a corner of nature used to create iconic illuminations of a temperament. Consequently, landscape painting is the main path to the modern because in landscape painting—from the very beginning with Constable and Friedrich, supported by various poets such as Wordsworth—was found the richest source for the iconography of the Self. One odd result of this was the late-nineteenth-century phenomenon of Symbolism, which used other than landscape configurations for the same purpose. What made this possible was the fact that landscape painting could be done with a minimum of mythological explanation and causality. Furthermore, the causal relation was perceived as emanating from the Self to the icon, rather than, as in previous cultural epochs, from the icon to the social individual. The immense innovative enterprise in all the arts in creating icons emanating from the Self led to a kind of art, in poetry as well as in painting and music, in which the innovation of the icon preceded the generation of an explanation, and indeed often superseded it. The result was art that gives the impression of being pregnant with meaning, but offers no clue as to what the explanation of that meaning might be.

This in turn led to a further odd but logical result. The artist, having taken upon himself the redemptive task—since he had no choice except to accept an innovative mythology of someone no better qualified than himself, some innovative theologian or metaphysician or some poet or novelist—saw himself as the innovator of mythological though inexplicable icons by virtue of the fact that he was an artist. Thus Art in the late nineteenth and early twentieth centuries became itself the mythological explanation which subsumed the Self. The absolutely isolated Self of the mid-nineteenth century found in Art a causal explanation for the emergence of the Self, as well as an instruction in Style to create or realize the Self. At the highest level of culture for the avant-garde tradition in all areas of culture Art becomes redemptive. Even scientists began claiming that they were really artists. For such people Art today is still the dominating redemptive mythology. An example may be found in the essay by Alfred Caldwell mentioned in note 2, above. The final sentence reads, "Art is the measure of Man," an interesting combination of Romantic and Enlightenment mythological reifications.

For advanced artists and thinkers, therefore, the nineteenth century was a mythological wasteland, although it must always be remembered that for the enormous bulk of the population Christian mythology and the Enlightenment secularization of it (and frequently a mixture of the two) continued to be operant. For those, however, who inhabited the wasteland, the task was the creation of innovative mythologies. However, there was a fundamental incoherence at work. To use Wallace Stevens' terminology, the whole effort of human culture has been redemptive, to satisfy the mind, and the first part of his "The Well-Dressed Man with a Beard," referred to above, is a brilliant and beautiful description of what such satisfaction is like. The last line, "It is never satisfied, the mind, never," is in the post-Kantian Romantic tradition. The poem is fascinating because it juxtaposes so ruthlessly the redemptive and the antiredemptive positions and so utterly rejects the redemptive. During the nineteenth century, therefore, there is an incoherence between the redemptive mythological effort, culminating in Art as the ultimate redemption, and the Kantian epistemological effort, which is antiredemptive. This incoherence and consequent instability accounts for the extraordinary cultural dynamism of the nineteenth and twentieth centuries, their immense outpouring of innovative creativity. It appears that for the past ten or fifteen years, however, artists have been arriving at the position advanced scientists achieved some seventy years ago, the rejection of the redemptive tradition. Today the avant-garde artists appear to be engaged in destroying the high cultural tradition of art, and in doing so it seems more than likely that they are actually engaged in destroying Art as a redemptive mythology. By violating the artistic tradition they are violating the tradition that every work of art is—whatever its subject matter or its motifs—an icon of the reified term "Art."

Yet the picture would not be complete unless some notice were taken of the two great mythologies of the past 170 years which, unlike the individual mythologies and even unlike the mythology of Art, have had a wide reception and have penetrated virtually all levels of the culture, though spottily. The redemptive tradition, which dates from at least the Neolithic and probably from the Paleolithic, permeates every aspect of our lives. As culture has become secularized, from the top down, it was only a few who have ventured into innovative mythology and even fewer who have been able to accept antiredemptiveness, and then only for the small intellectual realm within their total behavior. This cultural secularization, this demythologization, left, as we have seen, an immense mythological vacuum, an absence of causality. And into it have rushed two great and all-explanatory mythologies, complete with causality and reified terms that can be readily translated into visual, verbal, and even aural icons. These are Marxism and Freudianism.

The first is almost a grotesque parody of Christian-Enlightenment redemption, in which History takes the place of God, Capital takes the place of Satan, the Proletariat takes the place of Christ, and Socialist society takes the place of Heaven. All mythologies are therapeutic; that is, they redeem the individual from a deviant behavioral condition to a validated and normative behavioral condition. Marxism is a social therapy in which the deviation or sin is the alienation of the proletariat. Freudianism, on the other hand, is an individual therapy, and its mythology is less transparent than that of Marxism. Instead of the Self, it proposes the Unconscious as the terminal explanatory regress, and it is an Unconscious inhabited by ambivalent deities, both good and bad. These deities are, of course, our parents and siblings. But for the analysand, his Father has no more phenomenal existence than Zeus had for the Greek therapeutic dreamer. There is no discernible difference between being possessed by a devil and being possessed by a castrating mother. Possession is, of course, a causal notion, just as inspiration is. And it has the advantage of all mythological causality insofar as it governs the individual; it frees him of responsibility for what he has been and done, and thus creates a virgin soil for the implantation of normative behavior. "Know ye the truth, and the truth shall make ye free" is a slogan taken by psychoanalysis from Christianity. Psychoanalysis is not, as has often been claimed, an explanation for mythology, but a mythology of explanation.

If, therefore, the growing iconological effort to explain and justify and control the iconographical interpretation of the arts of the nineteenth and twentieth centuries is to be successful, it cannot be undertaken from either a Marxist or a Freudian position, since both of these are but two of the many innovative mythologies of the nineteenth century, and since both are redemptive, not antiredemptive. Of very few people can it be said, "It is never satisfied, the mind, never." Yet that is the direction in which more people must move if we are to be free of the destructive burden of Neolithic redemptionism.

6

HISTORIOGRAPHY AND

THE RING AND THE BOOK

[1967*]

The point has often been made that Browning derived the plan for *The Ring and the Book* from the Trial-Book, or Old Yellow Book. Perhaps it is not surprising that it took him so long to decide how to handle the matter. The death of his wife; the move to London; the great amount of time and energy spent in supervising Pen's education, first in lodgings with piano practice at his elbow, then in the more commodious Warwick Crescent establishment; the preparation of the 1863 collected edition of his poems; and the preparation of *Dramatis Personae*—all this consumed time. When he finally had leisure and opportunity to think about his murder story, he did not take long to decide how to handle it. By the time he ended his 1864 vacation trip, it was all in his mind, or so he said. A letter of October 3, 1864, to Julia Wedgwood, asserts, "I have got the whole of that poem, you enquire about, well in my head, shall write the twelve books of

* Reprinted by permission from *Victorian Poetry* 6, no. 3–4 (Autumn-Winter 1968): 243–57. Copyright © 1968 by West Virginia University.

it in six months, and then take breath again."[1] He had already promised her a sample of it when he had something to show. This status report is somewhat more precise than that in a previous letter to Isa Blagden of September 19; he had earlier told Julia Wedgwood that he had taken few books with him (p. 71), but in the letter of September 19 to Isa Blagden he wrote that he had only a Euripides, at which he had been "having a great read."[2] The implication seems to be that he had purposely brought few books and had confined himself to Euripides because he wanted to think without excessive distraction about his Roman murder.

However, it is not sufficient merely to assert that once he started thinking about the matter seriously, intensively, and at leisure he soon saw the solution to the problem. In the first place, the plan was absolutely novel, and in the second, he had never previously innovated a means of literary organization. To be sure, some of those means, such as in *Pippa Passes*, or in the various dramatic monologues, he had employed in a novel manner, but nothing in his previous career would lead anyone, including Browning himself, to expect a completely new way of writing a long poem. It is not enough to assert that he got the idea from his collection of sources; it is necessary to explain how it was possible for him to see that collection as his proper model.

Indeed, when one examines those documents, Browning's decision becomes even more of a puzzle. For years, ever since finishing his final play, he had been writing almost exclusively in terms of the dramatic monologue. In the old documents themselves, only three passages could be so conceived; the deposition of Angelica in Pamphlet Four, and the deposition of Francesca and the examination of Canon Caponsacchi in Pamphlet Seven. It is difficult to see how the journalistic accounts in Pamphlet Ten and in the Secondary Source—even though they might have inspired Books II, III, and IV—could of themselves have provided the catalyst that made it possible for Browning to break through traditional literary orientations and his own increasingly standard-

[1] Richard Curle, ed., *Robert Browning and Julia Wedgwood: A Broken Friendship as Revealed by Their Letters* (New York, 1937), p. 79.

[2] Edward C. McAleer, ed., *Dearest Isa: Robert Browning's Letters to Isabella Blagden* (Austin, Texas, 1951), p. 193.

ized way of handling any problem he wanted to write a poem
about. ("James Lee's Wife" is a mild exception.) If an explanation
is desired for the doubly innovative character of *The Ring and the
Book* it seems necessary to look farther and deeper than is usually
done.

Much of the criticism of the poem can be used to give us a
first clue—especially that of Gest, DeVane, and of various others
since the publication of the documents Browning used. There is
a considerable body of discussion as to whether Browning's construct of the case is correct at all, and his silent changing of the
date of the elopement to St. George's Day is often cited—with
a glance at his own Georgian rescue of his own Andromeda—as
proof that he was not even trying to find the truth, or that if he
was he deceived himself most outrageously. The assumption behind these arguments is that he was trying to find the truth, or that
he should have been, and his own statement that he had found the
truth is often called upon. Yet the poem provides sufficient warning: the extraordinary semantic lability of "truth" in Book I, the
virtual statement at the end of Book XII that poetry doesn't have
to tell the truth in order to be true, because it breeds truth in the
reader "obliquely"; and a peculiarity in the plan itself, which I
shall take up later—all these make it reasonably clear that one
point of the poem is that the truth cannot be told, ever. For one
thing, the poem makes it perfectly clear—in the manner of all of
Browning's dramatic monologues—that the human mind organizes its phenomenal perceptions according to its own interests,
and the end of the poem adds another touch—one that should
have warned its critics—in asserting that this general condition of
the cognitive process applies also to one's interpretation of language: it is not merely that the world is interpreted according to
one's own interests; it is just as true that statements about the
world—whether the statements of others or one's own statements
—are interpreted in the same way.

And this point is made in the organization of the poem. Book
I is a dramatic monologue uttered by Robert Browning—a Browning carefully identified as the historical Browning by the various
references to his wife in that book and in the last, when Robert
Browning is again the monologuist. But what Robert Browning?

Whose Robert Browning? Is Isa Blagden's Robert Browning the same as Julia Wedgwood's? Judging by the letters we have, one finds it impossible to think so. Is Elizabeth Barrett's Robert Browning the same as Elizabeth Browning's Robert Browning? Is the Robert Browning of this woman—or either of these two women—to be identified with Robert Browning's Robert Browning? Which Robert Browning's Robert Browning? The point is that the carefully identified historical Robert Browning of Book I is fatally compromised by the very plan of the poem, for that plan puts that Robert Browning in the same category as each of the other monologuists, including the two forms of Guido—or the at least three forms of Guido: the gentleman of Book V, the wolf of Book XI, and the jelly of that same book who suddenly reveals the interests that constructed both of these fraudulent self-conceptions. The marvelous collapse of Guido shows that the various monologuists not only interpret reality according to their own interests but also in the same way interpret themselves as part of perceived and cognized reality. Hence the Robert Browning of Book I is to be conceived as interpreting the documents according to his own interests—necessarily and ineluctably. And further, his self-conception is the primary source of that interpretation, as the careful self-portrait at the very beginning makes sufficiently clear.

Yet it is even more intricate than that. Browning's monologue of Book I and his re-entry at the end of Book XII, together with his careful insistence that the rest of the work is based *by him* on the documents he found in the Florence flea market, form a pair of brackets around the other monologues (and letters, in Book XII). We are to imagine the compromised historical Browning of Book I inventing the other monologues, just as the historical Browning of his previous dramatic monologues invented the speakers, their situations, and their discourse. The problem can be put in abstract form. Let a signify a speaker; let x signify the speaker's situation; let @ signify the act of interested and compromised interpretation; let B signify Browning. The earlier monologues, then, can be symbolized thus: (a @ x). But if it is true that dramatic monologue constructed on this principle shows a speaker interpreting a situation, then the author of that monologue must necessarily have the same relation to that complex that the speaker does to his situation. Consequently *The Ring and the Book* can be symbolized thus:

$$<B @ [(a @ x) + (b @ x) + (c @ x). \dots]>.$$

Hence, if the cognitive act of a monologuist is compromised by his interests, then Browning's cognition of that cognitive act is compromised by *his own* interests. Given the cognitive model proposed in the dramatic monologues, it was logically necessary, though not historically necessary, that sooner or later Browning would have to include himself in the dramatic monologue complex.

Yet in spite of all these warnings, of various degrees of subtlety and obviousness, any number of critics have insisted on discussing the work as if Browning were a historian trying to discover the truth behind a set of documents and succeeding, or a historian trying to discover the truth but failing, or a historian deliberately trying to deceive the reader into thinking he had discovered the truth when in fact he was—and knew he was—manipulating the documents for his own interests. Now the significant thing about this kind of criticism is not the conclusions arrived at; if the above analysis of what Browning was up to is correct, all the conclusions are quite irrelevant. Rather, the significant thing is that, in examining Browning's role in handling the documents, these critics used the historiographer as their model. Even when some of them conclude that though Browning proved to be a bad historiographer, he was a very good poet and did what a poet should do—utter noble truths—it is obvious that their prime interest is in Browning's success as an historiographer and their model is the historiographer's responsibility toward his documents.

It seems to have occurred to no one that this responsibility was precisely the problem Browning was concerned with.

One of the most important transformations for which Romanticism was responsible was the historicization of European culture. The overwhelming success of that transformation is attested to by the very innocence of the critics I have been discussing. Their line of reasoning is only too transparent: Browning is dealing with a set of historical documents; that he thought of them as historical documents is shown by the trouble he went to in order to find further documents—as he tells us in the poem, and as we know from the story of the discovery of the Secondary Source. The proper critical approach, then, is to examine the success with which he played the role of historiographer. But if my analysis of the plan of the poem and of the Browning kind of dramatic monologue is at all correct, Browning was saying to himself something like this: "I want to write a poem about a set of documents; to do so I shall play the historiographer's role. What, then, does it *mean* to play that role? What is an historiographer? What are his interests?" That Browning was concerned with the nature of truth is a platitude; that, like some of his most advanced contemporaries, he developed an instrumental theory of truth is not so firmly and widely grasped; that he developed a concept of truth as radical, nearly, as Nietzsche's and presented it in an almost Wittgensteinian mode is scarcely yet realized. For our purposes, however, it is sufficient to recognize that one of his central concerns, perhaps his absolutely centripetal preoccupation, was epistemology. Granted this, it is not at all unlikely—it is logically necessary—that he should have considered the nature of historical truth. Furthermore, given his conviction of the interested distortions of the cognitive process, it is logically coherent that he should have conceived of "historical truth" as "historiographer's truth" and ultimately as "an historiographer's truth."

The historicization of European culture is powerfully attested to not only by the critics of his longest poem but also by his own literary career. For him, until the time of *The Ring and the Book*, the most common way to grasp a psychological problem was to find an appropriate historical circumstance; or, to make the same point differently, psychological problems emerged for him when he studied an historical situation. Until *Prince Hohenstiel-Schwangau*, all of his long poems were historical, with the exception of *Christmas-Eve and Easter-Day*, but that poem is deeply involved with historical problems and deals directly with historical analysis. It is also, like *The Ring and the Book*, a poem in which he himself appears, though he is not self-compromised. *Paracelsus* is far more integrated into its historical situation than is generally recognized (as I hope the recent edition of that poem makes unavoidably clear). For *Sordello* he not only turned to

Sismondi's great history of the Italian Republics and to Verci's study of the Eccellini, and to the almost frightening richness of Muratori's superb compilation of chronicles; he also went to the scenes of the events he was describing, in the same way that Carlyle and Macaulay were to. All of the plays except *Pippa Passes* had historical settings; and even that requires a fairly detailed knowledge of Italian political history in the 1830s, as well as of the fate of the contents of Canova's studio after his death. Of the shorter poems through *Dramatis Personae* it is a general rule that the longer the poem the more likely it is to have an historically identifiable and dramatically significant setting. It is therefore helpful to the proposal of this paper to point out that—after *The Ring and the Book*—the next poem, *Balaustion's Adventure*, used an historical document by providing a constructed historical setting for a recitation of it, that is, an imaginary setting for a translation of it. Thereafter came his so-called Balzacian poems about contemporary or very recent actual events; some were historical in the sense that they had happened, but they were closer to journalism, sociology, and psychology than they were to history. Two of them were not even dramatic monologues.

Further, it is instructive to list, however briefly, some of the great historical enterprises that appeared during the years from Browning's young manhood to his decision of how to deal with his Roman murder case. The impact Carlyle's *French Revolution* had on him is of course well known, but during those years Carlyle also published his *Oliver Cromwell's Letters and Speeches* and above all his enormous and entrancing *Frederick the Great* (1858–65), which Browning read, although it made him "curse and swear."[3] There were Grote's history of ancient Greece (1845–56) and Finlay's series of volumes about ancient, Byzantine, Medieval, and Turkish Greece (1851–61). There were the fascinating Macaulay history (1849–61) and Froude's history of England in the sixteenth century, which, for all its faults, has never been entirely superseded (1856–70). Masson and Spedding began their great biographies of Milton (1857–95) and of Bacon (1861–74). In the 1860s Kinglake initiated his vast *The Invasion of the Crimea*

---

[3] William C. DeVane and Kenneth Knickerbocker, ed., *New Letters of Robert Browning* (New Haven, 1950), p. 112.

(1863–87) and Gardiner his great series on English history in the seventeenth century (1863–1903). In addition, of the numerous Continental historians, such as Chateaubriand and Michelet, perhaps the most interesting to Browning would have been Leopold von Ranke. *The Civil Wars and Monarchy in France* was translated in 1852, *The History of the Reformation in Germany* from 1845 to 1847, other works in 1849 and 1853; but, above all, the work which it is impossible to believe Browning did not read, perhaps in the original German (1834–36), *The History of the Popes in the Sixteenth and Seventeenth Centuries*, was translated in 1840, again in 1842, and by still a third hand in 1852–53.

For the problem being examined here, the important thing is not merely that these were great historical works in a period in which an educated public bought and read them in numbers still impressive, and that *The Ring and the Book* was written in a period in which the cultivated consciousness felt itself being transformed by a knowledge of the past such as no human beings had ever had before; rather, it is the gigantic scale on which these works were executed and the years of incredible labor that went into them. Nowadays very few professional historians would undertake anything so massive without the assistance of a team, not to speak of large research grants. Indeed, the only real example of this grand historiography in the mid-twentieth century is something of a curiosity, something of a fossil, the kind of thing, indeed, that many a professional historian believes should not be undertaken by one man: Lawrence Gipson's *The British Empire before the American Revolution*. But in the heyday of historicism —which corresponded with Browning's lifetime—the enthusiasm, the sense of inconceivably exciting and important discovery, the sense of contributing to a Hegelian transcendence of cultural limitations, all provided the energy to sustain fantastic achievements. To such enterprises, *The Ring and the Book*, on the corresponding and necessarily much smaller scale of even the long poem, was an equivalent. On the one hand the scale of Browning's poem corresponded to the great historical enterprises which preceded it and were contemporaneous with it; on the other hand, these great works were made possible by an investigation into original documentation other than chronicles, which was the great achievement of nineteenth-century historiography and the foundation for a scientific historiography.

This new attitude toward historical documents had already begun to have its effect on historical fiction. More than anyone else, Scott was responsible for the historicization of the European consciousness, and the "literary" historians—Carlyle, Macaulay, Michelet—were directly inspired by him, as were Hugo, Ainsworth, and an endless host of purveyors of historical fiction, most of it even more careless than Scott's, whose carelessness had at least something of a Shakespearean majesty. In the period, however, in which Browning was meditating on his Roman murdercase problem, a far more historically and intellectually responsible kind of historical novel was beginning to appear. A precursor was Kingsley's *Westward Ho!* (1855), based directly on Hakluyt; but much more modern and historiographically responsible was Charles Reade's *The Cloister and the Hearth* (as a serial, 1859; as a book, 1861), for Reade used the techniques of historical research as no English novelist had before. In 1862 came George Eliot's *Romola*, which for many tastes was too historically detailed and overworked; Browning's response is instructive.

I told you what I thought of the *two* first volumes of *Romola*: as honestly, I add now that I was much disappointed in the third & last: there was too much dwelling on the delinquencies of the Greek after he had been done for, and might have been done with, as a pure and perfect rascal—while the interests, Savonarola and the Republic, which I expected would absorb attention and pay for the previous minutenesses, dwindled strangely.[4]

He had already read *Salammbô*, also published in 1862, and his comment on that is equally illuminating:

Mrs. B. lent me "Salammbô"—don't you remember my old, and still continuing passion for "Madame Bovary?"—If you read *this* as probably you have, my immense disappointment will be easily understood. I take nine-tenths of the "learning"—the historical touches &c to be pure humbug—"all made out of the carver's brain."[5]

[4] *Dearest Isa*, p. 178. (Letter of November 19, 1863).
[5] Ibid., p. 173. (Letter of August 19, 1863).

It is obvious that what Browning wanted was more historical detail, not less, and detail that met the highest standards of accuracy. For the first time in English historiography that detail was beginning to be possible, as well as that accuracy. The Germans and the French had long since started publishing the most important material in their archives, as well as throwing them open—though neither took place until after the nineteenth century had well begun. In 1857 the publication of the English Calendar of State Papers was instituted, and in 1858 the Rolls series was initiated, two decades after serious work was first begun on caring for, preserving, and publishing the great mass of material in the governmental archives. It cannot be said that this had an important effect directly on Browning, but it would have been difficult for him to have been ignorant of the tremendous work Froude had done and was continuing to do in the Spanish archives at Simancas, in view of the publicity and the attacks upon his accuracy.

Thus the new style of historiography was something an educated and cultivated man of historical interests could scarcely avoid knowing about. As F. S. Boas observed, "It was in the 'sixties that organized academic teaching [of history] began in England, and that the professional historian took the first steps to supplant the amateur." "Froude," Boas adds, "showed that he belonged to the new era by his extensive use of documents."[6] The revolution in historiography initiated by Ranke had finally arrived in England. The older historians, such as the still active Carlyle, had proceeded essentially by collating chronicles, pamphlets, and similar printed materials It was a style of historiography which in methodology had not really changed for some centuries. It is important, therefore, to understand Ranke's revolution and his place in the history of historiography. It is true, of course, that in the infinitely more scrupulous use of sources as well as in the determination to use all possible sources as critically as possible, Ranke's great precursor and master was Niebuhr, who in turn learned his technique from Wolf, particularly from the famous Prolegomena to Homer (1795). Nevertheless, as G. P. Gooch has

[6] Quoted in John Drinkwater, ed., "Historians in the 'Sixties," in *The Eighteen Sixties* (Cambridge, England, 1932), pp. 189–90, 197.

noted, Ranke added something novel, "his determination to seize the personality of the writer and to inquire whence he derived his information. 'Some will copy the ancients, some will seek instruction for the future, some will attack or defend, some will only wish to record facts. Each must be separately studied.' "[7]

This formulation has, in the present context, an extremely familiar sound. Ranke's position, as interpreted by G. P. Gooch, is the formula for critical historiography, and it is evident that it is identical with—as well as concurrent with and derived from the same sources as—the meaning of "criticism" in the "higher criticism" of the Bible, and possibly is ultimately to be derived from Kant. "Whence did he derive his information?"—that is, in what situation was he placed? "Some will copy the ancients," etc.—that is, what are the interests of the writer? The critical study of history, therefore, depends upon analysis of the cognitive process responsible for the particular document the historian proposes to use, and the use he makes of it depends upon his analysis of that process.

It is obvious that this conception of the historiographer's relation to his document, thus formalized, is identical with the formula for the dramatic monologue as Browning handled it. Several conclusions may be logically drawn.

First, from this point of view it is evident that Browning's historicism before *The Ring and the Book* was the old-fashioned, noncritical historicism of Carlyle and Macaulay and Michelet, not that of Ranke and of Froude, Stubbs, and Gardiner. Like the literary historians, on the basis of extensive reading he created an imaginative construct of some period of the past, sometimes a very minute period, as for "My Last Duchess." Either the cognitive process he wished to handle emerged from that imaginative construct, or a problem he was meditating found its exemplification there. Probably both processes actually occurred. From such works both Browning and his sources were absent.

---

[7] G. P. Gooch, *History and Historians in the Nineteenth Century* (New York, 1949), p. 79. This work, first published in 1913, is, I should say, one of the absolutely indispensable works for the study of nineteenth-century culture. Obviously I have depended heavily on it for much of the material in the present essay.

However, when one reads Ranke's superb *History of the Popes* or Froude's fascinating *History of England from the Fall of Wolsey to the Defeat of the Spanish Armada*, one is intensely aware both of documents and of the author studying those documents. The *critical* aspect of modern historiography emerges in the footnotes; they are not merely authorities or sources but the very life of the historian's cognitive process, and both writers are intent on making them interesting. That is much of the excitement and intellectual grandeur of the Ranke school and its followers in England. This characteristic of the new school of historiography is precisely the obvious characteristic of *The Ring and the Book* when it is compared with Browning's earlier historical poems. There was ample opportunity for him to be aware of the change, even had he been unfamiliar with Ranke, and he probably was familiar with him; it seems highly probable, therefore, that an awareness of the change in historiography was responsible for the peculiarity of *The Ring and the Book* in its reference to the documents upon which it was founded and in the attitude of the author toward those documents.

Second, this formulation permits a further conclusion to be drawn, in the sense that the structural similarity between Ranke's conception of the historical document and Browning's of the dramatic monologue is the sort of thing that demands an explanation—or at least tempts the cultural historian to offer one. The fundamental character of Romanticism—that element which links Wordsworth to Wallace Stevens, Hegel to Polanyi, and Friedrich to Picasso—can be seen in various ways, but since Browning centered his thinking on the nature of truth, it is best seen here epistemologically. It is the question, to use old-fashioned terms, of the relation of subject to object, of the mind to the phenomenal (or a little more precisely, that character of the mind which makes it satisfactory to talk about the actual as phenomenal). What it amounts to is the cognition of an irreducible tension between subject and object, in the sense that the subject cannot be reduced to the object, nor the object to the subject. In terms closer, but not much closer, to the empirical world, it means that to the mind there is an irreducible surd which recedes forever beyond the utmost powers of explanation. Ranke endeavored to cancel, or at least reduce to a minimum, the distorting interest, or surd, of the authors of historical documents in order to get at historical truth, *wie es eigentlich gewesen*. Browning aimed at creating historical situations so that the irreducible surd of the interest of the speaker might be located. This is why it is so difficult to decide if the monologuist speaks for Browning: in one monologue, Browning might be seeking to identify his own interests; in another, to identify interests not his; in yet another the monologuist might share some of Browning's interests and not share others. But the monologuist and Browning always had one interest in common, to manifest their uniqueness, or irrational surd, in the cognitive apprehension and interpretation of a situation. Thus, if the structural identity of Ranke's and Browning's thinking is acceptable, the explanation can be located logically in their common source in the main Romantic line. However, this proposal makes it necessary to distinguish between Carlyle and Ranke, for Carlyle, whose *French Revolution* is most instructively seen as one long Browningesque dramatic monologue, was Browning's master in an important sense yet to be thoroughly explored.[8] The difference between the German historian and the English was in part their methodology, though it cannot be said that Carlyle was totally unaware of the distorting interests revealed in each document be examined. He could not have been, since he was if anything even more richly a product of German Romantic epistemology than Ranke himself. The distinction between the two approaches was not so much epistemological as a matter of their own interests. Carlyle deliberately used history to illustrate his philosophical interests; Ranke's interest was that of the professional historian. The one used history for his own interests as soon as he felt it was ready; the other aimed at postponing the introduction of his own interests as long as possible. Hence Carlyle trusted documents that felt right to him. (His feelings were often shared by subsequent critical historiographers.) But Ranke continued research until he felt he had done as much as he could to cancel out or at least balance distorting interests. Further, Ranke

[8] It is, for example, hard for me to believe that the striking stylistic shift between *Paracelsus* and *Sordello* is not at least in part due to the publication of the *French Revolution*.

was capable of standing apart from his own interests and correcting them, something Carlyle had no desire to do whatsoever. Thus Ranke, accused of being too generous to Catholicism in the *Popes*, quite deliberately wrote of many of the same events from the Protestant position in his *Reformation*.

This brings us to the third conclusion which the formulation makes possible, demands, and tempts one to make. It is obvious that the Rankean conception of the historiographer's task in estimating documents places historiography on an extremely equivocal foundation. The logic is precisely the same as that already illustrated in the proposal that logically Browning had to include himself in the dramatic monologue. If the author of the document is necessarily subjected to his interests in interpreting the events he writes about, then the historiographer is subjected ultimately to *his* interests in eliminating that author's interests and thus arriving at historical truth. Historical truth, therefore, is like any other truth: In the end it is distorted by the self-conception of the historiographer. Now as Ranke's behavior indicates, he was quite aware of this limitation on the historiographer's claim to be able to discover historical fact as it really was. So was Froude—as his essay "The Science of History" plainly indicates, and as does his frank assertion elsewhere that the coming of the Reformation to England was the best thing for England that could have happened.[9] This frank acceptance of what is sometimes called bias (an improper term, for it implies that unbiased history is possible) is responsible for the great charm and intellectual fascination of the new school of critical historiography: One is aware that the historiographer knows that his explanation of events, no matter how carefully they have been extracted from the documents, is inseparable from his choice of events to be explained. The success of the new history, however, meant its professionalization in

[9] The essay was first given as a lecture at the Royal Institution on February 5, 1864, and first published in the first volume of *Short Studies on Great Subjects* (London, 1867). One is tempted to think that Browning heard the lecture, or at least heard about it, as he very well might have in his constant dining out. Passages in it sound like directions for writing *The Ring and the Book*. It is enough, however, to cite the lecture as evidence of the fact that the educated and cultivated public was aware of the new historiography and interested in its problems.

academies, and, as always happens when an idea is professionalized and its methodology made available to inferior and less
modern minds, the methodology was sanctified and petrified. The
result was that "objective" historiography—an historiographical
mode that eliminates the subject—was conceptualized; standardized; and taught as the one possible, and only true, way of writing
history. This assumption, of course, is the assumption of those
critics of *The Ring and the Book* who have busied themselves
with deciding whether Browning's interpretation of his murder
case is historically "true."

Browning himself, fully accepting the irresolvable tension between subject and object—including the tension between himself
as subject and the subject-object tension he is examining—implies, on the contrary, "My interpretation I *believe* to be true,
because it satisfies my own interests; I do not *assert* it to be true."
If this is at all an adequate account of the matter, it is possible
to understand how, on the one hand, he could claim that he
found the truth, while being perfectly aware, on the other hand,
that he had changed the date of the elopement to St. George's
Day. He could scarcely anticipate that Hodell would one day
publish his documentary sources and thus make it possible to
discover what he had done. Rather, the falsification of the documents should perhaps best be conceived as a way of Browning's
telling himself that, no matter how carefully he studied the documents and incorporated in each of his speakers that speaker's
own bias, ultimately he too was biased by his own interests. On
the other hand, however, he could not have been unaware that
those few who knew his work were acquainted with his rescue of
Elizabeth from the Arezzo of London, and it is possible that he
expected his readers to take account of that fact. Indeed, in setting Book I at Casa Guidi and in referring to his dead wife he
virtually invites them to do so. It is logically correct that he
wanted his readers to be aware of his own interests; whether or
not it is historically correct is another matter.[10]

---

[10] Browning, of course, is notorious for having refused to explain his
poetry, even to the extent of allowing Mrs. Orr to publish not only inadequate interpretations—and sometimes incorrect ones—but even factual
errors. In this connection it is interesting that for the 1888–89 edition he

Finally, from all this it is possible to provide a further explanation as to why Browning, after *The Ring and the Book*, turned from historical situations to contemporary ones. In a famous passage Stephen Dedalus says that history is a nightmare from which he is trying to awake; and *Finnegans Wake* is itself the nightmare of history. One of Joyce's masters was certainly Nietzsche, and in 1874 Nietzsche published the second of his *Unzeitgemässe Betrachtungen, Vom Nutzen und Nachteil der Historie für das Leben*. It was the first powerful attack on the all-too-successful institutionalization of critical historiography. The importance of history to the Romantic tradition was that it offered a strategy to resolve the problem of alienation, for history can be a primary means of cultural transcendence. But, as Nietzsche points out, its very success within the culture had made it into a means for trapping the individual, since the Rankean tradition had been academically falsified into a means for achieving objective historiography, something quite impossible and absurd. Consequently, the subjective element, ignored and hence no longer controllable, becomes tyrannized by the culture which the Romantic was seeking to transcend. But an even subtler difficulty was involved. The acceptance of history as a means of cultural transcendence can, as the career of Carlyle all too plainly showed, entrap the individual in his own subjectivity; that is, it can persuade him that his self-conception is "true." But such a self-conception is based upon the individual's grasp of the phenomena of his personality, which is a product of his culture. Therefore, since cultural transcendence is also, for this reason, self-transcendence, to accept historiography as a final solution to the problem of alienation and cultural transcendence is to abandon the struggle for self-transcendence and therefore to surrender once more to the culture. Consequently, it is not enough that history should be used to reveal one's interests; it must also be used as a means to transcend those interests. Historiography as an instrument to escape from historiography—this may be the ultimate importance of *The Ring and the Book* in Browning's intellectual enterprise.

---

canceled the 1878 dedication to Mrs. Orr of *La Saisiaz and The Two Poets of Croisic*, although he retained the other dedications.

With this in mind it is now possible to express more exactly the logical structure of Browning's masterpiece. Let B . . . signify the historical Browning who wrote the poem over some four years, a Browning who even as author of the poem did not remain stable, since he necessarily interacted with what he had already written and was responding to. Let cB signify the compromised Browning in Books I and XII. Thus:

$$B \ldots @ <cB @ [(a @ x) + (b @ x) + (c @ x). \ldots] >.$$

The Browning who writes the poem is to be distinguished from the Browning who is in the poem. Thus Browning achieves toward himself the attitude he had previously established toward his monologuists. Freed from historiography, he could turn to the contemporary. Perhaps he was the first major nineteenth-century figure to awaken from the nightmare of history, for he had learned to perceive it as the construct of his own necessarily distorting interests.

7

AN INTRODUCTION

TO EMERSON'S ESSAYS

[1968*]

R alph Waldo Emerson was the first to appear of that amazing
  sequence of literary intellects which emerged from the provincial darkness of the young American republic. Emerson (born
in 1803), Hawthorne, Poe, Thoreau, Melville, Whitman—sooner
or later they have all been accepted into that grand European
culture which transcends and rises above the narrow considerations of nationalism; and it is from a supranational European
orientation that they are all best understood and best measured.
In recent decades Emerson has not been so admired, at least in
America, as he once was. Possibly his day is coming again.
Certainly for some readers he has always been the greatest of that
group, just as he was the inspiration and vital spark for almost
all of them, even when they rebelled against him.

Of Emerson's various literary achievements, most of which

* Reprinted by permission from *Essays / Essays: Second Series*, by Ralph
Waldo Emerson, from the Charles E. Merrill Standard Editions series, ed.
Matthew J. Bruccoli and Joseph Katz (Columbus, Ohio: Charles E. Merrill,
1969), pp. v–xvi. Copyright © 1969 by Bell and Howell Company.

began as lectures assembled from entries in the immense, flowing Mississippi of his Journals, his greatest are the two series of *Essays*, published in 1844 and 1849. Within a decade of their publication in England they had become volumes which every cultivated intellectual and literary figure there found it necessary to know well. Matthew Arnold, a young man then, later said that Emerson, along with Goethe and J. H. Newman, was of central and utmost importance in his own development as a man and as a writer, and Arnold was above all other English writers the one who castigated the English for their failure to know and be interested in the literature and learning beyond the limits of their little island, particularly that of Continental Europe. His notion that a man should be a good European was taken up by Henry James and became the formative idea of the latter's life and literary career. To Arnold—the good European—Emerson belonged in the company of Goethe, the man who, more than any other great figure of the late eighteenth and early nineteenth centuries, insisted on the fundamental unity and internal coherence of European culture. Goethe was of the deepest importance to Emerson, and when the thirty-year-old American went to Scotland in 1833, he sought out Thomas Carlyle, who for nearly a decade had been struggling to bring the richness of Goethe and other German writers to the provincial English. Emerson's task, his mission, his goal, was to join America to supranational Europe in a seamless continuum; it was a manifestation of his subtlety that one of his strategies was to endeavor to make his fellow Americans into good Europeans by making them exquisitely aware of what it meant to be an American, a matter on which there is still considerable confusion.

So Emerson flows from Europe and back to it again, and to think of him in exclusively American terms and categories is to miss much of his meaning and most of his greatness. Perhaps that is why to the young American of today, at a time when the weakest and least civilized of European cultural strata—those social and cultural strata which the most civilized Europeans have shamefully neglected—are themselves becoming so Americanized, Emerson's *Essays* may not be very appealing. If such a young American finds them pale, disjointed, wandering, faded, too optimistic, excessively bland, he will after all be but repeating the judgment of many of the critics and teachers only a generation or two older than himself. Yet for some men in their fifties and sixties, as they see death coming nearer, as—to borrow from Yeats what he has said better than anyone—they cast a colder eye on life, on death, as they increasingly take a half-concealed pleasure in watching the aggressive horseman of energy and achievement pass by, as they are increasingly torn between a certain contempt for men and an almost unendurable compassion for suffering and self-torturing mankind, the *Essays* of Emerson become always more satisfying and bracing. The affinities of Emerson, the bland optimist, with Schopenhauer, the most invigorating of pessimists, begin to become apparent. His affinities with Søren Kierkegaard, the Danish master of irony, become intriguing and engaging; ten years Emerson's junior, Kierkegaard wrote most of his works in the same decade that the older writer's *Essays* were published. The blandness, the optimism, fade away, and a vigor and intellectual toughness emerge which strike into the soul that iron in which the aging man delights. More than anything else, he has learned how to read Emerson. It is not easy.

Everyone knows that Emerson's style is aphoristic; everyone knows that the *Essays* were assembled from here and there in the Journals; everyone knows that they are disjointed, and that there is no particular reason why any sentence could not be omitted. It is easy enough to test this. Leaf through the essays, randomly selecting a dozen pages, and letting your eye strike any sentence by uncontrolled accident. You will find that almost any sentence you light on can be extracted from its context and savored, or dismissed, without reference to what precedes or follows it. In Emerson, it seems, there is no argument, no sustained discourse— philosophical or any other kind—but only a series of sentences stitched together under various grandiose titles of such a kind that almost any sentence could appear in almost any essay.

But that is not the only apparently damaging allegation that can be made against Emerson's style. As we read any *Essay* continuously, the connection between almost any of these aphoristic sentences and the one that follows it is by no means easy to grasp. Often the next sentence does not seem to follow at all.

One of the gravest and most difficult philosophical problems is this: Given sentences *a* and *b*, how do you know that sentence *b* properly follows from sentence *a* except by sheer contiguity? Between any two sentences in any discourse lies, it would seem, an abyss, and the task of the man we call the good writer is to bridge the abyss, to give the reader at least the illusion, if nothing else, that sentence *b* really and truly follows from sentence *a*. This is what we expect when we start to read an essay, even the essays of that most capricious of informal essayists, Charles Lamb. After all, even Lamb does more to get his reader across the bridge from *a* to *b* than does Emerson, at least much of the time. It is a most interesting and instructive exercise to take any piece of not remarkably good, but merely acceptable, prose and to explore the devices used to get the reader from *a* to *b*: the hints, the clues, the parallelisms, the contrasts, the quasi-logical connectives, the pronouns with their antecedents in the previous sentence, the conjunctions, the qualifying adverbs. The devices of style which go into constructing the bridges across the abysses that lie between sentences are innumerable, and every competent writer must master them. Emerson neglects them. He does not build us bridges; he makes us leap. And the matter is made worse by his fusion of a capriciousness greater than Lamb's with the philosophical earnestness and moral seriousness of Plato, Montaigne, Spinoza, Kant, Goethe, Carlyle. With the air of one bent on absolute lucidity, he devotes himself to eluding us.

It is not in traditional discourse and expository prose or even in inspiriting rhetoric that we must look for a model for what Emerson is doing. It is not in prose at all, but in poetry. That model is to be found in two kinds of poetry, the lyric poem and the poetic drama. When we start to read a lyric we do not expect a continuous discourse with bridges carefully built from one sentence to the next. Rather, we expect the speaker of the poem to fling himself from one proposition to the next, at times to leap from one proposition to the next like a predator flinging itself on its victim; what we expect is the tingling excitement of subjectivity, and when we respond adequately to the lyric poem, we glow with that same excitement. As Plato long ago said, poets cannot understand what they are talking about. He was quite right, but he should have added that neither can anybody else. Since he was a philosopher, he was scarcely performing a professional role that would permit him to admit that truth. Lyric poets do not conceal the abysses that divide sentences; they exploit them. Emerson is a philosopher who writes like a lyric poet and thinks like one. His individual sentences are dazzling. How does he get from one to another? He does not tell us, because he does not know. It is his pride that he does not know. He refuses to submit to the universal human illusion that we really know what we are doing while we are doing it. One who does not grasp the immense and magnificently self-centered pride of Emerson—the pride of a Lucifer who has fallen but knows that only in *his* kind of fall is there redemption—has not grasped an essential quality of the man and his writing.

The second model for Emerson's *Essays* is to be found in the speeches of the protagonists and other central characters of poetic drama, especially tragedy, and above all the tragedy of Shakespeare and his contemporaries. *Hamlet* is the greatest of tragedies because its central theme is what underlies the behavior of the heroes of all tragedy, and of all interesting noncomic characters whatever. It is the endless struggle of the hero to redefine himself. Each of us has a self-image and we have a similar image of each individual we know, for the images of both self and other are arrived at in the same way, by observing and making sense out of what we do and say. We can stabilize our world—ourselves, those we know, and the situations we live in—by making those images simple, coherent, and fixed. But we do this at the price of ignoring and repressing those bits and pieces of our behavior and the behavior of others which do not fit coherently and consistently into those images. In every tragic or serious work, the author puts his protagonist through a series of situations which shatters his self-image, and his images of those intimate with him and of his world—which forces him to be aware of unexpected or hitherto unobserved and unassimilated aspects of his personality and of his social and natural environment. His image is shattered, and he must remake it, only to have it shattered again. Only when he has assimilated the unassimilated is he permitted to die, and he dies because to do that assimilation is in fact to do the impossible. The falsity of tragedy and the spurious comfort we gain from it rises from seeing the hero arrive at a self-understanding which no man in the real world—rather than in the illusory world of art—can ever have. Shakespeare, greatly daring, kills Hamlet without permitting him that spurious self-illumination. Hamlet, dying, tells Horatio to explain him, because the truth is that he cannot explain himself, nor can any man.

That is why Hamlet utters his great soliloquies; why these, not the conclusion, are the heart of the play. Shakespeare denies Hamlet self-illumination. Ever since, critics have been arguing about what ought to be a consistent image of Hamlet, and they have never agreed, and they never will agree, because Hamlet is inexplicable. Hamlet is Man, as no writer before or since has dared or had the genius to present him. Thus, to Emerson, Shakespeare was a great philosopher, and the model for Emerson's *Essays* are the soliloquies of Hamlet, of Shakespeare's other tragic heroes, and of the heroes of Shakespeare's theatrical contemporaries. Hamlet's soliloquies emerge from dramatic situations in which self-image is shattered. Emerson's *Essays* emerge from a grander situation—the condition of man—which, truly apprehended (as it almost never is by anyone), shatters any man's self-image. That is why the first of the *Essays* is "History," which, Emerson tells us, is a spurious projection of our spurious self-images, and he shatters it. That is why the next essay is "Self-Reliance." To rely on oneself is to have the courage to doubt one's comforting self-image. This is the meaning of the famous statement, "A foolish consistency is the hobgoblin of little minds. . . . With consistency a great soul has simply nothing to do." A great soul may know that he must have a coherent and acceptable self-image to act at all, but he knows that at worst it is spurious and at best it is only an instrument.

The *Essays*, then, are a fusion of the lyric and the dramatic soliloquy. Emerson assembled them from here and there in his Journals because he knew that any self-image is an assemblage, not a coherent structure. Just as the lyric poet exploits the leap from sentence to sentence, so Emerson exploits the inconsistency of our personalities that our self-images endeavor to conceal. The tragic role he plays is that of Man acting his part on the stage of the World, and he sees that the personality of Man is an assemblage, the various bits and pieces of which come from he knows not where, and he does not conceal the fact. He glories in it; it is the source of his immense and magnificently self-centered pride.

A further genre of poetry can provide yet another model for reading Emerson's *Essays*—a kind of negative model. In the very decade of the essays, the 1840s, a younger contemporary of Emerson's, the Englishman Robert Browning, created the dramatic monologue. As with Emerson, his two sources were the lyric poem and the soliloquy of the Elizabethan theater, of Shakespeare and his contemporaries. But Browning adds a twist neither in Shakespeare nor in Emerson. Browning's monologues emerge from situations which, though they do not shatter the self-image of his speakers, certainly threaten to shatter them; the monologuist immediately throws himself into the effort to maintain his self-image. Consequently the reader sees through the self-image as the monologuist does not. He sees that the speaker is making an assemblage out of the rags and tatters of his personality in order to preserve his self-esteem. He sees the threat which could shatter the self-images were it not for the defenses of the speaker. It is the process subsequent psychologists have come to call rationalization, and nowadays we know all about it and perhaps can do it better because we know. It could be said, of course, that Shakespeare does the same thing in the soliloquies of such a villain as Iago, but that would be an error. Iago rationalizes because of a moral defect. Browning's monologuists rationalize because they are human beings. Browning's twist is that we rationalize because we are human; rationalization is what we pay in order to exist. Rationalization is the price of the ticket of admission to the great theater of human society and culture. Emerson's *Essays*, then, can be profitably approached as dramatic monologues by a man who is doing his best not to rationalize. To be sure, we can say that he sometimes fails. To affirm that he always falls into an easy optimism is to miss the *Essays* almost completely, just as it is a total failure of comprehension to call Browning an easy optimist. We lie to ourselves in order to exist, to act, and since writing is a form of action, sometimes even

Emerson lied to himself. But he knew, as Browning knew, that what we call honesty with ourselves is also a lie, because such honesty makes ourselves explicable, and we are inexplicable. Thus self-honesty is to ascribe to ourselves a moral defect which conceals from ourselves a condition of existence. And it must be added that in the 1850s Emerson became grimmer and developed something of the terrible insight of Browning.

Nevertheless, Emerson would not have been human had he not tried to justify his position and provide a rationale for his style. It cannot be denied that he succumbed to the philosophical temptation to explain the inexplicable. But then, not to have succumbed would have been consistent, and thus inconsistent with his inconsistency. His tragic role is that of Man, and Man's struggle to achieve a consistent vision of his condition is a part of that role and cannot be avoided. Yet such a consistent vision, once achieved, can be denied and transcended; that is what the essay "Circles" is about. To think at all we must have a ground to our thinking; or, as those German philosophers of the time, whom Emerson knew directly and indirectly, like to put it, there must be a ground to existence, if we are to exist. Yet there is no reason why we should not change that ground as often as we like—or can. That is why one cannot create a consistent philosophical position from Emerson's writings except by omitting a great deal.

In the fashion of his time he often used the terms *subject* and *object*, that is, the observing mind and what it observes. Ever since Kant, it had been realized that the subject—or observing mind—observes what it wishes to observe, or, to put it more delicately, what it is its interest to observe; and we know this is so because the object—that which is observed—is always tripping up the observing mind. The instruments, or categories, of the observing mind—the subject—are never congruent with the world—the *Ding-an-sich*, as Kant called it. We see, not the real world, which is inaccessible to us, but the phenomenal world, the world as rearranged to our satisfaction, or dissatisfaction, as the case may be. Thus we have two images, that of the subject and that of the object, and they never match; or, to put it another way—and Emerson liked to put it both ways—the subject projects onto the world an image which falsifies the world. What the world really is we cannot know. In temporal terms, we are always just missing the bus, but then we are always just about to catch it. In more abstract terms, Emerson, like all the advanced thinkers of his time and ours—though today we would put it differently—was convinced that between subject and object there is an irresolvable tension. We do not perceive the world, we create it; or, in perceiving the world we create it. And this act of perceptual creation is man's deepest interest and satisfaction. Here is the most important reason for Emerson's style. Like so many of his contemporaries, to him the perception of a work of art or philosophy was as creative an act as creating it. Kierkegaard called writing which forces the reader to create, teaching by the indirect method. At any rate, from this irresolvable tension between subject and object emerges an odd paradox. Everybody interprets the world a little bit differently from everybody else, yet we all find our way around in it reasonably well; and these two facts can never be put together, or at least Emerson could not do so except in a very special way. It is a way not completely acceptable to us today, but from it something of great significance can be rescued which reveals Emerson's modernity and relevance to our times.

In the essay "The Over-Soul" Emerson works out his position. To grasp it one must first seize vividly the way we ordinarily think about the relation of the mind to the world. To use non-Emersonian terms, our usual assumption is something like this: A stimulus or set of stimuli is fed into the brain by the nervous system. The brain processes these stimuli in various ways, usually called rational (i.e., logical), irrational, and emotional, and the result of that processing, which we call mental activity, is the generation of some activity, including verbal activity. We identify ourselves with mental activity, and feel convinced that we are in control of it. "My mind," we say, "is my own." Now Emerson cannot accept this picture of what happens. Rather, he recommends that we stand aside from our own activity, watch ourselves generating activity, and sunder our usual identification of ourselves with our mental activity. If we do that, it then becomes apparent that the usual picture is quite false. Rather, a stimulus or set of stimuli is fed into the brain by the nervous system. The brain processes these stimuli in ways we cannot possibly comprehend, and the result of that processing is our behavior, which is, therefore, inexplicable. Between stimulus and response lies a mystery, an abyss, the same abyss that lies between two sentences. Thus, if "mind" means awareness, or consciousness, then what happens between stimulus and response is not mind, is not mental activity. Or, if "mind" means what happens between stimulus and response, then awareness, or consciousness, is not mind. What happens in that abyss, Emerson thinks, is not only inexplicable; it is the source of everything that lends life its value. There, he thinks, subject and object are one; in that abyss, he believes, the divine enters the human.

It is interesting that in these very years in which Emerson was publishing the *Essays*, in Denmark Søren Kierkegaard was working out a remarkably similar scheme. In human life he discerned three possible stages, or three levels of orientation toward the world. The first he called the aesthetic, the orientation which satisfies one with the sensuous and the imaginative. Should a man, however, discern that the values of such a life are incoherent and contradictory, he develops the ironic vision. As a result he comes to realize that he must choose among these values if he is to have a life more meaningful than the pure entertainment of the aesthetic orientation. Thus he arrives at the ethical stage (or orientation), in which he believes that he has his life in control, that he determines his life. Should he come to realize, however, that his life is not his own, that his behavior is actually inexplicable, he will, if fortunate, be amused that men should entertain the illusion that they know what they are doing, and that the sense that they make out of themselves and their experiences is anything more than, at the best, comforting. Thus humor precipitates him into a third stage, or orientation—the religious—in which he realizes that each of his acts is a leap from a previous act, a leap which he can only perform but cannot understand. What sustains him in that leap is God, of whom, however, he can never hope to comprehend anything. Thus Kierkegaard's position is remarkably like Emerson's.

It is worth noting that anyone who does not wish to employ the word "God" in his thinking, can nevertheless find both Emerson's and Kierkegaard's schemes quite useful. It can be said that both, still dominated by something of traditional thinking, stripped the term "God" of all useful meaning and used it in order to have *something* to put into the gap between stimulus and response, the abyss over which man leaps from act to act. In the post-Freudian period Western culture is more inclined to use "unconscious" or "subconscious," but like "God" in the Emersonian and Kierkegaardian structures, these words simply mean that whatever is going on in that abyss—and we cannot know what it is—is very important, so important as to be the source of all value.

Although Emerson did not think in Kierkegaardian terms, the Dane's categories are helpful in understanding Emerson. Particularly they help us to understand what in Emerson has so often been condemned—especially by the terribly earnest; the irredeemably ethical; those moral bullies who are always trying to force themselves and everyone else to the irresistible choice, or what they fancy to be the irresistible choice; those who are so foolish as really to believe in reason and logic and man's self-possession as absolutes, not as dull and fragile instruments. What annoys such people is Emerson's radiant light-heartedness, which they think of as shallow optimism. It is nothing of the sort; it has gone beyond optimism. That is why Nietzsche so admired Emerson. If one reads Emerson's Journals, one comes to realize that Emerson achieved that light-heartedness only by paying a price of terrible strain and even suffering, a suffering which never left him. Emerson, like Kierkegaard, arrives at the religious stage through humor, and it is why, among their many other virtues, the *Essays* are so amusing. The essay "Compensation" is an instance. Here he is not humorous but ironic. The universe, he tells us, is a system of justice; for every action there is a corresponding reaction; for every crime there is a punishment. At first glance it seems like a position that affirms that the universe is a harmonious and coherent unity. However, if for every action there is a corresponding reaction, then everything cancels out everything else. His point can be seen if we realize that when we talk about the importance of justice, we mean the importance of justice for other people, not for ourselves. For ourselves we do not want justice, but favors, special consideration. We want the judges of *our* actions to render their judgments on our sins and errors with a full knowledge of the extenuating circumstances. But no—Emerson tells us—there are no extenuating circumstances; there are only our acts. Nevertheless he consoles us. In human life the compensation is that we transcend what we were, that we break through to a new vision of experience, we break down those defenses which preserve a spurious self-image and create a new one which is, hopefully, at least less spurious.

There is no doubt that Emerson, like Kierkegaard, was not an optimist but a redemptionist. The optimist thinks that the progress of the race is automatic. The redemptionist thinks that if man will truly understand his situation, he can redeem himself and the world and can permeate both with a radiant and permanent value. When Emerson was publishing the *Essays*, the young Karl Marx was struggling toward his vision of human redemption, of a society in which subject and object—for he thought in the same terms as Emerson and Kierkegaard—will be reconciled. But there is a difference between the German on the one hand and the American and the Dane on the other. Marx thought redemption could be achieved by the mass of mankind's freeing itself from its oppressors, who had alienated from the individual the fruits of his labor. Emerson thought that the peculiar historical circumstances of his country might conceivably facilitate the achievement of individual redemption, which he, like Browning, thought could be but momentary and must constantly be achieved anew. Kierkegaard came to the conclusion that redemption could be achieved only by the individual, working in profound isolation, utterly separated from his fellowman. Emerson, in the 1850s, moved in this direction, not in Marx's.

The theme of alienation is common to all three. To Marx, economic oppression has alienated man from his happiness, from the rewards of his work, those rewards being his natural right. To Marx, the immediate task was to overthrow economic oppression and its political instruments so that man might enter at once upon his happiness. To Emerson, redemption was a spiritual achievement, and, like Kierkegaard, he came to see that it lay, not in overcoming alienation, but in plunging into alienation, with no assurance of what—if anything—might lie beyond it. Thus, what is often called the optimism of Emerson is closer to a sunny and cheerful indifference. Marx would resolve the inconsistencies of society and culture into a coherent value-laden society and culture; Emerson denied that society and culture could be coherent and value laden. Value could be achieved by the individual only if he accepted his incoherence and his absurdity. For Marx, the goal is to create a society in which all men are equally heroic in their common mastery of nature. For Emerson, only the individual can be heroic, and only as an individual; and nature is not to be mastered, but to be loved. To put it with excessive baldness, Marx thought that redemption could be realized only by bringing people together into a common cause and a social unity. Kierkegaard and Emerson and Browning thought that the only way was to keep people apart, and that one must begin by keeping oneself apart. Marx is the energetic horseman; but it is Emerson who casts a cold eye.

These two ways, the Marxian and the Emersonian, are still the only ways of dealing with that alienation from society and culture which has been the experience of every modern and highly cultivated spirit of that last century and of this, our own. Which way is to be preferred? Alienation was the problem of the 1840s, and it is the problem of today. Certainly Emerson, in his *Essays*, has illuminated that problem as have few writers then or since, and with a brilliance that one can never, finally, tire of.

8

ERNEST HEMINGWAY:

SEXUAL THEMES IN HIS WRITING

[1971*]

Nowadays—when pornography is sold not only on 42nd Street
but quite openly in respectable magazine and paperback
book stores in small, conservative Southern cities; when almost
any city of any size has a store dealing exclusively with sexual
material, verbal and visual, of almost any degree of explicitness
one might care to buy; and when even unsophisticated towns
can have a movie house which shows stag films—it is hard to
believe that the veiled and subdued sexual material in the fiction
of Ernest Hemingway once was considered daring. Some of it
was actually unpublishable at the time it was written in the 1920s.
It is amusing now to see the blanks and dashes and euphemisms
his publishers made him substitute for the frank, masculine language he actually wrote.

It is important, then, to understand that Hemingway started
writing fifty years ago, for only with this historical dimension

* Reprinted by permission from *Sexual Behavior* 1, no. 4 (July 1971):
62–70. Copyright © 1971 by International Publications, Inc.

clearly in mind can it be understood that what appears now to be reticence was then of a frankness judged to be brutal. Brutal, ugly, hard-boiled, tough-minded, anti-intellectual, animal, perverted, immoral—these were among the epithets thrown at Hemingway and his work in the 1920s and the 1930s. But now such judgments also seem very strange. When we read him today, all these terms seem utterly inappropriate. On the contrary, what is obvious now is the sensitivity, the tenderness, and a fierce drive to be absolutely honest not only about what he observed but, more important to him, about what he felt concerning what he observed. In any event, the importance of the emotional content and its potential for arousing emotion in him come out strikingly in *Death in the Afternoon,* a book utterly misunderstood at the time and still generally misunderstood.

The book opens with the most explicit statement Hemingway ever made about what his aim in writing was. First, he conceived his task as putting down "what really happened in action." But this was not an end in itself. Rather he was concerned with "what the actual things were which produced the emotion that you experienced." The principal hindrance to this concern was feeling "what you were supposed to feel, and had been taught to feel," which prevented you from "knowing truly what you really felt." Hemingway was convinced that the best way to discover what one truly feels is by observing violent death. Since the war was over, he went to Spain to see the bullfights. There violent death was accessible for observation and feeling.

The difficulty of determining what one truly feels cannot be overestimated, and it is worth considering the strategies Hemingway used before we examine the peculiar emotion that he discovered. To discover and write down what you truly feel requires "deculturation." Human behavior may be divided into two aspects, that derived from culture and that derived from social institutions. Such concepts, however, are entirely too vague for comprehending what actually goes on.

For them can be substituted the terms "performance" and "instructions." Performances are sufficiently similar to be usefully classified into types of performance, or institutions. An institution, then, is a class, or type, or category of performance.

A social institution may consist of hundreds of people, or of merely two, as in a dyadic institution. Friendship, for example, is an institution, and it is one that Hemingway was intensely interested in. In friendship the interaction between two individuals is a conventionalized one. One has to remember that there are certain things one must not do in the performance of the kind of interaction we call friendship to realize this. Furthermore, the relation of an individual to himself is also an institution, even when it is absolutely private and quite unknown to anyone else. A performance need not involve interaction with another to be conventionalized. On the contrary, the phenomenon of behavioral convergence with one's own behavior indicates that the individual conventionalizes his self-perception and his relation to himself, and that different kinds of situations so affect him that he shifts from one self-relational convention to another. It is one of the major tasks of psychiatry—perhaps its only task—to uncover the individual as an institution.

This conception of the individual as an institution brings out clearly the other aspect of behavior, instructions. For any individual is constantly engaged in giving instructions to himself. Tying a string around a finger in order to remember something may seem perhaps too simple an example to be taken very seriously, but it is a model for all such self-instruction, except for one factor. It is overt, yet most self-instruction is covert. We call such covert self-instruction thought, but that is not a very explanatory term. Rather, we should think of covert verbal or other sign behavior. It is not merely words that serve as instructions, but visual imagery as well. Even dreams, at least at periods of individual crisis, can serve as instructions. Indeed, the general tendency for instructions is that, as the individual moves into an increasingly severe personal crisis, the instructional mode changes. It moves from verbal self-instruction to nonverbal. Dreams and visions become crucial to the individual, and he must perforce rely upon them, since his ordinary verbal instructions have failed. When even dreams and visions have failed and he is no longer able to produce them, he moves even farther away from self-produced covert verbal instructions into overt instructions, that is, into such instructions as he may find, in his confusion and uncertainty, in his environment. When those fail him, he is incapacitated for performance.

Thus reduced to the environment, we may begin at the other end of instructions—culture. There is nothing in the natural environment which of itself is capable of giving man instructions. Put in another way, this means that man can act only because he has a mind. But what is "mind"? It is a word that makes one nervous, for clearly in trying to understand behavior we do not want any nonempirical entities hanging around. Behavioral psychologists do not like the word, and quite rightly, since it has traditionally implied something which cannot be located in the empirical world—and that is what they want to talk about. However, the fact that a "mind" cannot be located does not mean that the word is meaningless or has no empirical foundation or justification. The real meaning of "mind" can be very easily understood. If you put several individuals in the same situation, their behavior always shows a variation in response. Likewise if you put the same individual twice in the same situation he will respond in different ways, even wildly different ways. And that is all the word "mind" means—variability of response. That is the empirical justification for its use.

It is clear from the preceding that some factor other than the natural environment is responsible for human behavior, and this factor is "culture." Since the natural environment does not dictate response, something else must dictate it, something purely human. The slightest examination of human behavior shows that an enormous amount of it is devoted to giving instructions to others as well as to oneself. In fact, in the older sense, as opposed to the anthropological or behavioral sense, "culture" consists entirely of instructions. Philosophy, the arts, science—not only are these instructions, but they are a special class of instructions. They may be called "meta-instructions," that is, instructions for generating instructions—general instructions for generating more specific instructions. But this necessity for meta-instructions reveals two further oddities about human behavior.

Returning once again to "mind," or variability of response, we may see that this notion suggests two other characteristics of culture. First, culture is incoherent. In a coherent culture all instructions would be consistent with each other. There would be no necessity for meta-instructions. Obviously, nowhere does man have such a culture, not even in the most primitive societies, in which discussion is necessary about what performances should appropriately be engaged in, whether to hunt animals or to search for grubs. Second, the notion suggests an enrichment for the term "mind." It points to the fact that the individual, faced with cultural incoherence, or inconsistency of instructions, is capable of generating novel instructions both for himself and for others. But there is a better term than "mind" for this capacity; it is, of course, "individuality." From this may be derived a notion of the greatest importance for understanding Hemingway and the place of sex in his writings.

An individual generates innovative instructions if, and only if, he experiences cultural incoherence. If, therefore, the individual is intensely concerned with his own individuality, with his "self," it may be assumed with great certainty that he is experiencing cultural incoherence. It is important to distinguish this from pseudo-individuality. That occurs when the culture, as at the present time, contains instructions that the individual should be concerned with his own individuality. If he engages in such concern without having actually experienced cultural incoherence, he will, of course, conventionalize his self-institution according to the current standards or roles for self-institutions. On the other hand, if the culture contains instructions that the individual should be concerned with his own individuality, he is quite capable of becoming aware of the incoherence of his culture. Thus a pseudo-individuality can bring about a genuine individuality; a pseudoself can produce a genuine self.

The kind of problem Hemingway was concerned with comes out in an odd passage in the first chapter of *Death in the Afternoon*. He is discussing the difficult moral question of the horses in bullfighting, the fact that the bullfight begins with the bull's attack on the horses ridden by the picadors. It is the first act in the drama. Many people, of course, are so upset by what happens to the horses that they find bullfights intolerable. Hemingway explains why he himself is not upset. First, he perceives the bullfight from the viewpoint of the bull; that is, he sees the bull's place in the whole intricate drama of the bullfight. But just as important, he also maintains that he does not care for horses as horses, or cats as cats, or dogs as dogs. He cares only for individual horses or cats or dogs. He is asserting that individuality in oneself can be affirmed only by affirming the individuality of others.

It is an interesting and important moral position, first emerging in the early nineteenth century, in the cultural tradition in which Hemingway was working. It is tantamount to saying that categorical perception is a denial of individuality, just as pseudo-individuality is a self-institution structured according to the fashionable categories of self-institutions. To love a horse merely because it is a horse is merely to love a category; it is to obey without question the cultural instructions. Hemingway is asserting that to love a cat because its behavior is not exhausted by the attributes of the culturally instructed categories is to love its individuality, which, he implies, not all cats have.

Here, then, is the ethical foundation for Hemingway's work, and for his life as well. An example may be found in his ultimate rejection of Gertrude Stein. His objection to her was not that she was a lesbian. Rather, his rejection was based on his comprehension of her gradual corruption. Though he does not use the term in reference to her, it is clear from his other writing that this is how he felt about her. Her corruption lay simply in the fact that she moved from a defense of homosexuality to the assertion that homosexuality is a proof of superiority. (It is the tragedy of homosexuals to come to this conclusion, and perhaps their only tragedy.) To Hemingway, to think in categories rather than to recognize individuality is the ultimate corruption. It is the basis for his attack on the Communists in *For Whom the Bell Tolls*.

In asserting, therefore, that his task as a writer was to discover and to set down what one truly feels and not what one is supposed to feel or is taught to feel, Hemingway revealed that he was experiencing cultural incoherence. Furthermore, in trying to put down what the actual things were which produced the emotion, he was responding to cultural incoherence in terms of a basic strategy. He was moving away from metadirections, and away from the culturally conventionalized self-institution of being a writer. He had perceived his individuality as a writer as a pseudo-individuality. Unlike individuals in a state of crisis who do not comprehend what is happening to them and move helplessly toward dreams and visions and ultimately a blank and noninstructive environment, Hemingway was purposely moving away from high culture, from meta-instructions, to the environment. However, he had no intention of moving outside of language, outside of culture. Rather, his intention was based on true feeling—feeling that he was not supposed to have or had not been instructed to have—to create a new kind of language, a new style, one that would be free both from pseudo-individuality and from those meta-instructions which he could no longer respond to, having discovered their incoherence.

It was wise of him, therefore, to turn to an alien culture, Spain, so different from the Anglo-Saxon world. To immerse oneself in an alien culture is a traditional strategy of those who wish an exposure to a culture that will reveal the inadequacy and incoherence of their own culture. And it was equally wise to turn to violent death. The encounter of matador and bull is the encounter of man and nature. That is, Hemingway at this point did not directly encounter nature but rather sought a ritualized and highly conventionalized drama of that encounter. Thus, he was in better shape than those who turn directly to nature itself and encounter its blankness, its failure to give instructions when the instructions of culture have failed. In violent death he sought that shock, that disorientation, so severe that the cultural instructions on appropriateness of emotion can fail. This is why in *Death in the Afternoon* he includes an appendix reporting the reactions of fifteen individuals to bullfights. He wishes to point out that the shock does not necessarily always work. He is defining his own individuality by contrast and is careful to give something of the cultural background of each individual he reports on.

What, then, was the true emotion he experienced? It is surprising. In his book on bullfighting Hemingway gives a great deal of information about every detail of the whole process, from breeding the bulls, which are descendants of a strain of wild bulls, to the eventual disposal of the bull's carcass. All of this has but one point: to enable the reader to understand the ritual so well that he can comprehend the emotion of its climax, the killing of the bull. Certainly part of Hemingway's interest is the skill and honesty of the matador. It is important that the matador should fake nothing, that he should be both honest and at the same time graceful, preserving always the purity of line of the human body. This may seem odd until one grasps that to Hemingway bullfighting was an art, specifically in modern times an art of sculpture. In studying bullfighting, then, Hemingway was studying art, attempting to discover a paradigm or model for his own art of fiction.

A second important factor is the skill of all of the members of the bullfight: picadors, banderilleros, matador, and the bull itself. It is of utmost importance that the bull also know how to fight, though not how to fight a man; a bull that has been in a bullring before would know too much, would be too skillful and hence too dangerous. The matador, oddly enough, must both teach the bull how to fight a man in the bullring and, at the same time, dominate the bull—and "dominate" was to become one of Hemingway's favorite words.

It is fairly evident that Hemingway used the matador's struggle with the bull as a model for his own struggle with writing. The analogy is very close. An experienced bull is too dangerous for the matador, whose prime interest is participating in a work of art. Likewise, language that is too experienced, too conventionalized, too literary, is capable of dominating and destroying the writer. The language that Hemingway struggled to master was the language of the ordinary man—the uneducated, "uncultured" man: the mechanic, the ranchhand, the fisherman. This is the source of Hemingway's peculiar rhetoric, which relies not only on the simple declarative sentence but more strikingly on strings of simple declarative clauses held together by repeated "ands." This is the kind of syntax that in school is carefully and severely trained out of the respectable writer. To use it in freshman composition usually means that you get a very low mark.

This factor of the skill of the matador led to another extremely important factor in Hemingway's own self-institutionalization as an individual. It is the notion of the "métier." He used the French term because no English term is its equivalent. To him it meant the craft by which a man maintains his existence, something more than merely earning a living. It is, therefore, a skill and at the same time something central to individuality. A man who is master of his "métier" knows perfectly the traditional and conventionalized modes of behavior required, and still is capable of adapting those modes to unexpected situations, of altering the conventions to meet the gritty recalcitrance of reality, without losing any of the skill and the grace of the tradition. He must innovate both skill and grace. The honesty, skill, and grace of the matador are essential factors, then, in producing the emotion.

The emotion itself is something else. If a bull is properly dispatched, the matador has so dominated it that he can lean over its lowered head, between the horns, plunge the sword between the vertebrae, and sever the aorta. This is the climax, to which everything else has led. To Hemingway, if the matador kills the bull without honesty, skill, and grace, the bullfight is a failure—as, he claims, most bullfights are. Certainly the rarity of perfection was an important factor in the appeal of bullfighting to Hemingway. Now at that moment when the sword is plunged into the bull, the motion of bull and man is momentarily arrested. It is a moment of stasis, Hemingway's "moment of truth." At that instant the bull and the man become one. And it is the perception of that oneness of bull and man that was, to Hemingway, the emotion of the bullfight. The sculptural group of bull and man united, fused into unity, was "the actual thing" which "produced the emotion that you experienced." Certainly the nature of that emotion is unclear, but it is important to understand it, because it is central to Hemingway's comprehension of sex and to the place of sexual experience in Hemingway's writing.

However, before proceeding directly to this problem, it is necessary to get rid of certain common preconceptions about the man which are part of the Hemingway legend, a legend which has made comprehension almost impossible, not only of his achievement but also of what he was centrally concerned with. As a boy spending his summers in upper Michigan he was trained in hunting and fishing by his father, and he learned still more from neighbors and Indians. When he returned to the United States from France in 1928 he settled in Key West, spending considerable time as well, for the rest of his life, in Wyoming, principally because of the hunting but also because of the beauty of the landscape and the sparsity of the population. Hunting and fishing became his principal interests—particularly the latter after he had discovered the fascination of the Gulf Stream and the excitement of fishing for marlin. In a few years he went to Kenya on a safari, marvelously recorded in *The Green Hills of Africa*. He once said that these sports were his only recourse when he could not write, and it was often enough that he could not. Indeed, considering the length of his literary career—more than forty years—he did not produce much. It was this mode of relaxation that was responsible for the greatest criticism he experienced. The New York intellectual, whom he came to regard as his greatest enemy, and with just cause, necessarily found an interest in hunting and fishing not only incomprehensible but rather shocking. It was offered as evidence of Hemingway's brutality and anti-intellectualism.

The injustice of such accusations is patent. In the first place, no one who sets out, in response to the experience of cultural incoherence, to devise a subtle strategy to discover what one truly feels, rather than feeling what one is supposed to feel, can be called anti-intellectual. To undertake such an enterprise is one of the most intellectual things it is possible to do. Furthermore, to resist the rhetoric of high and official and establishment "culture" because it is the source of cultural incoherence, and to turn to the ordinary language of common people as a source for innovating a new literary rhetoric—precisely because one is aware that the source of the cultural incoherence is language itself, is verbal behavior—is again anything but anti-intellectual. It is an intellectualism that transcends the conventions of the intellectual role and its instructions and directions.

And in the second place, it is obvious that his intense interest in hunting and fishing was modeled upon his study of bullfighting. He had tried bullfighting as an amateur—as so many Spanish do —and knew that he was not made for it. He was too big, too muscular, too clumsy. A matador does not need to be strong but he does need to be graceful. His physique is more of a ballet dancer's than a prizefighter's, and Hemingway was a boxer. But on the other hand, both hunting and fishing were "métiers"; both had as long a tradition of skill and of their own kind of grace as, nearly, the existence of humanity. In all his accounts of both sports Hemingway always emphasizes both the skill and the grace as well as the capacity to endure. And to him, to endure was everything, but of value only if the endurance were conducted with skill and grace. It is apparent, then, that there was no discontinuity between his writing and his hunting and fishing. Both endeavors, as he conceived them, required not only skill and grace but also the capacity to maintain that skill and grace while meeting the unexpected. In both, one exhausted the conventional limits of skill and grace and extended them. Consequently, Hemingway was always furious when he was accused of hunting and fishing in order to create and maintain an image and legend of masculinity, and was even more infuriated when it was implied that the drive to prove masculinity necessarily derived from a lack of conviction of his own masculinity. The truth of the matter is that neither masculinity nor pseudomasculinity had anything to do with what hunting and fishing meant to him. Although he had made it clear enough, the literary intellectuals were incapable of comprehending that his blood sports could have any other significance than brutality and anti-intellectualism. In both his vocation and his relaxation he was engaged in forging his individuality, and in the same way.

What hunting and fishing meant to him he made extremely clear in his posthumous novel, *Islands in the Stream*, published in 1970, nine years after his death. This work has been badly received by the critics. Yet I believe it will eventually be recognized as his greatest achievement. It is not difficult to understand why he did not give it a final revision and publish it. *Across the River and into the Trees*, also a moving and beautiful work, was received with execration and contempt. If his mature work was going to be misunderstood, there was no reason to be around and to suffer the attacks on it. In *Islands in the Stream* there is a long and brilliant narrative of how the son of the protagonist, a painter named Thomas Hudson, fought a giant swordfish all day, and eventually lost him. What the boy remembers as of greatest significance in the struggle was, toward the end, the feeling, first, that he and the swordfish were not enemies, and second, that he and the swordfish had become one. He became, he said, the swordfish, and the swordfish became himself. He asks his father if he understands, and the father says that he does, that he knows exactly what the boy means. Yet, interestingly, he wonders if he should have allowed the boy this experience, if it were too much to subject him to at so early an age. It is fairly clear that it was not the struggle, nor the physical effort, but rather that particular experience which he should have spared him. We are, after all, always of two minds about permitting the young to experience the most terrible truths of human life. We know that, to be men, they must, and yet we know but too well the suffering that such truths entail.

It is evident that this narrative is a subjective account of the objective experience of the unity of bull and matador. It is a loss of the distinction between self and world, between subject and object. It is a loss of identity. Such an experience is judged to be pathological, and no doubt it is sometimes the outcome of psychopathology, one of its symptoms. But it need not be pathological. On the contrary. It is normally assumed that the ego or the identity is "an existent," or, to put it bluntly, that we really exist. However, an enormous amount of culture consists of directions to the effect that we ought to believe that we do indeed exist. Religion, philosophy, and the arts (and science as well, if more subtly) are made up, to a great extent, of such instructions. It is reasonably clear that the sense of identity, the sense of an empirical distinction between subject and object, is a cultural phenomenon, not a natural one. The ultimate effect of "deculturation," then, is the loss of identity. It is as far as one can go in discovering a "true feeling." If such a discovery is the outcome of psychopathology it is terrifying; if, however, it is the outcome of a deliberate effort to divest oneself of an incoherent culture, to move from culture to the world, then it is inexpressibly rewarding. It is perfectly clear that the *Islands* boy's experience with the great fish is to be taken as the ultimate reward for dealing with recalcitrance of the world with a grace and skill that go beyond the convention of grace and skill. The boy, certainly, does far more than a boy is supposed to be able to do, or should be required or allowed to do. His subsequent loss of identity was, for Hemingway, the significant opportunity that sexual experience also offers. There is evidence for this in both his life and his work. With at least three of his four wives he was extremely interested in symbolizing this fusion of self and other. He wished, and at times proposed, that the woman should cut her hair much shorter while he allowed his to grow long. Each, thus, would become the other.

All his themes and fantasies are united in his most sustained attempt to put down in words the experience of fusion of self and world, the love story in *For Whom the Bell Tolls*. Three aspects of Maria are of importance here. First, she has been raped by Franco's troops. Second, her hair has been cut off, and when the hero, Robert, meets her, it is just growing out. Third, as he touches it he thinks of the fur of an animal. First, then, she has experienced the shock of violence, that shock which, to Hemingway, is necessary in order to strip away culture, to permit individuality to emerge from the swaddlings of cultural instructions. She is quite clearly presented as someone who has died and has been reborn. She is even given a new mother in Pilar. Second, her short hair offers what Hemingway had fantasies about, the possibility of fusing two identities. Third, her identification as an animal makes her an even better candidate for that encounter with the world which leads to fusion of subject and object and to loss of identity. Hemingway was in fact extremely fond of cats. In his Cuban home he had numbers of them. Moreover, in *The Green Hills of Africa* his regard and respect for the animals he hunted, even his love for them, is striking. The pure emotion of shooting the animal was the same pure emotion generated by the fusion of matador and bull.

Robert has been prepared for a culminating sexual experience with Maria. He is fighting on the Loyalist side in the Spanish war, not out of political conviction—he insists on his lack of political sophistication and interest—but because he has become aware of the incoherence of his culture, a culture which is destroying the value of the lives of ordinary men and women: peasants and workingmen and bullfighters and whores. He fights only because he respects their individuality as unique human beings.

It is another instance of what has been mentioned before—the only way to assert one's own individuality is to assert another's. This is the real significance of the "no man is an island" theme; it is not, as usually supposed, a sentimental and political humanitarianism. Hemingway respects individuals precisely as he respects animals, for their individuality; but most of all he respects individuals whose culture is extremely simple and straightforward. This must necessarily be the attitude of one who has sought to solve the problem of cultural incoherence by "deculturation."

The situation, therefore, is perfectly set up for the sexual scenes. The most important one is not, however, in the famous sleeping bag but rather by daylight on a hilltop. Pilar arranges this situation, but she must first overcome her jealousy. This has nothing, she insists, of the perverted, of the lesbian. Rather, her action is the abandonment of possessiveness, of the possessiveness of all parents—for she, as we have seen, is the spiritual mother of Maria. Probably the important theme here is that parents rarely abandon their possessiveness—Hemingway's own mother certainly never did—and respect the individuality of their children. Pilar gives spiritual birth to Maria: that is, she gives her up; and no doubt one reason Pilar is made such an extraordinary and powerful figure is that Hemingway wished to emphasize the strength it takes to do this.

The sexual experience on the hilltop culminates what had begun in the sleeping bag, the sense that each has of becoming the other. The culmination is the famous "the earth moved" passage, of which so much sport has been made. It appears that ordinarily it is interpreted as a reference to an unbelievably powerful orgasm, but that is quite clearly not at all what Hemingway was talking about. Both Maria and Robert speak of the earth moving away. They become detached from the earth. They themselves go away, but not together. In the light of what has been said above, it is reasonably clear that the pure emotion which Hemingway is struggling to set down here is that loss of identity, the first stage of which is the fusion of self and other. To one who experiences so deeply the incoherence of his culture and the inconsistency of its directions—and to whom the emergence of individuality is at first the only possible solution—the loss of that individuality itself as cultural convention must become the culminating human experience.

Two parallels are of some use in suggesting the possibility of this interpretation. One of the techniques of Yoga is the *tantric* technique, by which the shock of orgasm is used to precipitate the individual into a condition of the sense of fusion with the universe, precisely that loss of self which so fascinated Hemingway. The other parallel comes from Wagner's opera *Tristan und Isolde*. There is little or no indication in the biography of Hemingway by Carlos Baker that Hemingway had any particular interest in music. Painting was the art he cared most for, after literature, and there is some indication that painting meant more to him (more than the writing of others, that is, though less than his own writings). The parallel with *Tristan* is therefore all the more striking, since Hemingway was quite probably unaware of it. On the whole, people imagine that Wagner's opera is a love story, but it is more accurate to say that it is about the use of love to escape from love. At the height of the love duet in Act II Tristan and Isolde quite specifically, and verbally, identify themselves with each other. The culmination of their experience, however, is interrupted, to be resumed by Isolde alone, after Tristan's death. In performances she is usually presented as dying at the end, but in fact the text gives no indication of this, though I have seen only one production in which she does not die. Rather, she is transfigured. Imagining she feels the breath of the dead Tristan, she identifies that breath with the universe, and she herself loses her identity by fusing with what she calls the *Weltall*, the universe undifferentiated by human culturally conventionalized and instructed categories.

The centrality of sexual experience in Hemingway's thinking must be recognized, but it is a strange and rare experience. Its importance is that by means of sexual intercourse it is possible, if the conditions are right and the individuals involved are ready for that experience, to break through the ultimate illusion—the illusion which persists when all others have been abandoned—of individual identity. What is involved is the pure emotion of total "deculturation," and its value lies in its negation of culture. Once experienced, it assures the individual of a value which lies outside of culture; it assures him that human culture is merely a kind of artifact. It detaches him from culture, and this permits both an awareness of cultural incoherence and a criticism of that culture which nothing else makes possible. The question is whether or not Hemingway actually made use of that insight. The answer to that may be postponed for a bit until another question is taken up.

Why was it that Hemingway turned to sex for this experience? It is not enough that he had precedence in the two parallels cited. Others have found the way beyond identity through other paths. In India, of course, there was elaborate metaphysical and religious support for the *tantric* technique. There it can scarcely be called a "deculturational process" but rather obedience to well-established cultural conventions. Wagner, however, followed the same line that Hemingway did, and the reason is not difficult to find. Sexual experience is an area of behavior for which—in Europe and America, at any rate—the cultural directions are singularly incoherent, inconsistent, ill-defined, and inexact. It is an area which is difficult for most people in our culture precisely because it requires them to innovate. The result is that in sexual experience every variety of individual interest can find expression—particularly those which are culturally inhibited in most other areas of culture. The experience of total control of the environment, for example, particularly of the social environment, is desired by most people; in sadism is to be found its expression. In the same way the equally powerful desire to surrender all efforts to control the environment can be symbolized and satisfied in masochism. Sex, therefore, is a stage on which any psychic drama can be acted out. (For a more extensive discussion of this point, the reader might be interested in examining my *Art and Pornography* [1969].) For two hundred years and more the impact of rationalism, analysis, and science upon the metadirectional dimension of our culture has, not surprisingly, led to a steadily increasing interest in sex. It is there, more than in any other area of human behavior, that cultural incoherence is highly visible, that those interests which the culture cannot deal with, though it has created them, come to the fore.

It is not surprising, therefore, that Hemingway's writing is filled with sexual material, even though it is pretty mild by current standards. Nevertheless, it was daring enough for the time. In "Up in Michigan," a story which in 1921 he could not get published in the United States, the theme is the unsatisfactory nature of a girl's first sexual experience. Hemingway was already criticizing the conventionalized instructions about how one should feel about such matters. But he was particularly interested in sexual failure and misdirections. He must be one of the first writers to make use of the theme of masturbation. It appears in *To Have and Have Not* (1937) and again in *For Whom the Bell Tolls* (1940). Homosexuality of one sort or another frequently appears. One of the most striking uses is in the short story "The Sea Change" (1932). A young man has discovered that his girl, possibly his wife, wishes to leave him temporarily to engage in a love affair with another woman. At first he is horrified. To him, lesbianism is a vice and a perversion. But suddenly a change comes over him. She has assured him that she will return. All at once he accepts the idea, both of the affair and of her return. He urges her to go. She does so, gratefully. As he looks in the mirror behind the bar, he sees that he looks altogether different (though not to the bartender); and even as he told her of his implied acceptance of the whole situation, he felt that someone else was speaking.

Here Hemingway has described with great accuracy the behavioral process of experiencing cultural negation, the denial of the validity of cultural instructions—particularly about feeling—which one has learned. In the 1927 volume of short stories, *Men Without Women*, he was at last able to publish "Up in Michigan" in this country and could also include another story of the theme of homosexuality, "A Simple Enquiry." The latter is concerned with an Italian major who makes subtle advances to an enlisted man, but who is not quite sure whether he has been misunderstood, whether he has been rejected because the boy has no interest in or is frightened by homosexuality, or whether the boy prefers another homosexual partner. Cultural uncertainty is the theme, as it is of a nonsexual story, "A Clean, Well-Lighted Place," in which the consequences of cultural uncertainty are set forth with striking power. Those consequences are the sense of nothingness, the total indifference of the universe to the interests of man, and the collapse of all cultural supports. In this story, the pure emotion is the sense of identity without confirmation in and by another human being.

But of course the most thoroughgoing use of sexual material is found in the novel *The Sun Also Rises* (1926). As Hemingway later explained, the idea for the book came from his own experiences. Wounded in the legs on the Italian front in 1918, he also experienced an inflammation of the scrotum as the result of fibers from the cloth of his trousers being driven into it by an explosion. This got him to wondering, he said, about what it would be like to be completely emasculated. He was sufficiently concerned with the theme to take it up once more in "God Rest You Merry, Gentlemen," in which a pious boy is so driven by "impure lust" that he emasculates himself.

Actually, however, emasculation is not the theme of *The Sun Also Rises*. Hemingway later said that its real theme is that promiscuity is no solution. Brett Ashley, an Englishwoman, and Jake are in love, but of course they can give it no sexual expression since Jake has been emasculated in the war. Brett goes from one man to another, as indeed she had been doing before she met Jake. Jake compares himself to the steers who control the bulls in moving them about preparatory to the bullfight. He regrets—but does nothing to hinder—her affairs with Cohn, or with Mike, or with the young bullfighter whom Brett eventually leaves because she knows she would ruin him.

What Hemingway is doing in this novel is not merely examining the inadequacy of the current convention of the Paris expatriates that sexual promiscuity is fun and important and even redemptive—he is also examining the destructiveness of love when it is channeled into sex. Jake is isolated by such standards, trapped into himself, while Brett is driven. She becomes hysterical with desire. The young matador, however, has grace and skill; indeed he is the white hope of bullfighting, since he offers the potentiality, young as he is, of redeeming bullfighting from the decadence into which it has fallen. Jake, the steer, betrays the bull, the young matador, to the destructiveness of inflamed eroticism. Since it is only cultural instructions which give the world meaning, sex is, in itself, meaningless. As a purely natural phenomenon it has no more human meaning than any other natural phenomenon. The cultural interpretation of sex, and the conventionalized directions for reacting to it, are the source of eroticism, sex made humanly meaningful. Hemingway emasculates Jake in order to isolate the cultural phenomenon of eroticism and to indicate its hopeless inadequacy. It is not merely that his compatriots in the Paris of the 1920s thought sexual experience to be redemptive. They had, in fact, but inherited a cultural tradition already nearly 150 years old. It is a tradition responsible, for example, for the misinterpretation of Wagner's *Tristan und Isolde.* The final scene shows Brett and Jake locked in bondage to each other. To Brett it is still the bondage of erotic illusion. For Jake, however, that is an illusion he has abandoned. His bondage to Brett is the bondage of responsibility. The young matador, meanwhile, has escaped. He can go on to the kind of life Hemingway approves of, the life of skill and grace, the life which, Hemingway was to realize, leads to that detachment of which Jake at the end of the novel has but an inkling.

In *The Sun Also Rises* Hemingway emasculated Jake in order to separate love from eroticism, for the two had been confounded —and worse, confounded with sex. The values of love and eroticism create impossible difficulties; in the young matador is seen a way of life capable of transcending those difficulties, a way almost corrupted by the confusion of eroticism and love and sex. Hemingway, as we have seen, went on to fuse eroticism, love, sex, and the life symbolized by the matador in order to discover and lay bare the problem of identity and to go beyond identity to detachment. The question still remaining is whether or not he was able to put that detachment to use. I believe that he did so in *Islands in the Stream,* which are not only the islands of the Bahamas and Florida and Cuba in the Gulf Stream but also the islands of individuality in the stream of culture.

The latter book is divided into three parts, and each is concerned with different manifestations of love. The first part is the love of a father for his sons; the second is the love of men for women; the third is the love of men for men, what Hemingway once called the sweet stench of comradeship. Each kind of love is shown as both irresistible and destructive. Only in his painting does Thomas Hudson find that detachment which makes love, the fundamental relation of human beings, endurable. When he knows that he has been mortally wounded, his first thought is of the paintings that would not be done—those results of that activity which extends the possibility of skill and grace and achieves the fusion of self and other, of subject and object, and which transcends identity and leads to detachment. In his first story, "Up in Michigan," Hemingway began the exploration of the human condition in terms of the sexual relations between human beings, initiated by love. Sex, he concluded, can be redemptive only if it leads beyond love to detachment. The message of love is that no man is an island. The message of sex, for those properly prepared, is that every man is an island. *Islands in the Stream* ends with Thomas Hudson's death. One cannot live without the illusion of identity. One cannot live without the destructive bondage of love. The problem is to endure, but life can be made endurable only by momentary experiences of escaping from the culturally induced illusion of identity, experiences made possible by extending skill and grace beyond their conventional limits to a fusion of self and other. To the incoherences of human life, which become most salient in love and eroticism, the only final answer is death. When Thomas Hudson knew he was going to die, "he felt far away now and there were no problems at all."

9

THE PLACE OF SEX IN

THE WORK OF WILLIAM FAULKNER

[1971*]

In 1954 William Faulkner published *A Fable*. It confounded his critics at the time and has continued to confound them ever since. He rarely spoke of his books (and but once, apparently, of this one), but he did refer to *A Fable* when in South America, saying that it was either a great novel or it was nothing. It is not necessary to agree with either of these judgments to take the novel seriously—as many Faulkner critics have not done, most of them having dismissed it as a failure, an excellent way to dispose of something one does not understand.

It seems reasonable to assume that Faulkner intended it to be central to his work, in the sense that it embodied his ultimate conclusions about human life. He worked on it for many years, and after publishing it, he issued only two more major works—*The Town* and *The Mansion*—followed by the lesser, but delightful, *The Reivers*. The very title indicates *A Fable's* signifi-

* Reprinted by permission from *Studies in the Twentieth Century*, no. 14 (Fall 1974): pp. 1–20. Copyright © 1974 by Stephen H. Goode.

cance. A fable is a narrative that is meant to be interpreted, to bear a meaning—sometimes a moral meaning, sometimes a more general meaning—some statement about the human condition. Even the setting indicates its special place in the Faulkner canon. It takes place during World War I at the time of the false armistice of the spring of 1918. Indeed, it is a kind of mythological interpretation of that false armistice. To be sure, in his early years Faulkner had written a few stories about World War I (in which he tried to be a flyer), and his first novel, *Soldier's Pay* (1926), is about a returning flyer. Yet the vast bulk of his writing is about the South, particularly Mississippi, and the South is the setting of *Soldier's Pay* as well as of his second novel, *Mosquitoes* (1927). These two novels are not considered important works by most critics. Faulkner's serious work is held to begin with *Sartoris* (1929), itself a reduction to a publishable length of a longer and still unpublished novel, *Flags in the Dust*, the cutting having been done by a friend, not by Faulkner himself. After nineteen volumes of novels and short stories, all (except for a few stories) about the South, a major book with an entirely different setting and entirely new characters—instead of the repeated characters and families of most of the rest of the work—indicates a very special kind of effort. It is as if before the vast and densely populated stage of his world and his characters he had drawn a curtain—as, in a play or an opera, a curtain is drawn for an entr'acte. The curtain presents a new setting, and before it, entirely fresh characters act out their roles. But it is not that this surprising interruption has nothing to do with what the rest of the play is about. Rather, this curtain and these characters conceal and suppress the rest of the play, but at the same time reveal its significance. It is as if Faulkner announced with full orchestra, "This is what my work is all about." And the probability of the adequacy of this judgment concerning the importance and significance of *A Fable* is increased and made nearly certain by the theme of the work, the central theme of European civilization for nearly 2000 years—the sacrifice and crucifixion of Christ.

The Christ figure—the Corporal—and twelve other soldiers are in the French army. Mysteriously, not only do they have the proper papers to circulate freely all along the front, but they even penetrate the German lines, apparently without danger, and spread their word. The result is a simultaneous refusal to fight by both French and German soldiers, a refusal that spreads to the British and American sectors. Eventually the problem has to be settled, and the normal course of fighting resumed, through the intervention of the Supreme Commander of the Allied Forces; he is a very surprising figure, for he is also the natural father of the Corporal, and in this version of the Christ story he is the tempter as well. In short, God, Satan, and the Emperor (or more precisely Tiberius-Pilate) are made one. It is the will of the Emperor and of Satan that Christ be destroyed, but it is also the will of God. This conflation of the three makes it clear that Christ, or what he represents, must be destroyed, not to redeem man, but because —in the judgment of the new Trinity—Christ represents an intolerable threat to Man.

That threat is the threat of Idealism. The Corporal, or Christ, offers peace; hope; happiness; love; tranquillity; purity of morality, of motivation, and of intention; everything that man wants and thinks it possible to realize. But God-Satan-Emperor know that this idealistic vision is but a vision of the solution of man's problems and that man's problems cannot be resolved. They know—and this is why they are combined in the figure of a General—that the condition of man is war, and that the vision of the Corporal is an illusion. Yet the General also knows that man cannot exist without that illusion, just as man cannot exist without war. War itself, however, is not to be understood as merely war. What is war in *A Fable* is—in the full human situation—the endless and irresolvable struggle of man with his environment. The Corporal—Christ—represents precisely that illusory Idealism which is the only justification for seeing mankind as noble but which at the same time disqualifies man for facing his situation and dealing with its problems. It is the magnificent madness—the permanent and incurable insanity of the human mind —which makes man both awe-inspiring and absurd. *A Fable* is a fable of the irresolvable struggle and eternal tension between the splendid insanity of mankind and the reality of the situation in which humanity finds itself.

This provides a framework with which to explain and understand what seems to be a wholly irrelevant excrescence in the book, the story of the three-legged racehorse. The story itself is one of those fantastic inventions so typical of Faulkner, and which he has done better than any other writer. Faulkner's works are full of such stories, the triumphant fulfillment of the whole tradition of the American tall story, born on the frontier—exaggerations by which frontiersmen erected human potentiality into a possibility that was more than adequate to deal with the frontier's terrifying problems. In Faulkner's world these stories are magnificent parodies of the most resplendent achievements of the human imagination.

Faulkner's wild invention tells of a magnificent, an impossibly superb racehorse: bred in England, sold to a South American; resold to a millionaire of this country; injured in a train wreck while being shipped north from New Orleans; and stolen by its English groom, a Negro preacher, and the latter's nephew. In the wreck one leg is broken. Healed by the three thieves, the horse can now run on but three legs, but even so, can beat almost everything. So the three thieves race it, furtively slipping from one part of the country to the other, always a jump ahead of the agents of the United States government and of the millionaire and of the insurance company. Cornered at last, they kill the horse rather than surrender it. It is a long time before Faulkner lets us know why the horse is killed, and the explanation turns out to be both surprising and directly related to the theme of the place of sex in Faulkner's work. The three thieves have become totally devoted to the animal. They are rumored to have made great sums of money by betting on it, but in fact they have done nothing of the sort. They race it because, and only because, it is such a glorious creature, a pure idea, or better, a pure Ideal of what a racehorse should be. And they kill it rather than let it be humiliated and degraded to the fate they know awaits it, the fate of being a mere studhorse, of being reduced to a merely sexual function.

Thus the Idealism of man denies the value of his natural, his animal, origins. The story is an instance of that fierce hatred of sexuality so often found in Faulkner's madder characters, and the fear of it so often found in still others. But there is an even more surprising and bitter implication to be found. The Idealism that has made man noble, the Idealism that purports to be life-loving and life-affirming, has, again and again in Faulkner, the consequence of death. Just as *A Fable* is an entr'acte in Faulkner's work—a masque that tells us what is going on in the rest of his work—so the story of the stolen racehorse (which he published separately and before he published *A Fable*) is an entr'acte or masque that tells us what is going on in *A Fable*. The Christ-Corporal appears to be devoted to peace, love, and life, but is, in fact, death-bound. His very existence and his efforts threaten a whole regiment of men (three thousand of them) with death, and by a series of coincidences as fantastically wild as the story of the stolen horse he becomes the French Unknown Soldier. As he so often does, Faulkner compels our belief by inventing the wildly unbelievable. It is as if one of his basic convictions was that man is the animal capable of believing anything, particularly if it is untrue. By raising fiction to the most extreme and alpine heights of the improbable, he forces us to be aware of our infinite capacity to believe the unbelievable, to grant credence to the totally absurd. He forces us to accept the fact that the ideal-istic and death-bound illusionism of the Corporal-Christ is a universal attribute of all men, a condition of man's existence which denies him an adequate realization of the conditions of his existence.

Yet it must not be thought that Faulkner's was an either/or mind. Some critics have apparently believed that to present two antithetical views implies that one should be accepted and the other rejected. In *Requiem for a Nun* (1951) Faulkner continued the story of Temple Drake, which he began in *Sanctuary* (1931). Nancy, the Negro maid and nurse, kills Temple's two children to save Temple, she thinks, from a further sexual transgression. In the attempt to win a pardon for Nancy, the lawyer and district attorney, Gavin Stevens, forces Temple to go to the governor and tell her entire story, including the fact that she lied on the witness stand in *Sanctuary*. He fails to get the pardon and hence-forth identifies himself totally with Nancy, visiting her in jail and singing with her; forcing Temple to visit her; and encourag-ing Nancy, an ex-whore, in her religious exaltation. Most critics have been approving of Nancy and disapproving of Temple. Yet Nancy is, after all, a murderess, and Temple is faced with the problem of continuing to live—under the circumstances, much the more difficult thing to do. Nancy's religious exaltation is such that, not only does death not frighten her, it doesn't make any difference. Further, Stevens is too easily accepted as Faulkner's mouthpiece. One critic, however, Professor Noel Polk, has gone the other way, and has seen at least part of the truth. To this critic it is the Idealists, Nancy and Stevens, who are destructive, and his sympathies are with Temple. Temple's position is that of the God-Satan-Emperor General in *A Fable*. Yet with *A Fable* in mind, it seems more accurate to see *Requiem for a Nun* as an exemplification or illustration of the vision of the human condition in *A Fable*. It is the human task to prevail, and necessary for that task is the human capacity to create illusions, yet those very illusions destroy the capacity to prevail. In short, between Idealism or Illusion on the one hand and the demands imposed by the conditions of his existence on the other, man exists and must exist in a condition of irresolvable tension, caught forever in the vice of Idealism and Biology. To attempt to resolve that tension in either direction, as Temple once did in *Sanctuary* in her own experience in a brothel, is the way to disaster. It is the task of the General to force man into the acceptance of that irresolvable tension.

The word "Biology" was not introduced accidentally here, nor without justification from Faulkner himself. *Requiem for a Nun* is a play, but before each act is a long narrative passage. In these Faulkner gives a dual setting for the events. One setting is the history of the town, Faulkner's Jefferson, Mississippi, the county seat of Yoknapatawpha County, "William Faulkner, Sole Owner and Proprietor." But this in turn is placed in a larger setting, the history of man as an animal species. In his novel Faulkner for the first time explicitly stated what was implicit in his work from the beginning, man as seen from the perspective of Darwin and Evolution.

In the beginning was . . . that one seethe one spawn one mother-womb, one furious tumescence, father-mother-one, one vast incubant ejaculation already fissionating in one boiling moil of litter from the celestial experimental Work Bench.

And Evolution itself is apprehended in a sexual metaphor. One pole in Faulkner's thinking, then, is the creativity of nature, sex, evolution. The other pole is the dome of the state capitol in Jackson, "the gilded crumb of man's eternal aspiration." In between is the jail in Jefferson—for *Requiem for a Nun* is not about Temple, nor about Nancy. It is about the jail, the centrality and symbol of civilization, the place in which, Faulkner says again and again, man gains his identity as man, antithetical to both Nature and Idealism.

Man is driven by the fury of the initial creative ejaculation, and he is driven by the fury of that ridiculous but eternal aspiration, that gilded crumb of a gilded statehouse dome. It is the jail that makes man human; it is in the jail that the two furies meet and are contained and molded; it is the jail that holds the two furies in tension; it is in the jail that is meted out the punishment of those who surrender to one fury or to another. "Only believe," Nancy tells Temple. And critics have been impressed by this religious madness. They have neglected or sneered at or dismissed Temple's sensible and desperate reply, "Believe what?" and again, "Believe what, Nancy? Tell me." To which Nancy replies, "Believe." But Temple knows better, "Because there's tomorrow, and tomorrow, and tomorrow. All you've got to do is, just to die." The fury of eternal aspiration and the surrender to that fury condemn Nancy, and Gavin Stevens also takes the easy way out, saying that we are "doomed, damned." "Hasn't He been telling us that for going on two thousand years?" The fury of eternal aspiration—the fury of Christ—is a fury that leads to death and the desire for death, just as does the fury of pure sexuality; for Nancy has murdered because she thinks she sees Temple surrendering again to sex, just as she, Nancy, once had, "backing her behind into a buzz-saw." Nancy and Stevens do not understand the jail, but Temple, though unknowingly, learns its lesson. On a pane of glass in the jail was scratched a name, and that name meant, "*Listen stranger; this was myself: this was I.*" Nancy sees herself as an abstraction, once of sex, now of belief; Stevens sees himself as an abstraction of justice. Temple, alone of the three of them, sees herself as Temple, as "I." But she too once surrendered to the fury of sex.

Even in the early Faulkner there are hints that the background of his vision of the human condition was Darwinian evolution. Nor should this be surprising. He was born in 1897, and when he was growing up, Darwin and evolution were subjects of intense discussion and conflict, particularly in the still predominantly rural and small-town America. The climax came in 1925 with the Scopes monkey-trial, when Faulkner was in New Orleans and, probably, writing his first novel. To be on the side of Darwin and evolution was to be on the side of the modern, and all of Faulkner's fiction indicates his intense interest in advanced culture, although much of his work is, to be sure, about the past. But to write about the South is to write about a culture in which the past is extraordinarily present even yet, and was far more so when Faulkner was growing up in a society still heavily populated by Civil War veterans. Historical consciousness comes very naturally to the Southerner, such was the trauma of the Civil War. The South is still the most interesting part of the United States, especially to a Northerner, simply because it is the only part that has suffered defeat in war and the humiliation of a military occupation. The theory of evolution is a historical theory, and because of his past and the failure in that past, it is easier for a Southerner to understand what Darwin was really saying.

For Darwin has often been misunderstood—perhaps usually misunderstood. It is not entirely an error to identify evolution with a theory of human progress, but it is, at best, a gross simplification. The usual unsophisticated—and often the sophisticated —notion of Darwinian evolution is that evolution is purposive, and that man has emerged from a line of ever-increasing perfection, internally in terms of brain physiology and externally in terms of adaptation of organism to environment. But this is not what Darwin said at all. On the contrary, Darwin administered a shock for a great many reasons, but one of them was that his theory requires that evolution be the consequence of accident and maladaptation of organism to environment. Evolution is the consequence of failure, and there is no reason to think that man himself will not fail. We should not, after all, sneer at the dinosaurs for getting themselves extinct; they lasted longer than man has yet.

In *A Fable* there are several visions of man's evolutionary future. In one, man becomes a brain in an automobile and establishes himself on other planets. In another, man is simply still talking when the sun dies and the end of life on earth comes. In the Nobel Prize Speech of 1950 Faulkner said that man will not only endure, but that he will also prevail. In *A Fable*, however, published four years later, the General says that man will prevail, but the Corporal says that he will endure. It appears that in the Nobel Prize Speech Faulkner was quite deliberately resolving a tension as part of a public appearance. The words of the speech about endurance and prevailing are almost identical with those of the General and the Corporal in *A Fable*. It seems reasonable to conclude that Faulkner offered an illusionistic and idealistic sop to the public and that with irony and a certain contempt he played the part of the Noble Idealistic Writer—the kind the Nobel literary prize was instituted to reward. Why bother to tell the truth to the general public? Is it not kinder to indulge its illusionary idealism, since it cannot tolerate the irresolvable tension of admitting the two furies but not being destroyed by surrender to either? As Faulkner uses the terms, "to prevail" and "to endure" are two entirely different matters. The first is real Darwinism; the second is the illusionary and idealistic misinterpretation of Darwin. To prevail is to dominate nature, as man must do to survive, but it also means that man cannot survive forever. To endure means to accept a passivity aimed at endless, eternal survival and redemption.

There seems to be another ingredient of nineteenth-century English culture in Faulkner's vision of human existence and the human condition. His third novel, and his first in which he took up his theme of life in Mississippi, was *Sartoris*. (The accent, he often insisted, is on the first syllable.) Now one of the most striking and powerful works of nineteenth-century English literature, which is the literature nineteenth- and early-twentieth-century Americans principally knew, is Thomas Carlyle's *Sartor Resartus*. In the 1920s, though less so now, the allusion of Faulkner's title to Carlyle's philosophical quasi-novel would have been inescapable, though I have yet to encounter a critic whom it has not escaped. The title means "the tailor retailored," and Carlyle's point is that man clothes the world in symbols derived from his own spirit, that the meaning of existence is created by man. To be sure, Carlyle also believed that the source of that meaning is the divine. But when the divine is eliminated and the source of that meaning is located in the evolutionary process of maladaptation itself, we have something virtually identical with Faulkner's notions, or part of them. Carlyle is also fond of quoting Shakespeare's "We are such stuff/ As dreams are made on" as an instance of his philosophy of clothes. Both of these are remarkably similar to Faulkner's idealism and illusionism. Further, there is a passage in Carlyle which is an almost perfect description of human life as Faulkner writes of it, an almost perfect summary of the stories Faulkner tells. "Thus, like some wild-flaming, wild-thundering train of Heaven's Artillery, does this mysterious Mankind thunder and flame, in long-drawn quick succeeding grandeur, through the unknown Deep. Thus . . . we emerge from the Inane; haste stormfully across the astonished Earth; then plunge again into the Inane. Earth's mountains are levelled, and her seas filled up, in our passage." One of the themes of *Go Down, Moses* (1942) is the destruction of the wilderness by man's ruthless and furious surrender to that idealistic drive which raised "the gilded crumb of man's aspiration."

So man is caught, trapped, and torn between the two furies of spirit and nature. In between he attempts to carve out civilization. The finest symbol of that civilization is the jail, in which human identity and responsibility and community are forged. The jail, of course, is negative, and the use of the jail as the source of freedom is paradoxical, or at least superficially so. Almost as fine a symbol is the General—at once God, Satan, and Emperor—who defeats and must defeat the Corporal—Christ, the pure spirit, the source of illusionary hope. And this symbolization too is negative and superficially paradoxical. When Faulkner attempted to think and to present civilization positively rather than negatively, however, he is not only less impressive but at his least impressive. One critic has written a book on Faulkner in which it is apparent that

that critic believes in Man and even in Life itself, and it is clear that he believes that Faulkner's belief is the same. I am not sure we need to tolerate such sentimentalities, but there is no doubt that at times Faulkner did so. When, as in the Nobel Prize Speech, he speaks of "the old verities and truths of the heart, the old universal truths lacking which any story is ephemeral and doomed—love and honor and pity and pride and compassion and sacrifice," one tends to cringe from embarrassment. The fierceness and power of the jail and the General are destroyed by this sentimental moralism. It was that strain in Faulkner that made it possible for him to write short stories for popular audiences such as that of the *Saturday Evening Post*. When his sentimentality appears, his greatness disappears, as does his wild humor and his immense power and intensity. It makes one suspect that the resolution of enduring and prevailing at Stockholm was not entirely ironical and contemptuous but expressed a real weakness in his thinking, an area in which he escaped from the irresolvable tension of his own vision. With the jail and the General he can defend himself against the furies of spirit and nature, nor lose his awareness of them; but when he attempts to construct a positive and consoling vision of human life he can only fall back on the worst of platitudes, the platitudes of the world in which he grew up. There were times in which he could not endure the glare of his own truths, times when his sardonicism failed him and dissolved into sentimentality. It is such lapses that force us to admit that he does not quite deserve to be called the American Shakespeare, though for the rest of his work only such praise is equal to his greatness.

Faulkner can be fruitfully discussed under these four headings: the fury of nature, the fury of spirit, the civilizing tension of jail and General, and the civilizing, tension-resolving sentimentalities of the eternal and universal truths of the heart; and so it is with his treatment of sex. Under the last of these, sex, there is little to be said. Sex is absorbed into community and family. Now it may be true that the family is the foundation of the community (though it is probably the other way around, the family being a precipitate of the community), and that family and community are the source of everything good in human nature; but if we entertain such a notion, it is incumbent on us never to forget the one incontrovertible point Freud made—the family and the community are also the source of everything in human nature that is vicious. Certainly Faulkner is aware of that, as in the fine short story "Barn Burning." There, a thoroughly vicious father, Abner Snopes, tells his son, "You got to learn to stick to your own blood or you ain't going to have any blood to stick to you." Out of a vision of what civilization can be, the boy betrays his father and escapes him forever, knowing that what his father deserved was the jail. In the same way, in *The Town* the murdering Mink Snopes kills Flem Snopes because Flem had not gotten him off scot-free from a murder charge. In the same novel Linda Snopes, officially the daughter of the impotent Flem, arranges for Mink to murder Flem in revenge for the suicide of her mother. The whole saga of the appalling Snopes clan seems to be an illustration of the transmutation of sex as a fury of nature into the family, and that in turn transmuted into the fury of the spirit through the ideal of family loyalty, which in turn enables the Snopeses to escape jail and General, though not death. More than once in Faulkner, family loyalty is an instance of death-bound Idealism.

At the beginning of his career Faulkner certainly did not have the clarity of vision he later attained in *Requiem for a Nun, A Fable, The Town,* and *The Mansion.* Not having yet attained it, he was less prone to escape from it into sentimentalities. So his first successful novel is deeply concerned with the fury of Natural Sex and its complex place in family life. *The Sound and the Fury* (1929) is about the Compson family and its disintegration. There is Benjy, the idiot, who has been castrated because he is thought to have attempted a sexual attack on a girl. There is Quentin, obsessed with his sister's virginity—not the physical fact so much as the family honor it represented. An Idealist, he really longs for death and commits suicide. There is Candace, the sister, who uses sex and an illegitimate child to escape the doomed family and simply uses sex thereafter to get what she wants, ultimately a Nazi general. There is her illegitimate daughter, Quentin, named for her uncle, who falls victim to the full fury of Natural Sex, steals her Uncle Jason's savings, runs off with a bigamist, and is never heard from again—though Faulkner hints at a particularly degraded fate. And there is Jason who detests the natural sexuality of both his sister and his niece. That there was an influence of Freudianism at this stage of Faulkner's development seems reasonably certain, but looking back from the vantage point of his later novels, it is possible to see here the beginnings of his vision of the fury of nature, the tumescence and the ejaculation.

This exploration was carried further—and more freely and imaginatively—in *Sanctuary* (1931). This is the story of Temple Drake, a foolish, frightened girl who falls among gangsters and is raped with a corncob by the malignant and impotent Popeye. He installs her in a Memphis brothel and there watches—"whinnying like a horse"—while one of his henchmen, Red, engages in intercourse with her. But Temple surrenders completely to Red. She is, as the madame says, "wild as a young mare," fully sexually awakened, fully in the grip of natural sex; and Popeye has Red murdered. Even so, when Popeye is tried for the murder of an idiot youth, whom in fact he has murdered, Temple lies, and an innocent man is lynched in Popeye's stead.

This exploration of natural sex is carried even further in *Light in August* (1932). Lena, pregnant out of wedlock by a man who has run away, sets out to find him, placidly sure that he will marry her, indeed that he is waiting for her. She has been much admired as the Earth Mother, but this I believe to be a sentimental interpretation. Rather, Faulkner takes up a theme he often returns to, the absolute immorality of women, their complete indifference to the civilizing efforts of men, especially when men are in the grip of the fury of the spirit, and women in the grip of the fury of nature. At the end, Lena receives the man who really does worry about her—for the father of her child is interested only in escaping his responsibility—and a happy marriage is implied. It is significant that that final union occurs with the help and protection of a sensible businessman. Lena's sexuality is thus brought under the control of civilization. The pregnant woman, Faulkner implies, is one with the tumescent and ejaculatory fury of biological nature; only when she has given birth can she be civilized. Lena is a powerful character because of her implacable and ruthless sexual will.

In *Light in August* the story of Lena is a wonderful and grotesque tall-story comedy, but the story of Joe Christmas is tragic. He is a mulatto hounded and driven by a force he does not understand—actually his grandfather, who sees in Joe the fruit of the sexual transgression of his daughter, bad enough in itself but made unbearable by his racial hatred. Joe spends his life and loses it trying to find out who he is. Terrible and terror-ridden as his effort is, it is nevertheless the effort to achieve identity and civilization, and it is ruined by Idealists. The woman who befriends him, Joanna Burden, is the last member of a family come to Jefferson from the North to help the freed Negroes, and is therefore hated by the natives. She befriends him, then—victim of the fury of natural sex—seduces him and becomes sexually wilder and more driven even than Temple, and then sets out to redeem herself and him with religion. Joe—enraged by these disorienting metamorphoses, from spirit to nature and back again, and disoriented by his mysterious and incomprehensible life— kills her and flees. A victim of the spirit, Percy Grimm, organizes a quasi-military group in order to keep the town from a lynching-bee, but on finally tracking Joe down to the ex-minister Hightower's house, he kills him himself and castrates him in the most brutal fashion imaginable. The struggle between spirit and nature could not be more tellingly revealed. It is with this book that Faulkner's thinking begins to be clarified.

Hightower introduces a new theme into Faulkner's work, the theme of the past, particularly of the Southern past. Hightower too is an Idealist, dreaming of the chivalry and cavalry of the Confederacy, caught in the historical fantasy and illusion of the Southern legend. Enmeshed in his dreams, he drives his wife into neurosis by sexual neglect and also loses his pulpit. It is at this point that Faulkner's thought begins to develop that historical richness which leads to *Requiem for a Nun*. To be sure, his next novel is *Pylon* (1935), the time of which is still modern but the setting of which is New Orleans, not Jefferson. Faulkner returned to the scene of his second novel, *Mosquitoes*, as if to make a fresh start by moving away from Jefferson and Yok-napatawpha County. *Pylon* is about a young and disoriented journalist who becomes fascinated with a "circus" of flyers, left over from the war. This novel, which is vastly underrated, is a metaphor for Faulkner's own situation as a writer peering into the world of Northern Mississippi to which, although born there, he no longer belongs. It presents the first significant indications of a changing attitude toward sex. In the absolute devotion of the woman to her flyer and even in her furious natural sexuality there are signs of the transmutation of Natural Sex into the equally furious Spiritual Sex. After her lover's death, she gives—abandons—their son to the flyer's father, and this refusal of offspring and repudiation of children becomes hereafter in Faulkner's fiction a way of indicating spiritual sex.

Absalom, Absalom! (1936) may well be Faulkner's greatest work, though with such riches to choose from it seems pointless to argue about which is best. Certainly it is an astounding novel. When it was first published the intricacies of narrative technique were such that the book was almost incomprehensible, and comprehensibility was not aided by a new departure in style, the creation of an extravagant, terror-ridden, and exalted rhetoric. Though miscegenation and incest play their part in the story and though there is some fury of natural sex, the work marks a further exploration of spiritual sex. Those two appalling Idealists, Joanna Burden and Percy Grimm, fell from spirit into nature without an intervening stage of civilization. Sex was seen as belonging to nature. But now Faulkner, as his style and narrative technique grow more complex, attains a new clarity of the vision he was to reveal fully in *A Fable*.

The main theme is the one begun in the presentation of High-tower: the Southern Legend—created Faulkner sees with brutal clarity, to sustain the self-respect of a defeated, humiliated, and wounded people. So the story is about a humiliation and a wound, and the lifelong effort to compensate for it, and the failure of that effort. Thomas Sutpen is the most fantastic Idealist in all of Faulkner, and here Faulkner explores ruthlessly the source of Idealism—compensation for man's failure to adapt himself to the world of nature and to the tensions of civilization. One of the

characters, the one determined to discover the full truth of the
whole of Sutpen's story, and who with powerful will draws
Quentin Compson—the one who committed suicide that year,
1910—into the force of her determination, is Sutpen's sister-in-
law, Rosa Coldfield. Wounded and humiliated by Sutpen's proposal, after the death of her sister, to determine whether or not
she is fertile before he marries her, she utters at one point in her
reminiscences one of the most famous sentences in Faulkner.
"I who had learned nothing of love, not even parents' love—that
fond dear constant violation of privacy, that stultification of the
burgeoning and incorrigible I which is the meed and due of all
mammalian meat, became not mistress, not beloved, but more
than even love; I became all polymath love's androgynous advo-
cate." She becomes both a male and a female supporter and
defender of all love, which must be seen as universally, ency-
clopedically learned in all human relations. Here is announced the
theme of spiritual sex and its fury. It was to be the subject of
Faulkner's next novel.

The Wild Palms (1939), almost as much as Pylon, has been
decried and neglected by Faulkner critics. Yet it is, to my mind,
one of his greatest works. It is actually two quite independent
stories, "The Wild Palms" proper and "Old Man"; and the chap-
ters of the two stories alternate. "The Wild Palms" tells the story
of a young intern who falls in love with the wife of a fashionable
New Orleans doctor, and she with him. They go off together—to
Chicago, to a mining camp in Utah, to Texas, and finally to a
beach town near New Orleans. In Texas he attempts to abort
her, something which he has once done before for another woman, and successfully, but this time he fails. The fetus is killed,
but the woman dies; and he is imprisoned for life. "Old Man"
tells of an inmate of the Mississippi state prison. At the time of
the great flood of 1927 he is sent with other convicts to work on
the levees and to do rescue work. Caught in the flood and separated from the others, he rescues, in spite of himself, a pregnant
woman. A totally ignorant and inexperienced man, nevertheless
he helps her give birth on a flood island crowded with animals
and snakes. For a time they live with the bayou people; he hunts
alligators, very happily. But his one aim is to get the woman

back and to return to jail. After three months he finally delivers her to those who can assume his responsibility and gratefully returns to prison, where he now receives an addition to his sentence—for attempted escape. His last remark is, "Women—shit!"

It is with this novel that Faulkner's thinking becomes fully coherent, with the triad of the fury of spirit, the civilization of the jail, and the fury of nature. *The Wild Palms*, as Faulkner makes explicit, is the story of Tristan and Isolde and all the famous spiritual lovers. The abortion is done so that there will be no rivalry to the lovers' exalting and all-consuming passion. The intern is totally ignorant of sex, and at first he seems to be merely the passive victim of the woman's natural sex; but it soon becomes clear that this woman is a woman of the spirit—of the madness and fury of the spirit run wild, without control, without containment, without civilization. Her erotic exaltation is not only like the religious exaltation of Nancy in *Requiem for a Nun*; it is the same thing. Into this erotic exaltation she carries up her victim, the intern. But it must be understood that he is not the victim of natural sex but of the spirit, of spiritual sex. Eroticism, Faulkner is saying, is the spiritual transformation of biological sexuality, and nothing could be more destructive, except its counterpart, religion itself. When it is all over, the intern looks out from his prison and sees a woman hanging out clothes. For the first time in his life he has a glimpse of civilization—from jail.

The convict has been imprisoned because he too was once an Idealist. Inflamed by cheap popular literature, just as the intern and his beloved were inflamed by the great erotic legends, he attempted, armed only with a useless pistol, to perform a splendid train robbery. Sent out to help, he faces the flood—nature in its most devastating fury—described in some of Faulkner's most marvelous writing. The woman he rescues is, like Lena, a great placid cow, unworried, sure that man and civilization will take care of her. And with intense exasperation the convict does so. With the same responsibility he helps, superbly, in the alligator-hunting among the French-speaking bayou people and takes brief jobs in order to earn his way back to the prison and to get rid of the woman and return the boat he had set out in. On one of these jobs he has, briefly, a sexual life, yet he is happy to get back

into prison, and his unflattering remark about women comes, of
course, from his identification of the fury of nature and the implacable natural demands of a pregnant woman. An Idealist, an
Illusionist, a man of the Spirit, he has been civilized and made
responsible by jail. His experience is a mirror of the intern's.
The intern has been exposed to the fury of spirit; the convict to
the fury of nature. Jail is that civilization which man has created
in order to protect himself from the irresolvable tension of nature and spirit, and from which he issues forth to do battle with
both.

At the end of *Requiem for a Nun*, Temple Drake steps out of
jail to face the implacable demands of spirit, just as the convict
issued from jail to deal with the equally implacable demands of
nature. Implacable is the right word: Faulkner often uses it. The
furies of the spirit and of nature cannot be placated; they can
only be struggled against—and with. Thus man *must* prevail,
even though to prevail leads to a civilization both vulgar and
trivial. When Faulkner says that man can endure, he is being
sentimental; for endurance arises from a naturalistic or idealistic
acceptance of the conditions of human existence as good. Such
an acceptance can lead only to death and the disappearance of the
race. To endure is to be destroyed; to prevail is to be ridiculous.
Here, perhaps, is the source of Faulkner's magnificent humor.
Sentimentality is the resolution of the contradiction of nature and
spirit, and of the incoherence of the two ethical necessities, an
ethic of nature and an ethic of spirit. To be sentimental is to
permit oneself to be captured by one or the other, in the belief
that one has reconciled them. Humor is the acceptance and transcendence of that contradiction and that incoherence. Humor is
Faulkner's defense against his own sentimentality and his attempt, never fully successful, to overcome it.

II CRITICAL THEORY

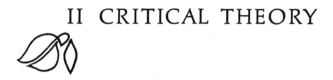

10

IS THE PROBLEM OF

LITERARY REALISM A PSEUDOPROBLEM?

[1969*]

The answer to the question of my title is, Yes, the problem of literary realism is very likely a pseudoproblem, for almost all critical problems are pseudoproblems, and by "critical problems" I mean here "literary critical problems." The explanation of this notion is that critical problems usually emerge from the assumption that such problems are unique to the category "literature." Now the first and most obvious thing to be observed about literature is that it is language. That is, the category "literature" is properly subsumed under the more general and inclusive category "language." The question then is, Does the particular critical problem one is concerned with also emerge from language?

No matter how we come at it, the question of realism appears to involve the question of how the literary work is related to "reality." Whatever notion we may have for that word, it cer-

* Presented at the English Institute, Columbia University, September 2, 1969. Reprinted by permission from *Critique* 12, no. 2, pp. 95–112. Copyright © 1970 by *Critique*.

tainly seems to involve the relation of the work to something or other that is outside the work. And clearly this is not only a problem of language; it is the central problem, to which all other language problems are subordinate. But before proceeding further, it will be useful to uncover what I believe to be a very common confusion. Indeed, it is a virtually universal source of confusion and error.

Consider such a passage as the following, from Pope's *Moral Essays*, "Epistle III. To Allen Lord Bathurst." It is the famous description of the Duke of Buckingham:

> In the worst inn's worst room, with mat half-hung,
> The floors of plaister, and the walls of dung,
> On once a flock-bed, but repair'd with straw,
> With tape-ty'd curtains, never meant to draw,
> The George and Garter dangling from that bed
> Where tawdry yellow strove with dirty red,
> Great Villers lies—

The fact that Buckingham did not indeed die in an inn or in poverty may be ignored; here it is sufficient to propose that most students of literature would call this a realistic passage. Now supposing some scholar did a great deal of research on the appearance and construction and furnishings of English inns in the late seventeenth century. The sources of his information would be of two categories, verbal statements and pictures—or nonverbal signs. On the basis of his studies, let us assume, he came to the conclusion that Pope's assertions about such inns are indeed accurate, and that all his specific details can be supported from other sources of information. Our scholar publishes his conclusions. What kind of relation has he established between Pope's poetry and the something outside the work?

First, he proposes that there is a relation between Pope and his own discourse, his article. He asserts that one possible appropriate response to Pope's lines is a scholarly discourse. The something outside the work, then, is more language. Next he proposes that there is a relation between his discourse and his verbal sources. He is still inside language. His final proposal is that there is a relation between his article and his picture sources, and between his verbal sources and his picture sources. Is he now outside of language? Yes, but not very far out. His pictures consist of humanly constructed, or artificial signs. But language itself is subsumed by the more general category "sign" or "semiotic system." Consequently, though he has gotten out of language, he has not gotten out of signs. The relationships he purports to have established are relationships between three examples of a subcategory of artificial signs—Pope's lines, his article, and his verbal sources—and another subcategory of signs, pictures. The something outside of the literary signs consists, then, of more artificial signs. Let me bring to the support of this position a passage from a recent book by a philosopher: *The Languages of Art*, by Nelson Goodman. In his introduction he writes:

Systematic inquiry into the varieties and functions of symbols has seldom been undertaken. Expanding investigation in structural linguistics in recent years needs to be supplemented by and integrated with intensive examination of nonverbal symbol systems, from pictorial representation on the one hand to musical notation on the other, if we are to achieve any comprehensive grasp of the modes and means of reference and of their varied and pervasive use in the operations of the understanding. (p. xi)

There are things here I do not particularly care for, especially the use of the word "reference," which seems to me to conceal a real abyss of confusion, but the general position is one I hold myself and the passage will serve my purpose.

Even in purporting to have established a relationship between verbal and nonverbal artificial signs, our scholar has remained within language, for his relationship is verbal. It is an act of criticism, for "criticism" as I shall use the term is a discourse which the critic asserts to be an appropriate response to a literary work, whether explicatory, explanatory, or evaluative. It can propose relationships between the work and other discourse, and between that discourse and other and nonverbal signs. Can it get any farther away from the work, to something beyond the boundary of nonverbal artificial signs? Beyond that boundary, presumably, lies reality, and if the critic purports to have established a relationship between the literary work and reality, he can, I suppose, claim that the work, if the relationship thus established is positive, is a realistic work, at least to the degree that the relationship is indeed positive; that is, it need not be, judging from practice, completely positive, just positive enough to justify the claim. Clearly, this turns the question of where the relationship can be placed in a continuum between the negative and positive poles. Obviously, such a view of the matter entails the conclusion that the placement depends upon criteria of judgment; but those criteria, just as obviously, vary from individual to individual and within the judgmental range of an individual along a continuum of time. This at least provides an explanation for the wide disagreements to be found on whether or not a particular work is indeed realistic.

This conclusion will be useful later. Here it is necessary to consider what the critic is doing when he asserts that he has established a relationship between the work and the "reality" that lies beyond the boundary of nonverbal and artificial signs.

The problem of what a sign is, is not too difficult so long as we do not think very hard about it, and so long as we do not ask what is not a sign. Most considerations of signs begin by assuming that they must be man-made, and there is nothing wrong in this so long as no claim is made that there cannot be non-man-made or natural signs. Within this definition a sign is any man-made configuration to which a response, or a family of responses, has been conventionalized. Such a definition makes it impossible to distinguish between a chair, let us say, and a picture of a chair and the word "chair." In giving instructions to a cabinet-maker, you can show him a chair and ask him to make one just like it; or you can show him a picture of that chair and ask him to reproduce it; or you can ask him to make a chair and be satisfied with what you get. In the first two instances you have given him directions such that the interchangeable responses are the result; in the third he has responded with one of a family of responses which you accept as belonging to what you judge to be one of an appropriate family of responses. In all three cases, however, he has responded to a sign. Perhaps it is possible to differentiate between man-made objects that are signs and such objects that are not, but such a differentiation must be purely conventional and arbitrary, for once we consider the response to the sign, the distinction disappears. And here that disappearance is the vital consideration, for the critic's judgment that a work is realistic is a response to a set of signs.

Worse follows from this, for if we apply the criteria of responses and families of responses to the world, it is evident that the world—that is, what I have hitherto called the world outside of verbal and non-verbal signs—also consists of signs. The distinction between artificial and natural signs is a very proper distinction for some purposes, but it cannot be sustained from the point of view that semiosis or sign-behavior requires. That is, when we consider responses to the world, the world, so far as human beings are concerned, consists of signs. Clearly, the distinction hitherto used between artificial and natural signs must be abandoned, and in its place I propose a distinction between immediate and mediating signs. Thus a tree is an immediate sign, while a picture of a tree and the word "tree" are mediating signs. The distinction I propose between the two is this: A sign which we understand as being a member of the category of which it is a sign is an immediate sign; a sign which we understand as not being a member of the category of which it is a sign is a mediating sign.

This distinction rests upon the proposition that all signs are categorical signs. When we use the word "sign," the implication is that it is a sign *of* something else. This is the source of the notion of "reference," to which I have already taken exception. It is said that a sign "refers" to something else. But if we consider what is going on in human activity, it is clear that signs do not refer. Human beings refer. A man *uses* a sign in order to refer to something else. Or sometimes he just uses the sign. This last leads to the notion that there is such a thing as nonreferential language or nonreferential signs. But that is an illusion, once we look at the behavioral situation in its totality. A man may respond to a sign only, let us say, by experiencing an intense emotional disturbance. Clearly he is not referring to something else, but it seems to be just as clear that this is a sign response. One may, then, respond to a sign by referring to something else, or one may not. It still remains a sign so long as one responds with some behavioral sequence; and experiment has shown that it is virtually impossible not to so respond to any configuration that the subject can discriminate as a configuration, that is, just about any configuration imaginable, after—in circumstances of extreme disorientation—a usually momentary condition of no response at all.

When I say that signs are categorial, therefore, I do not mean that they are signs of a category of configurations, though I can mean that if I wish to: that is, if I wish to confine my inquiry only to sign responses which result in referring to something else. Rather, I mean that a sign elicits a family or category of responses. A man can respond to a tree by painting it, or by classifying it botanically, or by cutting it down, and so on, but though each instance of painting may be, and indeed must be, different, all such instances fall into the response-family or category of making a painting.

This position does several things for us here. It makes it clear that the sign-character of a configuration is not immanent in that sign; rather, a configuration can serve to stimulate any number of response families. That is, a sign, whether mediating or immediate, is not confined to one semiotic function or, to use a very dangerous word, "meaning." Furthermore, since sign responses are matters of acculturated convention, it is clear that there is no necessary connection between sign and response; strictly speaking, any sign can be culturally linked to any response. Thus, the meaning of any sign, immediate or mediating, nonverbal or verbal, can be all possible meanings. Terrifying as this conclusion is, it at least serves to explain why human beings spend so much time disagreeing with each other, and certainly why there is so much disagreement about literary realism.

The second thing this position does for us is to make it a little easier to understand what the critic does when he wishes to establish a relationship between the work and what lies beyond mediating signs—that is, immediate signs. However, since the character of a sign is not immanent, whether a sign is mediating or immediate is not immanent either, but depends upon the kind of response. Thus we may discriminate between mediating-sign response and immediate-sign response. The first response involves substituting for a sign some other sign. This does not mean that the substitution has to result in identity. That could not be done in any case. Rather it means that a sufficient number of what are judged to be the attributes of the sign, according to the response-family engaged in, are signified in the mediating sign to a degree valid for what the sign-responder judges to be the requirements of the situation in which he is acting. A painter may find the merest sketch of a tree sufficiently valid, or he may judge that a great many attributes are required—color, height, number of branches, roughness of bark, and so on.

If mediating-sign behavior involves the construction of mediating signs, then its antithesis—immediate-sign behavior—involves the manipulation of signs, interference with the environment—the actual physical manipulation, which depends upon the judgment that the signs so manipulated are immediate signs. Such immediate response to signs is, of course, the foundation of science, and, so far as I can comprehend our situation, our only valid source for judgments about the world. The scientific revolution of the sixteenth and seventeenth centuries amounted to a decision to ascribe truth value to a proposition only if the conventionalized response to it involved a changing of the environment such that a predicted consequence of such changing was the result. To describe what one sees or feels or hears, therefore, is mediating-sign response; and so is to draw it or to use nonverbal mediating-sign behavior.

Insofar, then, as our critic remains within the realm of mediating signs, his claim that a work is realistic amounts to a claim that he has substituted for it other mediating signs that meet certain criteria. These criteria he tends to call "objective," but by that he means merely that his own statements purport to be substitutes for signs other than those of the signs of the work. That is, in response to the work, he has generated a discourse; in response to his sources, verbal and nonverbal, he has generated another discourse. In response to these two discourses he has generated a third which is a substitute sufficiently valid for the conventionalized demands of the situation and which is internally coherent. Thus he says that Pope's lines are realistic because certain of their attributes are to be found in late seventeenth-century descriptions and pictures of poor inns. Obviously, the crucial problem is the criteria. As we have seen, such criteria can vary along a very wide continuum, and anyone who has read much literary criticism—or even a little—which uses the terms "realism," "verisimilitude," and so on, knows that they do. But though the problem of criteria is crucial, it is also trivial. That is, you or I or any critic can propose any set of criteria we wish. These can be randomly chosen, or they can be very tightly deduced from some metaphysical principle. This is tantamount to saying that the critic cannot go outside of the boundaries of mediating signs. That, however, is not entirely so. Though the connection with immediate signs is remote and hard to come at, it does exist. It is often said that history has no regularity, no pattern; and certainly it is clear that those historians who propose to find such regularity in history have in fact merely organized certain statements which purport to be historical into a patterned or regular kind of coherence. However, an immediate regularity of pattern in history is to be found in the highly predictable circumstance that documents and artifacts are not distributed randomly over the surface of the earth but with a certain regularity and predictability. We can, in short, predict where we will find them and what they will be like when we do so. Leslie Hotson did not search for Shakespeare and Marlowe records in the archives of the Dalai Lama in Tibet. He transported a certain part of his environment, namely, his body, to London—for from the point of view of cognition or understanding, the body itself is part of the environment and can be understood as an immediate sign. We may manipulate it to predicted results, responding to it with sign behavior. Thus it may be said correctly that historiography has a scientific foundation, no matter how remote from any actual historiographical discourse that foundation may be. It is worth considering how, in spite of this remoteness, we tend to give credence to historical statements, by which I mean not merely formal history but also such statements as, "Yesterday I drove from Philadelphia to New York."

The basic function of language has, I think, been well formulated by Grace Andrus de Laguna: Language functions by coordinating behavior. The next level of explanation, I would say, is that language functions by giving directions for behaving. One such kind of directions consists of directions or instructions for finding something that cannot be found. There is no difference between directions for finding something that can in fact be found and directions for finding something that cannot be found. There is no difference between "The Empire State Building is at the corner of Fifth Avenue and 34th Street" and "The Empire State Building is at the corner of Madison and 72nd." The only way to judge the relative adequacy of the two sentences as sets of directions is to look and see, as Wittgenstein would say. That is, the only way to find out is to follow the directions. Hence there is nothing immanent in sentences or in nonverbal mediating signs that tell us whether or not they are substitutes for mediating or immediate signs. For that reason, it is necessary for the simplest kind of either social interaction or interaction with the nonsocial environment to take on trust sentences that strike us as adequate directions for locating something that can indeed be found, which, for brevity, I shall call the existent. This is the source for classifying some sentences as descriptive sentences. Such a sentence is one we take on trust as being capable of furnishing directions for finding the existent. Consequently it is futile to attempt to discover by linguistic or any kind of philosophical analysis whether or not a particular sentence should be categorized as a response to immediate signs. That can be done only by what, again for the sake of brevity, I shall call scientific behavior, although formal science is only a very tiny part of it. To say that a sentence is a descriptive sentence cannot be an assertion that something outside of itself corresponds to it; it can only be an assertion that it belongs to that category of sentences only some of which can function as directions for finding the existent. Historiography is constructed from that category of sentence. Obviously so is realistic literature. It is what makes such literature possible. And, of course, so is criticism that purports to decide whether or not a work is realistic.

Furthermore, this ambiguity inherent in the category of descriptive sentences is responsible for the varying definitions of reality. I think it is apparent that I am using an instrumental or operational or pragmatic conception of language, quite opposed to a constitutive or realist view. The latter proposes that statements about the world correspond to the world, and do so because meaningful attributes are immanent in the world and can be captured by language without significant distortion. It frequently goes on to propose that statements that explain descriptive statements maintain this relation. Or in some views, descriptive statements have a constitutive or realist relationship to the world, while at least some explanatory statements are metaphysical and therefore invalid. The view that I am using proposes, rather, that explanatory or metaphysical statements are directions for generating and combining descriptive, or, as I prefer, exemplary statements. It proposes that just as there is no way internal to descriptive sentences that makes it possible to distinguish between those that are existential and those that are not, so all sentences are, as it were, equally metaphysical, in that there is no way to tell whether or not any sentence is existential except by manipulating immediate signs, that is, by scientific behavior. The advantage of this proposition is that it offers an explanation of the constitutive or realist position, while the latter cannot, so far as I can see, establish an explanatory relation to the instrumental position.

But whether that is the case or not, at any rate the position I propose explains why the term "reality" cannot effectively be limited to any particular kind of sign or sign response. If we see the semiotic continuum as ranging from explanatory sentences through exemplary—i.e., descriptive—sentences, nonverbal mediating signs, and on into immediate signs, and if the mediative character of signs is something properly to be judged an attribute not of the sign but of the sign-response understanding, as we have seen, then the segment of that continuum designated as giving us valid information about reality is a matter of convention. Some will say that only those sentences are true which explain explanatory sentences, i.e., only those sentences are true and describe reality which are metaphysical sentences. Another position asserts that only those sentences are directly and immediately related to reality which are on the one hand descriptive and on the other hand logically subsumable under explanatory or metaphysical sentences. Still others claim such status only for descriptive sentences. Others, though it is a fairly rare position, will claim that language cannot have truth-value *vis-à-vis* what is outside of it; only nonverbal signs can. Others claim that only immediate signs can give us knowledge about what is real. (This may seem my position, but, as I shall clarify subsequently, it is not.) Consequently, one cannot say what segment of the sign-continuum gives us knowledge of the real world, but only what segment people say can give us such knowledge. But the case is worse than this, for the common-sense and almost universal position toward language is the constitutive or realist position. Thus the distinction between what happens between stimulus and response and covert verbal behavior, which is itself a response, is commonly concealed by a categorization of both as mental behavior. And that distinction is that the first is inaccessible and the second is accessible, if only to the person doing it. Thus, commonly, any sentence that someone interprets as referring directly and informatively about the world is identified as direct mental knowledge of the world.

Now just as we cannot say what is real, but only what people say is real, so we cannot say what is realism in literature, but only what people say is realistic, and for the same reason, it is futile to designate some segment of the semiotic continuum as realistic to the exclusion of all other segments. Naïve judgments in such matters are more instructive than sophisticated ones. Thus in theater lobbies and in nonprofessional discussions of literary works, one constantly hears such statements as, "It was (or was not) real to me," or "I could (or could not) believe in it." It is interesting that statements of this sort and arguments based on them are engaged in at all, for everybody knows that literature is all made up anyway. The above analysis, however, offers the possibility of an explanation. Any sign can be understood as an immediate sign or as a mediating sign. Thus in responding to immediate signs by manipulation two stages of response can be discriminated: the first is the categorization or understanding of a sign as an immediate sign; the second is the manipulation itself. The first may be called the preparatory stage. Thus, when one is walking through the woods at night, a bulky, darker object may be interpreted as a threatening man or animal, or merely as a bush one had forgotten about. In the first instance, assuming that subsequent manipulation shows it to be indeed a bush, it is interpreted as a mediating sign, since what is judged to be an appropriate substitution has occurred. But if it is indeed a threatening creature of some kind, then the preparatory interpretation was correct, and the immediate sign response was appropriate. To enter upon the preparatory stage of judging a sign to be an immediate sign when further investigation shows it to be a mediating sign is the source of what we call dramatic or literary illusion, as when people say, "It was only a book, but the people in it were as real to me as if they were actually in front of me." A striking instance of the switch back and forth between the two kinds of sign response is to be found in operatic performances. At one moment the audience, or some portion of it at any rate, is entirely caught up in the agonies of the heroine she is superbly expressing. When she finishes, the audience bursts into applause. When she was singing, the sign response was that of the preparatory stage for immediate sign response. When she finishes, the heroine signs are understood as mediating signs, and the singer signs are understood as mediating signs, as is indicated by the effort to manipulate the singer into a state of gratification or possibly into an encore.

More sophisticated discourse, however, does not use the terms "real" or "convincing" and so on, but rather such terms as "realistic" and "verisimilitude." The futility of trying to settle arguments about whether a work is real or convincing has made the sophisticated cautious. At the beginning I proposed that literature is properly subsumed under the general category "language," but I am sure that a good many felt quite indignant about this. Literature should be, an alternative position proposes, categorized under "art." Well, of course, anything can be categorized, quite reasonably, in all sorts of ways, and I myself would certainly call literature art as well as language. However, to my mind when the question of semantic function is present, nothing is to be gained by categorizing literature as art. Nothing can be said in literature which cannot be said in nonliterary language, and on the whole said better. To put it as economically as possible, poetry is badly written prose. Currently, to categorize literature as art probably most commonly means that it is a product of the creative imagination. I do not think it is possible for anyone to give me directions such that I can locate the "creative imagination" in space and time as an immediate sign. It is an explanatory term, not a descriptive term, i.e., an exemplary term. What the phrase "creative imagination" does is to put some man-made semiotic constructions in a special category, that is, to ascribe certain attributes to certain classes of semiotic construction. To subsume "realism" under "creative imagination" is to make use of a distinction proposed above: Only some descriptive sentences can function as directions for finding the existent, since there is no internal indication within the sentence to tell us whether or not an appropriate response is to look for an existent. All that "literary realism" tells us is that in discourses so categorized it is inappropriate to use descriptive sentences as directions to look for the existent. As I suggested, literary realism is possible only because this fundamental ambiguity is to be found in all descriptive sentences. Science attempts to discover which descriptive sentences are directions to look for the existent. Literature, so far as it is realistic, is indifferent to the matter. Thus it can use sentences like "The Empire State Building is at Fifth and 34th" and sentences like "The Empire State Building is at Madison and 72nd."

However, this is to consider only one mediating sign response to literature. The discussion of reference above suggested that only some sign responses are referential. This may be put another way. We may distinguish between two environments, that outside the skin and that inside. The internal environment is not merely nerves and organs, but rather—and far more important— our perception of changes in organs and in the nervous system, particularly the sympathetic nervous system. It is the internal weather. Now we have direct access only to our own internal weather, but not to someone else's. That does not mean, however, that other peoples' internal environments are not part of our own environment. If immediate sign-response involves manipulations of signs to a predicted result, even if the predictability is but a matter of probability, then the internal environments of others are immediate signs, though known by mediating signs and manipulated by such signs. In the same way, of course, we can manipulate our own internal weather to a predicted result. The writer, then, constructs a system of verbal signs to which the reader can respond in a variety of ways: He can simply understand, an activity which remains pretty mysterious but of which it will be possible to say something below; he can act the critic and construct a system of mediating signs; he can manipulate his internal environment, thus engaging in immediate sign response. But it does not follow that only artists create sign systems which are used as immediate signs for engaging in the manipulation of the internal environment, nor that such manipulation must be the result of response to literary signs, nor that it ought to be. Some schools of aesthetics, for example, affirm that positive value is to be ascribed to a work only if the internal environment is manipulated, while others maintain that such value is properly ascribed only if the internal environment is unaffected; still others claim that the work is valuable if the internal environment is manipulated to intense emotional disturbance; yet others maintain that the work is a true work of art only if the internal environment is manipulated to absolute quiescence, for rapt contemplation. So far as I can understand any of these positions—not very far, I fear—to maintain one to the exclusion of another is a matter of a blend of culturally conventionalized and individual gratification.

These considerations make possible, I think, a somewhat clearer understanding of what I have called the preparatory stage of immediate sign-response. Our perception of changes in internal physiological conditions are perceptions of preparations for action—for either, basically, attack or flight. It is, then, the inclusion of such signs in the act of cognition or understanding that appears to be responsible for such statements as "It was convincing" or "It was real" or "It was true to life." Still, the last of these suggests that something else is going on as well.

Whatever else we may say about cognition or understanding, it certainly seems to be the case that it depends upon perception, or even that perception is but one aspect of the cognitive-perceptual process. In any case, perception, considered by itself, does not respond to an entire field of signs but rather selects, simplifies, reduces. When we add the term "cognitive" or "understanding" to this process we add the notion of organizing. We make sense out of experience; we cannot help making sense out of experience; and the sense we make is not derived from the world itself. Rather, the world, as I have suggested, is known as signs. And if it is indeed the case, as I have proposed, that all signs are categorial, then cognition is categorial, and categorial activity, since it is not derived from something immanent in the world, is prior to the world. This is the sense of Hegel's concrete universal. In responding to the world categorially what we do is to employ, to speak metaphorically, a cognitive model, or an expectancy, or a mental set. To be Coleridgean for a moment, to use categories and the structure of categories of any cognitive model without changing them is an act of the fancy; to create new categories and to restructure the structure of categories is an act of the imagination. Yet if we are to use these unsatisfactory and extremely vague terms, I think we must recognize that imagination and fancy are not two different kinds of cognitive activity, but rather the poles or limits between which lies the continuum of what actually goes on.

These considerations provide another definition of the term "reality," one quite different from those explored above, and hence further explanations of the term "literary realism." We use the word "reality" when we are responding to a disparity between the cognitive model or set and the signs we are using it to organize. To be a little more explicit, a cognitive model prepares us for action in a category of situation, never for action in a unique situation. Consequently, to the degree that expectation is frustrated, to that degree we must engage in innovating categories, in integrating such categories into a structure of existent categories, and in restructuring the structure of categories. At least this, I think, is the kind of occasion in which sophisticated people at the higher cultural levels are trained for problem exposure, or awareness of disparity between model and data, and are trained in ascribing positive value to such awareness. This is another interest at work, perhaps, in the cautious tendency of the sophisticated literary critic, whether professional or not, to use "realism" rather than "real" or "reality."

On the other hand it must be recognized that we also use the term "reality" when the categories and the categorial structure are confirmed—that is, require minimal innovation in categorization and restructuring. It is less sophisticated individuals, or sophisticated individuals when they are not troubling to be sophisticated but are content to be naïve, that in such circumstances say that the work is "true to life," "real," or "convincing," or say "I know somebody just like that."

Both surprise and confirmation, then, can be occasions for ascribing such attributes as reality or realism or verisimilitude or convincingness to literary works. The ascription is evidently, as with all judgments, a blend of culture and personality, of convention and innovation. To justify such judgments—though a better term than justification would perhaps be rationalization—we summon criteria to our aid. The effort, of course, is to integrate the judgment into the individual's cognitive system. In any case, as I have suggested, the criteria can be absolutely anything at all, and the history of literary criticism is filled with heated and endless discussion over what are the proper criteria. The argument is futile, and will go on as long as literary criticism continues. One is perhaps permitted to hope that that will not be forever, at least as literary criticism is currently practiced.

There is one final point I would like to make, one problem in the use of "realism" which I have not touched on. Since any sign can be responded to by mediating or immediate sign-behavior, it is understandable that we should say that a literary work is as real as life itself. But what about those responses to works which result in our saying that the work is *more* real than life itself, realer than real? I shall confine my discussion to characters, though the point I shall make is also applicable to social circumstances and the physical environment. I think it is not uncommon that when we think about such fictional characters— to use my own favorites—as Hamlet, Uncle Toby, Carlyle's Friedrich Wilhelm, Bloom, and Proust's "I," they have a vividness which very few people we know have when we think about *them*. An answer to the puzzle of the realer-than-real lies in the material already presented. To use the Coleridgean terms once more, it requires far greater loss of energy and creates far greater difficulty for action if the cognitive activity is close to the imagination pole of the cognitive continuum than it does if it is close to the fancy pole. Consequently our necessary tendency in adapting ourselves to our environment—internal as well as external—is to confirm the categories and the categorial structure whenever we can. Imagination is fine when you don't have to do anything, but for action, such as escaping an enraged grizzly bear, the fancy is more practical.

So it is in interaction with other people, and even with ourselves. Insofar as possible, we prefer to confirm our cognitive models of personalities. It causes us distress, disorientation, and energy loss to have to change them. It is the theme of all stories of marriage which begin when the honeymoon is over. The literary experience, however, is blessedly irresponsible. We don't have to do anything. Consequently we can afford surprise, disorientation, and energy loss. Hence, certain great characters, the realer-than-real characters—ordinarily to be found in works unusually long for their genre—require a constant recategorization, a constant reconstruction of our cognitive model of them. Both fictional persons and real persons, after all, consist merely of signs, as we have seen. But some fictional persons elicit in the reader a discontinuity of cognitive activity. There is one very good test for such fictional individuals. If literary criticism shows a history of continuous reinterpretation of a fictional personality, obviously controlled by changing cultural interests, and if those reinterpretations show a constant effort to create a unified and coherent theory of that personality, then we have a realer-than-real fictional character. Such, of course, is Hamlet. No one will ever create a consistent and coherent theory of Hamlet's personality which will not be immediately and successfully challenged by some other theory. No explanation of Hamlet is lasting; the reason is that Hamlet's personality does not make sense. It is our illusion that personality, whether our own or another's, is coherent and structured. No, we are ragbags of behavioral patterns, but only the greatest writers have the courage to say so. They are the creators of the realer-than-real.

11

POET AND CRITIC:

OR, THE DAMAGE COLERIDGE HAS DONE

[1969*]

The fact that Dryden (not to speak of Ben Jonson and Pope) had preceded Coleridge as poet-critic may have encouraged Coleridge in being both. However, it seems more probable that his conception of himself as primarily a philosopher justified to him—if he needed such justification—his critical undertakings. After all, in spite of his remarkable achievements as a poet, he was, like Gerard Manley Hopkins, something of an amateur poet. He thought Wordsworth the poet of their generation, but in his intense philosophical involvement, he wanted Wordsworth to be a philosophical poet—not that the latter needed much encouragement. For if Coleridge was something of an amateur poet, Wordsworth was something of an amateur philosopher.

I do not wish to imply that there is anything to sneer at in

* Presented at the annual meeting of the South Atlantic Modern Language Association, November 7, 1969. Reprinted by permission from *Studies in the Twentieth Century*, no. 6 (Fall 1970), pp. 1–11. Copyright © 1970 by Stephen H. Goode.

amateurism. Quite the contrary. One must always remember that
Kant, for example, was the first professional philosopher, and
there were scarcely any professional scientists until late in the
nineteenth century. Professionalism as we conceive of it today
is a phenomenon of the past hundred or hundred and fifty years
at the very outside, while professionalism in the study of literature is considerably younger than that. Professionalism does
antedate this century, though not by much. Darwin himself was,
by modern standards, an amateur naturalist of a very traditional
English sort. It is never to be forgotten that European culture—
by which I also mean American—has almost entirely been created
by people who today would be classed as amateurs. It was, I
think, the amateur tradition, so vital in the life of Goethe, that
more than anything else was responsible for Coleridge's forays
into poetry and criticism, forays in which one is always conscious
of his home fortress, philosophy.

In the tradition of amateurism there was mingled a good deal
of the older tradition of the virtuoso of the seventeenth and eighteenth centuries, the man who collected and studied in any area
his fancy moved him to, and who was, incidentally, responsible
for the assembly of important materials for the future of scholarship and science. A reading of Coleridge's notebooks makes it
reasonably clear that the wide range of his behavior—so impressive to present-day specialists—was less, perhaps, the result of
his extraordinary intellectual powers than the consequence of
the behavioral patterns of the virtuoso tradition. Nevertheless, he
was obviously a thinker rather than a collector or an antiquary,
although it was, I believe, the tradition of amateur and virtuoso
that led him to a wide range of interests and observations. This
in turn brought into exercise his remarkable intellectual powers,
for it stimulated him to begin the categorial classification of what
he understood as similar phenomena, and this process in turn led
him to higher level explanations of similar categories. Given the
amateur-virtuoso tradition and his disposition, and given his
remarkable powers of abstraction, he was led automatically and
irresistibly not only into philosophy—that is, higher level explanatory systems—but also into the investigation of *how* he
had moved from phenomena into philosophical speculation.

Yet in addition to all this, there was a third force at work in his, and Wordsworth's, cultural position. They were men—like many of their generation in Europe, though to be sure in numbers a very small minority—for whom the explanatory systems of the Enlightenment had broken down. What happened to them can best be explained in terms of Hegel, their contemporary, for he devoted his life to understanding and explaining an experience that all three had. Hegel, it seems to me, had one central problem which all of his thinking was focused upon and derived from, the phenomenon of cultural transcendence. Hegel's explanation—which was *not* that of thesis, antithesis and synthesis, a triad which Fichte invented and for which Hegel had utter contempt—was that what appears to be the system of belief of a culture is not in fact a coherent system at all. He expressed this by saying that in any proposition is implicit its negation. In that form, I am inclined to think his notion more than a little ridiculous. But it must be remembered that he thought historically, and his problem was an historical problem. What he was in fact getting at was the observation that an individual assents to a proposition, not because of the nature of the proposition, but because of the situation in which he grants his assent. If the situation changes sufficiently, he may very well start saying "No" instead of "Yes." A woman brought up to believe that divorce is a very great sin may very well change her mind after she has been married ten years to a drunken bum who beats her and keeps her in a continuous state of pregnancy, without providing the income to support the children he is so carelessly fathering.

What this means when we apply it in Hegelian fashion to the apparent system of a culture's beliefs is that if the historical situation changes sufficiently, what traditionally appeared to be a coherence becomes in fact an incoherence. At that point, according to Hegel, the task of the artist, the man of religion, and above all the philosopher is to transcend the incoherence and innovate a new proposition which on the one hand will maintain the valid features of the incoherent beliefs and on the other will introduce genuinely novel features. The result is what Hegel called the *aufgehoben* and what I have called cultural transcendence. The history of man is, Hegel maintained, the history of *Geist*, the history of how concrete historical situations are constantly revealing cultural incoherence and how philosophy, as well as art and religion—though, to Hegel, to a lesser degree—are constantly trying to innovate an integration. When the fundamental assumptions of a culture, its ultimate explanations and explanatory systems, are thus disintegrated by concrete historical phenomena, then a culture is in a condition of crisis, even though only a very few people are aware of it and even fewer can achieve the cultural transcendence necessary. For those few who do, we may go on to say—and this is a point that, I think, Hegel never fully grasped—their transcendence puts them into a difficult position. Since they are in a tiny minority and ordinarily, at least at first, even unknown to each other, they are in a condition of being aware of a cultural incoherence which the vast mass of their fellows see as a coherence. Alienation is their lot, and from this alienation flows the intense friendships so characteristic of the first couple of generations of Romantics, of Wordsworth and Coleridge, for example. Moreover, alienation is not to be confused with polarization. The polarized respond to the incoherence by plumping for one proposition or another. The disaffected of our own day, for example, are merely polarized, and it is a source of great confusion to call them alienated.

Now although I have called Coleridge something of an amateur poet, there is no doubt that early in his life he took his poetic efforts very seriously, as indeed he should have. While he was desperately rummaging about in the attic of European culture to find something—the neo-Platonists for example—which he could use in his situation of experienced incoherence, at the same time he was moving toward cultural transcendence by writing an entirely new kind of poetry, though, regrettably, he did not write very much of it. In the *Mariner*, in "Kubla Khan," and in the unfinishable *Christabel* he was exploring his situation and the workings of his thought at what I have called elsewhere the exemplary level of language. There emerged the Romantic notion of symbolism, that is, the meaningful meaningless, a discourse which appears to exemplify some metaphysical explanation; but what that explanation might be cannot be grasped, nor does the symbolic poem contain any clues, the reason being, of course, that the poet does not have any clues himself. The events of his narrative discourse are, he feels—as does the reader—intensely meaningful, but what the meaning is one cannot imagine. It is the kind of discourse to which one responds by the conviction that an explanation is appropriate, but one finds it impossible to generate an explanation. Attempts to explain the *Mariner* have had a bit of success only in the past forty years, and no one would claim that a completely appropriate explanation has yet been forthcoming from anyone. We all make stabs at it, but we can scarcely convince ourselves, let alone anyone else.

Within a few years, of course, Coleridge lost the power to write serious poetry at all, and this profoundly novel kind of poetry he wrote for only a few months, or possibly a couple of years. We all know of his intense regret, his sense of desolation, at this loss, but it is easy for students of literature to exaggerate its importance. What had happened is in fact not difficult to understand. It is a well-demonstrated proposition of psychology that conceptualization is the enemy of memory. That is, to the degree we absorb phenomenal data, subsume them, and incorporate them into categories and propositions, it is those subsuming explanatory categories and propositions that serve our interests, not the data, which we tend to forget. The bare proposition contents us, and we move easily from one abstract or explanatory proposition to another, without the necessity for generating examples. Indeed, the more abstract thinking becomes—as is very obvious in Coleridge's case—the more difficult it is to think of examples at all. Coleridge had created a new kind of poetry because his explanatory system had collapsed as a result of what he had come to understand as its own internal incoherence. As he began, painfully, and slowly, to generate new explanations with what satisfied him as a growing internal coherence, poetry became alien to him. His new kind of meaningful-meaningless poetry was no longer possible for him, while the old kind of poetry, which exemplified unquestioned explanatory propositions, was equally impossible, since his thinking was at that stage of abstraction—or as Hegel would have said, that stage of the Absolute—at which it was not yet in a condition to be applied to the concrete world. He did not yet sufficiently understand it himself;

nor was it yet nearly complete enough or firm enough or flexible enough to be used. The effort to put it to use was to come only in the 1820s. Yet the fact that he had created a new kind of a poetry necessarily turned his attention to how such a phenomenon could be possible. He had achieved a cultural transcendence, and for him as for Hegel, that phenomenon, rather than the phenomenon of poetry itself, or poetry in general, was the object of his most intense interest. Any metaphysic, or general explanatory system, he might be able to construct must—for his own peace of mind, to resolve his own tensions and confusions—include and find a significant place for poetry.

Yet it must always be remembered that, when Coleridge writes about poetry, it is his own poetry of the golden years he is thinking of. That is why he so often misses Wordsworth and what Wordsworth was trying to do. Moreover, it was his own loss of the ability to write poetry that was central to the problem he was struggling to resolve. Furthermore, not only is his criticism exceedingly biased and slanted in his effort to integrate it coherently into the general explanatory metaphysic which was the most important thing in the world to him; not only was he, therefore, concerned with a philosophical problem and not with a critical problem; not only was he concerned, not with poetry, but with a philosophical explanation of how poetry is generated—that is, *his* poetry; but his criticism also, as a consequence of all this, is, I think, virtually useless. Moreover, the attempt to use it has, I believe, been exceedingly damaging to the critical tradition ever since. It is only fair to admit, however, that, in the whole range of English critical theory, there is but one essay I really like and can approve of; and that is Davenant's Preface to *Gondibert*, which cannot, incidentally, be understood unless one also studies and understands *Gondibert* itself—not a very good poem, perhaps, but in the history of culture an extraordinarily interesting one. In defense of what is obviously an outrageous position, let me point out that Davenant wrote his preface when his roommate at the court in exile at St. Germain was Thomas Hobbes. No wonder Hobbes wrote such an admiring epistle!

To begin with what may seem a minor point—minor at least in the sense that it involves a distinction we have all been trained in and which most people who worry about such matters now consider to be self-evident—Coleridge more than anyone else was responsible for the distinction between poetry and rhetoric. This distinction is, I believe, completely invalid. They are usually perceived as two mutually exclusive categories, whereas in fact they are independent categories, that is, not necessarily exclusive of one another. For, as we have seen, and as subsequent criticism has accepted, Coleridge conceived of poetry as the product of a poet, that is, as the consequence of a special kind of mental function of a special kind of personality. The trouble with "personality" and also with "mind" is that they are at such a high level of metaphysical explanation and—in the discourse of Coleridge and subsequent critics—are so completely hypostatized as to be useful in subsuming other propositions, but absolutely useless in subsuming empirical phenomena. Hence the hopeless wrangle that has been going on ever since. "Rhetoric," however, is a matter of empirically observable linguistic phenomena. A study of the classical rhetoricians—and an intensive study of these writers would be an immensely fruitful enterprise, still waiting for a good modern linguist—reveals that their classifications of rhetorical figures include just about any linguistic phenomena that can be found, not only in classical poetry, but in the poetry—even the hippie poetry—being written right now. I would propose for a general theory of rhetoric the term "linguistic overdetermination," that is, a more frequent appearance of linguistic phenomena than can be found in any random selection of spoken discourse. However, even this term is no doubt unsatisfactory. My impression—and such is our state of ignorance in this immensely important but grossly neglected matter that I can but have an impression—is that social roles (a metaphor, to be sure) are linked to rhetoric. Actually, to digress a moment, it is my own conviction that the proper subject of sociology is social management, that social management is accomplished by rhetoric, and that the proper study of sociology is the study of rhetoric.

At any rate, to consider poetry as rhetoric, that is, as a special mode or modes of discourse, is at least to consider it as a linguistic phenomenon which is accessible. And this is certainly far better than to consider it as the product of a special personality and a special function of the mind, hypostatizations which probably do not exist and are certainly inaccessible. Coleridge, in short, has persuaded us to go snipe-hunting, and we have yet to bag anything of the slightest value. Further, to conceive of poetry as a rhetorical mode is to see at once that rhetorical modes change, and that their changes are linked to other cultural changes. We all know this. Why, then, do we go on talking about poetry in the Coleridgean manner?

Well, for one thing it is marvelously seductive. It makes poetry terribly important, and therefore it makes us—its guardians, its interpreters, its cultural transmitters—terribly important. All this, of course, derives from the famous distinction between the fancy and the imagination. I have been confused by this for forty years, and I have never found anybody who could explain it or put it to any use at all. But after all, I have concluded, it is simple enough. What Coleridge is saying amounts to this. All configurations discriminable from their ground are signs. And a configuration is a sign because we judge it to be a member of a category of similar configurations and respond to it accordingly. Sign-perception is of two sorts. Signs perceived as immediate signs are members of the category of which they are a sign, as a tree is a member of the category of trees. Mediating signs are perceived as not being members of the category of which they are signs, as the word "tree" or a picture of a tree are not members of the category of trees. Now as a kind of Kantian, Coleridge saw that these categories, and the structuring of these categories, are not dictated by the signs but are a matter of human behavior. Sign-perception and sign-categorization are therefore cultural conventions. That is all that is meant by the notion that the mind transcends the world, and it is of course a good deal—and so far as I am concerned a reasonably correct account of the matter. Hegel's position was remarkably similar. The "concrete universal" is an immediate sign.

Now Coleridge says, more or less correctly, that we can discriminate two kinds of mental activity, though my own opinion is that these are not two kinds but two poles of sign-behavior. The one applies without change the categories conventionalized within the culture and, in the same rigid manner, the structure of those categories. The other innovates new categories—a metaphor is an innovated category—and manipulates in novel ways the conventionalized and culturally validated categories and their structure. To write poetry which merely exemplifies existent categories is to write poetry of the fancy. To write poetry which exemplifies novel categories and innovatively manipulated categorial structure is to write poetry of the imagination. This I think is what Coleridge was talking about, but I would be the last to deny that he did not talk about it very well. What his position amounts to is that imagination is a defining attribute of human beings, but poets have more imagination than others. There is, however, not the slightest reason to conclude that an excess of imagination in the Coleridgean sense has anything to do with whether a man is a poet or not. In the Coleridgean sense of the term, there is no difference between the scientific imagination and the poetic.

Now clearly what Coleridge calls poetry of the imagination is highly innovative poetry. It was what for a time he wrote himself, and he was fascinated and justifiably so by the phenomenon—but not by the poetry; rather, by the innovation. As a man responding to a cultural crisis of the utmost severity, as a man who found his self-respect in his power to achieve—at least in one area, poetry, and increasingly, though somewhat less impressively, in another, philosophy—he had obviously an intense interest in validating innovative poetry, which he called poetry of the imagination. His criterion for judging poetry, then, is "Innovative poetry which is culturally transcendent in a direction and in a mode I approve of." There are no reliable grounds in his position for relegating noninnovative poetry to the category of mere rhetoric or mere verse or mere fancy. The confusion in Coleridge, which we have been cursed with ever since, is the confusion of innovation and creativity.

Innovation is the norm of human behavior. The human brain is so constructed that nobody ever gets anything right. Innovation which is validated by the culture or by some subculture within the culture is called creativity; innovation which is invalidated is called error. Creativity is validated error; error is invalidated creativity. The confusion between error and innovation—which is by no means exclusively Coleridgean, but is generally Romantic—was in part inherited from cultural periods before Romanticism, as far back at least as Plato. Certainly, however, in England and America Coleridge has been more responsible than anyone else for the current phenomenon of labeling creative any innovation not economically important nor obviously threatening to the belief system. The results have been curious. Human behavior is maintained in channels and kept predictable and therefore socially manageable by the general phenomenon of policing: that is, invalidating any behavior innovative beyond a culturally established range of permissible innovation, and backing up that invalidation with force. The identification of creativity with innovation means, of course, the continuously delta-like spreading of a kind of behavior. The consequence is that in the art galleries and in the volumes of poetry and in the concert halls of today anything sufficiently innovative is now called creative, and is validated. The function of policing, of maintaining cultural standards and traditions, is consequently vitiated. How many of us have not, in our embarrassment, praised a student for the most revolting literary absurdity because it is creative, novel, self-expressive—to introduce another culturally damaging term for which Coleridgeanism is responsible. The consequence of Coleridgeanism is the deliquescence of the arts.

But do not misunderstand me. I do not say that this is bad. It may very well be good. Mankind has paid a heavy price for the high arts; perhaps the price has been too heavy. Perhaps mankind is right in casting off that burden. If Coleridge was the destroyer of high culture, he may have been the savior of man.

12

THE DEPLORABLE CONSEQUENCES

OF THE IDEA OF CREATIVITY

[1970*]

The problem of creativity is a very strange one. For quite some time there have been major research enterprises on the psychology of creativity and of the creative personality. For reasons I hope to make clear, I do not think that such undertakings will arrive at any conclusions at all, let alone conclusions of any significance. The problem needs to be looked at in quite a different way, as a term, or word, rather than as a presumed mental or personal attribute. Now the most striking thing today about the term is its fantastically widespread use. Virtually anything can be called creative, and we are constantly urged and we constantly urge our children to be creative. It almost seems as if the word had been reduced from any possible significance to a mere intensifier, so that it means little more than "good," hardly even "good" in some special way. Yet that is to exaggerate. The term does, at

* Delivered at the annual meeting of the Western Association of Art Museums, October 1970. Edited transcription of tape recording.

least ordinarily, appear to imply an additional attribute, and our task must be to attempt to locate it.

The most striking thing about creativity, particularly as the term is applied to the arts, is what we might call the hagiolotrous atmosphere in which creativity is discussed. Hagiolatry is the worship of saints, and hagiology is the study in general of saint worship and in particular of writings about saints. A couple of years ago, the Catholic Church said that a good many saints were being worshipped who had in fact never existed and officially withdrew them from the canon of saints. A great many people were upset by this, and quite a few have gone on worshipping saints anyway, very sensibly; for, after all, it makes very little difference whether a saint actually existed or not so long as he does the job you want him to do.

We are all, of course, entirely familiar with the notion of art as religion; and in the late nineteenth century there was in sophisticated cultural circles a triumphant affirmation of the religion of art. We tend to think that that stage of cultural history has been left behind, but the very notion of creativity indicates that the religion of art has by no means died out. "Creativity" was originally an attribute of Deity, and only of Deity. The transference of a divine attribute to humanity, however, has by no means done away with the idea of divinity. It has simply meant that sainthood has spread from religious saints to a great many other kinds of saints. The present interest in the arts shows all the manifestations of hagiolatry. We have art museums instead of religious shrines, and if you examine the architectural layout of art museums, you will find that they have striking resemblances to religious shrines. The assumed importance and significance of art and the artist—and the somewhat sacred character of the artist—indicate that the hagiology of art continues. This is true, of course, not only of the visual arts, but just as strikingly of literary criticism. The study of art leads not only to a willing suspension of disbelief, but even to a willing suspension of common sense. The source of this notion, therefore, of the religion of art needs to be detached before we can discuss the problem of creativity, and to be separated from the general course of cultural history so that we can observe with some precision, perhaps, what has happened to us, and momentarily, at least, can free ourselves from the hagiolatry of creativity. Thus we may be able to observe in a somewhat more objective way—with less commitment, possibly, and even less moral bullying—what is really going on when we are talking about creativity.

What are the situations in which we use this term? Because the term has gotten out of hand, this is one of our problems. The kindergarten child busy with fingerpainting is called creative, and so is Michelangelo. There does seem to be a difference, but when we put it in the light of the present use of the term "creativity," the difference is almost impossible to locate. Now when people talk about the religion of art they continually act as if the term "religion of art" were some kind of metaphor. It is by no means a metaphor; it is a very exact description.

To the degree a culture becomes secularized, to that degree it becomes more and not less concerned with religion. Religion becomes more widespread, more pervasive through the culture as religion proper becomes less pervasive. Secularization means, more or less, the disappearance of institutionalized occasions and symbols for the religious experience, but it does not mean that the religious function has vanished from the culture, or is even weaker. It is probably stronger.

What, therefore, is the religious experience? If we go back in history a few centuries, it is apparent that one of the most significant aspects of the religious experience as it has generally been discussed in Western culture is the notion of Grace, as in John Bunyan's *Grace Abounding to the Chief of Sinners*. However grace may be described or defined, there is one basic definition on which there is no disagreement: Grace is the revelation in one way or another of the divine to the individual human being. It is the penetration of the divine into the human being's behavior in such a way that he himself will experience the sense of grace and other people will recognize its presence or manifestation. The result is hagiolatry. A saint is one on whom, by definition, grace has descended, and the Holy Ghost is the instrument of the descent of grace. We have, therefore, already something of a triad of the divine, of grace, and of the saint; and to that we may now add the public recognition of sainthood, or the descent of grace upon the individual. At the time of the Reformation and the Renaissance, the problem of grace became highly important in the Catholic Church. In the seventeenth century, for example, a tremendous controversy surrounded the movement called the Port-Royal movement. The quasi-Calvinistic Catholicism of Port-Royal revolved around the problem of grace, and at the same time in England and the other Protestant countries grace became a central problem. There were men in the seventeenth century one might call Calvinistic Catholics, but the traditional Catholics, represented by the Jesuits, were ruthless and savage in attempting to extirpate completely this Calvinistic notion of grace. The reason was that the new notion meant that grace could descend upon the individual without the intervention of religious ritual, and without the intervention of the Church. The church, therefore, became the occasion for the reception of grace, but not the cause. This meant a very profound difference in the conception of the relation of the human to the divine. It meant that the individual and friends of the individual could recognize in the individual the descent of grace apart from its authentication by the official church. Thus the whole function of the church suffered a severe attrition. In time it became even less than the occasion for the reception of grace; it became something that merely facilitated the descent of grace. For a man like Bunyan a church was hardly necessary at all, and for a man like Fox, the Quaker, it became quite unnecessary, even quite useless. There was no reason for the church's existence.

Thus the problem of grace became a central problem in European culture. However we define grace, the entry of the divine into the individual and its manifestation through behavior to others became something that could be validated by others and could be conceived as extremely useful to others—all without the intervention of a church. And if it could descend upon any individual, it could descend upon this individual as well as that; it could descend upon you and you yourself could authenticate it and validate it. Thus sainthood, the official canonization or public recognition and validation of the manifestation of grace, became separated from the notion of grace. Thus grace became separated from the notion of the church. It was, so to speak, a free concept within the culture, no longer bound to a social institution.

In the course of the seventeenth century, culture became, also, further secularized and rationalized. The religious function—and with it the notion of grace—began, though concealed, to be attached to secular notions. At this time Longinus' famous treatise on the sublime once again became available. It was in the Platonic tradition of poetry as the result of divine inspiration. Though Plato presented the notion ironically, the irony has been ignored, and for the most part still is. The Platonic discussion became the foundation for the notion of the poet as the receiver of divine inspiration—or grace—in a non-Christian tradition revived at the end of the seventeenth century. That tradition, as well as we can tell, goes all the way back to the Neolithic conception of the shaman, who is himself the instrument of the divine and is divinely inspired. We have, therefore, at the end of the seventeenth century a cultural situation in which the Christian notion of grace has become secularized and in which that secularization is supported by a non-Christian source and tradition. Hence the general conception of the eighteenth-century Enlightenment is that, so far as poetry and the arts are concerned, and so far as the individual is aware of the grandeur of the natural world, the poet is somehow or other superiorly endowed to recognize the existence of the divinity in the world, specifically in the natural world. He has a peculiar psyche which makes him more sensitive than others. This notion of sublimity-grace-poet is fused in the notion of the *imagination.*

The background is the deistic conception of God. Deity can be known only through the rational analysis of the natural world, but that knowledge must be supported and indeed made possible by an enthusiastic recognition of God in Nature. God is known through an inspired perception of nature, that is, through the imagination. "Imagination" originally meant simply the ability to have covert nonverbal images—in dreams, hallucinations, and so on,—and that is all. In *The Faerie Queene* it is regarded as a very dubious, and even a dangerous, faculty. As

Shakespeare said, in the lunatic, the lover, and the poet the imagination is running wild. Its danger arises because it is based on sensory experience and can therefore divert the mind from the reference of all problems to the existence of God. It has a tendency to separate the mind from God. In the eighteenth century the situation is entirely reversed. The imagination becomes, not something separate from or threatening to the reason, but the support of reason. It is the imagination which gives the individual the sense of meaningfulness and value that supports and motivates and is the spur for the reason. The poetic imagination, therefore, and the artistic imagination become highly central. The imagination, since it is the faculty by which the divine is discovered, becomes the equivalent of grace. Or rather, the notion of grace is detached from the word "grace" and is attached to the word "imagination."

Thus we have exactly the same kind of pattern that obtained before. We have the divine, the descent of grace or the imagination, and the saint, the *hagios*, that is, the artist; and we have the recognition of the artist and the validation of grace in the artist and his works by the critic, or more likely the virtuoso, the enthusiastic perceiver and collector of art—the informed collector, the ancestor of the museum curator. Validation within the church is accomplished by the priesthood, and the critic becomes the counterpart of the priest. The museum curator takes on another function of the priesthood—perhaps that of verger or sexton, who exhibits the manifestations of grace in the shrine-museum. The Museum, after all, is the place of the muses, those semideities who are the symbolizations of particular modes of the descent of grace on the imagination, on the arts. We have exactly the same structure, including the worship, that we have in religion. It is not careless to talk about the religion of art. It is not a metaphor. It is precisely the same thing. With the coming of Romanticism we have an even more striking manifestation.

In the eighteenth century the imagination as a means of grace was operant through the artist's observation of the natural world and through his creation of the vision of the natural world, a vision which would create a perfect harmony of the individual soul, the structure of society, and the natural world itself. In epistemological terms, the notion was that the categories of the object exhaust the attributes of the subject. Insofar as there is a separation and disharmony among the individual, society, and nature, it is the result of error and ignorance in the past. Once these are corrected we can have a perfect world. That this notion is still extraordinarily powerful today I think the events of the last years of the 1960s make clear. Yet the Romantic notion is quite different. Instead of seeing a desirable, or possible, fundamental harmony between the subject and the object, the Romantic saw in the relation of subject to object an irresolvable tension. Thus the basic human problems cannot be solved, and the problem therefore of value and meaning became extremely pressing. The Enlightenment secularization of traditional belief simply converted the idea of return to Paradise or ascent to Heaven into a notion of a perfect society. Hence arose the perfectibilitarianism and Utopianism of the eighteenth century. To the Romantic, such notions now became unavailable. Nature became something that is perceived as unknown and unknowable. The Romantics felt that the Medieval notion of absorption of object into subject had merely been reversed by the Enlightenment. The Enlightenment was, then, merely Medievalism upside down, as the Marquis de Sade so devastatingly pointed out. The Romantic notion of an irresolvable tension between subject and object made the traditional religion and the Enlightenment religion of nature untenable. Thus Philipp Otto Runge, the German artist, said in so many words that the artist is not inspired by nature, but directly by God. It is at this point that among advanced thinkers throughout Western Europe the notion of the unconscious emerges. The divine penetrates the unconscious mind and thence descends to the conscious mind. (Freud simply reverses this and has instinct ascend to the unconscious and thence to the conscious.) The artist is peculiarly open to such a penetration and is thus the instrument by which the divine, that is, meaning and value, enters the world. The artist becomes the saint. The imagination is the penetration of the divine into the world. By the end of the nineteenth century the divine had been more or less eliminated, but that is the only elimination from the pattern.

At this point a new difficulty arose. The imagination as the means of grace and value had been available solely to the artist and possibly also to the enthusiast, who, however, was inspired by and modeled on the artist. And this was initially the attitude of Romanticism. However, Coleridge, like Schopenhauer and Hegel and a good many others, concluded that the mind cannot know the world except in terms of the mind's own interests. Thus its interests cannot be separated from its actual knowledge. Our knowledge of the world, therefore, is necessarily a construct. This does not mean that the world is an illusion; the Romantics had, in fact, a much stronger sense of reality than had appeared in any preceding period. The strength of that sense, however, emerged from the conviction that reality can be known only in terms of human interest. The power, therefore, by which we make sense out of the world is not, as in the eighteenth century, a power by which we discover the meaning and value immanent in the world; it is a *creative* power imposed upon the world in terms of human interest.

Thus everyone is imaginative because the imagination now becomes the power of making sense out of experience. An incoherence arises because the creative imagination is the unique function of the artist, but is also a function common to all men and necessary to all men, even to their very existence. A kind of resolution of this incoherence was reached in the notion that, though the artist does what everybody else does, he does it better. It was nevertheless an unstable resolution, because the proposition could be easily reversed and was, thus: Everybody does what the artist does. Art, then, and the artist are left without a defining attribute. It becomes impossible to distinguish the artist from anyone else or the work of art from any other artifact. Further, since the imagination was in origin and function a religious conception, the activity of the creative imagination—creativity being the attribute of the divine—had to be extended to everyone. One consequence, for example, was that the perception of the work of art, the so-called aesthetic experience, became as creative an act as making a work of art. Yet, since the artist was, after all, the one who did create the work of art—though by no unique power —and made divine creativity accessible to the nonartist, he became a functional equivalent of the saint, with the result that the work of art became the functional equivalent of the saint's relic. The nineteenth century even developed the pilgrimage to the home and tomb of the artist, an activity that increased, it was felt, one's susceptibility to the divine grace that flows through the artist into the world.

Let us now, however, look at this with a skeptical eye and with some detachment. Let us abandon this mythology of creativity, this religious conception of creativity, and look at it somewhat more coolly. There are two things, it seems to me, that the human mind cannot avoid doing: First, it cannot avoid making sense out of experience, and second, it cannot resist constructing experience, or at least attempting to construct experience, as a coherence. This is where Hegel is still so extraordinarily instructive, for he points out that in cultural or social life no two beliefs or values are coherent with each other, but that the characteristic of a cultural epoch is that certain beliefs are conceived as essential and coherent with each other, and that a cultural crisis arises when, because of a change in the culture's total situation, that which has been perceived as coherent comes to be seen as incoherent. The spread of the notion of creativity to its present indeterminate usage is the result of the attempt to keep in coherent stability the incoherence of a unique attribute of the artist, which is to be found in everyone.

Now there is another thing which human beings cannot avoid —innovation. If we take a good old psychological term, "stimulus-response," and examine it from the point of view of modern knowledge, we find that we cannot talk about stimulus and response at all any more, because we cannot locate a stimulus. We can only talk about the stimulus situation, but what it is in the stimulus situation that is responsible for the response cannot be located. The reason is that the human brain is *not* a causal system—i.e., something like a telephone switchboard—because of the very nature of the brain cells and the relationships among them. The result is that nobody ever gets anything right.

One of the most interesting phenomena for understanding the fine grain of human behavior is printing, or more specifically, the composition of type. Anybody who has put anything through the press knows that it is impossible to get anything more than a few lines really correctly set up. The explanation is that no behavior pattern, no matter how thoroughly validated, can be learned to absolute perfection. Language itself is a stochastism; it is not a system, a structure with universal laws. It can be understood only statistically, not causally. It is constantly manipulated and constant innovations are being made. An infinite number of new sentences is available in any language. Language is a stochastic system; it is a random system. And the reason is that the brain itself is a stochastic system. No matter what the stimulus situation, or how often the brain has encountered it, the brain necessarily produces infinite innovations.

Innovation is the norm of human behavior. On the whole, to be sure, behaviors fall into recognizable families. This gives us the illusion that behavior is stable; that is, we mistakenly categorize two similar behaviors as the same behavior. Language itself is constantly in a drift of change, and likewise all behavior, no matter how patterned, is characterized by that same drift of change. What I have discussed above is an excellent example. Given the basic pattern of God, grace, sainthood, the priest, and worshippers, we can recognize the same pattern in the attitude toward creativity and the arts even today. Even though a great many factors have been changed, the factors within the system remain much the same, in spite of the fact that for many people an important factor, God, has disappeared. But Jung substituted for God the racial unconscious, and Freud substituted sex, and Bergson substituted the *élan vital*. One incidental result, oddly enough, is that for a great many people sex has become the means of grace.

But a problem arises in the fact that, though innovation is the norm, a behavioral pattern can remain sufficiently true—to use a term from biology—to make it possible to categorize an innovative behavior in an already existent and long-standing behavioral pattern. To refer to this second phenomenon I shall use the term "cultural convergence" to mean the convergence of people's behavior with the behavior of other people. It is obvious of course that there has to be behavioral convergence for there to be any interaction at all. Moreover, we know about other people exactly in the same way we know about ourselves, by observing our behavior. And we control our behavior as we control the behavior of others, by cultural convergence with our own behavior.

What happens is that we construct our conceptions of other people's behavior and adjust our behavior so that it will successfully interact with theirs, or manipulate them so that their behavior will successfully interact with our own. Likewise, we construct notions of our own behavior and so direct our own behavior that it is coherent and convergent with our own preceding behavior. We must recognize that cultural convergence and self-convergence are the identical phenomenon. Self-convergence is responsible for the notion of style. Style is a problem more apparent in the arts simply because the rate of change in the arts is more rapid than in other forms of behavior.

A little examination will make it possible to see how this cultural convergence works. We may begin by considering the phenomenon I would call the delta effect, or the deviancy effect, since deviancy spreads in a delta-like formation. Insofar as any cultural mode is badly transmitted from one generation to the next, to that degree the delta effect, or the spread of deviance, will occur. An example is sex. Sexual behavior in our culture is badly transmitted. For the young it consists mostly of folklore which, when they really start their sexual life, turns out to be extremely unreliable. They are forced to do an amount of innovating which is uncomfortable and sometimes seriously disturbing. The result is that in each generation you get the full spread of sexual deviancy. Deviancy is not something that is a characteristic of a disturbed personality. It is a stochastic or statistically random effect. Another example is college teaching, which, like sex, is something that is badly transmitted. Since the teacher has no idea of how to do what he is supposed to do, in any department there is a very interesting spread of teaching styles. The individual teacher, in order to create a predictable role for himself, creates a self-convergence, a certain style of teaching. He begins by using a paradigm, some model or some professor whom he has admired. But in any department you will find much the same range of deviance.

The first stage of behavior, then, is the divergence within a particular family of behaviors. It must be something so divergent from the norm that it is recognized as a divergence. Here at the beginning we must recognize that divergence is already a social matter, something that is recognized and defined socially as a divergence. Within any mode of behavior in a culture there are certain tolerable limits of divergence within which the behavior is still regarded as sufficiently close to the ideal of that behavioral mode that it is not regarded as sufficiently divergent to be recognized as divergence. However, we are constantly engaging, in all the modes of behavior, in kinds of divergence which are of a random character. Probably the vast bulk of shoplifting in the United States, which is costing us all enormous sums every year, is considered by most people to be culturally linked. It is not. Nor does it seem to be true that a small group of people is responsible for all of it. Apparently it is mostly done by respectable middle-class housewives. The reason seems to be simply that many stores no longer have the number of personnel that they had, nor is virtually everything behind counters or inside of cases. There is no longer constant observation and segregation of goods from the public. That is, there is now an underpresence of signals in supermarkets and department stores. There is not nearly so much information that one should pay for what one wants and not simply take it. The decline of such instructions has been accompanied by a rise in shoplifting. Without constant and continuous repetition of instructions, divergence has crept in. The removal of information from behavior has meant that increasingly larger numbers of people have begun to be dishonest. Now when a divergent pattern of behavior is repeated in the individual, or in a mass of individuals, it is called deviance. A unique divergence is not important, but the patterning of divergence in behavior is a deviance. So long as the ideal of the behavioral mode does not change, patterned divergence is regarded as deviant behavior.

At this point two very interesting things can happen. Either of two stages in behavioral development can ensue. Suppose you take a kid who swipes a bicycle. You say he's just a kid and he's done this just once. It is just divergence. But suppose he starts to swipe bicycles steadily. His behavior now becomes a patterned divergence and therefore a deviance. It has already been in-validated by cultural norms, and if the boy keeps it up, he is sent to prison, the graduate schools of our criminal classes. In prison he is trained to be a professional criminal. On graduation he enters, professionally, the crime world. However, he turns out not to be an interesting criminal, because his patterns of diver-gency in criminal behavior are not sufficiently creative. His bosses judge that his deviancies as a criminal are not worth standardizing and adopting.

That is, a divergence which has been patterned into a deviancy is judged to be a deviancy by social validators, and likewise a patterned divergence which is judged to be socially useful by social validators is taken up and adopted, because it has been judged to be *creative*. Deviancy, then, is socially invalidated patterned divergence, while creativity is socially validated pat-terned divergence.

We are now in a position to understand a little better how it is that cultural convergence and self-convergence are brought about. The effective force is the phenomenon of policing, of which the official police are but one small part. Policing is a universal charac-teristic of human behavior. To eavesdrop is one of the most in-structive things it is possible to do. If you eavesdrop, you will discover that most conversation consists of value statements. Looked at from this point of view, value statements are policing statements. As the example of shoplifting shows, continual polic-ing of a behavior is necessary if it is not to be badly transmitted and if it is to be maintained within tolerable limits of divergence. And such cultural convergence includes self-convergence; the individual, to maintain his own behavior within tolerable limits, must continuously police himself, even in behaviors which are always totally private.

We can now turn to the peculiar behavior modes of the arts, and the problem of creativity in the arts as the medium of divine or functionally divine grace. The most important thing about the arts is their irresponsibility. A work of art does not require us to do anything, not even to respond to it, if we do not care to. It does not require us to manipulate the environment for our own benefit or anyone else's. Aristotle's famous theory of the cathartic effect of tragedy may simply mean that when we are watching a tragedy we can take pleasure in seeing a noble man killed. Shakespeare said that we are to the gods as are flies to wanton boys; they kill us for their sport. Well, in the artistic experience we are such gods; we kill for sport. This divine irresponsibility is significant in the arts and the artistic experience because artistic experience is a withdrawal from social interaction. Such withdrawal makes possible a breakdown of behavior patterns, and that in turn makes it possible for us to generate cultural innovations more freely. The removal from social interaction permits a disorientation, and it is through psychological disorientation that useful innovations enter into culture. This is just as true of the culture of rats as it is of the culture of human beings. No society can continue to exist without occasions and strategies for withdrawal and disorientation. However, the innovative products of that disorientation and withdrawal are by no means all validated, that is, brought into social interaction and subjected to policing. Many of them are invalidated, as one sees easily if criticism in the arts is examined. The critic is the priest-like validator. It is but necessary to observe the ups and downs in the reputation— that is, the validation—of various artists to see this phenomenon of validation and policing at work.

Art, therefore, being an activity of withdrawal and irresponsibility, is subjected to validation on the grounds of other cultural interests. Since the coming of Romanticism, however, the grounds for validation have been creativity. But creativity is only innovation, that is, behavioral divergency sufficiently striking to be recognized as divergence. The result is that in the arts we have arrived at a cultural situation such that anything that is sufficiently divergent to be so recognized is validated as creativity. The interests of the critic—the validator—are not controlled now by policing or by cultural interests external to artistic acts; they are controlled solely by the recognition of a divergency and a pattern of deviancy. That very factor is responsible for his saying that the work was the consequence of a creative act, or of creativity.

We have, therefore, the present situation in which in all the arts there is a deviational spread, a delta effect. The result is that the only barrier for the artist is the publicity barrier. If he can only get some validator, someone who runs an art gallery, someone who knows what he can get away with—namely, practically anything—or some critic to say that his work is creative, then his career is made. He can sell anything. The confusion of innovation and creativity has meant that innovation becomes the most important factor for validation. The result is not merely the delta effect, but also an enormous increase in cultural change and the rate of cultural change, so that there are two or three latest art movements per season.

But in spite of this the artist today is in no enviable position. Quite the contrary. When Schoenberg abandoned tonality, he found that though he could put down any note he wanted to, in fact he could not write anything that lasted more than a minute or two unless he was setting a literary text. Therefore, in the early 1920s he invented the twelve-tone system. On the one hand it generated possibilities from which he could select, and on the other hand it provided a self-policing device. The oddity is that it is not freedom but policing and cultural validation which is the occasion for the occurrence of divergence and deviancy. Some of these can be validated and made culturally convergent. If there is no such policing and validation, and if things are validated only on the grounds of their innovation, you simply get a spread of increasing cultural change. And you also put the artist into a desperate situation: Since he can do absolutely anything he wants to, there is no reason for him to do anything, but only a reason to do something.

That reason to do something is that the function that now remains for art is the religious function. The artist creates creativity. Therefore creativity is what the artist creates. This seems idiotic until we recognize that the creativity that the artist creates is actually the works, the stigmata, and the relics of a saint. However, the absence of a set of demands that will enable the artist to do something to create possibilities from which he can select by validation and offer to others for validation on grounds other than mere creativity has put the artist into an enormously difficult situation. I think the appearance of concept art is symptomatic. It is the crisis of the artist that has forced him to think about concepts because the culture is not providing them. But the validational criterion of creativity makes it quite unnecessary for him to embody the concepts.

Further, since the criterion of creativity cannot distinguish between the artist and the nonartist, anyone who calls himself an artist is an artist, and anyone called creative is creative. The result is the possibility of the total disintegration of the whole artistic enterprise and particularly of the kind of art associated with high culture. The cultural level of the high arts becomes increasingly indistinguishable from the middle and lower level of the arts. Everything is running together. Hence Pop Art. To be sure, so far has the situation deteriorated, the old official Pop Art by now looks like the old masters.

Will this disappearance of the high arts, created and produced for an aristocracy, be unfortunate? Man has sacrificed a great deal for high art. It has been a tremendous burden and a tremendous expense. So if man says art will be just for fun and if anything innovative in this irresponsible area we call artistic behavior is to be validated as art, will there be a genuine cultural loss? The economic burden of the arts and the burden the high arts have imposed upon the spirit will be lifted. The high arts will disappear, except in museums, where they will be increasingly disregarded and abandoned to the dust. Instead, there will be something very, very inexpensive and highly dispensable. The result of the confusion of creativity and innovation which has resulted in the deplorable consequences—or perhaps not deplorable —of the idea of creativity will be the turning of art as we have known it into a kind of art best designated as "kleenex art," a simple and cheap way of generating and discharging religious feelings. But if art indeed does have a function other than a religious function, and if this is particularly true of high art, then emergence of kleenex art, the use of art solely to fulfill a religious function, will be, can be, must be—even though it is but temporary—a cultural disaster.

13

LITERATURE

AND KNOWLEDGE

[1972*]

The continual recurrence of the problem of whether or not literature may be regarded as offering knowledge suggests that the problem is incapable of solution. Certainly, solutions have been offered; if anyone is so minded, he can choose to his satisfaction among a variety of solutions. So long as his choice satisfies him well enough so that he can forget about the problem, it probably makes little difference which selection he makes. If his decision makes it possible for him to go about the business of encountering literature and, if he so wishes, of studying it, and of doing both with what he judges to be greater satisfaction and efficiency, his selection of a solution or solutions can be reasonably regarded as quite satisfactory. On the other hand, should he wish to present to others the consequences of his encounter and the results of his study in such a way that his

* Presented at the Sixth Conference on Comparative Literature: Literature as Knowledge, at the University of Southern California, May 11–12, 1972. Reprinted by permission.

efforts are validated, the problem threatens to rearise. The question of whether or not the results of his study of literature are to be offered as matters of knowledge—to be validated as such by others—is a matter with which I shall not be concerned here, though it is a problem of the greatest possible interest and one, I feel, insufficiently explored. Rather, I shall be concerned only with the problem of whether or not literature can in itself properly be judged a source of knowledge.

To be a bit more explicit, I shall not be concerned with the problem of whether or not the literary work can be regarded as an expression or realization of the knowledge of its author. Indeed, it appears to me that the notion of knowledge-and-literature I shall be concerned with—whether or not it can be said that the literary work provides us knowledge of something outside of itself—subsumes the problem of the author's knowledge and whether or not it gets into the work, since the assumption that literature gives us knowledge must be either prior to or independent of deciding questions about the author's knowledge. Indeed, the assertion that the author knew, consciously or unconsciously, what one asserts to be the knowledge the work offers seems to be hardly more than an effort to improve the reliability of one's assertions about the knowledge one claims to have obtained from encountering and, it may be, studying the work. But this leads back to the question of whether or not one's knowledge of the knowledge the work purportedly offers is correct or adequate, a problem I shall not be concerned with, as I have already indicated.

The attempt to determine whether or not it can be said that a literary work provides knowledge of something outside of itself appears to arise then from an interpersonal and intrapersonal disagreement about the validation of assertions purporting to be reliable accounts of the knowledge said to be derived from the work. At the first level this is a simple disagreement about how the work *should* be interpreted. Obviously the interpretation of a work is prior to the question of whether or not the knowledge the interpretation makes available is to be relied on, is true knowledge. Disagreements at this level can be resolved in several ways, in addition to resolution achieved by abandoning all interpretational alternatives but one. One resolution, often encountered, is that literature should not be interpreted at all, but only experienced. This purely experiential attitude can be employed in either of two ways to eliminate the question of whether the work can be said to yield knowledge of something outside of itself. One way is to assert that the value of literature is to be found in the total experience it makes available, but that that total experience does not include anything that can properly be called knowledge of something outside of the work, except for the minor proviso that the experience will improve the quality of subsequent literary experiences; in the sense that each such experience makes us more knowledgeable about how to gain such experiences, each literary experience can be said to yield knowledge. But such knowledge, of course, is knowledge about how to go about having adequate literary experiences. A knowledge of how to catch a fish does not, it would appear, improve our knowledge of fish, but only of fishing. We may say that thus we learn more about fish, but it appears to be more accurate to say that we have improved our behavior, including our tool manipulation, in such a way that the probability of catching fish is statistically improved. Such knowledge is not to be regarded as ineffable knowledge. On the contrary, just as it is not only possible but common to give directions about how to improve one's fishing performances, so it is possible to give directions about how to improve one's reading performances.

Such behavioral knowledge is obviously of the greatest possible importance, but, except for one matter, is independent of the question I am concerned with. The exploration of that one matter, however, may well serve to clarify that question. That matter arises when it is desired to test the adequacy of the reading performance. Some such tests are not, to be sure, concerned with the problem of whether or not the literary work offers knowledge of something outside of itself. I have in mind such testing questions as, "Did you visualize the imagery?" though to be sure some people do not visualize; for them such a question is not only useless but baffling. One of much wider applicability for poetry is "Are you able to transform syntactically distorted sentences into syntactically normal sentences?" or for a novel,

"Can you list the attributes of the chief protagonist and demonstrate their coherence and incoherence with each other?" or "Can you discriminate the rhetorical styles of various sections of the work?" We are getting closer to the issue when we ask, "Can you subsume the data, or at least what you regard as the significant data, in a proposition or propositions more general than the sentences in the work itself?" To be sure, to put the question in that form would terrify most of our students and perhaps ourselves, but that is what we are asking when our test questions are in the form, "What does the work mean?" This in fact immediately raises the problem of whether or not the work offers knowledge of something outside of itself, for if the "meaning" is more general than the sentences in the work, then it would certainly seem that the propositions in question can subsume less general sentences not found in the work, sentences found elsewhere. Such a question is the preliminary to such a question as, "Did the work give you a knowledge of the living conditions of the poor in the mid-nineteenth century?" or such a deliciously vague question as, "Did the work give you a profounder understanding of human nature?" Let me add here a justification for the use of the term "proposition," about which there has been such passionate discussion. I use the term to point out what seems to me a recognizable fact of behavior, that individuals accept different sentences as being sufficiently equivalent for some verbal situation to be regarded as interchangeable. The term "proposition" classes such sentences together.

Several things are apparent from this glance at testing for behavioral knowledge of adequacy in reading literature. It points out the difference between behavioral knowledge and propositional knowledge, and the tendency to move from one to the other. Further, that tendency suggests that between the two kinds of knowledge, behavioral and propositional, there is no ultimate difference. The further suggestion arises that the more important kind is frequently judged to be the propositional knowledge, the "meaning," and that the behavioral knowledge is often judged to be justified by the fact that it leads to propositional knowledge. But this judgmental tendency indicates that "knowledge" is an honorific term. On the other hand, the point from which we started, and to which we have now returned, is the resolution of interpretational disagreements by appealing to the experiential value of reading the work, a value that excludes knowledge of any kind, except increased behavioral knowledge of how to read.

The second experiential mode of resolving questions of interpretation is to assert that the work of literature does indeed give us knowledge of something outside of itself but that such knowledge is ineffable. Such knowledge is to be distinguished both from behavioral knowledge and propositional knowledge. Obviously the ineffability resolution does not assert that literature says what cannot be said, but rather that the work of literature gives us knowledge that cannot be said except in the language of that particular work. Such a theory obtained for considerable time and was, of course, the radical form of that orientation toward literature known as the New Criticism. It is scarcely news by now that the New Critics dishonored their own theory and frequently, to put it mildly, told us in different discourses exactly what the literary discourse in question said. They can scarcely be blamed; they were teachers and critics, and if either is confined to behavioral knowledge, and is limited to giving instructions on how to read effectively, there is little, perhaps, that he can do, and constant repetition of that little is not amusing. On the other hand, it may be said that they could have done far more with behavioral knowledge than in fact they did and also that there seem to be reasons why they were, perhaps inevitably, drawn toward propositional knowledge.

One reason was their desire—a desire with interesting historical sources, a desire that may properly be called a redemptive desire—to assert the supernal value of literature. It is a common assumption that such supernal value is to be found in general propositions or universals which are properly labeled "true." Thus if literature has supernal value, it must be capable of yielding true universals. Since, in point of fact, the universals that literature often yields are far from supernal, are in fact quite untenable and even absurd, the ineffability resolution was appealed to. The proper form in which to defend the resolution by the ineffable is that any propositions the work yields are to be regarded, not as true propositions, but as propositions that put us on the way to a knowledge of the ineffable truth of the sort that only literature can yield. This leaves room for the critic to engage in interpretation without asserting that his knowledge is final; it also permits him to dodge the issue of testing the knowledge the work is said to yield. In fact, of course, the ineffability theory of the New Critics did yield to an extraordinary diversity of modes of determining the knowledge the literary work can be made to yield, and it has created a situation which can only be justified by the proposition that any propositional knowledge purportedly derived from a literary work is true knowledge. Thus the problem of interpretational disagreement is resolved by claiming that no disagreement is possible. All interpretations are equally valid, since all give knowledge, not of the ineffable truth, but of the paths to the ineffable truth. The emergence of hermeneutics as a central problem of literary study suggests that such a position has made and is making a great many people very uncomfortable.

The second reason why the New Critics were inevitably drawn toward propositional knowledge is that it appears to be the norm of linguistic behavior to respond to a set or category of "concrete" or "particular" statements by subsuming them under a more general statement. On the other hand it does appear to be the case that some works of literature are peculiarly resistant to this kind of subsumption, are peculiarly recalcitrant to the effort. It is not that it is heretical to paraphase—the term heretical providing another indication that the effort of the New Critics was redemptive and was designed to ascribe to literature the function traditionally assigned to religion—it is rather that sometimes it is virtually impossible. However, the works of which that can be said are pretty generally the products of the last eighty years or so, such works as, to my mind, *Billy Budd* and *Ulysses*. The claim, so often made, that only such works can be truly designated as literature or, to use an even more honorific term, "art," is an instance of what so frequently happens. Whenever there is a cultural metamorphosis, there is a new mode of art, and critics respond by asserting that only this mode is properly to be called art. From this point of view it can be said that there is a mode of literature that does not yield propositional knowledge and yet can be claimed to yield a knowledge that is somehow ineffable *for the time being.* Thus it is not ineffable in principle, as has been claimed of such literature, but is ineffable in practice. That is, there is no reason why at some future time it should not be possible to make it yield a propositional knowledge on which there could be and would be considerable agreement. Thus the claim that literature yields ineffable knowledge can be seen as an effort to validate literature that was in practice ineffable. But why was it asserted that such literature yielded knowledge? (To be sure, the more usual form of putting this was that it yielded truth.) Somehow, it was asserted, the world looked different after encountering such works. To use Wallace Stevens' great phrase, they made possible "a new knowledge of reality." Yet what that knowledge amounted to could not be said. This kind of literature was so novel that it is not surprising that the conclusion was leaped to that only literature (or art) can make it possible. That may not be the case, yet on the other hand the problem such literature presented appeared to put the problem of literature and knowledge in an entirely new light. This is a problem to which it will be necessary to return, and, for the sake of reference and making the problem recognizable when it is returned to, I shall give this kind of knowledge the name "reorientational knowledge."

I return to the point at which the problem appears to arise of whether or not a literary work provides knowledge of something outside of itself. The question assumes a formidable and threatening aspect at two stages in responding to the work in the direction of its possible knowledge-yielding properties. The first is the hermeneutical problem. Is the interpretation reliable? Can an interpretation be reliable? If that stage can be successfully passed in such a way that it can be said that a reliable interpretation is possible, then and then only can the question be raised as to whether that interpretation yields knowledge.

At the present time, in part for reasons I have already touched on, there is certainly a hermeneutical crisis in the study of literature. I suspect that this conference itself is a symptom of that crisis. The immediate cause for that crisis is the consequence of the New Criticism, as I have already suggested, which was so feeble theoretically, as well as value-oriented, particularly with its interest in validating the emergent literary styles of the early twentieth century, that it provided no hermeneutical constraints. But the New Criticism in turn rested upon the Romantic theory of the creative imagination, possibly as confusing and vague a notion, at least in its effect, as has ever entered the language of critical discourse. The objections to the term are that "imagination" gives no instructions on how to look for and locate a phenomenal existent, while "creative" assumes what it attempts to assert, that there is a difference between innovation sufficiently emergent to be noticed to which a positive value ought to be assigned and similar innovation to which a negative value ought to be assigned. However, it appears to me that a phenomenally useful translation of the term "creative imagination" might be possible, and for it I would substitute "socioculturally validated cognitive innovation." To be sure, this expression needs translation itself into less technical language. By "innovation," then, is meant here that the innovation is interpreted as implying in of some established mode of behavior sufficiently gross and sufficiently deviant to raise the question of whether or not it ought to be validated. "Kubla Khan" was such a work. By "cognitive" is meant here that the innovation is interpreted as implying in addition to grossness and deviance an innovative knowledge of whatever it may be said that "knowledge" is of, whether it is "knowledge" of a transcendent or divine world, or whether it is "knowledge" of the phenomenal and public world which all individuals, by virtue of their humanity, have access to. By "validated" is meant that, in the cultural tradition in which it appears, the work is assigned the attributes of "excellence" and "importance." Thus within the cultural tradition in which they emerged, "Kubla Khan" has long since been designated as "great," while the status of *Sordello* and *Clarel* is still questionable and undecided. By "socio" is meant that the validation is maintained through time by the assimilation of the validation within a social institution. This means that the positive validation of "Kubla Khan" is maintained by the reiteration of that value by individuals who play roles in social institutions, that is, persistent patterns of interaction involving both traditions of cultural directions and performance, and that such institutions are maintained by continuous economic investment—not necessarily of a profit-producing sort—as an English department within a college or university. Further, by "sociocultural" is meant that the institution, as part of its behavioral tradition, assigns to literature certain tasks. Thus at midcultural level the obscene limerick was until recently assigned the task of presenting content not permitted in other literary modes, while greeting-card literature is still assigned the task of formalizing such socioculturally sensitive interactional patterns as crisis and celebration situations. Thus "sociocultural" is designed to draw attention to the task of individuals in assigning and maintaining validation and content-assignment as a factor in the general enterprise of social management.

Now in all this the most dubious term is "cognitive." What is meant within the Romantic metaphysic is that the task of the artist was to innovate content, that is, statements and nonverbal sign complexes in practice (though not necessarily immediately) susceptible to interpretation and of which it could be asserted that it offered hitherto unknown modes of knowledge. Initially that content was conceived as providing knowledge of a reality transcending the phenomenal and publicly accessible world. It may further be said that such a claim for literature rested upon and was made possible by the prestige of literature at the level of high culture, literature being circularly defined as the literature validated at that cultural level. Literature's traditional task before the nineteenth century was to exemplify the "propositional knowledge" of the high cultural level, a knowledge which consisted of metaphysical and validational language employed by socially ultimate power centers to control and validate the exercise of social management by the application of social power. Thus it may be seen that the Romantic ascription to literature of the task of the innovation of knowledge created an interpretational crisis, since the propositional knowledge it exemplified was as yet unformulated. As I have already suggested, to "interpret" literature means to subsume the statements of literature under more general statements, or universals, to which is ascribed the attribute of knowledge, which is necessarily propositional knowledge, that is, it consists of interchangeable sentences. Since Romantic literature exemplified as yet unformulated propositions (as "Kubla Khan" had to wait a long time before it could be subsumed under universals of which there is currently a considerable variety and about which, as yet, only partial agreement, or interchangeability), it was in practice ineffable and believed to be ineffable in principle. This is the reason that the New Criticism was incapable of formulating interpretational constraints, while at the same time claiming for literature ineffable cognitive innovation.

Thus the crisis in literary hermeneutics can be seen to emerge from a general and a historically local sociocultural condition. Any culture assigns to literature specific contents, and within that culture each cultural level makes similar though ordinarily different content assignments. Since there are normative constraints, therefore, on the interpretation of literature and since the virtually universal tendency is to accept a theory of immanent meaning, the conclusion necessarily makes its appearance that literature has a unique kind of meaning. Whenever there is a cultural transformation or metamorphosis such that literature is assigned new content-tasks, there is temporarily a confusion in how such literature ought to be interpreted. At such times the older content-task eventually descends to a lower cultural level and continues within the culture. No individual lives exclusively at a particular cultural level, and the higher the cultural level he lives at, the truer this is. To maintain the emergent cultural task for literature at the high cultural level, it is therefore necessary to deny at that level the honorific term "literature" to literature of lower cultural levels and at the same time to assert that the interpretational mode for the literature of high culture is the proper mode for interpreting any literature. This further reinforces the notion that literature has a unique kind of meaning. In the early nineteenth century, Romanticism, with its demand for innovative cognitive meaning, produced literature for which there was currently no interpretational mode. This produced the notion that literature is in principle ineffable, although in practice much

literature once judged to be such has become amenable to interpretations on which there is considerable agreement and for
which there is fairly weighty cultural validation.

If it is the case, as I propose and believe, that the notion that
literature has unique semantic properties is a cultural illusion,
it follows that literature presents no unique interpretational problems. The only question is this. Can an individual arrive at an
interpretation of any linguistic utterance acceptable to the originator of that utterance, that is, what is judged to be a correct
interpretation, in the absence of the originator? Since in ordinary
human behavior this happens all the time, I think the answer
must be, Yes, he can. It will be useful for what follows to suggest
that he does so either by possessing or by acquiring sufficient
knowledge of the situation in which the utterance originated to
produce what has been defined as a correct interpretation. This
is the condition that makes historical interpretation possible,
since the relation of the interpreter to the absent originator is
always historical, though the historical distance may be only a
few minutes. Indeed, any interpretation of an utterance is strictly
a historical interpretation, since the situation in which the interpreter produces his interpretation is, he assumes, sufficiently
similar to the immediately preceding situation to make his interpretation pertinent. This brings out the notion that the condition of successful interpretation is sociocultural persistence but
also that in the absence of such persistence it is theoretically possible to reconstruct cognitively sociocultural situations in which
there has been little or no persistence. This in turn assumes that
there are behavioral universals. This is to say that such universals
are the properties of the biological species, man, properties which
are not shared by other animals, though certain behavioral universals apply both to man and to some or even all other animals. One
such behavioral universal specific to man is generally assumed
to be language itself.

If in theory, therefore, correct interpretation of any utterance
is possible, then, since literature does not have unique semantic
properties, the correct interpretation of literature is possible. If
the interpretation of any utterance can give us knowledge of

something outside of language, then the interpretation of literature can give us knowledge of something outside of language
and literature. It would be very gratifying to be able to terminate
here this examination of the problem of literature and language,
but, alas, it is not possible. There is the second stage of responding to the work in the direction of its possible knowledge-yielding
properties, and it is even more formidable and threatening than
the first, hermeneutical, stage. The reason is that we can say that
literature yields knowledge if, and only if, we assert that any
utterance always yields knowledge. If only some utterances yield
knowledge, then it is possible that literary utterances never yield
knowledge, and it is equally possible that only some literary
utterances yield knowledge. If the latter is the situation, then
the question of the relation of literature to knowledge is a useless
question. The only question is, "Does this particular work yield
knowledge of something outside of itself and of language?" But
this, since the interpretation of literature presents no problems
not found in the interpretation of language, is the same question
as "Does this particular utterance, whether literary or not, yield
knowledge?" Further, if the former—that literature never yields
knowledge—is the situation, it is only a special case of the latter
—that literature sometimes yields knowledge. This is so, it seems
to me, because in either case the decision rests upon the existence
of criteria for determining whether or not a given utterance yields
knowledge. Granted such criteria, one can decide both problems:
whether literature sometimes yields knowledge, or whether it
never yields knowledge. Are there such criteria? One can only say
that there does not seem to be universal agreement on them. But
this condition may offer us a way out of our dilemma.

A glance at the history of epistemology is enlightening; happily, a glance will be sufficient. That history is a record of the
attempts to establish once and for all the criteria for determining
whether or not a sentence, or more precisely, the interpretation
of a sentence, does or does not yield knowledge. For example, at
one time the following sentence was held to be knowledge-
yielding: "There is a transcendental realm of being"—"transcendental" in this instance being interpreted as "of another order

of being than either the human or the natural." For most professional academic philosophers today that particular sentence is no longer regarded as capable of an interpretation that would yield knowledge. On the other hand, there continue to be a great many philosophers who cling to the notion that it is indeed knowledge-yielding. The blood spilt in the battles about such sentences could drown the seas in sorrow, but one who remains undecided as to whether or not the desired criteria can be established, and who looks on the struggle as an interesting, though not entirely enlightening and edifying, phenomenon of human behavior may not unreasonably conclude that the effort to establish with finality the desired criteria is futile. More briefly, he may not unreasonably conclude that the effort is normative. That is, the effort is, not to establish what the criteria are, but rather what they ought to be. A normative effort is always related, no matter how obscurely, to social management and to the cultural milieu in which that effort is a factor. For example, there is no doubt that in the past hundred years the physical sciences have achieved extraordinary victories. Is it surprising that scientific language should have come to be regarded as the model for knowledge-yielding language? From this point of view it is impossible to differentiate between the quarrels of philosophers over the criteria at issue and a quarrel in the street between two semi-literates in which the issue is the same. I do not wish to denigrate philosophers, for whom I have the profoundest respect, though they do not frighten me as they once did, or at least not to the same degree. It is to the credit of philosophy that it has determined what is really at issue in the quarrel in the streets, that is, the criteria. Further, in this century they have made an important advance. They have come to realize that what they thought was the problem of how the mind is related to the world is rather a problem of whether sentences can be interpreted to yield knowledge of something outside those sentences. But I submit that those philosophers with whose writings I am acquainted, and they are not nearly so many as they should be, have yet to realize that their effort is normative. That is, the various solutions to the problem of the theory of knowledge are properly put not in the form, "Knowledge is x," but "One ought to assert that knowledge is *x*." From the point of view of the perfectly respectable effort to understand human behavior, the problems of epistemology and of philosophy in general are not sacrosanct, something no one but a philosopher has a right to examine, but rather are best understood as subsumed under the general category of social management. To put it another way, philosophy, in spite of the claims of linguistic philosophers, is not something that can explain language. On the contrary an adequate theory of language provides an explanation for philosophy, which is, after all, a mode of linguistic behavior manifest in a wide variety of rhetorics. Or, to be a bit less dogmatic, a theory of language is in as good a position to explain philosophy as is philosophy in its efforts to explain language. The relative claims of philosophy and language to explain each other cannot be resolved, but exist in a condition of contradiction with each other which cannot be resolved, and which we must live with.

In view, then, of the instability of criteria for knowledge-yielding utterances, and in view of the normative and dependent character of the epistemological enterprise of philosophy, the question is not, "What are the criteria for discriminating knowledge-yielding utterances?" but rather, "What are the kinds of utterances for which such criteria are sought?" It is perfectly apparent that in ordinary verbal behavior such criteria are constantly being sought for all kinds of utterances, no matter how we classify them. Thus it is not a question of whether literature sometimes is knowledge-yielding, or never knowledge-yielding, or always knowledge-yielding. Literary utterances are like all utterances. They are always subject to being questioned as to whether or not they are knowledge-yielding. On the other hand, it is not true that all utterances, literary or otherwise, are invariably challenged upon utterance, or upon being encountered in written or printed form, on their knowledge-yielding properties. Any utterance can be so challenged at any time, but it is equally clear that that is what does not happen. Clearly, there are somehow stabilizations of criteria. What needs to be explained is what is going on when particular utterances or classes of utterances are either stabilized as knowledge-yielding or are challenged. What is the character of the verbal behavior involved?

I have already suggested that the proper form of the question "Is this utterance knowledge-yielding?" is "Is the interpretation of this sentence knowledge-yielding?" Put in this way the same problem that emerged for criteria emerges here. That is, are interpretations stable? Clearly the answer is that they are not. For example, the history of philosophy is filled with varying interpretations of the utterance "philosophy," each claiming to be knowledge-yielding. And, of course, the history of discourse purporting to be about literature is marked by the same instability in the interpretation of that term. Assuming that stable interpretations are desirable—and that is always the assumption in both philosophy and criticism—it does not seem probable or even possible to achieve stability without some insight into why instability in these terms is, so far at least, the norm.

Claims as to the knowledge-yielding character of interpretations of utterances are inseparable from claims about the interpretation of the word "meaning"—claims that, in recent decades at least, invariably, judging by my experience, are involved with the word "refer." If it is asserted that the utterance refers to something outside not only of itself but of language, it is said to have meaning. This neglects, I think, two important points. It neglects the fact that it is not the utterance that refers but, if anything, the interpretation of the utterance that does that referring. Likewise it neglects the extremely dubious status of the word "refer." It does not seem to me that a word or a proposition or any utterance can refer. Referring is something that human beings do, as the formulation "the interpretation of the utterance" suggests. "Refer" is a term that categorizes those behavioral acts in which, in this situation, an utterance is a stimulus to which a human being responds by locating a configuration outside of that utterance, whether it be another utterance or an extralinguistic configuration. And of course such referring behavior is as unstable as are criteria and meaning. In short the neglect in such a sentence as "The sentence refers to x" of a sceptical attitude towards "refer" and "interpretation" is the result of assuming that meaning is immanent, when meaning is rather a matter of response. But further it must not be permitted that the formulation, "locating a configuration outside of that utterance, whether linguistic or extralinguistic," go unchallenged. This located configuration is not necessarily the configuration or a member of the category of configurations to which the utterance has directed the individual to refer. Here again instability reappears. Hence, a fuller formulation for "The utterance is knowledge-yielding" is "The utterance is a stimulus to which an individual responds by interpreting it as a directive to locate outside of the utterance a linguistic or extralinguistic configuration which he interprets as the configuration or member of a category of configurations the interpretation directed him to locate."

But this formulation is not yet complete, for the presenter of the hopefully "knowledge-yielding utterance" has not yet been taken into account. He appears at the beginning of the process, of course, but he also reappears at the end, for the only way the responder can know that his location is correct is the concurrence of the presenter that he has indeed located the configuration or a member of a category of configurations the presenter's utterance directed him to. But can "know" here mean anything more than "have some assurance that"? I think not. Moreover, since the presenter can also evince instability in his assurance that what was directed to be located has indeed been located, it must be recognized that the preceding formulation must have added to it "The presenter concurs that the responder has indeed located the configuration or a member of a category of configurations which the presenter *also* interprets as that which the presenter's utterance directed the responder to locate." This instability in the presenter's interpretation and concurrence is of great importance, because it makes it possible, in the absence of the presenter, to experience the assurance of conditional knowledge: that is, the responder can say, "If the presenter were here, his interpretation of the utterance and his interpretation of the located something would concur with mine." Further assurance may be obtained subsequently by displaying the something to the original presenter, but it must not be forgotten that here also the presenter interprets that something. It may also be added that, if the presenter and the responder are one and the same individual, the character of the sequence does not change an iota.

Of any utterance, therefore, the assertion may be made that it is or is not knowledge-yielding; any set of criteria may be adduced to adjudicate the assertion; if the assertion offers "reference" as a criterion, the testing of reference involves a multistaged behavioral sequence, each stage of which is marked by instability. Thus nonnormative efforts to determine whether or not an utterance is knowledge-yielding, or to decide what knowledge derived from utterances really is, or to fix the meaning of "meaning" and "refer" are bound to be abortive; such efforts are necessarily normative.

Further, I think it is possible to provide an explanation why this should be so. Either an utterance determines the response to it, or it does not. It seems to me that the merest glance at verbal behavior indicates that it does not. In other words, as I have already suggested, meaning is not immanent. If it is not, then any utterance can in theory elicit all possible responses; and likewise, all possible utterances can in theory elicit but one response. It is equally obvious that neither of these is in fact the case. There is something that limits responses and channels them through time. If it is the case that an utterance determines the response to it, the explanation must be that the response is genetically transmitted—or at least that appears to be the only explanation currently available. If such is not the case, then the explanation must be that the response is culturally transmitted. That is, it is a matter of convention. The limitation of responses to utterances is carried out by a wide variety of constraints. One such constraint is the use of such terms as "know" or "knowledge." To paraphase slightly the formulation of Dr. Robert Combs of George Washington University (in his 1971 dissertation at the University of South Carolina, "Hart Crane and the Psychology of Romanticism," p. 18), the term "knowledge," is one mode of limiting response. To put this in a kind of shorthand, an utterance does not determine response; it issues directions for behavior; and this formulation is adequate so long as we remember all the factors responsible both for the stability and the instability of that behavior. Thus when we assert that an utterance yields knowledge, we are engaged in the process of limiting or conventionalizing response. But the situation is even worse than this. If it is true that, when the responder in carrying out his response locates an extralinguistic something, he interprets that something as ful-filling the directions of the utterance, then the extralinguistic world is also subject to interpretation and involves the herme-neutical problem. Bluntly, the extralinguistic world does not con-sist of objects which determine response, but of signs which elicit response exactly in the manner that utterances elicit re-sponse. The meaning of any nonverbal configuration, as well as of verbal configurations, is once again the response, with all that that statement entails. Thus our response to the world is as much a matter of convention as our response to utterances.

From this position, I think, it is possible to amplify the notions of the three kinds of knowledge I have already suggested, that is, the three modes of limiting the channeling response by using such terms as "know" and "knowledge" and "truth" and "em-pirical," and so on. The three kinds of knowledge are propo-sitional, behavioral, and reorientational.

Propositional knowledge, of course, consists of propositions which we validated with the word "knowledge" or with other members of its family. As we have seen, any utterance which is claimed or judged to be a response to a literary work can be called knowledge, if we so choose. However, in practice I believe it to be the case that ordinarily the term is used for repetition and interpretation. One is tempted to add to this "description"; but descriptive propositions themselves involve interpretation. "In this play Macbeth kills Duncan" would no doubt be accepted by most readers as a correct description, but it is possible so to interpret the language of the play that the reader concludes that Macbeth becomes insane before the murder and that there-fore it is uncertain who the murderer is, or that Duncan commits suicide and that Macbeth is thrown into such turmoil by the sight that his disordered imagination accuses himself of the guilt. Since the interpretation of *Macbeth* is by now highly stable, it would be difficult to get anyone to agree, but I certainly have read statements that purport to be descriptive statements in response to literary works, but are considerably wilder, in my judgment, than these. A repetitive proposition, then, repeats exactly the words of a work or some sequence of those words. All else is in-terpretation. Interpretation proceeds by subsuming selected sentences or bits of sentences or sequences of sentences under a more general proposition, or universal. Thus the universal may properly, I think, be said to explain the sentences in the work, and those sentences may be said to exemplify the universal. This is the position of Sir Philip Sidney in claiming higher truth for poetry than for history. Further, it is possible to interpret—that is, to explain —sets of sentences (or fragments or sequences) by a series of universals, which in turn are subsumed under a smaller series, and so on in a regress of explanation to a single proposition. This, I suspect, is the structure of much interpretational discourse. For such interpretation the honorific and normative term "knowledge" is often claimed to be the proper term. That is, we say that an individual possesses a knowledge of the work if he is able to offer a convincing interpretation, and we say that such an interpretation gives us such knowledge. To be sure, a work of literature can and often does include within it such explanatory propositions. If we accept them, we say that the author exhibits knowledge of his material. Likewise, interpretational construction is often claimed to be evidence of the same sort, knowledge on the part of the author.

There is yet another occasion for using the term "knowledge." The explanatory universals having been formulated, an effort is made to locate outside of the work sentences which have already been accepted as knowledge-yielding. Thus, certain sentences in Dickens—a great many of them, in fact—are explained as possibly exemplifying general propositions about the condition of the poor in nineteenth-century England. In Mayhew or in Parliamentary Blue Books, other sentences are located which are judged to be knowledge-yielding sentences exemplifying general propositions about the condition of the poor. In such a situation the tendency is very strong to validate the works of Dickens by asserting that they yield us knowledge of the conditions of the poor in nineteenth-century England.

A different mode of this kind of occasion for using the term "knowledge" is to subsume selected sentences under general propositions of a psychological character. We then seek sentences which can be subsumed under such propositions in discourses which we have judged to be knowledge-yielding about the life of the author; on these grounds we assert that the literary work can yield us knowledge of the author.

A different kind of occasion for using the term "knowledge" appears when the responder generates utterances of the same sort as the utterances to be found in the work, or some selection of such utterances, without initially generating an interpretational universal. We can accept these ourselves with or without generating such a universal. This is the normal way of claiming knowledge-yielding properties for a work in practice resistant to interpretation.

These, I believe, exhaust the occasions on which we use the term "knowledge" in validating a response as something which ought to be maintained, that is, conventionally channeled. And I believe this statement to be correct because these are the three verbal occasions, aside from repetition, in which we apply the term "knowledge," no matter what the character of the utterance, literary or not.

As for behavioral knowledge, it would appear that literature is not only the source of behavioral knowledge, with the proviso that such knowledge entails interpretation and convention, but even that it is the most important kind of knowledge that literature can be said to yield. When Dr. Johnson asserted something to the effect that no one would fall in love were it not for amorous romances, he was getting at this aspect of literature. Thus literature is not only an occasion for uttering propositions to which the normative term "knowledge" is applied, it is also a means for limiting and channeling behavior, that is, for transmitting behavioral knowledge. If, however, this proposition is acceptable, the definition of literature must include obscene limericks as well as *Hamlet*, improvised literature in a workingman's bar as well as *Paradise Lost*. That is, literature cannot be an honorific term limited to a particular category of discourse validated in that subculture we call high culture. The definition of literature must be formal. I would propose that a work tends to be judged as literature if the discourse in question exhibits a sufficiently greater concentration of focusing or overdetermination of the universal linguistic features of the language in question. (This is a necessary, but not a sufficient, condition: a sufficient condition adds the attribute of discontinuity within the sequence of each kind or instance of overdetermination. However, the term "literature" can be applied—and often is—in response merely to linguistic overdetermination.) That is, the overdetermination is enough to rise above the normal horizon of some observers' linguistic expectancy. It goes without saying that the presenter of the work of literature channels his overdetermination according to the conventions of the tradition in which he is performing, but it is equally obvious that he can innovate conventions by overdetermining linguistic features in a new manner or by overdetermining features not previously conventionalized. A formal definition of literature makes it possible to separate literature as a definable and observable mode of discourse from both the propositional knowledge it yields and the behavioral knowledge it transmits. Furthermore, just as propositional knowledge of literature can be innovated—that is, can present "new knowledge"—so literature can innovate behavioral patterns, or can invert a validated behavioral pattern. But this is true of literature only because it is true of all behavior. Indeed, the human brain appears to be so constituted that all behavior is at least minimally innovative. The term "creative" is applied to behavior if it is sufficiently innovative to be noticeable and if the response to it is validational. Thus, to understand literature properly as a source of behavioral knowledge, it must not only be given a formal definition; it must also be separated from the term "creative." That is, a work of literature can be properly called literature whether or not it yields innovative behavioral knowledge. Moreover, it would appear that a formal definition of literature illuminates further its function as yielding behavioral knowledge (whether already validated or innovative), that is, as presenting behavioral knowledge as a candidate for validation, and therefore for channeling. The concentration or focusing or overdetermination of linguistic behavior is a kind of italicizing, a sign of importance, of something that ought to be paid attention to. Thus the formal character is a normative use of language, in that it is part of the behavior-channeling process. If this is indeed the case, we would have an explanation for the fact that a culture tends to present in literature what is particularly important to it, especially its crucial behavioral knowledge; that innovative behavioral knowledge tends to be presented in literary modes; that literature is so commonly, across many cultures, granted the status of the sacred; and that the aura of the sacred envelopes the poet, the presenter of that literary mode more characterized by overdetermination than any other.

Finally, there remains reorientational knowledge. This could be conceived as a special case of innovative behavioral knowledge, but by that I mean innovative for the culture, although to be sure the innovation is presented by an individual and is also overt, phenomenally observable innovation. Reorientational knowledge is innovative for the individual, though it may be recurrent, i.e., channeled, within the individual's culture or subculture or literary tradition within that subculture. The term "orientation" may be justly determined, I think, as proposing a metaphorical explanation for the phenomenon of selective and patterned (i.e., recurrent) perception and cognition or, perhaps preferably, interpretation. One must be careful not to hypostatize the term, as in, "The orientation controls the perception," which would be an error. The term opens the way, as it were, to proposing explanations of the character of particular perceptual-cognitive selections and patterns within an individual or common to more than one individual, and to explanations as to why such orientations are as they are and not otherwise. Orientation, however, is a static term; orientations—remembering always the term is an explanatory metaphor—are unstable. The individual is actually, to the degree that he is mentally sound, in a continuous process of reorientation. A reorientation is "a new knowledge of reality" for the individual, though Stevens' phrase, of course, could just as well be applied to the culture. As an instance of reorientation induced by language, consider Ruskin's discussions of clouds (or indeed of any natural phenomenon) in *Modern Painters*. In my experience, most people, after reading that passage, assert that they have never really *seen* a cloud before. Or, once a student—after one-third of a course in poetic analysis—said to me with tears in her eyes that she had never really read a poem before. The use of the term "really," so often encountered in utterances in response to a reorientational experience, indicates that what is asserted to be a knowledge event has occurred; the use of the word "knowledge" is the validation of the reorientational event—usually followed by limitation and channeling.

There appear to be several reasons why literature should be particularly amenable to the reorientational process. The concentration or overdetermination of linguistic features increases the probability of perceiving those features in ordinary linguistic behavior and also of making an overdetermined use of them in non-literary utterances, that is, utterances which, for whatever reason, we are willing to call rhetoric but not to call literature. If we wish to preserve the traditional distinction between rhetoric as directions for immediate or at least shortly ensuing action and literature as not giving directions for action—a distinction derived from the social consequences of rhetoric and literature but not from their formal character—then literature can be said to improve the individual's rhetorical performances. Further, the overdetermination requires a more rapid reorientation to linguistic features, a rate increased by the cognitive-perceptual linear discontinuity of literature, that is, of those features. Moreover, literature as distinct from rhetoric, probably in part because of its sacred aura, can be morally irresponsible; it can negate or offer alternatives to validated modes of limiting and channeling behavior. This possibility is further strengthened if a formal definition is accepted. That is, the kind of behavior literature subjects to reorientation or channeling—including the behavior responsible for the concentration of linguistic features—is not limited by any but culturally local constraints. This provides an explanation for the constant instability of such constraints, whether they are internal to literary criticism or external to it. To be sure, all constraints to behavior are more or less local and temporary (though in "temporary" I include a constraint that lasts for millennia), but the frequency of disagreement and conflict over what constraints should or should not control literary behavior, the striking instability of literary constraints, suggests that more than any other mode of verbal behavior literature offers occasions for reorientational knowledge.

I have proposed that the term "knowledge" is a normative term which can justly be linked to the term "literature" if we use the phrases "propositional knowledge," "behavioral knowledge," and "reorientational knowledge." Further, I have suggested that these modes of using the word "knowledge" are appropriate to literature simply because they are extraliterary and extralinguistic as well; literature presents no peculiar mode of knowledge. On the other hand, I have also proposed that literature is better suited for the presentation of cultural innovations to be called knowledge than any other kind of verbal behavior, and this is even more true for the presentation of occasions for reorientational knowledge. At the moment, at any rate, I think that these three modes of using the term "knowledge" subsume and exhaust all other modes. But this means, of course, that I cannot think of any more.

III BEHAVIOR, EDUCATION, AND SOCIETY

14

THE VIRTUES

OF SUPERFICIALITY

[1969*]

Some fifteen years ago I started to use the word "orientation" pretty much as most people use it—vaguely, indefinitely, and with the assumption that there is something in the mind that corresponds to the word. It was certainly naïve of me to think that for any word there is something that corresponds to it, but after all such is the belief not only of almost everybody in the world but even of a great many philosophers and linguists, even today. In a book published nearly a decade ago, *Beyond the Tragic Vision*, I wrote: "In any situation in which our senses give our minds messages about the world, two elements are present. On the one hand is the real world, the public world, which we all agree is there: the mountain, the tree, the table, the contents of the test tube, the pointer on the measuring scale. On the other is the pattern in the mind, the Gestalt, the neural path, the orientation, with which we organize these public data." Now there is

* Reprinted by permission from *TriQuarterly*, no. 20 (Winter 1971), pp. 180–93. Copyright © 1971 by Northwestern University Press.

nothing terribly objectionable in this; it is perhaps somewhat less dangerous than Platonism, and far less so than neo-Platonism, which can be useful if one knows how; but it is also clear that such terms belong to the Platonic tradition, and that they are filled with all the traps that that tradition sets for the unwary. The passage is full of words which can scarcely support any serious examination: "situation," "senses," "minds," "messages," "world," "mind," "Gestalt," "neural path." To be sure, such words as these are rarely given any serious examination; indeed, there is a silent conspiracy in the intellectual world that we should all agree that they do mean something or other and that we should not inquire too curiously exactly what. It is to my credit, I think, that I added that I used "orientation" because it "is the most general and least demanding word we can use." At least I knew that there was something seriously questionable and dubious about the term, something that made me uneasy and that should have made me uneasy. My defense is that at least I knew it, and that innumerable writers—some of them very serious philosophers and scientists—use it without a trace of nervousness. Still, I sinned; and even though my sin was only the necessary consequence of Original Sin, it is right, I think, that I should do public penance. Now, I think, I can be a little more demanding.

Certainly, "orientation" is a term filled with difficulties. It seems to be a mentalistic hypostatization, and as ordinarily used it is. It is like such terms as "will," "motivation," "expectation," "intention," and, of course, "mind" itself, all of which are sources of imprecision and confusion. That all these terms are useful is undeniable, and perhaps that is all that we can ask of any term. However, they are exceedingly brittle. When one attempts to use them in any careful analysis, they tend to break in situations of any intellectual stress. Moreover, as such a term, "orientation" tends to be somewhat defenseless. If one uses it, any opponent of one's position can say, "Well, what, after all, is an orientation?" It is very hard to think of an answer. Definitions, to be sure, are easy enough, like all definitions, but the attempt to locate an orientation in the phenomenal world is frustrating.

Anyone with a behavioristic orientation, of course, has no trouble in pointing out that mentalistic terms, beginning with "mind," are empty of content, and it is easy for him to embarrass the user of "orientation." However, it is equally easy to embarrass the behaviorist. One has but to ask, "Now tell me, what really *is* a stimulus? What really *is* a response?" and he is just as helpless as the orientationist. It is enough to point out that the behaviorist's efforts to isolate a stimulus in the perceptually sterile environment of the laboratory are in vain; the very sterility affects the response to the supposedly isolated stimulus. Above all, the psychic insulation of the laboratory, its reduction of the perceptually irrelevant to as close to zero as possible, alters drastically the perceptual activity, since the normal filtering and selective and reductive attribute of perceptual activity is correspondingly reduced. The revealing thing about such experimentation is that it can be made useful only by statistical analysis. It is probably a mistake to pay much attention to averages, means, and norms. Deviancy from those norms is the significant factor. The range of response, not the fact that a set of numbers can be mathematically manipulated, is the striking phenomenon.

The difficulty of the stringent behaviorist seems to lie in his assumption that somehow or other the response is immanent in the stimulus, that there is a necessary connection between stimulus and response. If he did not assume this, the phenomenon of mathematically arrived at statistical averages could not acquire for him the importance that my reading of psychological literature certainly seems to indicate. The truly significant matter for psychological theory (as opposed to practical consequences, for which statistical probabilities are admittedly of the highest imaginable importance) as well as for philosophical and semiotic theory, is precisely that, faced with the identical configuration, biologically similar organisms—including that very special and deviant breed, the laboratory rat—show a *range* of responses.

The notion that the response is immanent in the stimulus is identical with the notion that terms "have" meaning—that the meaning of a sentence, for instance, is "in" the sentence, and that our job is to extract it "from" the sentence—and with the notion that it is useful to ask, "What does the term really mean?" The fact of the matter is that it is not even useful to ask, "To what does the term refer?" Human beings, and apparently some animals, "mean"; it is they who "refer"—not terms, not sentences, not words, not signs of any kind. The behaviorist—for whom, indeed, I have for many reasons the profoundest respect, and in whose activities I take the greatest possible interest—is in the position of Hegel when he said that every proposition implies its negation. This seems like a very profound notion, and even those philosophers, almost all of them, who have repudiated Hegel and the Hegelian tradition still proceed in very much the same way. Aside from the fact that it is probably impossible for human beings to say anything profound, and that all we can hope to do is to utter the superficial with the utmost lucidity, all that Hegel is saying is that it is possible to say yes or no to any proposition; and his great insight into history amounts to the notion that, as situations change, some individuals find it irresistible to say no to propositions to which anything but yes had been unimaginable.

The notion that a stimulus dictates its response and the notion that a term (or a sentence) dictates its interpretation are, then, identical. Whether he knows it or not, or likes it or not, the behaviorist is studying meaning behavior, and insofar as he thinks that the mean, or average, or any other statistically arrived at number is more important than the range of the meaning behaviors he has isolated, to that extent he accepts an immanent theory of meaning, and to that extent he operates on a magical theory of semiotic behavior. He is no better off than the sorceress who bestows an enemy's name on a wax image and then melts the wax image in the fire. If she lets the enemy know what she has done, of course, and if he shares her stimulus-response theory, the chances that her activity will produce the desired result, the death of her enemy, are statistically significant. Human beings are really very obliging and cooperative in such matters. But there is also, to be sure, the chance that the sorceress' enemy, no matter how well-informed about her activities, will not cooperate. Like the behaviorist, she must proceed pragmatically on a statistical basis, and she must await the outcome of her acts. Her enemy's orientation may be such that he can employ a countermagic, or that he has sufficiently transcended their common culture to be no more than amused by her efforts. This gives us one semantic function for "orientation." We use the word when we wish to

draw attention to the fact that a range of responses is possible to
a configuration we have identified as a stimulus in a given situation. Even though we may be mistaken in identifying that
stimulus, our mistake is of little importance for the successful
use of the term "orientation." At this point, all that it has to do
is to serve us in raising the possibility, or pointing to the fact,
of a responsive range.

This may be clarified by examining a fine old philosophical
notion: that the essence of a tree is its treeness. For some centuries this sort of thing has seemed quite pointless and has often
been cited as an instance of metaphysical absurdity. Yet by rein-
terpreting it, it can be made quite useful. One need have no
qualms in such matters. As Hegel abundantly proved, the history
of philosophy is the history of drastic and shameless innovative
interpretations of ancient propositions. The statement that the
essence of a tree is its treeness can be interpreted as a statement
that what makes a tree a tree is its attributes, or better, that what
makes a configuration identifiable as a tree is its attributes. However, the difficulty is that, in the ascription of those attributes,
there is no inherent stability. A lumberman, a botanist, and a
landscape painter ascribe partly or entirely different sets of attributes to a tree. The ascription of the defining attribute "treeness"
to a tree can best be seen as a strategy for resolving this problem.
It is a recognition of attributional variability, an assertion that
surely, after this variability is removed from the situation, something must be left. There must surely be something immanent in
the tree, something that continues, something that is constant,
some defining attribute free from attributional variability. That
there should not be is apparently intolerable to human beings,
is apparently so disorienting that any kind of action, including
verbal action, becomes impossible. That is, if the tree has no
attributes, we do not know how to respond to it. Or, better, if
we are unable to ascribe attributes, we cannot respond. Consequently we cannot behave in a way which either we or anyone
else would or could recognize as tree-responding behavior. This
does two things for us: it reveals that responses, and hence the
ascription of attributes, are matters of cultural convention, and it
suggests that conventions can be innovated. Thus a defining at-

tribute is left over, after all, and it does make the essence of a tree its treeiness. As stimulus, that defining attribute is the tree's emergence from its perceptual ground as a configuration, and as response, the defining attribute of a tree is simply that there is a response to it. Obviously such defining attributes are worthless, since they do not distinguish a tree as stimulus-cum-response from anything else as stimulus-cum-response. To define the essence of a tree as its treeiness, then, can once again be seen as a desperate strategy to establish theoretically the stability of attribution, which can be done only by draining from either a configuration or its corresponding term all attributional variations— that is, unhappily, all attributes.

To say that the essence of a thing is its thinginess, then, is merely to say that it is possible to respond to it, without indicating what kind of response is necessary. As such, it is a very valuable proposition, for it permits us to raise the term "orientation" from the mere level of using it to point to the fact of a responsive range to the level of using it to point to the fact that responses to a configuration can be seen as falling into families, or sets, or categories of responses, according to the attributes we ascribe to such responses—just as a tree is defined as good for lumber, or for botanical study, or for landscape painting, according to the attributes ascribed. "Orientation" is a term used to categorize sets of behaviors which we cognize as sufficiently alike to be grouped together, "to cognize" meaning "to ascribe attributes to." When we assert that a man has such-and-such an orientation, we are calling attention to the plausibility of perceiving his behavior in a given situation as being similar to his behavior in other instances of what we cognize as the same kind of situation—to the plausibility of cognizing his behaviors as similar in what we cognize as different kinds of situations. The individual who responds in precisely the same way, no matter what the situation, we call an extreme psychotic of a particular type. Whatever happens, it "means" the same thing to him; that is, he has only one mode of responsive behavior, no matter what happens. To call attention to this we say that he "has" an absolutely fixed orientation.

"Orientation," then, turns out to be not quite such a mentalistic term as our triumphant behaviorist suggested. Or if it is purely mentalistic, it is so because all terms—including terms like "tree" and proper names—are equally mentalistic, since responsive behavior is not possible without the ascription of attributes. This suggests that we have here an explanation for philosophical idealism, built on the observation that response to the identical stimulus is characterized by a range of responses—as Socrates delighted in pointing out. It follows, he claimed, that we must be capable of responding to a configurational stimulus by ascribing attributes to it *before* we encounter that particular stimulus. All philosophical idealism amounts to, ultimately, is that, at least for human beings and for some animals, stimulus is not ineluctably linked to response, does not dictate response; or, to put it another way, meaning is not immanent, neither the meanings of the configurations of the nonverbal world nor of the verbal. The foundation of idealism is an observation that everyone makes. But in spite of this a priori "knowledge," —this advance preparation for ascribing attributes—whatever its source, we find our way around in the world reasonably well. So, says the empiricist, we do know that "things" really "are." And all *his* position amounts to is that the ascription of attributes has predictive value. It is not necessary to sweat over a choice between idealism and empiricism. Both are perfectly acceptable and quite useful, but more useful if both are simultaneously held and are seen as based on common, everyday observation. This position has, if no other merit, at least that of meeting the criterion of superficiality.

Now, to incorporate the notion of responsive variability with the notion of orientation, or discriminable families of responses, it is useful to use the term "sign." In this sense, a sign is a configuration for which different families of responses are observable or possible, that is, constructible. But that, of course, means all configurations. Hence, insofar as a configuration is a configuration—that is, discriminable from its ground—it is a sign, even though the perceiver of that sign may be unable to respond because he cannot ascribe to it any attributes. If he feels an impulse to respond, but cannot, the configuration is nevertheless a sign. The only immanent meaning in any stimulus is that it is a stimulus because there are responses to it—not a very helpful solution, but of some use. For example, some children, before they can speak, practice sentences by uttering nonsense syllables with all the pitch and stress variation and even in the phonemic formula of the linguistic environment, of "meaningful" sentences. One feels an urge to respond, but one is entirely at a loss as to what to say. But the crisis is easily met. The child's "orientation" is an interest in practicing sentence-sounds in nonsense syllables, and the "need" his "orientation" grants him is the need to elicit a similar response. One can say anything or merely imitate the child's nonsense speech to satisfy the needs of his orientation.

From the position that we use the word "sign" to call attention to the fact that a configuration is capable of eliciting a responsive range—or families of responsive behavior, including verbal behavior—certain other terms can be clarified, a possibility which will help to give a little more content to the term "orientation." The difference between a sign and a signal is that the response to the latter is ineluctable. But for human beings and for some animals there are no such signs, except reflex responses. It is often enough asserted that the signs of logic are ineluctable and that the meaning of a logical sign is immanent in that sign. In that event they would be signals. But I see nothing in the history of logic to make me think this must be so, all the passionate asseverations of logicians to the contrary. Rather, we use the term "signal" in situations in which our orientation elicits a need to exclude even the consideration that all possible responses except one could be appropriate. "Signal," therefore, is most appropriately used in military sign terminology, for a military operation depends upon rapid and undeviating responses. We use "signal" to indicate that it is appropriate to refuse the possibility of any response but one or, at its most liberal, but one family of response. We use "sign," then, in situations in which we recognize that differing families of response are possible but only one family is appropriate. We use "symbol" in situations in which we recognize the appropriateness of employing two or more families. And we use "irony" in situations in which we exploit that possibility of the appropriateness of several response families but wish to assert that at least one is in fact inappropriate to the situation.

These are stimulus terms. Since "signal," "symbol," and "irony" are terms more limited than is "sign," it seems reasonable to use "sign" as the general term and the other three as subclasses of "sign." Signs, then, are stimulus terms, and the corresponding response term is "orientation." This formulation gives a little more content to "orientation," but it is still somewhat too mentalistic, though certainly, I think, less so than it was at the beginning of this discussion. Sign and orientation are inseparable, for a sign requires an orientation to be responded to, while an orientation requires a sign to be elicited. As the Hegelians would have said, the actual is the union of essence and existence. Thus, though orientation is now more out into the open, it still has something of mentalism about it. We have got "sign" to the phenomenal point, but "orientation" still falls short of that. It is desirable, to please the behaviorist, to reduce that mentalistic aura to the minimum.

The trouble, as with so many words, particularly those of a mentalistic character, is that "orientation" is used for a number of different semantic functions. Reasonably respectable is the function already suggested: to categorize sequences of behavior into sets or families. But second, in such a sentence as, "A sign requires an orientation to be responded to, while an orientation requires a sign to be elicited," there is certainly the usage by which an orientation is that mental phenomenon responsible for a given behavior. Between the stimulus and the response, the suggestion is, is an orientation, since orientations account for responsive variability. Third, and similar—but out in the open and observable—are sets of signs, verbal and nonverbal, which are said to be orientations responsible for such variability. It is these last two semantic functions which appear to be badly confused, one with the other.

The source of this confusion can be traced to the confusion in such terms as "mind" and "thought," which apparently are most generally assumed to subsume "orientation." This confusion can be straightened out by making the observation, which meets the criterion of superficiality, that both "mind" and "thought," as generally used, confuse two quite different sets of behavior, one observable and one not; that is, the latter is a verbal construct.

One set consists of covert verbal behavior, or other covert semiotic behavior, as in dreams, visions, daydreams, and imaginings, in the old-fashioned sense. The other set consists of what we suppose must happen between stimulus and response that accounts for responsive variability. The distinction is usually made by the terms "conscious mind" and "unconscious mind" or "conscious and unconscious thought." But if we make the distinction between covert semiotic behavior and mental behavior, then it is apparent that "the mind," whatever it is, is entirely unconscious and entirely inaccessible, or very nearly so, in the sense that we cannot say anything about its content, as we can of covert semiotic behavior, but only of its functioning, and then probably only metaphorically, at least for the most part. If we restrict "mind" to what happens between stimulus and response, since covert semiotic behavior is itself quite obviously a response and not something subsequent to stimulus and anterior to response, then it seems clear enough that "orientation" in this semantic function is not to be subsumed by "mind" but is another word by which we ascribe different attributes to the same presumed phenomena to which our use of "mind" ascribes attributes. "Mind," "thought," and "orientation" are all on the same level, though each has somewhat different semantic functions.

Each of these words, thus restricted, is the same bridge by which we cross the abyss of ignorance that lies between stimulus and response. Nevertheless, the vague outlines of some of the primeval monsters busy in those depths can, I think, be discerned. (Could they be called, by a wilder metaphor, instinctual computers?) For one thing, the way they busy themselves running the machinery of perception can be talked about a little, however crudely and superficially. Briefly, experimental psychology shows us that perception in establishing a configuration as a configuration selects, simplifies, reduces, and organizes. Cognition, made possible by perception, ascribes attributes to configuration, though this notion is dimmer than one would like. At any rate we know that we can alter behavior by ascribing different attributes to configurations and sets of configurations. This is done by controlling behavior through further sets of signs. We can, so to speak, introduce into an individual an a priori novel to him, and so alter his behavior. Like a stage manager, we can alter the scene by changing the lighting. Such manipulation is commonly called —and quite properly, I think—reorientation. Thus our mysterious primeval manipulators from within so arrange matters that the perceptual-cognitive process is categorial. Every sign is a sign of a category of configurations, not of an individual configuration. And that is why we can't say what an orientation, or a stimulus, or a response really is, or locate one in the phenomenal world. We can only locate members of a priori categories. Once again, the actual is the union of the essence and the existence. (It must not be forgotten that just as we can alter the behavior of others by ascribing different attributes to a category of configurations, so we can alter our own behavior by picking up perceptually attributes which the category, to speak mythically, had not led us to anticipate. But the process in both cases is identical.) Next, two configurations are cognized as either sharing or not sharing whatever attributes we are currently looking for, that is, are interested in ascribing. The analogy between structured and cognized configurations is the only way, it would appear, that mental activity can proceed beyond perception and cognition. Finally, all it can do with that extension of its functions is to predict.

Scandalous—but, happily, superficial—as this position may be, it is all, I suspect, that at the moment can be said about mental activity in the sense of what happens between stimulus and response. Since it has been said in one way or another for some thousands of years, by the neo-Platonists, among many others, it is perhaps all that ever can be said.

The actual is the fusion of essence and existence—or, in other, rather more satisfactory words, for human beings the world consists of categorial signs. There remains, if possible, to illuminate the notion of orientation in its third sense, that of a set or family of signs, including verbal signs. At the most primitive level of analysis, signs function by coordinating the behavior of human organisms, and at the next level, by controlling the behavior of those who have been prepared beforehand to be controlled. That preparation beforehand is what we call education, and the study of it is called learning theory. At the next level it can be said that signs function by giving sets of directions for behavioral performance. It is hardly necessary to proceed beyond this level, and even here what happens is so complicated that it can be understood only in the grossest way, though statistics and computers give us some hope of better comprehension. However, it is possible to say something about signs themselves and how sign-functions may be categorized. Signs and sign constellations and sequences can be seen as falling along a continuum from such statements at one end as "The ultimate nature of reality is the Absolute" to, at the other end, existent trees and rocks and people. Along this continuum two articulations can be observed with some ease. The first is the distinction between signs which are cognized as members of the categories of which they are signs, and those signs which are not. If a tree is cognized as a categorial sign, the members of which are other trees, then it is the former. If it is cognized as a sign of a god, or of a compass direction, then it is the latter. Within the category of signs which are not members of the categories of which they are signs a further categorial articulation may be made between verbal and nonverbal signs. Thus there can be proposed three categories of signs. The first— i.e., signs which are members of their own categories—may be called immediate signs, while those which are not members of their own categories are mediating signs, of which there are two sorts, nonverbal and verbal.

Since we cannot begin at the beginning of any learning process, once we have passed the point in infantile development at which categorization (or cognition) begins, whatever that point may be, orientative behavior is best understood as reorientative behavior. The study of orientation is necessarily the study of reorientation. The historical continuum of orientative behavior, whether for an individual or for a culture, must always begin at a point on an historically constructed continuum. That is the problem Hegel, who may be called the first great student of verbal reorientative behavior, was wrestling with. I suspect that he has never been equaled and that in his work there is still much of great value which has never been used. Be that as it may, it is also reasonably evident that reorientative behavior can take place along the ahistorically conceived continuum of sign-behavior at any point, from cognitions of the physical world to statements about the ultimate nature of reality, or even such entrancing statements as, "The nothing nothings the nothing," which can be made to yield fascinating propositions if treated with sufficiently drastic shamelessness. Such statements as those offered, or the statements of theoretical physics, can be rightly called explanatory statements. That is, only in verbal behavior, only in language, it is possible to generate explanations. The continuum of signs from the remotely mediating to the immediate manifests itself within the category of verbal mediating signs as a continuum from the explanatory to the exemplary, from explanation to exemplification. That is, verbal explanations do not explain the world; they only explain, by subsumption, exemplary sentences. Language cannot itself break out of the magic circle within which it functions, but it can prepare individuals beforehand for reorientative behavior in response to mediating nonverbal signs and immediate signs. Thus language can be seen as having its sole function in human behavior as reorientative activity. This can happen in myth, which is verbal behavior at the exemplary end of the continuum, which functions as explanation without explanatory sentences. This is why the mythology of any culture is in a constant state of flux. And it is why metaphysics, or ultimate explanation, which is verbal reorientative behavior at the explanatory end of the continuum, is likewise in a constant state of flux.

Mental reorientation, as defined above, is the process, the means, the form, if you will, of reorientative behavior, and signs are the consequence, the deposit, the content, perhaps, of such behavior. Metaphysical explanation is man's most powerful tool for stimulating the mental processing of signs, for preparing the organism beforehand, for implanting—to be old-fashioned—the novel a priori. Language does not constitute the world, nor describe it, nor predict it, nor does it have a direct instrumental relation to it. Rather it subjects man to a continuous, unremittant, reorientative massage. It is what enables him to survive, for his orientative activity is always inadequate to the demands of the existent. The actual is *only* the union of essence and existence; when the figure emerges from the ground, then error and illusion begin. Man's most magnificent, and most amusing, adaptation to this ineluctable state of affairs is his development of the power to generate explanations. As Swinburne put it, "Silence is most noble till the end." And Wittgenstein agreed.

Thus I would propose giving "orientation" a little more content than it currently seems to have. But after all, it is only an explanation, and the best explanation in the world is still only an explanation. This one, I hope, has at least the virtue of superficiality.

15

THE CORPORATION'S ROLE

IN TODAY'S CRISIS OF

CULTURAL INCOHERENCE

[1971*]

Of the major institutions involved in social management, one of the most recent and impressive is the great business corporation. In this instrument we see, whether we like it or not, one of the most astounding social inventions in human history. The modern corporation has inconceivable possibilities, but it has as yet scarcely realized what it is and what its potentialities are. Its dependence on profit as a measure of success has concealed from it what it is already doing—transcending the nation-state in the exhausting task and unrewarding responsibility of social management. And its potential for social management has been concealed from those *outside* the corporation by the social sins business has committed. These social sins scarcely need to be detailed. Business has done terrible things to people and to the environment. Yet it has produced real wealth and genuine human satisfactions on a scale no previous social institution has ever

* Reprinted from *Innovation*, no. 21 (1971), pp. 30–40. Copyright © 1971 by Technology Communication, Inc. Reprinted by permission of Executive VideoForum, Inc., New York, N.Y. 10017.

achieved, even remotely. Even though the corporation has so far been used for relatively trivial purposes, it has probably done less damage than two other institutions: governments and universities.

Universities on the whole are not as impressive in generating change as are corporations. It is reasonably clear that in the past one hundred and fifty years, the brains of America have gone—just as brains always go—where there is the greatest challenge and the greatest reward. In this country the area of challenge and reward—the challenge being by far the more important of the two—has been business. Yet the corporation has a kind of symbiotic relationship to the university, a relation that needs further exploration if we are to understand the potential of either for social change.

The weakness of both governments and universities is that they have a great many functions and a great many social tasks to perform. The result is that an enormous amount of the energy available to them is wasted in intrainstitutional struggles over how that energy should be used. Their strength is that they are extraordinary machines for gathering and processing information. What keeps the corporation from similar effectiveness in this area is its very efficiency.

The strength of the corporation arises from its single-mindedness of function, but its weakness also lies in that fact, for the information it gathers is preselected by its unitary function. Consequently, it is more than a little prone to neglect (or simply to fail to gather) information that does not fit its current conception of its function and its measurement of success. The corporation is like an individual of such fixed orientation toward experience that he cannot adapt his orientation to changing situations, which necessarily require a restructuring of his interests. Nor is this analogy inapt, since corporations are, after all, not entities but persistent patterns of human relations and interactions, like any social institution. The corporation is not an individual. Rather, it is a kind of mythical god which categorizes the attributes of its members, and facilitates the process of social management by which individual attributes are shaped, imposed, and discarded according to the judgments of individuals already shaped by the corporational institution. The corporation is not an entity; the word "corporation" is rhetoric, and rhetoric consists of those verbal and nonverbal signs by which social management is carried out.

"Government," of course, is a similar rhetorical term. When we say that the United States has decided to do something, what has really happened is that a few individuals (or perhaps only one) in a position of power have made a decision and have the power to effectuate it. The term "government" is one of the instruments of power, or control, or social management. Similarly, when it is said that U.S. Steel has decided to do something or other, it is an error to imagine that U.S. Steel has decided anything, for the simple reason that U.S. Steel does not exist. To be sure it is a legal entity, but legal entities themselves are part of the rhetoric by which society is manipulated.

As entities that act and cause, both governments and corporations are fictions. As persistent patterns of interaction the members of which share a common socially managing rhetoric, they are very real indeed, not fictional at all. Rhetoric is the instrument of social management, and the social role that carries with it command, decisional control, and manipulative control over rhetoric is the position of social power. Corporations and governments— and universities—have public relations departments and always have had them. For long periods in European history the principal role of the church was that of public relations officer for governments. The struggle between church and state in the Middle Ages was a struggle over the problem of whether rhetoric was the source of social power or its instrument. The subduing of the church settled the matter. Rhetoric is an instrument, not a source.

The corporation, which pays more attention (an increasing attention) to rhetoric than does government, and is certainly far better at it, is a kind of synthesis of government and church. The question now arising is an interesting one. There are already plenty of indications and have been for some time that the corporation is transcending the nation-state. The possibility appears that just as the state subdued the church, so the corporation is now subduing the nation-state, turning it into an ancillary or instrumental institution. There are certainly plenty of signs that the nation-state is already an outmoded institution, but attempts such as the League of Nations or the United Nations to transcend the nation-state have been unsuccessful, principally because the weakness of governments, the multiplicity of functions, is simply compounded. The result is not synthetic, but merely additive. It is interesting, however, that—insofar as the United Nations has been able to accomplish anything of value—it has done so, as with UNESCO, by setting up a corporation. This suggests that the only available model for dealing with genuine nontrivial problems is the corporation, even though so much of its effort has been trivial, providing immense amounts of what nobody needs or even particularly wants, and—with its mastery of advertising rhetoric—doing so in an excessively wasteful and redundant manner.

Within nations, and particularly extremely advanced nations such as ours, it is hardly an exaggeration to say that government operates principally as an ancillary or instrument of corporations, whether on moralistic grounds we like it or not. In areas in which corporations have no particular interest—such as in poverty—government flounders. University education, however, is quite a different matter. It is vital to the existence and persistence of corporations, and the interest of corporations in universities is obvious. One has but to look at boards of trustees, whether of public or private universities and colleges. The simple facts are that the corporations of this country own the universities, and that the universities are primarily instruments of the corporations. The legal aspects of this are not in question. We need not be concerned with legal fictions. By "own" I mean that the universities exist primarily to provide the corporations with replacement parts for worn-out or otherwise discarded personnel and with additional parts for expansion. To be sure, the universities also produce replacement and expansion parts for government (though government is pretty much an ancillary to the corporations) and for the universities themselves as well as for primary and secondary education. Replacement and expansion parts form the bulk of the university products, and most of that bulk goes to the corporations.

Secondarily, the universities produce a very small number

of products—graduates—characterized by what is perhaps best called "wisdom." Such individuals, possibly because of personality attributes which the university does no more than foster and develop, have sufficient detachment to recognize when a social institution is malfunctioning and sufficient insight to deal with the malfunction with some effectiveness. The usual response to malfunction, whether of the individual or the institution, is defensiveness, or guilt, neither of which is of the slightest value in dealing with the problem. The most important ingredients of wisdom, however, are sustained problem exposure and solution postponement, which prevent premature termination of data gathering. These, together with detachment, require not only superior intelligence but also two other attributes: the ability of the individual to put himself under severe intellectual pressure and the ability to postpone gratification, that is, specifically, to tolerate tension and internal disturbance.

At the present time, it is reasonably clear that the universities are facing several severe difficulties and that these difficulties are already having an adverse effect on the corporations. First, it has been assumed until recently that the immense productivity of the corporation, the cornucopia of goodies it has given American society, is such that increased productivity will automatically and necessarily absorb and trivialize the amount of damage done to the society and the environment. John Ruskin coined the useful term "illth" for such damage—as opposed to the term "wealth." However, it is the increasingly powerful conviction of ever-larger segments of the society that the production of illth is at least as great as the production of wealth, and that the by-products of creating the cornucopia are such that we are being deprived of the ability to enjoy and profit from its productivity, perhaps irretrievably. The result is a devastating cultural incoherence.

Sociologists tend to talk about cultural values as a system. In reality, however, the term "system" is extremely misleading. The values of any society or culture or individual have originated at different times and in response to different situations. A society or culture or individual is a loose package of diversities—an incoherence—not a structured system of compatible entities. Whether or not such a package is seen as coherent is a consequence of the cultural situation of the perceiver. As situations change, a perceived coherence can metamorphose into the perception of an incoherence. Such a metamorphosis produces in the perceiver a sense of cultural crisis. The perception of a social incoherence by a sufficient number of strategically placed individuals means that the society is in a condition of cultural crisis. And that is the condition we are in.

Hence the disturbances within the universities. The production of replacements means that the universities are simply maintaining a socially destructive force, the corporation, as well as the government, insofar as the government has become the ancillary of the corporation. As for the production of those with the attributes of wisdom, up to the present they have been produced to deal with malfunctioning of institutions within a social coherence (and, as any corporation president knows, not nearly enough of them have been produced even for the needs of a coherent system). It would appear that to deal with the problems of cultural crisis, more individuals are needed who are characterized by a greater detachment than was required in the past and by greater capacity for problem exposure and solution postponement.

At this point the university is faced with a problem of the utmost severity, which, to my knowledge, has never been recognized. The attributes of wisdom, as I have defined them, are the attributes of the aristocracy and the haute bourgeoisie, that is, the new aristocracy of the industrial revolution that replaced the old pre-industrial or agriculturally based aristocracy. Social management—including above all the manipulation of the principal instrument of social management, rhetoric—requires detachment, not defensiveness and guilt, and requires postponement of gratification together with problem exposure and solution postponement. The tradition of university education is an aristocratic tradition. It is designed to refine, intellectualize, and cultivate individuals who arrive at the university with the value of the attributes of wisdom already instilled in them. Or more precisely, it was designed to select and cull from the potentially wise provided in various ways by the socially managing class. The fantastic growth and immense success of the corporations, however, has increasingly required the universities to produce replacement parts as well as the wise and has indeed required far more of the wise than could be produced, since the field of candidates for selection and culling was too limited. The universities, in short—compelled by the corporation—had to start mass education of the petite bourgeoisie, or lower middle class. (The position I take here does not claim to be elitist in the sense that the values of the aristocracy and haute bourgeoisie are better or more essential to the social process than those of the petite bourgeoisie and the working classes. Rather, it shows why elitism remains—in spite of efforts to remove it—a central problem in attempting to understand culture, society, and individual.)

The tradition of university education, however, is hopelessly maladapted for such an enterprise. The values of the petite bourgeoisie and of the working classes—into which it has been necessary, rather gingerly, to dip to meet the personnel requirements of the corporation—are exactly the opposite of those of wisdom. They are the values, not of detachment, but of attachment—or commitment, defensiveness, and guilt—reduction to the minimum of problem exposure, and of immediate problem solution. The reason is simple. For the attributes of wisdom, a considerable degree of disposable income is necessary, because only disposable income makes it possible to achieve that degree of psychic insulation and social protection necessary for both the application and the production of the attributes of wisdom.

The universities, therefore, are attempting an impossible task: With the by now pretty ragged remnants of an aristocratic educational tradition, they are attempting to educate individuals to whom the values of such an education are almost entirely alien. The situation is compounded by the fact that, as the universities —under the compelling demands of the corporation—have expanded, they have had to expand their faculties, and they could do so only by recruiting them from the petite bourgeoisie and, to a far lesser degree, from the working classes. Vast numbers of such faculty members, in spite of undergraduate and graduate education, have never learned or comprehended the attributes of wisdom, the values of social management. Instead of becoming themselves cultured and aristocratically educated, they have merely learned various pedagogical and professional technologies.

It has not been recognized, then, that the problem of the universities is not the cultivation of students already prepared for such cultivation but is, rather, a massive acculturation problem. The typical university student today is precisely analogous to a Peace Corps volunteer for work among the peasants of Peru; he must be given lengthy and intense training in the language, the culture, the history, the whole way of life of the people he is supposed to live with.

If this analysis is on the right track, the universities are faced with a monumental task. They must retrain their faculties. Currently, those faculty members who are imbued with the values of aristocratic education are relatively helpless before their students. They can only complain about the petit bourgeois values, since they do not recognize that their task is—in the traditional university—not education, but acculturation. As for those who have never learned such values, but have only learned technologies, they need to be trained in such values pretty much from scratch. This class of university teachers is increasingly predominant even in the humanities. The fact that an English professor writes a publishable scholarly article usually means no more than that he has learned an intellectual technology, and such technologies do not operate at a very high intellectual or cultural level.

Thus one kind of faculty member needs to be trained to perceive the acculturational problem, while the other needs to be trained in both the aristocratic values *and* the acculturational problem. This retraining of faculties is, moreover, essential not merely to the survival of the universities as other than technological institutes but also to solving the problems of the corporation. Not only must the corporation deal with the profound suspicion of American society that the corporation is as destructive as it is constructive; not only must it therefore surmount the current crisis of cultural incoherence in order for its potentialities as an extraordinary new event in human history to be realized; in addition, as its role becomes increasingly important, the attributes of wisdom need to be in operation—not merely at the upper executive level, or at the lower executive level, but even at the management level, at which, until fairly recently, the values of the petite bourgeoisie were sufficient for successful operation.

As I suggested earlier, the corporations appear to be taking over the primary tasks of social management from nation-states and their governments. As social institutions, they are transcending governments. It is perfectly obvious, for example, that the European Common Market exists to facilitate the operations of the corporation and the corporation's transcendence of the European nation-states and their petty territories. But this process is being hampered and may be irretrievably damaged by the current cultural crisis and the failure of the universities to provide the kind of personnel without which the corporations can scarcely continue to exist.

We must not imagine for a moment that biological theory assures us that man is going to be a successful species; there is reason to believe that he has not yet even been evolutionarily tested, and he may very well fail that test. From this point of view, the corporation is usefully seen as an adaptational mechanism which may or may not have survival value, though there is so far good reason to think that it does. Certainly the survival value of the nation-state as an adaptational mechanism is more than seriously in question. What keeps a species going at one stage in its history may very well destroy it at another stage, and the destructive capacities of the nation-state are becoming increasingly obvious.

However, members of corporations—and, often enough, high-level members—are themselves responding to the current cultural crisis by losing confidence in the corporation itself, particularly in the responsibilities of social management and in hierarchical organization. To comprehend the problem facing the corporation it is necessary to examine two aspects of the problem, the corporation as an institution and the immediate reasons for the cultural stagnation of the universities, upon which the corporation must necessarily depend for its lifeblood.

So far I have used the term "culture" rather vaguely. To understand the symbiosis of corporation and university, it is necessary to give "culture" a more precise definition, and particularly to spell out such vague and currently suspect terms as "aristocratic culture" and "wisdom."

Human behavior may be seen from two aspects, or it can be understood as a general category subsuming two further categories. One aspect or category is culture; the other is social institutions. If for the terms "culture" and "institutions" we substitute the terms "directions" and "performance," respectively, it becomes reasonably easy to discover what we are talking about. The most obvious kind of directions is language. Language cannot say what the world really is, fundamentally, it can only tell us how to find something, provided we have been trained to respond in an appropriate manner to the directions— that is, to find what we are told to find.

But language is merely the most obvious kind of directions. The world is filled with innumerable kinds of directions. Most of them are nonverbal. A tool, for example, is a set of directions for how to grasp it and what to do with it. But like all sets of directions, it is inadequate. It needs supplementing by further directions; that is, the individual needs to be trained to respond appropriately to the directions the tool gives, just as he needs training to respond appropriately to the directions of language. This supplementary training is all the more necessary because any configuration can be used to provide a great variety of directions. The universal characteristic of language is polysemy, or multiple meanings of the same word.

Innovation, more than anything else, is the generation of a deviant or inappropriate response—inappropriate, that is, judged by current standards. If such a response turns out to be useful and worth social validation, then it is called a creative response. If not, it is socially discarded by being labeled an error. I'll return later to another function of directions, but it is essential first to understand more clearly the character of performance or institutions.

An institution, as suggested above, is a persistent pattern of interaction. This is true even of the private performance of an individual. Insofar as the individual gives himself directions which he then performs, he is a social institution. The process is no different from giving directions to somebody else. What we call "consciousness" amounts merely to learning the ability to give oneself self-generated directions. It is the internalization of directions first given by whoever is rearing the infant. The institutional interaction with oneself, therefore, is no different from the institutional interaction with another.

Of institutions, three kinds may be observed, and these three kinds are exhaustive. The crucial kind is the economic institution, one that exists to provide goods and services and solve the problems involved in such activity. Such institutions, for reasons I shall get to later, are invariably hierarchically structured and must be. They are characterized by two kinds of tension for the individual: the vertical tensions of exercising authority and challenging authority, that is, ambition; and the horizontal tensions—among peer groups at any hierarchical level—of rivalry and acceptance.

The success of the individual in a hierarchical or economic institution depends upon his ability to handle these tensions. Such handling is learned and facilitated by two other kinds of institutions. One is the para-economic institution, of which the prime example is the family. As any society develops beyond the point at which all members are involved in simple food gathering, as it gets to the point at which various possibilities for getting energy are at its disposal and at which, therefore, decision making becomes necessary, it develops hierarchical economic institutions and the family. The family is an unstable hierarchy, for its task is to train the individual to handle the tensions of economic institutions, and for such training and retraining, which is continuous throughout the individual's life history, instability is essential to cast the individual into a bewildering series of hierarchical situations in which he is exposed to all vertical and horizontal tensions. Thus it is the rare child who experiences a trauma when he enters school, for he has already been trained to handle the tensions of relating to his superiors, his teachers, and also to his peers, his schoolmates.

On the other side of the economic institution are relief institutions, or clubs. These are either hierarchically structured, so that the individual is relieved of the tensions of peer relationships, or they are horizontal in structure, so that the individual is relieved of vertical tensions. It is highly instructive that all visions of the good society are either hierarchical or horizontal (egalitarian).

The necessity for the hierarchical structure of economic institutions arises from the nature of culture, or directions. This may be understood from two points of view. One lies in the character of language itself, and particularly in the character of explanation. Explanation proceeds by what I call an explanatory regress. For example: Why are there stones in this pasture different from the rock outcroppings? Because a glacier deposited them there. Why did the glacier happen? Because of changes in the earth's meteorological system. Why are there changes in the meteorological system? Because of the character of the solar system. Why does the solar system have such a character? At one stage in the development of science, the answer simply was, because God willed it so. In such a scheme of explanatory regress, the word "God" merely terminates the regress, which is in theory indefinite. Explanation proceeds by subsuming less explanatory or, one might call them, more exemplary statements.

The further along a regress an explanatory statement is, the more exemplary statements it can subsume, but also the less precise directions it gives. An explanatory regress is constructed, moreover, not merely by simple subsumption, but by reconciling apparently incoherent statements or by rejecting a statement in favor of another, parallel statement that is incoherent with it.

Now the interesting thing about explanatory regresses is that they are hierarchical in structure, and therefore have the same structure as economic institutions. The reason is not difficult to find. Because of polysemy, the fact that two or more responses to any direction are possible, a subsuming direction is necessary to eliminate inappropriate and divergent responses. But subsuming statements do not come into existence all by themselves. They are uttered by human beings. And so are incoherent or rival statements. So it is not rivalry between incoherent statements that a subsuming human being resolves, but rivalry between human beings whose responsive statements to the same stimulus situation are divergent and incoherent. Whenever two human beings are interacting, dominance and submission pass back and forth; but when three are interacting, dominance is rapidly stabilized on one of the three and submission on the other two. The nature of language, of directions, of culture, is such that decision making involves interactional subsumption, or stabilized dominance and submission, or hierarchy.

Recent efforts to assert that economic institutions can be egalitarian are but another instance of what has happened so often throughout European history. At a time of severe cultural crisis, an effort is made to impose the organizational pattern of egalitarian relief institutions on economic institutions. Such an effort is not a solution to the cultural crisis but merely a symptom of such crisis.

The structure of explanation, then, is identical with the structure of economic institutions, and both are capable of indefinite regress, depending upon the complexity of the situation with which the explanation or the institution is attempting to deal and on the amount and kinds of information available. The corporation is the most efficient fusion of explanatory and hierarchical structure the world has yet seen. If, as suggested above, it becomes as efficient an information-processing institution as governments are, it will outmode and transcend the nation-state. To a certain extent it already has.

There is one factor, however, which has not yet been mentioned but only hinted at. That is the factor of power. As the hierarchical stabilization of three-member interactional situations indicates, dominance or power is the stabilizing factor. The reason for this again lies in language and other directions. It is impossible to disprove a statement to someone who does not accept your methods of disproof. It is a sad fact of human existence, and one that explains much of human history, that the only way to get rid of a proposition one disapproves of is to kill the man who holds it. This is the basic reason in culture itself for the fact that social organization depends upon naked power. Furthermore, the higher the level of hierarchy, the greater the necessity for naked power, because, as we have seen, the higher the level of explanation, or the farther from the real world the explanatory regress, the more exemplary statements or information can be included but the less precise the directions for performance.

To put it another way, the higher the level of explanatory and hierarchical regress, the wider the range of situations in which the directions can be used, and therefore the less precise the directions. This explains, for example, the difference in military organization between strategy and tactics. Strategy consists of general directions, given appropriately enough by generals, but tactics, the directions for the execution of the mission on the fighting front, are left up to captains and corporals. Thus a corporation may assign a salesman a territory as part of its sales strategy, but the tactics of selling are left up to the salesman. If he fails, power is exerted and he is either retrained or dismissed.

Directions, as we have seen, need to be supplemented by additional directions. But there is another kind of directions which can best be called meta-directions. These are directions not for performance but for generating directions for performance. When we look up the hierarchical regress of explanation, we see theory emerging from specific directions, or exemplary statements. But when we look down from the top, we see specific directions emerging from theory; we see meta-directions giving birth, as it were, to specific directions, or to more specific directions. By generating increasingly specific directions, the physicist moves from a theory of the electron to specific instructions for building equipment and performing an experiment. So in a corporation a policy, or theory, is generated at the top of the hierarchy and is then successively broken down at each level of the hierarchy into more specific operations, the order downward at each level taking the form of, "This is what you *must* do [observe the domination or power term] but *how* you do it is up to you."

The meta-directional level, then, is the theoretical level. In theory-construction and in corporation organization alike it is the level at which policy or theory is generated by the transformation, manipulation, permutation, and innovation of highly regressive explanatory statements. It is the level at which the flow of information reveals incoherences in the theory. It is the level at which incoherence is resolved. It is, in short, the level of high culture. It is the level from which social management emanates.

And whether we like it or not, it is the level which supports the high intellectual, humanistic, scientific, and artistic enterprises of man and on which such enterprises are economically dependent. High culture, to subsume these enterprises under a single term, processes and manipulates the rhetoric which hierarchical power uses for social management. It justifies and validates, intellectually and artistically, the decisions of social management. This function of high culture must not be thought of as occasional. The task of high culture is to be sensitive to the constancy of situational change and therefore to the constancy of cultural crises, which may range from mild to severe. Information flows to high culture, where it is applied to the cultural situation or critical aspects of it. High culture perceives the disparities within and between information, the current mode of structuring that information, and the general cultural situation. It subjects, one might say, explanatory modes to a continuous and never-ending intellectual and artistic massage. As corporations have developed, they have, for example, become increasingly interested in the arts. This has always been true of power centers and it indicates that the corporation is becoming a true power center for social management.

Furthermore, it is now apparent where the values of "aristocracy," of "wisdom," have their origin and why. All high-culture and high-power centers are alike characterized by psychic insulation and social protection—as can be seen in the office of the corporation president (who is protected by several layers of assistants and secretaries and by spacious, luxurious, and noise-free surroundings). The same is true of the quiet, secluded laboratory of the scientist, study of the philosopher, and library of the humanist; the remote studio of the artist; and the silent museums and theaters and dark concert halls in which the high arts are presented and performed. The processing and innovation of meta-directions require problem exposure and solution postponement, and these in turn require situations in which decisions can be postponed until theoretical manipulation is exhausted and information is processed, sifted, and integrated into theory.

High-corporation policy making, the construction of scientific theory, and the listening to music composed at and for the high cultural level all involve elaborate techniques for prolonging a behavioral sequence, for postponing decision, for theoretical conclusion, and for the sense of psychological closure. They involve the postponement of gratification and the ability not only to sustain tension but to seek it out, the ability of the individual to impose upon himself extreme pressure.

Since the complexity of modern society, the incoherence of the current cultural crisis, and the increasing domination of the corporation require far more people inculcated with these values of high culture than the universities are currently producing or seem able to produce, the question arises as to whether or not it can be done. I believe the answer is that it is indeed possible.

Nearly twenty years ago I was a newly tenured associate professor at the University of Pennsylvania. The then president of the Bell Telephone Company of Pennsylvania approached the president and the provost of the university with the idea of setting up a program for preparing successful management-level personnel to be capable at the executive level. I was given the job of attempting to prepare such a program. The problem was—as I saw it—that at the management level the individual was rewarded for solving problems and answering questions, but at the executive level he was required to ask questions, to discover and pose problems, and to decide whether specific questions were worth answering and problems worth solving. He was promoted to the executive level in order to do something completely different from what he had been doing successfully.

The president of the Telephone Company had become convinced that humanistic education somehow or other held the key to success as a corporation executive. He had observed a tendency of individuals with a humanistic background to continue developing beyond that point at which those with a purely technological background tended to level off, even though the former might move at first more slowly.

Since the problem was basically a psychological problem I perceived it as one that involved attempting to bring about the kind of personality reorganization and value reorientation ordinarily accomplished by some sort of psychotherapy, and to do this by intellectual and artistic manipulation.

The men, most of whom were in their late thirties, participated in the program, at full pay and with expenses taken care of, for ten months. All of their time was devoted to the program. The immediate psychological aim was self-criticism without anxiety. The ultimate aim was criticism of the corporation without anxiety. My object was, for the sake of the corporation, to train the individual to be independent of validation by the corporation. If an individual identifies himself in terms of the corporation, he must necessarily accept entirely the values of the corporation; and this disqualifies him from the primary task of the executive, which is to see when the values of the corporation have become inappropriate to the situation with which it is trying to deal.

The method of the program was to expose the individual to extreme cultural incoherence, and in particular to subject his principally petit bourgeois values to the corrosive analysis of high culture—to introduce him, that is, to the whole world of meta-directional processing and manipulation. The courses were drawn from history, philosophy (particularly the philosophy of science), the various arts, and the behavioral sciences (especially anthropology and sociology) and were so arranged that problems of similar nature appeared simultaneously in quite different courses. No effort was made to put all this together for the student. Rather, he was put into a situation in which he was encouraged to penetrate through intellectual barriers between disciplines, an activity of high culture but so rare in universities today that their claim to high culture must be seriously questioned. The first three weeks, for example, were devoted to a simultaneous and intense study of logic and of history, so different in method and content that the students were disoriented from the start. For the last eight weeks, as another example, the men pursued an intense study of Joyce's *Ulysses*, since this was the most linguistically disorienting experience I could think of which would be at all accessible. (Since then I have concluded that the study of high-culture literature must be at the center of any humanistic education aimed at developing wisdom. Such literature presents simultaneously the most complex mode of linguistic behavior and the most difficult and complex problems of interpretation. Both of these are at the heart of rhetorical manipulation, so closely allied, as I suggested above, to power centers.)

In a situation of psychic insulation and social protection the men were trained in that endurance of tension, problem exposure, and solution postponement which are the attributes of the activities of social management and of the manipulation and innovation of high-level meta-directions. Subsequent studies and the subsequent careers of these men indicated that the program was more successful than I myself believed at the time it possibly could be. Most of the men involved in that first year felt a freedom from the immense power of the corporation and have gone on to high executive positions. Unfortunately, after seven years the program was abandoned, principally for lack of support from cooperating members of the Bell Telephone System. Part of the reason was that, to attract more participating companies, a considerable amount of practical business training was introduced, thus damaging the men's social protection and introducing extraneous career anxieties into a situation already full of intellectual and cultural anxiety and tension (purposefully full, of course). The protection and insulation were further damaged by having an individual identified as representing the interest of the corporation in constant supervisory attendance in the classroom and by permitting members of the executive level of the corporation to be present.

The program was not nearly so effective in the second and subsequent years. In the first year the men felt free to abandon their corporation self-image—by wearing casual clothing, for example—but no such effect obtained in the second and subsequent years. The real trouble was that the program was probably at least twenty years ahead of its time; in addition, though the program was initially effective, my own rationale for it was, as I now see it, inadequate, though on the right track.

To me, the program was enormously illuminating, because it made me realize how profoundly ineffective college and university education is, considering the resources at its disposal. Some of the factors at work here have been indicated above. Certainly every day, it seems, the universities, not understanding their acculturational problem, yield a little more to the inroads and demands of popular or petit bourgeois culture. Certainly the corporations are in part at fault here, because of their demands that the universities provide technologists and because of the corporations' failure to comprehend their nature as institutions, their possible future as adaptive mechanisms, and their necessary alliance and dependence upon their ancillary high culture, a term to which I have attempted to give some empirical and theoretical content.

Nevertheless, much of the failure of the universities is due to the universities themselves. The universities are in fact culturally stagnant, for the proliferation of research and publication carried out according to well-established and professionally validated paradigms is no sign of cultural vitality. All over the country, university administrators at the high executive level are aware of this, but their efforts to push the universities in the direction of cultural renewal are blocked by the faculty. The power centers of faculties are the departments, and it is interesting to observe that newly founded colleges are simply not permitting departments to be set up. The effort appears to be the same as that in the Bell Telephone program: to put the faculties in situations in which professionally erected barriers around the disciplines are penetrated and hopefully torn down. Nevertheless, the real problem has scarcely been faced. The bitter truth is that no profession is so destructive to enterprise and talent as the profession of college and university teacher. Briefly, three factors for this tragic situation may be identified.

First is teaching itself. The university or college teacher is virtually unique in that he receives no social validation which can convince him that he is doing a good job. He does not really know what he is doing; he does not understand how he does it; and he permits no peer or superior to observe his performance (a matter of relative indifference, since such an observer, himself a teacher, knows no better what is going on than does the teacher observed). This lack of validation places the teacher in a stance of defensive and guilt-ridden anxiety against which he has virtually no recourse. Clearly, one cannot set out to be a good teacher. Teaching must be a by-product of intellectual and cultural vitality, and of sustaining that vitality, in the absence of validation, throughout an entire career. If you have a wonderfully rich, complex, and informed mind, it is difficult to be a poor teacher.

Here, however, another factor enters. The university and college teacher has to be someplace and do something only from six to eight hours a week. The rest of the time he must decide for himself what to do, and even when he is in the classroom he has absolute freedom of choice over his activity. He lives, in short, an unstructured life. Now such a life, given the protection and insulation granted to the university teacher, is clearly designed to permit the maximum degree of problem exposure and solution postponement. The difficulty is that very few people have the personalities to sustain such freedom. Most teachers go in for a kind of pseudostructuring, which does nothing to further their primary job, teaching, but gives the teacher the impression that he is extremely busy and active. It is make-work. The situation is the situation of high-level culture, but in any population only a very tiny proportion operates at that level, and not all of these few are successful. Mass education, however, requires thousands and thousands of college and university teachers. The personalities capable of accepting and profiting from an unstructured life are far fewer than the number needed to fill the teaching positions.

The third factor is perhaps the most vicious of all. It is the publish-or-perish policy, better called the publish-and-perish policy. It has been a disaster. It forces individuals to publish who have nothing to say and know it, while on the other hand it forces individuals who have nothing to say and don't know it to imitate paradigms of intellectual technologies. It forces brilliant young men to violate their minds by committing themselves to print when they know perfectly well they are not ready, and to publish something that in the future they will regret and even be ashamed of, providing their intellectual vitality survives the destructive factors of academic life. The contempt for such intellectual technology is unbelievably widespread in the academic world, especially among young men who are active publishers, but such contempt is sooner or later extended to themselves for participating in such activities. The nonpublishers, on the other hand, have been driven into a corner and given no alternatives. If, in spite of all the discouragements, they do in fact maintain their intellectual vitality—and it is the minority that does so—they are not rewarded, but punished. One of the best ways to maintain intellectual vitality, for example, is to give a course one has not given before. If the teacher in publish-and-perish departments does do that and does not publish, there are two consequences. He learns more and renews himself far better than if he had ground out a publishable article, and he is punished for doing so.

These few lines are, indeed, but a hint of the deep-seated malaise and intellectual corruption and stagnation which is characteristic of the universities today. It is clear that the first task of the universities is to devise a way for identifying and rewarding those faculty members who maintain their intellectual vitality, instead of withering on the vine, but who do not publish. For older men it is probably already too late, but the universities are full of splendid and promising young people who are being destroyed. I have watched that destruction growing and spreading for twenty-five years, and it is a sickening sight.

The corporations, to whom the universities are ancillary, in truth own the universities; the corporations—whose existence depends upon the services of high culture, who are faced with a cultural crisis and a cultural incoherence from which only high culture can rescue them—cannot afford to ignore this intellectual cancer in the universities, nor can they afford to permit what they are in part encouraging: the destruction of the universities by turning them into technological institutes. As I stated at the beginning of this analysis, the modern corporation is an astounding social invention. However (and it has not yet realized this), it cannot achieve its potentiality—or perhaps even maintain its existence—without the aid of the values of high culture.

At the present time of cultural crisis the university appears to be the only institution capable of cultural renewal. Since the corporation controls the university through the latter's board of trustees, it appears to be the task and responsibility of the corporation to enable the university of revitalize itself, instead of simply exploiting it as a machine shop for spare parts, as has been the case in the past. Nevertheless, it is necessary to be aware that to revitalize a deteriorating social institution requires a far greater capital investment than it takes to start a new institution to carry out the same function. Perhaps it would be better for the corporation to allow the university to go its declining way and instead to start new academic institutions for the sole purpose of preserving and inculcating those values of high culture so essential to the corporation's survival.

16

ARTS FOR THE CULTIVATION

OF RADICAL SENSITIVITY

[1971*]

The problem with which this paper proposes to grapple is, as I see it, whether or not our educational institutions, particularly those of higher education, can be so revitalized as to overcome their current cultural stagnation, a stagnation by no means limited to educational institutions but on the contrary obtaining throughout our culture, whether we conceive of it as European-American (i.e., Western) or as increasingly international and worldwide. As to the latter alternative, it is obvious that as the undeveloped countries develop they adopt, with little adaptation, the cultural patterns of the West, and in so doing lock themselves into the problems of the West, particularly the problem of cultural stagnation, before which the West itself appears so far to be relatively helpless. It hardly seems possible that the little lever of higher education can move the enormous

---

* Reprinted by permission from *Educational Reconstruction: Promise and Challenge*, ed. Nobuo Shimahara (Columbus, Ohio: Charles E. Merrill, 1973), pp. 201–21. Copyright © 1973 by Bell & Howell Company.

and lethargic mass of the world. It seems even more unlikely that a radicalization of so small an element in the curriculum as the arts—one which has so little status and prestige, judging by the insignificant sums devoted to them; one which affects such a minor part of the university student population and a much smaller part of the population as a whole—can possibly be capable of changing anything one way or the other. The arts at a high cultural level—for that is what I shall be concerned with—are not economically self-supporting, but even the little money needed is difficult to come by. Moreover, the high arts themselves are currently in a condition of extreme crisis; not a few artists have actually given up.

The most logical place to begin is with a discussion of the general cultural crisis of stagnation, but that, as I hope to show, is best considered in terms of education in the arts, at least for the purposes of this paper. Insofar as academia is stagnant, its cultural difficulties are subsumed and explained by the general stagnation. However, there obtain in higher education both endemic and epidemic sources of cultural stagnation which are special to that social area and which need to be disposed of so that the general crisis and the possibilities in the arts for responding adequately to it may be more clearly disengaged from the weakness of higher education in general. The endemic infection is to be found in the very nature of faculties and of faculty life; the epidemic infection is to be found in current faculty policy, particularly as it is administered in major institutions and as it affects the most talented of young faculty members.

The effect of the endemic faculty infection is that the social role of university or college faculty members, more than any other social role, destroys talent, innovation, and enterprise. This should not be the case. Indeed, the situation is so powerfully conducive to just the opposite that the destructiveness is little noticed. The faculty role is given more social protection (as in tenure) and more psychic insulation (as the very design of a campus indicates) than virtually any other. Throughout society, when we find psychic insulation and social protection as prime elements in the circumstances or social situation of a role, we invariably find associated with it the prime duty of problem exposure and solution postponement, for these are the necessary attributes of roles devoted to social management and, above all, to the examination and analysis of the failures of such management and the innovation and implementation of more adequate techniques of management when the inadequacy of established techniques is revealed by a changing historical situation. Thus, when a society is working with relative smoothness, the task of social management is the reinforcement of such techniques and of those validational and explanatory activities which are the particular assignment of high culture. At such times the task of high culture is to rationalize away cultural and social incoherences or to incorporate them with the appearance of logic into the current system of explanation and validation. However, when a society and a culture are in a condition of crisis—particularly when the crisis has developed to stagnation, so great are the incoherences—then the task of high culture is to expose the incoherences and to generate novel systems of validation and explanation. Clearly, the social situation of the academic world calls for the exercise of these high cultural duties. Yet just as clearly, with rare exceptions, the academic world does neither at all well. From this point of view the great social investment in institutions of higher education produces very little and has but a trifling effect on the society as a whole. Organized religion does a better job of rationalizing away incoherences or, by casuistry, incorporating them; while the great innovative modes of explanation and validation rarely come from academia. A famous economist has recently asserted, for example, that academic economists have simply given up on the central economic problem of today, the wage-price spiral. They do not understand it, and they have abandoned any attempts to understand it. (My own feeling, for the little that it is worth, is that the explanation lies in our having reached the limits of economic development, while our ideology demands endless economic growth.)

I believe the sources for this failure can be found in the endemic infection of academia, the situation of the faculty member. It has three aspects. First is the problem of value. How does the faculty member know whether or not he is doing a good job? Unlike other social roles, no validation is forthcoming from superiors, peers, or subordinates (students). The situation calls for privatization, but the price of this is that no superior or peer can validate, simply because he does not know what the faculty member is doing in the classroom; while no teacher, except the most naïve, can take more than temporary and therapeutic comfort from validation emanating from students. In general, self-validation is by no means impossible. The individual is most usefully considered as a dyadic social institution, capable in theory of validating his own activities, having learned validational propositions and attitudes from his culture. But this makes it clear that validation, as already indicated, is a social activity. Hence self-validation requires very firm and objective values; self-validation is easiest in handicrafts. But no one quite knows what he is doing when he is teaching at the university level, and since it is an activity that has always been privatized (except for unreliable subordinates), there is no system of validation which enables the teacher to validate his own performance. Hence the oft-heard statement that a teacher who does not often think that he has no right to be teaching cannot be a good teacher. This may or may not be true; it looks more like a rationalization of an impossible validational situation; it is certainly cold comfort at best. Just as in Calvinism the only sensible thing to do is to assume that one is among the saved, so for the teacher the only sensible thing to do is to conclude that his self-doubts are proof that he is doing a good job, a rationalization that tends to vitiate the effectiveness of self-doubt and is obviously a strategy to deal with the absence of validation. It is but one of many such strategies which divert the energy of the teacher from his task into an endless and futile and time- and energy-wasting effort to achieve validation.

The second aspect or factor is the problem of freedom. Human behavior may be considered as having two aspects, any behavioral bit manifesting both—directions and performance, or culture and society. Now self-directed activity is of course perfectly possible—and, as with the housewife, very common—but like self-validation it depends upon a rich, complete, firm, and well-transmitted set of directions. These directions are almost entirely absent for the role of college-university teacher. At best he must

depend upon a role-model derived from some admired teacher
of his own. But in the absence of adequate directions and of
virtually any means of transmitting them to rising generations,
any role-model must have been developed to suit the contin-
gencies of a unique personality. Consequently it provides, not a
lasting model, but only a rough sketch which requires innovation
on the part of the teacher who adopts it. Such role-models invariably produce a wide range of deviation, not necessarily a
bad thing but certainly a condition which forces the teacher into
emphasizing his own uniqueness and frequently produces a useless, though entertaining, eccentricity. Worse, it forces the teacher's attention onto the technique of teaching, technique for which
there is neither an empirically derived foundation or scientific
justification nor an adequate set of directions. There is really very
little that deserves the name of the "culture" of college-university
teaching. Now in the absence of such directions, a more general
principle must be generated, though it rarely is. Teaching, judging
from what has been proposed, cannot be a direct aim; it can only
be a by-product, specifically a by-product of intellectual vitality.
But should the teacher arrive at this very vague and general conclusion—though he rarely does, in my experience—he is once
again faced with the problem of freedom and of innovation for
unique purposes that cannot be understood or can only be understood after many years of fumbling and intellectual wandering.
Freedom ordinarily means freedom to direct one's own behavior,
but there seems to be no wider range of behavior in free societies
than in controlled ones, and little difference in behavioral result
between self-direction and direction by others. In short, the
teacher is faced with the problem of genuine freedom, a social
anomaly, one with very little social support and reinforcement.

The third factor or aspect is closely related to the preceding
one, so closely that it may be the same thing; yet it is worth
distinguishing. It is the problem of time. Except for six to twelve
hours a week, the college-university teacher has all of his time
at his disposal. There are only a few hours, then, during which
he has to be at a particular place and engage in a particular activity—though for the latter, of course, there is such a wide
range of possibilities that it need not be burdensome. A graduate

seminar, for example, in which the time is spent by the students in listening to each other's papers is not far from downright fraud as far as the teacher is concerned. The result of the free time is that the teacher *must* decide what to do. In terms of time, his life is virtually unstructured. An unstructured job for which one is paid is as much of a social anomaly as a life of freedom. I have heard more than one unusually sensible psychiatrist insist that the temporally unstructured life of the college-university teacher is such an unendurable burden that its destructiveness is incalculable. The rate of alcoholism among university-college faculties seems to be, on the most reliable accounts, considerably, very considerably, higher than among the population as a whole. The consequence of this lack of structure is that most teachers either idle their time away or structure their lives by inventing make-work in order to give themselves the impression that they are really earning their pay. There is little evidence that giving lots of tests and assigning lots of papers and spending lots of time correcting and grading both is pedagogically very productive, though it would be very difficult to get many teachers even to admit that possibility. Yet, like calling the roll and spending twice as much time (or more) in a committee as its problems need, testing and grading and correcting can consume immense amounts of time. So valuable are these activities for consuming time and creating structure in a role in which lack of structure is the prime source of value that they are powerfully institutionalized and have great prestige. Spending a lot of time with students—usually a demanding and attention-appetitive few—also has great therapeutic value for meeting the problem of free time, though the same amount of time spent with, for example, a good encyclopedia would have much greater value for all of one's students.

These are the endemic infections of the body academic. The epidemic infection is much more easily recognized and at least affects only a few institutions instead of all of them. It is, of course, the policy which is best known as publish-*and*-perish. This epidemic began to rage, it would appear, in the 1920s. Lacking a means of distinguishing a good teacher from a bad, administrators noticed—it was pretty obvious—that those teachers who were also publishing scholars and scientists had the reputation of being the most effective, or at least the most attractive, teachers. The lesson seemed clear. To create good teaching, whatever it might be, one had but to reward publishing, since publication provided social validation for the existence of intellectual vitality. To reward on the basis of publication—which became the consequence, in spite of lip service to "good teaching" —appeared to ensure the encouragement of intellectual vitality and certainly made the task of handing out rewards of rank and salary much easier. The result, however, was far different. In spite of complaints, faculties in which this policy was instituted were in fact much happier, not because intellectual vitality was encouraged, but because more binding directions were given and an embarrassing freedom was curtailed. At last, faculty people had something to take up their time, and the policy was used by faculties to force a reduction in teaching hours and student load. Further, since those who published were rewarded, they shortly became the managers within the faculty, only too eager to maintain a system from which they had profited and which, they discovered, could be mastered without too much difficulty. In fact, the difficulty became less as time went on. The pressure to publish produced a corresponding pressure for media of publication. Once the scholarly journals were created, for economic reasons it was necessary to publish a certain number of pages each quarter, that is, to fill each issue up. The same effect was shortly discerned in university presses, which were tooled up to produce annually a certain minimum number of titles. To produce less than that minimum sent the cost up. It is less expensive to produce, let us say, six reasonably good books a year and a dozen or so very ordinary ones than it is to produce merely the six good ones. The result has been what can with some accuracy be described as humanistic and scientific scholarly technology. Instead of cultural vitality, one has the endless imitation of a limited number of scholarly paradigms. Just as a competitive grading system forces the majority of students to psych out their teachers, so competitive publishing forces a greater majority of faculty to psych out journals and presses. I have even heard an excellent press director give a lecture on exactly how to do it, although he thought he was doing something else.

The build-up in publication had a still further effect. When any intellectual activity confronts a public, the effect is professionalization. That is, certification and standardization are necessary to gain the confidence of a public ignorant of the intellectual activity but desirable as a part of that activity's market, now that a market for that activity is being sought. In the practical arts, such as medicine and engineering, this seems socially beneficial, since behind them is scientific research which is channeled through the practitioners to the market—though this, of course, is less true than it was, since scientific research is now somewhat more likely to seek the market directly. But when the intellectual activity directly enters the market and becomes professionalized, it loses its intellectual vitality. The reasons are three: First, the individual's interest turns away from the intellectual activity and becomes focused on his status within the profession; second, he is equally interested in the status within the profession of his particular institution—in the academic world, of his department and his university; third, perforce he becomes interested in recruitment, the result having been since the last world war the professionalization of undergraduate studies, with disastrous results. Finally, the result is an easily managed system with only one path to status and reward. In any publishing department and in academia as a whole this has created a two-class system of haves and have-nots—the latter of whom are permanently disgruntled, and to a great extent justifiably so. Since they do not publish, they perceive quite clearly that the bulk of publication does not emerge from irresistible intellectual pressure within the individual but from an entirely exteriorized desire to share in the gravy. They feel that they are morally superior and they know that they are poorer—always an explosive and socially dangerous situation.

Moreover, there is a further consequence which bears directly upon the problem with which this book is attempting to deal. Any educational reconstruction requires risk-taking and above all the creation of new curricula and new courses. So long as there is but one system of rewards, through publication, anyone who attempts the risks of educational reconstruction will not be rewarded, but punished, since the time necessary for such reconstruction must be taken away from time reserved for writing and publication. Any attempt at educational reconstruction that does not recognize the endemic infection of the academic world and try to deal with it, and that does not deal with the epidemic infection by creating a number of alternative systems of reward, is doomed. I know of but one place, not that there are not others of which I am ignorant, in which a certain educational reconstruction shows promise and is developing. It is working, or at least shows promise of working, simply because the president set up a separate college and promised and has kept his promise to reward its faculty just as well as the faculties in the other colleges in the university but without requiring from them anything whatever in the way of publication. What we need is a number of alternative paths to reward, since publishing now is the only possible validation available to members of academic faculties. The result of our present system is that the large majority of faculty personnel have withered on the vine by the time they are fifty —and a very large number, including our most intelligent and active publishers, by the time they are thirty-five. However, alternative systems of rewards mean a sharing of the gravy by a greater number of people than now share it. From the latter can be anticipated the most intense opposition and the most violent outcries against "violating and compromising professional standards." Nor would even large infusions of new money make any difference. That happened in the 1960s, and those who had the gravy simply got more of it. Thus it must be recognized that the present system has a built-in economic principle which resists any change in the direction of encouraging intellectual vitality instead of cultural stagnation. Unless this problem is met and resolved, the proposals contained here will be purely visionary, not much more than idle activity, another way of adding to one's bibliography. The rest of this paper will assume, therefore, that this problem can be resolved, though I do not think that can be under the present system. I suspect that the only possibility is the creation, not of alternative paths to rewards within the present system, but rather of another system, of an alternative academia, uncompromised by the past.

II

If educational reconstruction is to occur through the cultivation of a radical sensitivity, on the basis of virtually all aesthetic theory the arts are the last place in which to attempt to produce such a sensitivity and which could possibly be affected by educational reconstruction. Art has traditionally been identified with order and has been praised or validated as the source of order, as the area of human behavior in which, above all others, order is created. Educational reconstruction will require considerable disorder before it is accomplished (if it can be, in itself rather doubtful), and certainly to cultivate a radical sensitivity requires that the individual in whom it is cultivated experience a probably fairly lengthy process of disorientation or cultural disorder. I have argued elsewhere that in fact in one aspect, the formal, art is not characterized by order, but by disorder, and that in the other aspect, the conventional or semantic, it can be characterized by either order or disorder, or a mixture of both. (See *Man's Rage for Chaos* [Philadelphia, 1965; New York, 1967].) Although I shall return to this, here I wish first to consider what kind of statement the identification of art and order may be and second what its social source may be.

By "what kind of statement" I mean "What its place is in human behavior, and what it is doing there," if that place can be located. Preliminary to defining "what kind of statement" is some notion of the most circumscribed area of behavior in which that place is to be found, language. The problem of language is inseparable from the problem of "meaning." A behavioral definition of "meaning" is that the meaning of any segment of utterance to which some behavioral response is possible is that very response. To my mind the weakness of contemporary linguistic philosophy is that it hypostatizes language. I do not mean that it hypostatizes meanings, in the sense that the language is identified and confused with the world, its referent, in the largest sense of reference. Rather, I am of the opinion that such philosophy hypostatizes language itself—that is, meaning—by at least talking as if the meaning of an utterance were immanent in that utterance. This hypostatization emerges in such expressions as "the statement refers to" or "the referent of the statement is." Now obviously language does not refer; humans do the referring. However we may explain or account for it, between any utterance and its "referent" is a human being who is responsible for deciding what that particular utterance shall in fact "refer" to, if anything. That is, a human being decides what the meaning of any utterance shall be, or, briefly, "the meaning of an utterance is the response to the utterance." The question is not quite, as Humpty-Dumpty claimed, who is to be master, the word or the person; rather, the person cannot avoid being master. Yet it is a responsibility the person does everything he can to abdicate, to surrender to convention.

The reason for this attempt to avoid semantic (or meaning) responsibility is most instructive and indeed is of the highest importance, particularly for the problem immediately at hand. If the person assumes mastery and contravenes or transcends convention, communication breaks down. What we mean by this is— in these terms—that the person receiving the utterance either cannot respond at all or responds in a way inappropriate in the judgment of the originator of the utterance in question. What makes the breakdown of communication possible is the fact that every utterance is capable of eliciting any one of all possible meaning responses. This realization brings out into the open the fact that the only thing that keeps communication not merely from breaking down but from dissolving into absolute chaos is an incredibly complex web of convention. Verbal education consists of instructing children in the conventions of response to an increasingly wide range and an increasingly complex quasi-system of utterance. Meaning, in short, is a matter of learning conventionally appropriate responses.

Furthermore, language is but one of many sign systems that human beings use. A play is a good place to observe a wide variety of semiotic systems: words, juncture, stress, pitch, volume, tempo, intonation, facial gestures, trunk gestures, extremity gestures, makeup, costume, motion, properties, scenery, lighting, music—the list can be continued. Scenery, for example, is clearly on the stage a semiotic system, but it is so only because the world consists of semiotic systems, each element of which, such as a tree or a cloud or a stone, is capable of eliciting a wide range of responses, all of which have to be learned, together with the conventions governing their appropriateness. Insofar as a human being is capable of responding to anything, it is because and only because that thing is a sign. "The world means," Browning said, but what he should have said is that the world consists of signs linked to responses established and maintained by convention.

We may now go back a step and pick up the point that the meaning of a term or other utterance is a response to that utterance. Such a response may be of one of two kinds—or of both simultaneously—verbal or nonverbal. If we call the nonverbal response an action, then it is clear that that action is governed by conventions. That is, an action in response to an utterance is behavior generated in response to conventions. But this formulation is clearly inadequate, since it defines the action as response to utterance and conventions. The difficulty lies in the fact that "convention" is a kind of intervening variable. That is, unlike the utterance, it has no phenomenal existence. It is a metaphor. Conventions are pre-established utterance-responses learned from other utterances—or from other signs, such as, for children and even on occasion for adults, manipulation by another person. An action, then, is a response to an utterance controlled by previously experienced utterances designed to train the actor in appropriate actions. He has, in other words, been given directions on how to respond to a particular utterance when it appears. Taking our metaphor from the stage, as we have already in "action," "actor," and "directions," we may usefully call an action a "performance." But since there is no difference between learning appropriate verbal responses and learning appropriate nonverbal responses, a verbal response is as much of an action—that is, a performance —as a nonverbal response. Language then does not tell us what the world is, nor does it refer; language is directions for performances. But what is true of language is also true of nonverbal signs, those created by human beings and those found in the world. The world, then, consists of directions for performance.

Human behavior may be thus reduced to two aspects, directions and performance—aspects, because any performance is a set of directions and any set of directions established by human agency, including those found in nature, is a performance, even though it may be only a covert performance or a mere emotional performance. We are moved by a beautiful seascape because, and only because, we have learned the convention, or fashion, of being moved by beautiful seascapes, the distinction between beautiful and nonbeautiful seascapes being itself a convention, as defined above. But we may go further than this in understanding the terms we use to talk about human behavior. Such terms as "society" and "culture" are high-level abstractions subsuming vast amounts of data. There is no such phenomenally observable entity as society, nor culture either. Because of their extreme abstraction, both terms have been given innumerable, elaborate, and differing definitions. The definition problem is this: Given the word "society," with what verbal formulation may I respond so that I may ensure appropriate responses to that word? A definition, then, is an additional set of directions for a performance, verbal or nonverbal, as the case may be. It is a substitution, and a glance at a dictionary shows evidence of the point made above; there is no theoretical limit to the range of performances a verbal direction is capable of eliciting. It is my proposal here that all definitions of "society" may be subsumed under the definition "performance in response to directions"; and likewise that all definitions of culture may be subsumed under the definition "directions for performance." We have only to add that every performance consists of directions and that directions are always performances, to realize that these terms do not locate factors in human behavior, but aspects; that is, they are low-level abstractions, perhaps as close to the empirical phenomena of behavior as one can get and still talk about behavior at all. Furthermore, the two aspects of behavior may be unified or synthesized by the term "communication." Thus human behavior is identifiable with communication. We are not animals that use communication; insofar as we are human beings we *are* communication, and that is all we are.

It is necessary to bring in this concept in order to reintroduce the notion of the breakdown of communication. If communication can break down, then human behavior can disintegrate; that is, the conventionally established links between directions and performance, between culture and society, can dissolve. Because of the enormous complexity of those conventional links, because of the lack of natural or other limitation to response to directions, and because of the inability of the human brain to learn any but very simple behavioral sequences with absolute exactness, culture and society, directions and performance, communication, and therefore human behavior itself, are inherently unstable. We are always threatened with and constantly experience the inability to respond to directions—the failure of our resources of performance. The central concern of humanity is and must be the stabilization of responses, that is, the stabilization of the conventions of appropriate performance. A moment's reflection on behavior from this point of view will bring to mind the constant and pervading demand for additional directions and the equally constant and pervading provision of them. The often bewailed inadequacy of language is rather the inability of the human brain to master the infinitely complex and infinitely extensive web of conventions of directions. Only if two people, or sometimes a large group, have engaged over a long period of time in the same set of performances in response to the same set of directions can behavior flow smoothly. It is not surprising that—in spite of the abrasiveness of close and continuous interpersonal contact—long-term, even lifetime, association should be a constant in behavior, or that those individuals who cannot or will not engage in the never-ending and always incomplete effort to learn the conventions of response should be segregated. The immediate dislike most people feel for individuals who speak the same language with a different accent can also be traced to this phenomenon. So much in verbal directions depends on constancy of pronunciation that a deviation is bound to be profoundly disturbing, since it brings to the foreground the constant threat of communicational dissolution, of the dissolution of behavior itself. This, I suspect, is the ultimate source of an emotional constant—thoroughgoing relief from which is rare and fleeting—anxiety.

But we may go further than this. It certainly appears to follow from what has been so far proposed that a dominating expenditure of available human energy must be devoted to stabilizing communication, that is, to stabilizing directions and performance. To put this concept into a word, I would propose the term "policing," under which is to be conceived as subsumed both the policing of others and self-policing. I propose this term because at the present time traffic-police and deviation-police are the most obvious modes of stabilizing behavior; but they are merely a surface manifestation of what must be man's central concern. Since self-policing is perhaps the more troublesome kind of policing to understand, a couple of examples will perhaps suffice to show the subtlety as well as the pervasiveness of policing.

One of the more puzzling aspects of human behavior is the phenomenon of collecting. Our first clue comes from the fact that collecting appears when there is a surplus of energy and time. The affluence of the United States in the 1960s saw an astonishing surge of collecting; more and more people became interested in collecting something—rocks, streetcar transfers, old cigarette coupons, baseball cards, paintings, cut glass. The list is almost endless. When one collects, one disposes of free time and energy by buying or otherwise acquiring examples of some category of artificial or natural phenomena. Even the simultaneous increase in tourism can be seen in this light; the tourist collects means of transportation and places. The most effective kind of collecting, of course, is to collect something well established, such as stamps or the famous tourist clichés of Europe. These latter become more crowded, while less well-known places, frequently enough of equal interest, are increasingly neglected, or only very slowly move into the prime tourist market. The reason for this, explained by the concept of self-policing, is that a disposable income makes it possible to increase the range of one's behavior, but in actual practice this does not happen. Rather the individual pounces upon a strategy for disposing of his disposable income by moving into a severely limited or heavily policed area of behavior; the explanation, of course, is that to increase the range of behavior is to increase the possibility of being unable to respond to novel directions, and thus to experience sharply the ever-present threat of behavioral dissolution. Self-policing therefore takes often enough the form of a self-imposed limitation of behavior, and this principle further answers the baffling question of why anybody is interested in anything. An interest is a self-imposed and self-policed limitation of behavioral range.

Another example cuts even closer to an anxiety of our times than does the anxiety-provoking disposable income. It is the phenomenon of drug use. The effect of any popular drug—alcohol as well as marijuana, heroin, and the barbiturates—is obviously to limit the range of behavior. The use of such drugs, whether they are derived from mushrooms, from fermented grape juice, or from various weeds, is to be found in virtually all societies. For a thousand years or more Russia has been a social failure. Communism has improved things a little over Czardom, but it has really created little more than a ripple on the surface of a society so stable that it is more than lethargic. In Russia the range of behavior is extraordinarily limited, and the rate of alcoholism and alcohol consumption is extraordinarily high. The stability of the far more adequate Scandinavian societies seems likewise linked to high alcohol consumption, as is the immense conservatism of France. Bolivia appears on the surface to be unstable, but it is only the government that is unstable—so unstable, and with such constancy, that one suspects that unstable government is part of the total social stability of Bolivia. In Bolivia the use of drugs other than alcohol is very high, and it is a society that knows little change. This principle of the use of drugs to limit the range of behavior may be successfully employed to explain the extraordinary link between our recent youthful rebelliousness— considerably calmed by a real and prospective reduction of disposable income—and drug use. Our youthful rebels talked up a storm and even frightened faculties into a momentary consideration of their own behavior, but the behavior of the rebels was actually very limited, considering the immense possibilities for social disruption that lay easily at hand. A few hundred well-placed charges of dynamite could have made Chicago or any other city impossible for the 1968 convention. The convention itself could have been easily prevented. Fortunately perhaps—or perhaps not—the rebels had already established in drug use a very effective means of limiting the range of behavior. Pot and

LSD rescued American society; but if it had not been pot and LSD it would almost certainly have been some other drug. The young, one understands, are now returning to the traditional American drug for limiting behavior—alcohol.

Drug use, then, is a mode of limiting behavior, of self-policing, of social stability. But it is by no means the only mode, nor is sex, which is a not very close rival. Central to the purpose of this paper is the most interesting mode of policing, high culture.

III

I have proposed that a direction is a performance and a performance is a direction, but there is one mode of generating directions which destroys the symmetry of this relation. This mode consists of directions for issuing directions, or meta-directions. Again, a dictionary is an obvious example. A definition is, on the one hand, a substitute direction, but an alternative use is as a direction for using a word, that is, a direction for a direction. Clearly, dictionary making and dictionary using belong to high culture. Dictionaries emerge when a culture has become at once so complex and so self-conscious that it is fully aware of the threat of behavioral dissolution, that is, of failure of communication. A dictionary—whether or not its editors propose a purely descriptive dictionary—is, as the critics of Webster's Third insisted, prescriptive, whether or not the editors wish it to be. It "establishes" the range of meanings for terms of multiple meanings, which are virtually all terms in common use. The more common the usage, the greater is the range of meanings, that is, of conventionally appropriate responses. It has long been virtually a ritual that when one enters college one of the first purchases is a dictionary, as it is traditionally a high-school graduation gift. It is a sign that one is about to enter upon the world of high culture and a direction to do so.

Another instance of meta-directions may be found in the emergence of logic on the Greek cultural scene. Logic followed on the dissemination of the metaphysical writings of the pre-Socratic philosopher. A metaphysic is an explanation of the world, but of such a nature that it determines and limits both meta-directions and directions. Further, metaphysics are covertly or overtly value laden, and indeed are often broached specifically in order to establish value priorities and hierarchies. The general twist of traditional metaphysics is "This is the way things are; and this is why they ought to be as they are; and these principles properly govern your behavior." A metaphysic is at once explanation and justification. The pre-Socratics introduced a variety of, for their time, sophisticated metaphysics which challenged and for some superseded the traditional metaphysics of Greek culture, exemplified in Greek religion, but not yet abstracted into higher-level explanatory principles. This multiplication of metaphysical explanations required the development of logic, that is, of sets of directions for controlling both syntactical and semantic language behavior at the metaphysical level. As culture becomes more complex, and as more of a population becomes aware of that complexity and is afflicted more self-consciously with the anxiety of behavioral dissolution, logic is introduced at progressively lower culture levels; that is, an attempt (never fully successful) is made to exert its control not only over meta-directions but also over immediate directions for nonverbal performance.

The consequence of this line of analysis can be proposed briefly, though a trifle baldly: High culture equals meta-directions equals limitation of the range of meta-directional and directional behavior equals policing. It may seem strange that alcohol, drugs, collecting, touring, metaphysics, logic, and high culture in general can be subsumed under the general term "policing," but such I believe to be the case. I think that this point is made more transparent if it is realized that the central position of all metaphysics is either the construction of a theory of an ordered universe or the ordered construction of a theory of the universe or the ordered construction of an ordered theory of the universe. Whenever we find the word "order" we can be reasonably sure that what is at work is the construction of a defense against the constant threat of behavioral dissolution, the ultimate source of which is the possibility that any sign can elicit all possible meaning responses. It is not surprising that "value" is so identified with "order" that the two terms are nearly interchangeable. To assert that an order exists is virtually to assert that whatever is said to manifest order is valuable. Moreover, whenever we encounter the word "order" we may be sure that the primary interest at work is limitation of the range of behavior, or policing. And thus we are provided with an explanation of what kind of statement the identification of art and order is and an explanation as well of the social source of that identification. So long, therefore, as art is justified in college teaching in the name of order and so long as the individual work of art is explained and validated by discovering in it a principle of order, art cannot possibly be used for the creation of a radical sensitivity nor as an area of study in which educational reconstruction can take place or even be attempted. To teach art in the name of order is to use art for the purpose of interactional policing and for the strengthening of self-policing. This comes out sharply in artistic evaluation, in which either the art of high culture is identified with art and the art of low culture is called non-art, or anti-art, or mere entertainment; or the art of high culture is called good art and the art of lower culture bad art. The inculcation of taste, or the limitation of the range of art to which it is appropriate to respond, is a clear instance of policing. It makes no difference that "good taste" is constantly changing. So long as hierarchies of value within the various arts are established, it is of no importance what those hierarchies are.

Nevertheless, the study and teaching and experience of art does hold a hope out for the development of a radical sensitivity and for educational reconstruction. The way to use it for such purposes is to use it to penetrate the armor of policing. And it is penetrable, for the whole enormous and central human effort is to police, to limit the range of behavior, to prevent behavioral dissolution, to stabilize directions and performance—is, in fact, self-defeating. Or rather, humanity is self-defeating, for the condition of its existence, stabilization by policing, is antithetical to that existence. What makes mankind (communication) possible destroys communication (mankind).

Scientific laboratories can tell us why. Scientific experiment depends upon a severe limitation of meta-directions, or theory, upon an extreme limitation of sources of stimulus, that is, of signs, and upon an extremely severe and lengthy process of behavioral limitation, or performance policing. Even so the bulk of scientific experimentation produces negative results. This is by no means to denigrate science. On the contrary, scientific method is the most remarkable way man has yet created for overcoming the inherent deficiency in behavior—dissolution. Yet the failure of so much scientific experimentation suggests that these three limitations are not directly responsible for scientific discovery, but indirectly. Significant scientific discovery is in fact the consequence of a hunch, a guess, an intuition, a scientist's leap into the dark. It is not scientific method that is responsible for significant discovery but the total scientific directions-performance complex, not the method but the cultural-social situation. It is a situation that privatizes behavior, and in so doing frees or separates the scientist from the immense, incomprehensible, and fluid network of normal communication. Scientific method—theory, isolation of experimental material, and performance, or laboratory techniques—creates a miniature or model of human behavior, small, stable, and comprehensible, which acts as a defense or barrier against the real thing. Encased and protected in his tiny communication world, the scientist is free from the normal situation in which everything involves everything else, in which no individual segment has any limits. Thus encased and free, he is capable of the *acte gratuite,* of the transcending hunch. He is, in short, in a condition of estrangement, of alienation—true alienation, not the spurious alienation currently so popular. He does not develop existent principles of order into a new concept. He overthrows them. The more significant his discovery, the greater the confusion into which it throws the theoretical principles from which he began. His discovery is a deviation. One of the first great scientific discoveries, Galileo's, was clearly labeled for what it was, a crime. For the present problem, the clear lesson is that human behavior at any given moment is inadequate for its own needs. To exist it must stabilize itself through policing, but stabilization prevents the criminal correction of a necessarily inadequate directions-performance state. The importance of science is not its discoveries—rewarding and damaging as they have been—but its constant proof of that inadequacy.

Another kind of scientific laboratory, the psychological laboratory, reveals another source of the self-defeating character of behavior. Here the interesting factor is not the scientist but the human subject. What happens in such a laboratory is that subjects are exposed to a single stimulus in a behaviorally neutral environment. The scientist records and makes a statistical analysis of the frequency of different categories of response. In spite of the enormous investment in such laboratories, very little of significance has been revealed. The reason is that in normal behavior no single stimulus can ever be isolated. That is, a response is a response not to a stimulus but to a stimulus field, made of an indefinably large number of stimulus sources—each of which is a sign capable of eliciting an indefinably large number of responses and together so interacting in the brain that only policing can produce any commonalty of behavior. The norm of brain activity is the production of random innovation. This, probably, is the significance of dreams, which after all can be interpreted only to confirm the interpreter's interpretational mode. However, as the behavior of the scientist shows, behavioral dissolution is the source of corrections to the "system." But not all behavioral dissolutions. The scientist makes his discovery by hunches, but only the very rare hunch is fruitful. Yet if policing is the channeling of behavior and the suppression of innovation, it is clear that normal interactional behavior is responsible for the loss of an incalculable number of possibilities for correcting the inadequacies of any current directions-performance state, as well as, of course, for an equally incalculable number of possibilities for damaging it. We must further recognize that the very success of science, it can no longer be denied, has already done an enormous and perhaps irreparable amount of damage. Yet it is only fair to admit also that the reason for the damage has been that the correction of the state has not been nearly thoroughgoing enough.

IV

This last point leads us finally to the real subject of this essay. Can the study and teaching of the arts contribute to the creation of a kind of human being capable of a more thorough-going correction of the system than has yet existed? Let me make it clear that I have no notion of what such a correction would be like or how it could be effected. I am merely sure that the most radical corrections yet proposed are childish in their grasp of the problem and in their solutions. Marxism, which may be the most radical, assumes that it is possible to so correct the human directions-performance condition that it becomes a true system, entirely adequate to the demands made upon it, entirely comprehensible, because completely coherent (logically!), and entirely learnable. I do not see how it is possible to take Marxism or the pseudo-alienation of the 1960s seriously. All radical proposals assume the possibility of creating a harmonious humanity, but I can see no possibility other than an unresolved tension between maintaining the directions-performance condition and correcting it, a situation compounded by the fact that only policed behavior is predictable and that therefore it is forever impossible to know whether a condition is overpoliced or overcorrected or, as may be the reason for the current stagnation, both at once. Surely, however, correction, as the scientist in his laboratory has shown us, depends upon disengagement, estrangement, alienation, dehumanization. To use the most current of these terms, I frankly propose that alienation is the unexploited possibility, the way out of our current impasse, something not to be overcome but something, rather, to be incorporated into the human condition in order to provide a stable constant for correction. I further propose that though the arts cannot produce corrections, except insofar as a work of art exemplifies a proposed correction produced outside of art, they can contribute to the introduction into human behavior of a constant and socially protected alienation, an alienation which can be entered into and departed from with the minimum of anxiety and energy loss, and which has a status that makes it available to all men capable of it. I propose that, given the desirability of alienation, the arts offer one of the better ways of producing it.

Two points, however, need to be made before proceeding. The first is that I am not proposing "alienated personalities." There is no such thing, nor can there be. Such a notion assumes that a personality is a structured entity, but on the contrary, it is a nonstructured, random package of directions-response patterns. The Romantics, whose great contribution was the discovery of alienation and its establishment as a viable and valuable mode of behavior, were alienated in but a few very small segments of their total behaviors, and on the whole confined their alienation to high-culture metaphysics and art. It is the Romantics, in fact, who suggest the possibility that art can be used as a means for creating alienation. The history of Romantic high culture in the nineteenth and twentieth centuries has proved that it is possible to institutionalize alienation. Therefore, what I am proposing is not alienated personalities but the institutionalization and stabilization of alienation as a viable mode of behavior. It is no accident that most of the great scientists of the nineteenth century had a youthful background of intense experience in Romantic culture and the Romantic tradition. At the present time, however, this is no longer true; science has become professionalized into a technology and, in comparison with the nineteenth and early twentieth centuries, is culturally stagnant.

The second point is that art cannot be depended upon to produce alienated behavior. On the contrary, it can be and usually is used exactly as alcohol, other drugs, sex, collecting, and tourism are used—to name only those already discussed. Like any drug or alcohol or sex or collecting or touring addict, the art lover can become an addict, for addiction is but an extreme devotion to a mode of limiting the range of behavior, a mode of self-policing. Since self-policing is the core of individual behavior, the existence of addiction can probably be explained most simply and satisfactorily as a statistically unavoidable phenomenon. Simply to support and encourage the study of and exposure to the arts will only create a greater number of people who use art in the way sex and drugs and alcohol are used and increase the number of art addicts. This is made the more probable if the extension of the high arts to a wider share of the population is justified in the traditional way, in the name of order.

Nevertheless art does present real possibilities for preparing the individual to engage in an alienated mode of behavior. The probabilities for this are historically strengthened by the experience of the Romantics—the discoverers of the possibilities of alienation—most of whom were artists, while those who were not, such as Hegel, were intensely interested in art and gave it a higher rank in the hierarchy of behaviors than it had been accorded before. The early Romantic notion of art as redemptive can perhaps be best understood as an attempt to validate and institutionalize alienation. I have proposed that the condition for correction of the behavioral (directions-performance) condition is alienation. It is essential here to present briefly the conditions for successful alienation. These are social protection, psychic insulation, the capacity to endure over long periods problem exposure and solution postponement, the preference for tension rather than for tension reduction, the capacity to tolerate tension, the ability to tolerate disorientation and the desire to seek disorientation actively, a sensitivity to cultural incoherence, a capacity for self-validation which in other circumstances would be condemned as arrogance, and an ability to exist without the constant flow of validation which is so constant and pervasive a part of non-alienated life and the absence of which for faculty members is so destructive. That all these are dangerous to the individual cannot be doubted, for every one of them is capable by itself of producing behavioral dissolution. Again, however, the history of Romanticism in the nineteenth century shows the dangers and in the twentieth century shows that the dangers can be resisted. The reason is simple. For the twentieth-century artist, alienation had become, through the struggles of nineteenth-century Romanticism, institutionalized for a small but accessible part of the population of the West. It had become economically viable, partly of course because of the very old tradition of the artist as genius, and of art, therefore, as a mode of behavioral limitation and self-policing.

I believe the artistic experience, by which I mean here the behavior of the artistic perceiver and consumer, can offer an admirable training ground for learning the conditions of alienation and for learning to tolerate them. But this potentiality can be put to use in teaching the artistic experience only if the aesthetics of order and the hierarchies of value are abandoned, for this sort of policing tends to drain away from the artistic experience the conditions of alienation. Nevertheless, those conditions are available. First of all, there is the almost divine irresponsibility of art. Certainly a work of art is a set of directions, and the artistic experience or response is a performance, but that performance need not and ordinarily does not become a set of directions to the artistic responder himself for a further performance on his part. This is not to deny that the work of art usually exemplifies a metaphysic, whether its explanatory or validational aspects. It may even exemplify a specific morality. There is no doubt that art is an extremely important tool of social management or policing. All art is, in fact, propaganda and rhetoric. However, the irresponsibility of the artistic perceiver can combine with an explanatory analysis of the exemplificatory aspect of the work in question to objectify the directions being exemplified, or, as often happens, being presented baldly and overtly. The teacher needs to be governed, not by "Oh the greatness of Michelangelo's soul," but rather by "Look what the son-of-a-bitch is doing to you." Thus the study of art can be used to abstract the patterns of directions-giving social management. That the Sistine ceiling is a prime instance of such social management cannot be doubted for a moment.

This marvelous irresponsibility of the artistic experience—an irresponsibility so necessary for the correction of the behavioral condition—is made possible by the fact that the artistic experience generally takes place in a situation of social protection and psychic insulation; and the higher the cultural level of the work and of the artistic experience, the truer this is. Indeed, the cultural level of a work of art can be readily determined by the degree of protection and insulation in which it is ordinarily presented. The prime function, however, of these factors in artistic experience is that art is characterized by perceptual discontinuity, or by the violation of the norms of expectancy. I have argued this extensively in the work mentioned above, *Man's Rage for Chaos*, and I can scarcely argue it again here. One point must serve. Whether or not an artifact was made in order to be an occasion for the performance of the artistic perceiver's role can be determined if an historical series of such artifacts, when juxtaposed in historical order, shows nonfunctional stylistic dynamism—shows, that is, stylistic change which is not related to the semantic aspect of the work. Women's fashions provide a ready example. The disorientation consequent upon perceptual discontinuity is ordinarily

tolerable only in psychically insulated or otherwise socially protected conditions. Moreover all social roles which require sustained problem exposure and solution postponement, such as that
of the corporation president, require the same protection and
insulation. Such sustained problem exposure and solution postponement is the mark of fictional narrative; while in the drama,
disorientation is often achieved by presenting information more
rapidly than it can be assimilated and sorted out and by inter-
weaving informational series so that overlapping and switching
from one series to another, without logical or other completion, is
maximized. The teacher of art—who normally does not teach
art, but directions for responding to art—must abandon the
aesthetics of order and give directions in such a way that the richness of the possibilities for perceptual discontinuity in the particular work are fully extracted. That this can be done and that
students respond very well to it I know from experience. They
are in fact grateful, for the aesthetics of order directly contradict
what they see before them. Students are very capable of recogniz-
ing the aesthetics of order as brainwashing, but they have no
vocabulary of invalidation with which to counteract it. In this
way, the teaching of art can become an admirable training in the
toleration of tension and disorientation.

Discontinuity is a matter of the formal aspect of a work of art.
Turning to the semantic aspect, it must first be recognized that
no semantic function is to be found in art that is not to be found
outside of it. The currently popular and even dominating doctrine
is that a work of art consists of semantic functions unique to that
work—of a semantic order or coherence unique to that work—
which is why it is value laden, and that the work has a capability,
therefore, of presenting "truths" not accessible outside of the
realm of art and artistic experience. This patent nonsense, a
rationalization of the Romantic's claim to the right of semantic
innovation, is obviously in the service of and sustained by a metaphysical notion of order and is a prime instance of high cultural
policing. It exploits the irresponsibility of the artistic experience
by converting it into an experience of great though absolutely
indefinable moral value. It is clearly training in social and cultural responsibility, the antithesis of that alienation which is the

condition of behavioral correction. On the contrary, the teacher of art should emphasize in his semantic analysis the incoherence of the work as a set of directions, thus showing why the historical conditions in which the work was produced have been transcended and abandoned. The theory behind this is that the dynamics of cultural history are to be found in the fact that changing circumstances of a society reveal incoherences in its culture which were once felt as coherences. Alienation has always been the mode for dealing with the discovery of cultural incoherence. That is why I suggested above that the Romantics did not invent alienation but discovered it and abstracted it from the matrix of behavior. The presentation of such incoherence is one of the best ways of training the individual to tolerate tension and even to seek it out, the aim being to direct his awareness toward the irresolvable tension between policing and correction.

The final point is that the teaching of art must be absolutely value-free. An introductory course in any of the arts, for example, or in the various arts, should select what is taught by a random sampling of all cultural levels, all cultures, and all historical periods. No mention of value should be made at all, nothing of "How beautiful this is," but only, "That is what is going on here," as outlined above. This value-free teaching is of the highest importance for training students to tolerate alienation and to see its possibilities as a means of correcting the current behavioral condition. The traditional method of teaching art is, above all, giving the students directions on value hierarchies. To have value settled in an area so remote from the concerns of ordinary life as art makes the artistic experience a prime source for self-policing, for limitation of the range of behavior, and therefore for a devotion to art of an addictive or nearly addictive character —a phenomenon that is currently increasing, though mostly at a fairly low cultural level. For this reason, to present a work of art without value directions is a useful way of exposing the students to an altogether desirable condition closely approaching panic. Beyond this it is desirable to expose the interests that govern the current valuation of the work and its place in the hierarchy of art value, and also the interests that governed such valuations in the past. The two strategies together should be so handled as to expose the student to his own interests in art valuation and in valuation in general. Thus the goal of training in alienation will be reached: self-alienation, or self-estrangement.

Several matters are now, I hope, fairly clear. Since education is primarily a matter of policing and training in self-policing, higher education, if it is to be reconstructed, can only be reconstructed to institutionalize more deeply than at the present alienation as a mode of existence. It is also clear, I believe, that such reconstruction can only be brought about by training faculties, or at least key faculty members, in alienation. Finally, it is equally evident that though the study of art and the training in artistic experience can be of great importance in preparing individuals for alienation, to use education in art in that way requires a total revolution in the way art is currently taught and validated. It does not seem to me that any of all this is possible, at least in universities and colleges as they now exist and are likely to continue to exist.

17

CULTURAL STAGNATION IN

AMERICAN UNIVERSITIES AND COLLEGES

[1971*]

The problem with which I propose to grapple is whether or not our educational institutions, particularly those of higher education, can be so revitalized as to overcome their current cultural stagnation. As I proposed in chapter 16, that stagnation is by no means limited to educational institutions but, on the contrary, obtains through our culture, whether we conceive of it as European-American (i.e., Western) or as increasingly international and worldwide. As to the latter alternative, it is obvious that as the undeveloped countries develop, they adopt with very little adaptation the cultural patterns of the West, and in so doing lock themselves into the problems of the West, particularly the problem of cultural stagnation, before which the West itself appears so far to be relatively helpless. It hardly seems possible that the little lever of higher education can move the enormous and lethargic mass of the world.

* Presented at a conference on the humanities at Converse College, Spartanburg, S.C., January 27, 1972.

Insofar as academia is stagnant, its cultural difficulties are subsumed and explained by the general stagnation. However, there obtain in higher education both endemic and epidemic sources of stagnation which are special to that social area (for a discussion see chapter 16, "Arts for the Cultivation of Radical Sensitivity").

It does not seem to me possible that any reform of the curriculum can be accomplished unless both the endemic and the epidemic infections are dealt with. Though I am aware that some colleges require publication, henceforth by "universities" I shall mean that publishing is required and by "colleges" that it is not, and by "required" I mean "required for tenure, promotion, and salary raises above the average." The structure of the problem is that the endemic infection is to be found in both universities and colleges, while the epidemic infection is to be found obviously only in the former. However, the consequence of the epidemic infection, professionalization, is to be found in both. The endemic infection manifests—as I have already suggested in discussing the question of value of the faculty member—in teaching. What is good teaching? Who knows? The confidence with which my colleagues talk about good teaching never fails to astonish me. I have been called a good teacher, but if I am, I haven't the slightest idea why. Moreover, though I rather think that the majority of students rather like what I do, and a minority like it very much, I also am quite aware that a respectable minority detest the ground I walk on. Students have been known to turn purple with fury at the mere mention of my name. I can console myself, of course, with the rationalization that since the only function of the teacher is to disturb, at least I have disturbed those who hate me. For all I know, I may have been of greater intellectual value to those who hate me than to those who are enthusiastic about me. I have no way of knowing. In the same way I am so dumbfounded by the behavior of my colleagues in sessions of committees on promotion and tenure that I will no longer serve on such committees. A man's life is disposed of, so far as I can see, on no evidence whatever—except the evidence of reputation, which is notoriously unreliable. Once when I was an acting head, it was represented to me that we should get rid of a young man because several students had said that he was the worst teacher they had ever had. Since we had a student committee working on faculty evaluation, I decided I would get some good out of it and asked it to make an ad hoc survey of student opinion about that particular teacher. It was true that several students said he was the worst teacher they had ever had, but it was equally true that even more said he was the best teacher they had ever had.

These are old stories to all of us, but I bring up such a weary subject in order to make a point which I rarely hear made, and then only by myself. It takes two to make a teaching situation. The relation of teacher to student is a charismatic relationship. Some adolescents like—or I should say, I suppose, liked—the Beatles, and some did not. Who can understand this? Teaching can be neither measured nor judged, and our talk about good teaching is, I think, absolutely idle. That is why, in universities, teaching cannot be an alternative to publication, which always wins out. Publication is something, but teaching is nothing. Hence a good many university teachers sneer at teaching. It is a way out of the dilemma, but not the best way. One of the best administrators I know frankly judges both teaching and publication on the same grounds—reputation. It is a way to make decisions, but it does absolutely nothing to meet any of the problems I have suggested as the central and destructive problems.

John Stuart Mill said that happiness could not be achieved directly, but only as a by-product, and I think the same point is true of teaching. But this leaves us with the question, "A by-product of what?" I think the best that can be done with this is to answer, "A by-product of intellectual vitality." It is one of those vague notions that can easily be torn apart; hence I shall not argue it, but merely assert it. There are a thousand ways good teaching can manifest itself; I suspect the dynamism is a continuous questioning of one's own assumptions. I try to teach my graduate students that they must force their ideas to the wall, put a knife to their throats, and kill them without mercy if their pockets yield nothing of value. One thing I am reasonably sure of, though it is only a negative definition. Intellectual vitality is not paradigmatic behavior. It is not the continuous exemplification of a socially validated and unquestioned theoretical model, as, for example, most publishing today is, and from what I hear, most teaching.

The first step toward meeting the problem of endemic infection is creating a situation which encourages and rewards intellectual vitality. But this is not easy. On grounds I can scarcely go into here, I have come to the conclusion that most human energy is directed toward the limitation of the range of the individual's behavior—both the range of categories and the range of behavioral deviation within any given category. The general term I use to refer to this phenomenon is "policing," which includes self-policing. Socialization consists of learning strategies for limiting the range of behavior, and to be interested in anything is to have found a satisfactory way of limiting one's behavioral range. The important matter is the limitation, not the character of the interest. Thus if intellectual vitality is nonparadigmatic, it works counter to the central thrust of human behavior. One of the main difficulties in implementing humanities programs is the resistance of faculty members to innovating programs. Here, I think, is the reason.

But how does one encourage and reward intellectual vitality? How does one even recognize it? It is as elusive as teaching. I think the answer is "by imitating reward by publication and quantifying it." In rewarding for publication, the first criterion is bulk, the second is the prestige of the medium of publication, and the third is quality—but quality doesn't mean much, because by that term is generally meant "conforming to a professionally validated paradigm." These are devices that certainly have resulted in an enormous amount of publication, though the notion of quality has just as certainly contributed almost nothing to intellectual vitality and has had no effect at all that I can see on the cultural stagnation of this country, except very probably to make it worse. I have suggested that it was thought that requirement for publication would increase the level of intellectual vitality, but I suspect that, if anything, it has lowered it. Nevertheless it is a model worth imitating because it had results. It is the only thing in the academic world that we can be sure has had any results. Publication is evidence that something has happened. We need similar quantifiable evidence for intellectual vitality.

Actually it is not at all difficult to find a way of getting it. The first step is to reward an individual for taking a graduate course beyond the Ph.D., in a field other than his own. In universities each course taken can be made the equivalent of a published article. The chances are enormous that the individual will learn more than he will by writing an article, and that is the important matter, that he learn something he did not know before. It would be quite possible, though the idea will necessarily encounter considerable resistance, to make such an accumulation of course credits official, in the sense that the individual can earn another Ph.D. But this is not essential. All that is essential is that the individual administering the course certify that the student has completed the equivalent of a graduate course. Nor need such a plan be limited to universities that award graduate degrees. Any college has a large number of faculty members capable of teaching at the graduate level, though the accidents of life have landed them at a place where they have no opportunity to do so. Nor need the courses be formal. They can be as informal as this. Suppose I should go to the professor who teaches the graduate course in Goethe's *Faust* and ask to take it. He might well reply, "Good heavens, it's not at a high enough level for you. You have written about *Faust* and I have quoted you in an article. Instead, I'll give you a list of the fifty best books and articles on *Faust* that I am aware of. You come over to my house once a week and we shall discuss them, and you write me a paper on why you think the valuable ones are valuable. It will be a pleasure to discuss these matters with a colleague, and at leisure, rather than with even the best graduate student." Moreover, if the individual takes enough courses to acquire, either officially or unofficially, the equivalent of the courses needed for a degree and in addition writes a dissertation, the reward should be commensurate. In universities it should be made the equivalent of the publication of a book, whether in fact it is published or not, and like almost all dissertations it probably will be better that it not be. The results of such a policy might be very great. At the time of the campus disturbances, not only newspaper editors but even faculty people (who should have known better) lamented that such explosions should affect the intellectual community of a university. This is absurd. An intellectual community is the last thing any modern campus is, university or college. Almost nobody really talks seriously to anybody else. If you want some decent intellectual conversation you have to form a group or a club, and keep it secret. My proposal might very possibly do something to bring to life the intellectual deserts in which we all live.

The second step is in two parts: first, to limit the number of times in close succession anybody can teach the same undergraduate course, and second, to reward an individual every time he teaches a new course. If this looks like the stick and the carrot, that is exactly what it is. To the objection I have heard that this would create course-charlatans as well as publication-charlatans, the answer is that there is no reason to be prejudiced in favor of only one kind of charlatan. There is no system that cannot be beat. It is the task of the administrator, never fully successful, to keep beating the system to a minimum. I would go even further. The term before the individual is to teach the new course, he should be required to give a public lecture on the subject. Such inaugural lectures should be made important and dignified occasions. For the students it would be a preview of a coming attraction. For the faculty it would be a chance to see one's friends, and one's enemies, and oneself, performing under pressure and, one hopes, at the highest level of their abilities. For this would not be an expert speaking as a professional, but an intelligent man grappling with problems and ideas new to him. This is the way paradigms are broken.

There are two points in this plan. First, by teaching a new course—and I am referring to undergraduate courses—one learns considerably more than it takes to write an article or even, for that matter, most books. Second, teaching a new course requires the individual to take risks. The social protection and psychic insulation we enjoy as faculty members are the conditions for social roles which require risk-taking, yet in our calling there is very little intellectual risk-taking, and, once again, the publication policy has reduced what little there once was.

These two steps will provide the qualifiable evidence we need for intellectual vitality. They cannot of course ensure such vitality, but they can increase enormously the probability that it will be forthcoming. It is my considered opinion that most faculty people have withered on the vine by the time they are fifty, and most of our young and eager publishing scholars by the time they are thirty-five or forty. The object is to reward the individual for learning something and for taking intellectual risks. To study a different field is bound to have a reflexive effect upon your own, even if you are an English teacher and study physics, certainly if you study any of the behavioral sciences or a humanity other than your own. To study outside your field forces you to question your own assumptions and forces you to question the paradigms of your own discipline.

It has been imagined that faculty members are in a social situation in which they undertake such efforts on their own, without stimulus and reward. But that is certainly not the case, for the reason I have already given: The central human thrust is to limit the range of one's behavior. If we are to accomplish anything, this is what must be fought against, but it is not the only enemy.

It is, I think, obvious that the two devices I have proposed would be enormously beneficial in creating an atmosphere favorable for innovative humanities programs and for providing the personnel for them, but before discussing that matter it is necessary to get another problem out of the way.

In any institution in which there is only one effective mode of achieving status and reward, a mode unavailable to or refused by some members of that institution, the result is disastrous. That is exactly the situation that obtains in universities. In any hierarchical situation—for that, in spite of our democratic rhetoric, is what we live in—the normal mode looking down from the top is contempt, and up from the bottom is resentment. In publishing departments, contempt is the mode of the haves, and resentment is the mode of the have-nots. The fact that there is no alternative mode to becoming a have instead of a have-not creates an atmosphere of such fierce resentment that it does not seem possible to me that the have-nots can perform at anywhere near their best level, or even at their median level. Moreover, both contempt at the top and resentment at the bottom are sources of righteousness, and righteousness is a strategy for avoiding the problems of the institution. Possibly there are good departments in very small colleges, but probably in the larger colleges and certainly in the universities I do not think that there is a good *department* in the country. In universities "good department" means a number of nationally known faculty members, but this has absolutely nothing to do with whether the department is good as a department. On the contrary, it prevents the existence of a good department in any other sense. If my analysis is correct, what is needed are alternative modes of achieving reward and status, and I have proposed such modes. But I do not think there is the slightest chance of their being implemented in universities. The reason is simple. The publishing haves make the policy decisions. The mere suggestion of the alternative modes I have proposed would arouse their most intent opposition. There would be outcries of the utmost violence against violating and compromising professional standards. But what these outcries would really mean is that those who have the gravy have no intention of sharing it with anyone else. Nor would large infusions of new money make any difference. That happened in the 1960s, and those who had the gravy simply got more of it. For the question in hand—innovative humanistic programs—it is useless to imagine that the universities are capable of accomplishing anything. It must be recognized that the present university system has a built-in economic principle which resists any change in the direction of encouraging intellectual vitality instead of cultural stagnation. No leadership can be expected from the universities. If anything is to be accomplished, it can be done only in the colleges. To be sure, I know of one university, not that there are not others of which I am ignorant, in which a certain innovation shows promise and is developing. It is working, or at least shows promise of working, simply because the president set up a separate college and promised, and has kept his promise, to reward its faculty just as well as the faculty in other colleges in the university but without requiring from them anything whatever in the way of publication. So far he has kept his promise, but the experimental college is but a few years old and the faculty is young. Either salary levels will not advance to the levels obtaining in the publishing colleges of the university, thus driving out the talented men now in the experimental college, or a publication requirement will be imposed or an excuse will be found to destroy the experiment. (Since first writing this, I have learned that my prediction is coming true; faculty members are still part of their original departments, through which rewards are processed. The departments are holding back on raises, promotions, and tenure. The college is suffering seriously.) The growing academic depression, which will probably last at least another ten years, and probably much, much longer, can only exacerbate the situation.

But a further factor which will prevent the development of innovative humanistic programs in the universities needs also to be mentioned. It is relatively minor, but crucial to the interests of this discussion. If a faculty member, particularly a young faculty member, engages in one of those abortive interdisciplinary or humanistic efforts which every now and then crop up in universities and usually wither away, he is not rewarded, but punished. Such programs require enormous amounts of time and energy. They require for some years an intense devotion, and it is really a self-sacrificing devotion, for the time he spends on the program is taken away from time that could be spent—far more profitably to himself and his family, often approaching or going through its maximum needs—on publication.

Nothing, then, can be expected from the universities. If anything is to be done, the colleges must do it. But here another difficulty lies in the way. I have suggested that my two proposals would do much to work against the fundamental inertia of human life which affects faculty people as much as anyone else. In the colleges also, however, there is the difficulty of stagnant professionalism. This emerges forcefully in the extremely common term "interdisciplinary." A true story will illustrate why "interdisciplinary" is a term that is far more of a hindrance than it possibly can be a help. In the 1950s Professor Michael Woolf established at Indiana University a new journal, *Victorian Studies.* His aim was interdisciplinary. However, he wanted both the innovative character of interdisciplinary studies and the prestige that comes only with obeying the paradigms of the professional disciplines. The result was that his journal published nothing that could not have been published in a scholarly journal of one of the professional disciplines. The trouble with the term "interdisciplinary" is that it tells everybody engaged in interdisciplinary efforts that they must meet the standards of their respective disciplines. It informs them that they must simultaneously maintain the standards of their professional disciplines and, at the same time, transcend those standards, abandon them. What is needed is not interdisciplinary programs but interdisciplinary teachers. Even assuming that professional standards in intellectual activities are worth maintaining—and for some purposes they are, though increasingly unimportant ones culturally—it is impossible for one man to maintain those standards in a number of fields, or if it is possible, it is so for such a tiny number of people as not to be worth considering. "Professional standards" means a mastery of the minute details of professional discipline, but all that at the best can be hoped for an interdisciplinary teacher is that he grasp the theoretical structure of that discipline, provided it has one, and not all of the academic professional disciplines do—literature, for example. An interdisciplinary teacher cannot be a professional; he must be an amateur. But to my mind this is by no means discouraging. Virtually all the major contributions to European culture have been made by people we would today call amateurs, not by what we mean today by professionals. Darwin was not a professional biologist but an old-fashioned English naturalist. Not one of the great figures of the seventeenth century, the century of genius, was a professional in the modern sense. If the colleges genuinely wish to accomplish something in humanistic programs or, better yet, in humanistic-scientific programs, they must abandon professionalism to the haves of the universities and embrace happily and wholeheartedly the reamateurization of their intellectual life. What this amounts to is that those faculty members who engage in such programs must be re-educated, they must be rewarded while they are being re-educated, and they must be rewarded for having been re-educated. Moreover, it is probably relatively futile to attempt such programs unless matters are so arranged that faculty participation carries with it the highest status and prestige available in the college undertaking them. Success in the kind of program under consideration depends upon solving two problems, a problem in social management and an intellectual problem. It is relatively fruitless to deal with the second without having made considerable progress in the first. The prospects for doing anything effective about the first are almost certainly negative for universities and not, I fear, very promising for the colleges. Yet if anything can be done, it must be done in the colleges.

Assuming that effective action can be taken in dealing with the problem of social management, the intellectual problem can be considered, but I shall have less to say about it than about the social problem. First I must utter another caution, I fear. There is no use in building a program designed to have an intellectual appeal to sizable numbers of the faculty. Faculty personnel are middle-class Americans first and intellectuals second. Considering that their primary task is to turn out replacement and expansion parts for the great corporations and their ancillaries— since the corporations in effect own the academic establishment through boards of trustees—this condition is probably all for the best in what is clearly the best of all possible worlds. What I mean is that the major life decisions are not made on intellectual grounds but on grounds of class membership, a situation directly responsible for publish-and-perish and for professionalism. Moreover, the effect of the destructiveness of faculty life, its endemic infection, is not to increase intellectuality but to emphasize the sense of class membership. If one's position in society is anomalous, and if one is gainfully employed in an institution deeply embedded in the social quasi-system, one longs for a reduction in the anomaly, and the university and college teacher longs to become, not more intellectual, but more middle class. Mind you, I am not attacking anti-intellectualism. It is not love that makes the world go around, but anti-intellectualism. Profound intellectuality discloses the inadequacy, the irredeemable inadequacy, of human adaptational strategies. Yet as I understand it, what is being proposed in the kind of program under consideration here is an increase in intellectuality, and therefore a deliberate introduction into college education of a factor that, if successful, will increase the probability of turning out both faculty and students characterized by sociocultural detachment, disengagement, alienation, and estrangement. Yet these modes are as essential as anti-intellectualism, however, for the social task of intellectualism is not knowledge for its own sake—an absurd rationalization—but the discernment and correction of those inadequate adaptational strategies that, in any given historical situation, can be discerned and corrected. It is the business of the academic establishment to turn out personalities carefully trained in specific ways of limiting their behavioral range, ways modeled on middle-class and socially validated paradigms. It appears to be the position of this conference that it also should be the business of the academic establishment to turn out nonparadigmatic intellectuals in somewhat greater numbers than are now produced by, it would seem, accident and inadvertence. Moreover, when I assert that it is the business of the academic establishment to turn out paradigmatic personalities, I mean turning out not only students but also teachers. Nor do I mean training people to be teachers; I mean the consequence of the lifelong activity of teaching. Humanistic programs designed to use the existent knowledge and skills of individuals regarded as successful teachers cannot amount to much. A successful program must be designed to have at least as much effect on its faculty as on its students.

Only those faculty members can be useful who are willing to engage continuously in a disorienting and deeply disturbing experience, who are willing to run the risks of sociocultural detachment, disengagement, alienation, and estrangement. We tend, like everyone else, to think of a college or university as a social institution in which the faculty shapes and molds the students. We neglect the obvious fact—and thus we have little or no control over the process—that the university and college are institutions which shape and mold the faculty, and have forty years to do it in, not just four.

For such purposes I believe that one of the most valuable lines to follow is the line of cultural history. Its immediate advantages are, I think, obvious. It is not a professionally recognized field; it is not a discipline; it is even sneered at by academic professionals. Historically, after the failure of nineteenth-century efforts to create *Geistesgeschichte* on a Hegelian and neo-Hegelian model, it fell into pretty thorough-going disrepute. Almost entirely deficient in theory, it lacks even a theoretical means of selecting material to be studied from the ocean of material available. It has no way of distinguishing between the Gothic novelists and the contemporaneous writings of Immanuel Kant. To attempt to move into it requires exactly that kind of risk-taking, both intellectual and professional, that our social role demands but that is so rarely tried. Further, it fits in extremely well with both strategies I have proposed for increasing intellectual vitality. Moreover, there are various indications that if the humanities and the social sciences are to develop and if humanists and social scientists are to transgress their professional constraints, it is one of the directions they can and must move in and in fact are already doing so. For the humanist there are three promising directions of transgression: theory construction, the behavioral sciences, and cultural history. In the study of literature, theory construction has been exceedingly feeble and pretty generally is based on an untenable aesthetic. In the historical fields, theory construction, also feeble but a little stronger, has been based on an inadequate philosophical model. In both literature and history so far, movement in the behavioral sciences has been mostly in the direction of psychoanalysis, which I cannot but feel is an intellectual cul-de-sac, more metaphysics than science. On the other hand, cultural history, for all its vagueness, is what the historical study of literature and history has been all along, without, for the most part, knowing it. Moreover, both those disciplines are filled with explanatory statements about human behavior, for the most part intuitive and unsupported. On the other hand, sociology and psychology are, here and there, beginning to move into an historical dimension, though again the liveliest area is also, I believe, the most unpromising—psychoanalysis, which is, whatever else it may be, unquestionably an historical discipline, arising from the pervasive historicism of the nineteenth century. There are signs, then, of a convergence upon cultural history. Moreover, having tried cultural history myself, and being currently engaged in teaching it at the graduate level (though of course it is called something else) and in attempting to construct a theory of cultural history, I know that it is capable of having a profound and truly intellectual effect upon intelligent students, though the less gifted tend to be somewhat bewildered. Either I have not found a way to reach them, or in spite of my rhetoric I am not really concerned with reaching them, or very possibly cultural history is not for them. But its greatest advantage is this. I have suggested that there is a necessary, or at least a desirable, connection among intellectual vitality, professional transgression, and amateurization. I know of nothing that engages all three of these factors so well as cultural history.

Moreover, there is a further and far more pragmatic reason for exploring its possibilities. One of the problems, perhaps the most important problem, in the current sociocultural circumstances is information overload. We are deluged with far more information than we can possibly absorb and organize into some kind of cognitive order. As Browning suggested eighty years ago, the invention of printing may have been a disaster. For our purposes, the most important matter to recognize is that we gain knowledge of our current world exactly as we gain knowledge of the world of the past, through various media. There is no difference between the way we learn about the events in Bangla Desh and the way we learn from a medieval chronicler about the battle of Poitiers, nor is there any difference between background journalism, as in *Time*, and historical discourse. Both are explanatory of reported events, or of nonevents, as the case may be. The real value of cultural history and its real thrust is not the accumulation of historical knowledge, entertaining as it is for history buffs, both academic and nonacademic. The real value is that in studying some segment of the past there is less information to be controlled; there is more accurate knowledge, since reports have been examined and sifted; there is far less emotional involvement; and the information is relatively stable, by comparison with current information; these factors together make it possible to construct an explanation for the data. But it is not the explanation that is important here. The important matter is that the construction of a reasonably satisfactory explanation for past events can provide a cognitive model for constructing a reasonably satisfactory explanation for current events. The study of cultural history, therefore, should have three aspects for the purpose of undergraduate education: the intellectual engagement with a relatively stable and controllable body of data, the construction of a cognitive model for organizing that data, and, this above all, the self-conscious awareness of the interests at work in self-and-culture in the construction of that model.

The last two considerations bring out the significance of the proposal that the kind of program we are thinking about must involve the education of the faculty as well as the education of the students. Thus the model is not something to be created by the faculty and then presented to the students; it must be fluid, it must be used dialectically, its instability must be exploited, just as, in the best of modern science, advances are made by exploiting the instability of theories, not in attempting to stabilize them. The faculty member must himself become a role-model for the students, in that he is, first, actively engaged in constructing and dismantling his cognitive models, and, second, engaged in discovering his own interests at work in that activity. Looking at oneself from right angles—or disengagement from one's self— is the same thing as disengagement from one's culture. Not learning appropriate behavior, but learning the capacity to behave inappropriately is the proper aim of the kind of program we are talking about. If the student can learn to endure the risks and dangers of disorientation, detachment, disengagement, alienation, and estrangement in a limited and protected environment— if he can learn under such circumstances to place himself, when needed, in an ironic relation to his own culture—some students may be able, after graduation, to use these attitudes in the real circumstances of life in our culture and society. If we are serious in what we are considering, we must, I think, recognize that we are proposing to produce nonparadigmatic and culturally disruptive intellectuals, men and women capable of struggling with some success against the central thrust of humanity—the limitation of the range of behavior—a thrust which makes human life possible but also makes it a failure.

18

THE ARTS

AND THE CENTERS OF POWER

[1971*]

The intimate relation between centers of power and the pro- duction and possession of the high arts is a problem that has long troubled me. One reason for my annoyance is that I have an intense interest in the high arts and I have devoted my life to studying them; but like many people who have little or no social power, I have little fondness for centers of power. The reason for my distaste is quite obvious, at least to me. In any hierarchical system—and all societies are hierarchically organized, and must be, as well as the institutions that make up those so- cieties—the prevailing attitude looking down from the top is contempt, while the corresponding attitude, looking from the

* Delivered at The Cooper Union School of Art and Architecture, Feb- ruary 3, 1972, and at the annual meeting of the Conference of College Teach- ers of English of Texas, March 10, 1972. Reprinted by permission from *Proceedings of the CCTE*, XXXVII (September 1972), pp. 7–17. Copyright © 1972 by Conference of College Teachers of English of Texas. Reprinted from *Critiques 1971/72*, The Cooper Union, 1972. Copyright © 1972, by Morse Peckham.

bottom up, is resentment. Both, to be sure, are strategies for avoiding the problems of the institution; and this avoidance explains why, although societies and their institutions work, they do not work very well.

And there are other reasons as well for avoiding the problem of the interrelationship I have spoken of, aside from the fact that the higher the art, the greater its economic dependence on power centers. Partly because of that resentment I have alluded to; partly because of the abuse of power by those who possess it (a situation to a great degree accounted for by the contempt that corresponds to the resentment of those without power); and partly because the possessors of power—who, if anyone does, have access to adequate information—so frequently make bad mistakes; the famous statement that all power tends to corrupt is one that receives immediate and enthusiastic assent from those without social power or with very little. That happy approbation in itself suggests that Acton's famous remark might be a sentimentality, and I suspect it is. When it comes to social power, the virtuous tend to be those who do not have any—just as, for example, although I have always been perfectly willing to sell my soul, it was only a few years ago that I received an offer, which of course I accepted without hesitation. But since I did not sell my soul for power but only for money, I continue to be troubled and indeed defensive about the association of the high arts and power. Actually, when I try to disengage and estrange myself from the normal attitudes of the powerless, I am forced to conclude that Acton's famous statement is quite inexact. On the contrary, it seems to be somewhat nearer the true state of affairs to assert that only the possession of social power in considerable quantity makes it possible for any individual not to be corrupt. This is somewhat comforting. Only the noncorrupt possessors of power are the supporters of the high arts. But the briefest meditation on the association between socially powerful moral monsters and their support of, and occasionally even passionate devotion to, the high arts deprives one of the sentimentality.

Looking elsewhere for that unease about the relationship of power and the high arts—an unease which most sociocultural products like myself share—it is quite obvious that those who are devoted to the high arts, in whatever capacity, and to high culture in general think of both as occupying in human affairs a special, unique, transcendent, and altogether superior position, while they perceive power, at best, as engaged in the somewhat degrading and, by contrast, impure activity of social management. Shelley put it in words no teacher of literature ever forgets or permits his students to forget: "Poets are the unacknowledged legislators of the world." This is believable, I suppose, only because it is such patent nonsense. *Credo, quia impossibile est.* We like to think that we are devoted to the high arts and to high culture because they are superior, but if we compare ourselves to the norms of human valuing, it seems more appropriate to conclude that we assert their superiority because we are devoted to them. And there is good reason to be devoted to them. The high arts and high culture are expensive; they never have been self-supporting; in any society it takes a lot of people to create them, to preserve them, to transmit them, to study them. All these people have to be paid, and they are paid of course out of the surplus funds available to those in positions of social power. If one cannot have power, one can at least have money; and in spite of the financial lamentations of scholars and artists throughout history, a devotion to high culture and its arts is not at all a bad way of getting it. To be sure it takes a lot of work to get very much of it—and often some talent—but one can scarcely hope to develop a marketable soul without some investment of energy. The surprising thing is that it is possible to make a decent living, and sometimes a splendid living, out of an activity that seems economically entirely without function.

One can of course explain the link between the high arts and power centers by appealing to some such argument as this: The arts provide the display necessary for status symbols. There is certainly much that is convincing in this argument, but it does not take care by any means of all the pertinent data. In a bourgeois society such as ours or Communist Russia's it does not hold very well. The great foundations, and in some countries the government, not only support the arts but seem purposely to divorce themselves from anything like splendor, nor do they use the products of that support to maintain that splendor. The Nobel prizes add nothing to the satisfaction of Alfred Nobel, who is dead; they only create a sociological puzzle. Moreover—though I think, for reasons to be forthcoming, that art is always rhetorical and always propagandistic—the freedom of the artist to present his own version of his employer's propaganda, and even to deny its validity and instead to offer his own propaganda, is today considered the very mark of a democratic and free society. The artist, for nearly two hundred years, has insisted that attacks on power centers must be supported by those very power centers and their surplus funds. It is as fascinating as it is mysterious that this claim has so often been granted. And even before this the artist claimed the right to be free from ordinary morality, and as Cellini's memoirs tell us, was granted that right. To bring the puzzle home, how can we explain the existence of such an institution as the Cooper Union? It is not satisfying to account for it by ascribing to the founder the noblest of noble sentiments. Why did he have such noble sentiments? And why did he devote such a large fortune to expressing them? We must, I think, look elsewhere, and to my mind when one is faced with a puzzle in human behavior it is often advisable to begin by looking to language, for language seems to be the activity that makes man human. And when one turns to language to find the answer to a riddle, one must turn to the central problem of language, meaning.

For half a century philosophy has been deeply preoccupied with the problem of language; indeed, the philosophical revolution of this century has emerged precisely from that preoccupation. At the same time modern linguistics has emerged, some of whose practitioners have had harsh things to say about the philosophers. The latter have directed their attention toward logic and somewhat less so toward the question of meaning, while the linguists, particularly the predominating school, are not pursuing a promising line, for their whole investigation, including that of syntax, is, I believe, philosophically regressive. The philosophers have not been much more successful. One school has, in the traditional philosophical way, as we now realize, set out to correct and improve language, to discipline it and straighten it out. Another school insists that language is perfectly all right as it is; all we have to do is to find out how it is really used. But the first school seems to ignore the fact that the correction of language is a constant in linguistic behavior, while the other school seems to ignore the fact that because language is constantly being corrected—as well as constantly changing for other reasons to which I shall return—it is impossible to find out how it is really used; there is no such thing as "ordinary language." But both schools certainly appear to proceed on the assumption that meaning is immanent in the language, that words are somehow the carriers of meaning, and that to find out what a statement really means is analogous to pulling olives out of a bottle.

But meaning is nothing of this sort at all. The carriers of meaning are not words but human beings, and they know how to ascribe meanings to words because they have been trained to do so by other people—parents, peers, teachers, all the culture carriers or transmitters, that is, everybody, all the time. In short, the meaning of any utterance it is possible to respond to is in fact that response. (This looks like a simple stimulus-response theory but it is not, as I shall make clear shortly.) But once we have sundered meaning from words and put it where it properly belongs, in the human being responding to those words, we are faced with the peculiar fact that in theory every word is capable of eliciting all possible responses. This proposal brings the problem of meaning right out into the open and above all provides an explanation for two phenomena of meaning, which otherwise, by a theory of immanent meaning, can only be stated but not accounted for. These are polysemy, or the fact that words have multiple meanings, as any dictionary can tell you, and semantic drift, the fact that meanings are constantly changing, as any historical dictionary can tell you. But semantic drift requires further explanations, of which two are available. The first is the very nature of the human brain. We can no longer talk about stimulus and response; we can only talk about stimulus field and response. And this makes it impossible to locate the specific stimulus for any response. In language, any utterance is encountered in a situation extremely rich not only in other utterances but also in other signs, nonverbal signs. So the stimulus field is a field of signs, and the human brain combines them in all kinds of ways. Anyone who has had a disagreement with someone else about how a painting should be interpreted or explained is quite aware of the possibilities for responding to a field of signs, even one limited by the edge of a painting, and of the extreme difficulty of coming to a decision acceptable to both parties. The second explanation is even more pertinent to our problem here. The brain is so constructed that it is virtually impossible to learn correctly anything more elaborate than very simple patterns of behavior, such as a sequence of seven numbers. Even such a sequence is an abstraction from the context in which it is encountered. The consequence is that in human behavior there is a constant flow of innovation. If we approve of the innovation we call it creativity; if we disapprove of it, we call it error. But most innovation is so slight that it goes unnoticed, and the accumulation of such innovations, as well as those both approved of and disapproved of, results in behavioral drift, of which semantic drift—the drift of meaning—is but a special case. So polysemy and semantic drift are the same thing, semantic innovation considered at any moment in history and considered historically. Or rather, since innovation is the predominating character—taking in the dimension of time—it accounts for polysemy, or, to use a useful word, subsumes polysemy. Or we can put it thus: Polysemy is a special case or an example of semantic drift. Or, polysemy exemplifies the more general case of semantic drift.

These alternative ways of putting it are very much to the point, for I want to consider the structure of the argument I have proposed. Observe that I have not said, "Semantic drift causes polysemy," and for two good reasons. When we use the word "cause" in connection with observable events in the world outside of language, all that we mean is that if x happens, in all probability y will happen. And all we can do is to wait and see. But when we are engaging in language behavior and utter such a sentence as "Semantic drift causes polysemy," all we are saying is that word x causes word y, which clearly cannot be the case, because in uttering "causes polysemy" I was responding to my own utterance "semantic drift," as well as to the full context, verbal and nonverbal, in which I uttered "semantic drift." If anybody "caused" "polysemy," I did, but I cannot possibly understand how. In language, "cause" links, not nonverbal events, but utterances, and that is all it does. (There is, however, another way of putting this, to which I shall return.) All the difficulties about "cause" have arisen from the confusion between two quite different meanings of a polysemantic word. That is, responding to two quite different kinds of stimulus field, verbal and nonverbal, with the same word, we judge that we have responded to two instances of the same kind of stimulus field. I emphasize this because I wish to analyze the structure of the verbal stimulus field I have offered, that is, how the key terms fit together.

Polysemy, then, is a category of meaning response which is a verbal exemplification of the more inclusive verbal category, semantic drift. Semantic drift, then, explains polysemy; that is, it has an explanatory relation to polysemy. But semantic drift is a special case or exemplification of behavioral innovation, which has an explanatory relation to semantic drift; that is behavioral innovation is a more general category which subsumes semantic drift. But behavioral innovation is explained by certain statements I have made about the brain; it is an example of those statements considered as a single proposition or concept. If I wish to explain why the brain performs the way it does, however, I am at a loss, or I can say, "It is the will of God," or "God caused the brain to be what it is." Whatever else the word "God" may do in other situations, here it merely terminates an explanatory regress. I purposely introduced here the word "cause" for the reason that it is inappropriate. I should have said that the proposition about the brain exemplifies the will of God. Had I used "cause" throughout, instead of exemplification and explanation, the impression I should have conveyed is that these various key terms have a horizontal relation, parallel to the events in time in the nonverbal world. What I wish to bring out is that in fact they have a vertical relation, a relation of subsumption by explanation and exemplification, and that from our arbitrary termination "the will of God" down to "polysemy" we have a hierarchy of terms, not a succession of events.

But why should this be so? And what explanation would be

most fruitful for our purposes? If an individual responds to an utterance made by another individual, his action can properly be called a performance, and the utterance can with equal appropriateness be called directions. Language, then, does not tell us what the world is. In *Appearance and Reality* (1893) F. H. Bradley proposed a scepticism which insisted that the ideas of the mind do not tell us what reality is, but only give us information about appearance. In more modern terms, language—not ideas—does not tell us what the world is, nor does it, to my mind, give us information about appearance. What it can do is to give us instructions or directions on how to find something or simply directions on how to behave in various kinds of situations. Moreover, as I have suggested above, language is but one of many sign systems to which human beings learn to respond with more or less appropriateness. Indeed, the world itself is such a sign system, or semiotic complex. We do not spontaneously respond with feelings of awe and beauty to the Alps; we have done so only because we have been directed to do so. Three hundred years ago we would have been directed to respond with a sense of fear and horror. We say that such responses are part of our culture. It is enlightening therefore to say something a little bit different, to say that the directions that nonverbal and verbal signs give *are* our culture and that society consists of the performances in response to those directions. But further, any response is also a set of directions to ourselves and to others. Thus behavior can be looked at from two points of view, or can be said to have two aspects—directions and performance, or culture and society. This is why it is so hard to make distinctions between anthropology and sociology. Both are concerned with human behavior, which is all there is, just human beings doing things. Culture and association, or society, are not two different modes of behavior, but merely two different ways of looking at it, every performance being a set of directions and every set of directions being a performance.

From this we may make two further steps toward understanding the symbiosis of high art and centers of power. A puzzle so far unnoticed is how it is that, given behavioral innovation, human behavior is in fact relatively stable, i.e., does not dissolve completely into a condition in which no one could respond in a way considered appropriate to the person giving the directions, even if that person should be himself. How is behavior channeled and kept, as the geneticists would say, true? I think that the explanation may be found in what is quite easily observed. First there is the enormous amount of human effort that goes into providing additional directions. Thus, when you ask what an individual's intention is, you are in fact asking for additional directions, the original directions not being to you complete enough or sufficiently exact. Second, there is the fact that the human individual is characterized by a self-imposed limitation on the range of his behavior, both the varieties or modes of behavior he engages in and the range of deviation from the norm of each variety or mode. Indeed, I have reluctantly come to the conclusion that the core of human behavior is precisely this limitation of the range of behavior. Were it not so, the directions-performance conventions would dissolve; that is, behavior itself would dissolve. The threat of such dissolution is, for the reasons I have already given, a constant in our lives; the anxiety of not being able to perform appropriately in response to directions or of not being able to produce directions which others—or oneself —can appropriately respond to is the fundamental and pervasive human anxiety.

Now one way of channeling or limiting the range of behavior —an activity which for the sake of brevity and, I think, accuracy I shall call policing—consists of a special kind of directions. These are directions for giving directions, or meta-directions. From this point of view, an explanatory regress, such as that from polysemy up to God, consists of a regress of meta-directions, each hierarchical level of which is a set of directions for controlling the utterance of directions at the next lower level. The explanation limits the semantic range of the terms which exemplify that explanation. What do you mean by "polysemy"? I mean "semantic drift." What do you mean by that? I mean "behavioral innovation." And so on. It will also be noticed, I think, that each higher level in the hierarchy of explanatory regress is vaguer, but is capable of including a wider set of terms. "Polysemy" is quite limited in what it directs you to look for. "Semantic drift" is much less so; it can control or police terms other than "polysemy." A word, such as "God," that terminates an explanatory regress can direct us to look for everything.

Now when we look at human association or interaction we find the same phenomenon. An institution is a persistence of a mode of interactional behavior—that is, directions and performance— a persistence that may last for a few minutes when strangers meet on the street or that can last for centuries, like the Catholic Church. But the longer it lasts, the more likely it is to develop into a hierarchical structure. Thus university classes for instruction developed from a loose association of teachers and students into the elaborate hierarchical structures we have today. Each level subsumes a number of institutions on a lower level. Thus a department may be called, in relation to the classes given in that department, a meta-institution, and so on through various levels of meta-institutions to the board of trustees. Moreover, each lower level is an exemplification of the directions of a higher level: a class of a department, a department of a college, a college of the university—once again ending with the will of God, in this case the trustees. Every institution that provides goods or services is organized the same way. Just as an explanatory regress can be terminated only by an appeal to the all-powerful—be it God, or Fate, or whatever—so a hierarchical institution is terminated by power, and this really means the ultimate regressive level which determines, without appeal, how the directions and the performances, how the behavior pertinent to that institution, shall be channeled and limited in their range. If you examine the behavior of people at the various levels, you will find that, the higher the level, the more they are engaged in a purely verbal activity—that is, in deciding what the meaning of the terms which run the institution shall be, what for example the term "humanities" shall mean in that institution, whether or not it shall subsume "history of art." Not too long ago it did not. Or, to give another example, what the term "academic freedom" shall mean. It is a term that means very different things in different universities. Institutions are hierarchically organized in order to control the meanings of words and other signs, of directions, therefore of culture. The structure of institutions is the same as the structure of explanation because a hierarchical institution is a hierarchical explanation. Both are terminated by absolute power because—since any sign can elicit all possible responses (or any direction can elicit all possible performances)—there is no natural limit to responses to signs and no natural limit to the range of human behavior, since human behavior is response to signs, conventionally established and maintained by policing. And "policing" is the right name for it, because the police are but the immediately visible manifestation of what is the foundation of human behavior, naked arbitrary power. Only power can limit the range of meanings—or can determine the response to directions, something we all learned, whether or not we choose to recognize it, when our parents first punished us for exceeding a permissible limit of the range of response. "Johnny, you can go out and play, but that does not mean you can get covered with mud. In fifteen minutes we're going to see your Aunt Helen." And we did get covered with mud and were smacked and were none too gently cleaned up. Thus we learned, or should have, something both about meaning and about power.

We are now equipped, I think, to explore more closely the relation of the high arts to the centers of power, a relation I have already suggested might well be called a symbiosis. The high arts and high culture are economically dependent upon the centers of power, since they cannot command a market wide enough nor remunerative enough for self-support. But the centers of power depend upon high culture and the high arts for their survival. The explanation is this: The control of meanings (that is, the control of directions for performance) by arbitrary power is necessary for human survival; it is also a failure.

To sustain this explanation needs a little preparation. So far I have lumped together the high arts and high culture, but it is now essential to make a distinction. The high arts exemplify high culture, as the Sistine ceiling exemplified the high culture of Catholic Europe, a culture already beginning to disintegrate and be superseded while Michelangelo was at work. Generally speaking, throughout human history the explanations the artist exemplifies are explanations generated by an intellectual other than the artist, though he is often permitted modifications and innovations within, usually, a fairly narrow range. Within the last two centuries, however, artists have often themselves become intellectuals, generating their own explanations, a matter to which I shall return. High culture is a verbal activity, the generation and manipulation of meta-directions, though there are, to be sure, the verbal arts—arts in which, because they are verbal, the artist is somewhat more likely to be an intellectual than is the nonverbal artist. Thus high culture has two branches, the intellectual, which manipulates meta-directions, and the artistic, which exemplifies them. The Sistine ceiling again provides us an example. It was commissioned by Julius II, and the task of Michelangelo was not only to exemplify Christian theology as the ultimate explanatory mode but also to exemplify the Papacy as the ultimate source of power over that explanatory mode (a power it still claims), and to exemplify as well the policy of Julius II, who, continuing that of the Borgias, was determined to make the Papacy into a powerful secular state, a state with the political and economic power to sustain its power over the Christian explanatory mode. Accepting without question that explanatory mode and endowed with a genius for exemplification as great as his artistic genius, Michelangelo was able to fulfill his task triumphantly. But let us not permit our admiration for his genius to obscure the symbiosis his behavior manifests of power, high intellectual culture, and high artistic culture.

On the other hand, as I have suggested, this particular symbiosis dissolved. What Julius and Michelangelo perceived as a coherent explanation has become incoherent. The difficulties were already apparent and became very obvious in Milton's *Paradise Lost*. To earlier Christians the ways of God toward man were just; Milton felt he could exemplify that justice in poetry only if he worked out that justice, and justified the ways of God to man. By the middle of the eighteenth century, at the highest intellectual level it was no longer possible to reconcile the power, knowledge, and goodness of God with the existence of evil. For God was substituted Man, as empty an abstraction, but capable of terminating an explanatory regress in a manner sufficiently coherent to validate the arbitrary exercise of power, as in the American and French revolutions, the Napoleonic empire, and subsequent political history, to the present. Just as the coherence of the concept "God" became incoherent, so in what I am saying here the coherence of the concept "Man" is becoming incoherent.

Be that as it may, the twofold task of high intellectual culture becomes more understandable. On the one hand, it is to maintain coherence by incorporating in it through logical resolution incoherences within the culture. Such incoherences are always there; a system of meta-directions can be coherent only at the highest explanatory level. As you move down the hierarchy of explanation and exemplification and thence out into the empirical world, incoherence emerges, because the lowest level of directions applies to only a small segment of the world, instead of to all of it; because semantic drift and polysemy become more uncontrollable; and because the use of low-level directions modifies those directions by the process we call feedback. On the other hand, as negative feedback invades a system, it can spread like a contagion to the topmost level, just as the creation of modern science in the seventeenth century on the basis of experimentation destroyed the existing explanatory system. One can trace how in science the once all-important and terminating concept "God" has become in less than four centuries "the behavioral patterns of scientists." Thus the second task of high intellectual culture is to innovate new systems of explanatory coherence.

I have suggested that a high-level meta-directional system, or high intellectual culture, validates power centers. It does so by controlling or policing the language of those power centers, by giving directions on how the language of the highest level of those power centers shall be used to generate and police directions downward through the hierarchical structure. Thus the language of Adam Smith, his explanation of economic activity, was taken to be what it was not, a complete explanation of human activity, and was used to control the development and application of capitalism. "The Invisible Hand" was used to terminate an economic explanatory regress, thus fulfilling precisely the same function as the concept from which it was derived, "God." It was used both to justify and to control the utterance of meta-directions in the business world.

What I mean by incoherence and how it affects meta-directions can be illustrated by several incoherences currently emerging, which it seems cannot be resolved within any of the high intellectual meta-directional systems currently available. Until very recently, unrestricted scientific activity and human welfare were seen to be coherent. More and more, at all levels of culture, they are being perceived as incoherent. Again, endless economic growth was seen to be coherent with both human and national welfare, just as unrestricted population growth was perceived as coherent with human survival. It has occurred to a few people that our present economic difficulties may be the consequence of our having reached and even dangerously gone past the environmental or ecological limits of economic growth, and likewise that the economic gap between the wealthy nations and the poor cannot possibly be overcome within the present system of meta-directions; nor has any alternative system put in more than a vague hint of an appearance.

Why incoherence must develop and why coherence at the highest intellectual levels is necessary can also, I think, be understood. Coherence in a meta-directional explanatory system means that the terms and propositions are judged to be without contradictions internal to that system. At any cultural level we demand consistency in the directions given to us. Without consistency we are unable to act. We are faced with contradictory directions, and behavior dissolves. This is as true at the highest levels of power as it is in digging a ditch. Nevertheless, incoherence must develop, simply because language does not tell us what the world is but only gives directions for performance. Thus a high-culture meta-directional explanatory system always says what the world is, and is always wrong. To be sure, it may work quite well for a while, especially if the total system it is policing is more or less economically closed and culturally protected. But once two modes of performance and two modes of directions come into contact, either one is destroyed—as primitives are always destroyed by more powerful explanatory systems—or both are damaged and riven with incoherence. It is my own conviction that culture contact between the European West and what we call primitive cultures has not only destroyed the latter but has seriously damaged the former by introducing material inassimilable in European high intellectual and artistic culture.

A glance at logic will illuminate this. Logic is the policeman of high explanatory systems. It emerged in Greece after the pre-Socratics had developed a number of alternative terminating explanations, high-cultural meta-directions beyond which further levels of explanatory regress were at the time impossible. The task of logic was to police such explanatory systems, with the aim of constructing a single explanatory system which would subsume or eliminate the others—a task which Plato attempted to carry out and which, with the aid of Aristotle, was in time completed in Christian Europe. Logic is concerned wholly with the construction of abstract coherence, but it was also believed that the language of logic was ultimately coherent with ordinary language. This was the belief which sustained the construction and reconstruction of meta-directions. But in certain areas of the highest culture, this coherence is no longer believed to be the case. The emergence of symbolic logic has revealed that logical coherence is at best a model of ordinary language, in which meta-directions are constructed, but that certainly between the two languages there is an unbridgeable abyss. Consequently, no high system of meta-directions can be, at best, more than a makeshift —doomed to reveal, under the pressure of reality, its fundamental incoherence. My proposal that the control of meanings by arbitrary power is necessary for human survival and is necessarily a failure is an exemplification of this more general notion, which subsumes it.

And where does this place the artist? Let us stand back from human behavior, let us estrange ourselves from it, let us, indeed, dehumanize ourselves for a bit. After all, when one considers man's record, especially for the past sixty years, a record which seems steadily to be getting worse and which appears to indicate, if the Club of Rome is right, that a hundred years is about the most we can expect this civilization to last, unless we change our ways drastically—when we consider all this, dehumanization does not seem a particularly unattractive or reprehensible strategy. I have already suggested that the main or central thrust of human energy is the limitation of each man's range of behavior, both the kinds of behavior he engages in and within any individual kind of behavior. The reason for this, I have also suggested, can be traced back to or explained by the fact that meaning is not immanent in the world but is a matter of human response to the world. Thus any sign, verbal or nonverbal, is capable of eliciting all possible responses. This, of course, is not the case, but why is it not? How is response limited and what is the effort that attempts to keep response true? If we look at it from the point of view of society, I think the right word for that effort is "policing." If we look at it from the point of view of the individual I think the right word is "interest." An interest in something is social policing which the individual imposes upon his own behavior. An interest in high culture and the high arts is one of my interests; it is my way of limiting the range of my behavior; it is my way of limiting my social interaction for the most part to a very small segment of society, to those whose interests are the same. Even so, it is a constant struggle, even within this narrow interest and even with only these few people to interact with, to limit the range of response to works of art and other products of high culture in such a way that communication with my colleagues in this tiny segment of society we inhabit does not, in fact, break down. So far as I am concerned, it is constantly breaking down, a matter that possibly I should regret more than, in fact, I do. If you wish to say that I am addicted to high culture and the high arts, I would not only be forced to agree with you, I would be happy to. But since addiction of any kind—since addiction limits the range of behavior whether it is to art or alcohol or sex or business or drugs or politics—is but a particularly intense and almost all-inclusive way of limiting behavior, it follows that this is one of the most important ways we have of stabilizing individual behavior and therefore society, which is but the sum of interactions of human beings with others and with themselves. I know of no society that does not use a drug to stabilize its behavior, and I cannot imagine that a society that has no stabilizing drug can possibly exist. If there are drugless societies, they are certainly very primitive ones; all civilizations use drugs. If you wish to say then that high culture and the high

arts function as a kind of drug for me, I am scarcely in a position
to disagree. However, I would add one point. A true aberration is
behavior that violates the stabilizing forces within the limits
or framework of any interest. I think I can claim that my approach to high culture and the high arts can with some justice be
called an intellectual aberration.

Art can be used in two ways. It can be used addictively or it
can be used to prepare us to be aberrant, to be genuinely deviant.
After all, what sociologists and psychologists call aberrations are
merely modes of limiting behavior, but modes which they happen not to approve of. It is difficult to see the difference between
alcohol and marijuana when both are used, as both commonly
are, to stabilize society. What we too optimistically call the
counterculture is, so far as I can see, as depressingly stable as
the established culture. It is the sad fact of human history that
it does not take long for a genuine aberration to become just
another mode for limiting the range of behavior.

Art, then, can be as much of an addiction as anything else
can. At least it has the advantage of providing economic support
for artists. But art can also be used to prepare the individual
personality to innovate a true aberration. Our culture is so
stagnant, since excessive social stability is the American vice, that
we can certainly use a few more aberrations, aberrations that will
stay aberrant. Thus, in claiming to present at least a mildly
aberrant attitude toward high culture and the high arts in that
I see them neither as modes of "creativity" (a word I have come
to detest), nor as modes of almost superhuman superiority, but
as modes of policing—in claiming this position as aberrant—I
am, to my mind, making a very high claim indeed. Paradoxically
—at first glance—I am claiming membership in that tiny group of
contemporary artists who are aberrant from the artistic tradition
itself.

Let me first explain what I mean by a tiny group. Art is said
to be an expression of the human spirit. To be sure, I am not
quite clear what I am talking about when I use the phrase "human
spirit," but I am sure enough to say that a dirty joke told in a
bar is as much an expression of the human spirit as Hamlet or the
Bible, or that a Playboy foldout is as much an expression of the

human spirit as Michelangelo's Sistine ceiling. Art indeed is not something restricted to high culture. It is all over the place. Some years ago in *Man's Rage for Chaos* (New York: Schocken, 1967), a deviant book about the arts, I concluded by saying that the only moral justification for the immense investment of time and energy it takes to respond with any adequacy to art at the highest level is that one can be free of it, at least if one is very intelligent and very old and very lucky. However that may be, art is pervasive in human life, culture, and society. Furthermore, it is unquestionable that the mindless adulation of art is infinitely more widespread than it used to be. At one time it was strictly a high-culture phenomenon, but it is penetrating to lower and lower cultural levels. The addictive character of art, even of high art—although it is mostly old high art—can no longer be evaded. Nevertheless, a tiny group is resisting that addiction, and in that tiny group I hope to claim membership. But if this analysis is at all correct, it is a very strange state of affairs indeed. Traditionally, high art has been used to exemplify the explanations of the world created at the high cultural level. But if these explanations are indeed modes of policing the language of validation and social management, then insofar as high art exemplifies those modes, high art itself is part of policing. Do not imagine that I am here objecting to policing. It is the condition of social existence. However, there are times when more aberration is needed than is currently forthcoming. We are in such a time and have been for nearly two centuries.

About 170 or 180 years ago something very strange happened. Here and there in Europe, for the most part unknown to each other, a few individuals operating at a high cultural level—artists and philosophers—came to the conclusion that the modes of explanation, validation, and social management were no longer working. I have suggested that the control of meanings by arbitrary power is necessary for human survival and is necessarily a failure. A cultural crisis appears when a great many individuals—a critical mass, as the metaphor has it—come to believe that the explanation of human existence, which is necessarily always wrong but is ordinarily believed to be right, is in fact wrong. An individual crisis appears when the individual has the identical experience. But when a number of individuals, unknown to each other, independently have that experience for the same reasons—then a cultural crisis is in the making.

The effect of the conviction that the only explanations of human existence available are all failures, all inadequate, is the loss of the sense of value. In a minor way it is a common enough occurrence, as popular songs can tell you. But it is also the dynamism by which an individual climbs up from the lower or popular level of culture to the highest level. Ordinarily he is satisfied when he gets there. The full power of high culture and its exemplificatory arts tells him he ought to be satisfied. It is a power hard to resist. He has every reason, he thinks, to be satisfied, and in ordinary historical situations high culture is enough. But there are times when a few individuals emerge, so to speak, at the top of the explanatory regress; they have gone through the ceiling. They find themselves outside culture. This is true estrangement, or alienation, or dehumanization. The sources for value have all failed them. Freud said that to doubt the value of human life means that a man is already sick. Possibly, however, at times it can mean that a man is taking the first step toward health.

In looking for a general term with which to talk about the sense of recovering the conviction of the value of human life, I would propose the word "redemption." To be redeemed is to enter into a state in which the question of the value of life never arises. That is what we mean by Heaven. In the past, before the nineteenth century, redemption was the peculiar task of religion. The failure of religion at the end of the eighteenth century— again, let me remind you, for a few individuals only—meant that new sources of redemption had to be found. Those few artists and philosophers who had burst through the available explanations of the world set out to find such sources for themselves. For those who were artists, this created a wholly novel problem. Their task had been to exemplify the socially validated explanations. Now they were in a position in which they had to create explanations to be exemplified. Otherwise—as they necessarily conceived it, given their cultural situation—they could not be artists. The first conclusion that they came to was that the redemptive power lay in themselves; such was the traditional prestige of high art because of its symbiosis with high culture and with the centers of power, they further concluded that the redemptive power lay in themselves because they were artists. Interestingly enough, a number of philosophers agreed with them. By the 1830s art had emerged as a mode of secular redemption. Moreover, by the 1850s all other modes of secular redemption —whether philosophical or social or psychological modes—had betrayed their inadequacy, at least for the most advanced artists and thinkers. By the end of the nineteenth century, in the high culture of Europe and America there obtained what was known as the Religion of Art. That is, of the various modes of secular redemption innovated in the early part of the century, only the mode of art survived. Since this mode has become popularized, it resulted in the extraordinary decision of the United States Congress to build a Center for the Performing Arts as a memorial to the assassinated President Kennedy. It was an expiatory act that redeemed the nation from its sin, as the general public has recognized, for it is tearing it to pieces in order to obtain Sacred Relics of the Martyred President.

It is almost incomprehensible that art should have assumed this role, that art should be the ultimate mode and explanation for validating human life. Yet, at the highest cultural levels, such has been the case. The explanation I think lies in the irresponsibility of the artistic experience. In seeing a tragedy we can frankly enjoy the destruction of a great man or nowadays even of an ordinary one. To be sure, before the nineteenth century, art was justified because it gave pleasure and also instructed, that is, exemplified. But it was irresponsible in that, though propaganda and rhetoric, it was but preparatory propaganda and rhetoric. At no time has art ever given instructions for doing anything to the world. Now this general character of art was even more powerful when the task of art came to be merely to instruct you to *feel* the sense of the value of human existence, to feel redemption. At the beginning of this century a new kind of art emerged, in all of the arts. It was an art that resisted all explanation, even explanations the artist himself proposed. As MacLeish put it, "A poem should not mean but be." That is, the responder

to the art should not respond by providing an explanation of what
he was experiencing but merely by feeling his own sense of
being and the value of the existence of that being. Art itself
offered the experience of redemption.

But now the situation is moving into a new phase and has been
doing so for nearly thirty years, though the consequences have
begun to emerge only in the last four or five. What sustained the
artist as artist until very recently was the very explanation of art
that enabled him to get the economic support from the culture,
the inadequacy of which he was exposing by offering an alternative mode of redemption, validation, and explanation. The difficulty lay in the fact that although art was no longer busy
exemplifying the modes of explanation that police high culture,
it was nevertheless exemplifying the fact of explanation. Art
continued to be explained, and so long as art continued to be
regarded as redemptive it must necessarily be given a redemptive
explanation. The meta-direction for art was that art should
exemplify redemption. This was still apparent in the work of the
abstract expressionists. In a period of postwar exhaustion it asserted that pure feeling is redemptive. The rhetoric and propaganda, that is, the cultural directions, of abstract expressionism
have by now penetrated deeply into our culture and are probably
the historical sources of what we call today the counterculture,
which is so deeply redemptive that bits and pieces of it have
regressed to religious redemption. The message of pop art was
that pure feeling at any cultural level is redemptive, and its
rhetoric and propaganda also penetrated deeply, and was again an
important historical source of the counterculture. Op art and mini
art propagated the rhetoric that pure perception is redemptive.
It was the source of the psychedelic art of the counterculture. It
is hard to imagine a more tenuous hold on redemption. And this
message also penetrated deeply.

Yet the general tendency of this progressive reduction of redemption has scarcely penetrated at all, though with the emergence of concept art, and funk art, and earth art, and packaging
art it should have. Since the beginning of the last century, art
has been attacking, in the name of redemption, the redemptive or
explanatory modes of the society in which it was operating. But

now art is attacking itself, or at least many people so believe. Certainly all traditional notions of art are either under attack or have already dissolved under the severity of the questions art has proposed to aesthetics. The horror so many people feel at what is happening in the arts today is not, however, as they think, a horror at what is happening to art. It is a horror at what is happening to redemption, to what is the last stronghold in our culture of the redemptive ideal.

What redemption amounts to is the conviction that the individual, ultimately, is a coherent entity and that human life can ultimately—though perhaps not now—be given a coherent explanation. In undermining a coherent explanation of art, the artists of today are attacking explanatory coherence itself. The result certainly appears to be the dissolution at the high cultural levels of the artistic enterprise as we have known it in the past. The distinction between high art and popular art is vanishing. Since we cannot respond to incoherent instructions, we identify value with coherence, and on these grounds we erect the desirability of coherent man, coherent society, and a coherence of man and society with nature. Man, we conclude, can be ultimately validated by attaining that coherence. If you look back through the course of human cultural history, you will find that human effort has always been directed toward living by a coherent explanation of the world. Even if all other coherent explanations have evaporated, so long as art remained the very symbol of coherence itself, the coherent ideal remained, but when art reveals its own internal incoherence, then the last exemplification of explanatory coherence vanishes at the highest cultural level. This seems to be the significance of the dissolution of the artistic enterprise of high culture which, I believe, is currently taking place.

This looks like a gloomy picture, but I do not intend it as such. It is, I think, the realization in artistic terms, the manifestation in artistic activity, that all meta-directional explanations of the world are wrong. The illusion that mankind is as responsible for his disasters as for his successes arises from the illusion that somewhere, somehow, in human nature and in the world is an ultimate coherence. It has led us, I think, to our present difficulties, our present threat of disaster. What the artist is doing today is exemplifying the proposition that this illusion is indeed an illusion, that the pursuit of redemption is ultimately destructive, that the hope of man lies in abandoning the illusions of coherence and redemption. The artist is exemplifying the nonexplanatory character of explanation, the ultimate incoherence of human nature, and in so doing he is performing for mankind the greatest service, I think, that in our present conditions can now be performed. Except for a few logicians and philosophers, he is the only one who is doing it. His task is painful but salutary, brutal but necessary, a destruction that is one of the few activities today with any promise, that holds out the hope of a genuine and fruitful aberration.

19

HUMANISM, POLITICS,

AND GOVERNMENT IN THE

NINETEENTH CENTURY

[1973*]

When I began this paper I thought I knew what I was going to discuss, but the more I thought about it the more puzzled I became. What is a "humanist"? What is "humanism"? I have, like most of us, been used to the terms most of my life, and of course I have been perfectly aware of the vagueness in the ordinary use of the words. Still, I had the impression that, though others were a little uncertain about the meaning of "humanism," I, at least, had a clear idea. However, the more I meditated, the less certain I became that any stable meaning was involved at all. More and more it seemed to be a term used primarily to ascribe positive value to some activity or individual. In academic talk a humanist professes one of the humanities, and a humanity is not a physical science or a social science. However, the NEH has recently included the social sciences among the humanities. This seems reasonable. If a study is not concerned

* Presented at the annual meeting of the Southern Humanities Conference, Houston, Texas, April 13, 1973.

with the physical world, it is concerned with the human world, and surely sociology and psychology are concerned with human beings, even though psychology does so much of its work in investigating the subhuman world of rats and college freshmen. Still, recent studies have made it impossible any longer to assert that all animal (non-human) behavior is genetic. Culture, in the anthropological sense, no longer can be said to be a uniquely human attribute of behavior. And if the study of human culture is not humanistic, does "humanism" have any meaning at all?

On the other hand, to include the social sciences among the humanities—to say that sociologists and psychologists are humanists—seems a very strange use of the word, and does seem to violate the tradition of its meaning. And where does history belong? In a recent reorganization of my own university, it was placed with the social sciences; but a number of members of the history department are rather unhappy with this. Historians are not at all sure that their activity is scientific, and if it is not, then surely it must be a humanity and historians must be humanists. Still, a good many historians are eager to claim that their intellectual activity is indeed a scientific activity. But if that is the case, is the historical and biographical study of literature the activity of a humanist? And indeed, a good many students of literature whose activity is self-defined as criticism assert that they are truly humanists but that the historical scholar of literature is not. And how about textual criticism? Is this a humanistic activity? Claims by the dominating school that its activity is properly to be considered a science would suggest that it is not. But these same individuals also claim that ultimately a decision about a textual crux can only be made by a humanist. Indeed, the original humanists of the fifteenth century were passionately concerned with textual matters, and modern textual criticism descends from them. And is the textual criticism of the Bible a humanist activity? It certainly has been done by people called humanists. But in that case, is a theologian a humanist? Not always, but often, "humanism" seems to have a coloring of "secularism," of "antisupernaturalism." Nonetheless, departments and courses in religious thought are usually administratively associated with the humanities in American universities and colleges, but is this merely an administrative convenience arising from the fact that there is nowhere else to put them?

In short, as I thought about the problem, my puzzlement steadily increased. My original subject was "Humanists' Views of Politics and Government in England During the Nineteenth Century," but what is there to say on this subject? Whether I interpret "humanists" as "some humanists" or "all humanists" or "representative humanists" or a "random sampling of humanists," the result is the same. That is, if I think of "humanists" as individuals, the answer is obvious and certainly not worth talking about. No matter how I define the term, no matter whom I include in this category, it is obvious that among the nineteenth-century English humanists all possible views of politics and government are theoretically to be found. And a rapid running over in my mind of a very random sampling showed that this is indeed so. The reason is that there is no more a necessary connection between the fact that a man is a humanist and his view of politics and government than there is a connection between the fact that a man is a grocer and his view of politics and government. I can think of no a priori reason on these grounds to spend any time even considering the subject.

But this is not the only possibility. If I think of a humanist, not as an individual, but as a social role, an answer more than a mere truism might possibly be forthcoming. To be sure, one can arrive at an immediate answer that, though a truism in itself, might have some fruitfulness. A humanist's view of politics and government is a function of the support politicians and government officials give to the social role of humanists. The merest glance at the situation in my own lifetime demonstrates the validity of this proposition, quite marvelously uninteresting in itself. As long as I can remember, my teachers and my colleagues who define themselves as humanists have been quite bitter about the virtually total lack of support the humanist role gets from politics and government. The story about the legislator investigating the state university budget who wondered why more books were needed when there was already a library full of books—most of them used very little, if at all—is a horror story I have heard so often I cannot even remember when it was first told me with that grim and bitter humor which humanists invariably employ when they talk about support from politics and government. To be sure, contemporary humanists occasionally point with pride to the fact that though scientists require enormous sums to do anything at all, even the most trivial research, *we* can do our extremely significant and culturally important work on virtually nothing at all, though it is very nice to get a Guggenheim. In short, humanists think of themselves as social, political, and governmental orphans, even outcasts; but our bitterness is mitigated by our awareness that we nobly carry on our work in spite of that. To be sure, occasionally one finds a humanist who permits himself to wonder if the fact that humanists lack such support may mean that they are doing nothing of any importance, nothing that deserves such support, that we *ought* to be social orphans.

On the whole, however, the establishment of the NEH was received as a great triumph for the humanist cause, and initially there were happy visions of immense sums flowing in our direction—though there was some bitterness that so much of it seemed to be flowing toward the questionable and even (by some) despised textual work of the Editions of American Authors. This phenomenon has often been interpreted as an indication that, in spite of all the talk, the government bias is still scientific—or better still, pseudoscientific. Generally speaking, a rather sad awareness has developed that though there is an impressive sum of government money (at least compared with nothing at all), there are an awful lot of humanists who want some of it—that is, as much as they can possibly get. And now that, in one program, the humanities have been associated with the social sciences, and the humanists with the despised social scientists, fear and gloom have struck those who know about it.

With this contemporary attitude as a model, there still seems to be little advantage in investigating the attitudes of nineteenth-century humanists. No matter how they defined humanism—or used some other word for it, such as Coleridge's "clerisy"—how is one to know that they defined themselves as playing the humanist social role when they made statements about politics and government? The fact that the statement is found in a human-

istic context is no guarantee that the social role was being maintained when the remark was made. People, in fact, slip easily and
readily from one social role to another, and from a straight playing of the role to an ironic playing of it; and in the latter case
it is by no means easy to determine whether or not irony is
actually present.

I think, then, we may safely postulate that an individual who
defines himself as playing the humanist role and values himself
because of that role will approve whatever politics and government may do to support the activities and values involved in that
social role. Thus, if he regards the preservation, study, and ap-
preciation of great works of art as a humanistic activity, he will
approve the governmental founding and support of historically
oriented art museums, and he will think of the politicians in a
parliamentary system as more than mere politicians, as true
statesmen. But if this is more than a truism, it is certainly not
much more. Nevertheless it allows us to rephrase the question,
let us hope in a nontrivial manner, as a series of questions. Do
politicians and governments do anything to support the humanist
role? If so, what do they do? Why do they do it? These may be
summed up in a single question: What is the relation of the
humanist role to governmental power centers?

One aspect of the question may be disposed of immediately.
In the nineteenth century, throughout Europe and even America,
there was an enormous increase in government support of humanist activities. The pattern was set by the Napoleonic regime,
and initiated by the French Revolutionary regime. Support of
humanist activities, hitherto dependent upon economic support
from private sources of surplus wealth or upon the whim of some
reigning monarch or other, now came to be taken over by the
government as government policy. To this phenomenon it will be
useful to return, but at this point it at least establishes a connection between the humanist role and government. Governments
recognized the support of humanism as either desirable or necessary. Even in this country, notoriously backward in such matters,
the Library of Congress has long since ceased to be a mere library of Congress. It has become a national institution, predominantly of a humanist character. It is impossible to pursue this

line of inquiry without a more precise conception of what the humanist social role involves, but at this point it is at least possible to hypothesize that humanism has something to do with social management. It is necessary to begin, however, with some notion of social management and its necessity.

"Social management," to be sure, is a term which we tend to find disturbing and even objectionable. We are free men, and so social management is bad. I am using the term, however, in a value-free way. Thus, to tell someone that he should fight for his political freedom is as much a matter of social management as to tell someone that he must submit abjectly to a monstrous tyranny. Likewise, for the individual to tell himself that he must do one or the other is as much a matter of social management as having someone else tell him. The reason is that the biological individual is a social dyad; in any given situation the relation of the individual to himself is no different from his relation to someone else. Thus in any given situation the biological individual is made up of two social individuals. From this point of view I believe that what we call the autonomy of the individual is a name for unpredicted behavior—sometimes innovative—in a socially dyadic situation. The biological individual in society is thus primarily engaged in suppressing impulses that would lead to behavior unpredicted and sometimes innovative in particular situations—his own impulses and those of others. He is thus primarily engaged in limiting behavior—his own and that of others—to socially validated channels.

That is social management, and it is a necessary condition of social interaction, including the biological individual's interaction with himself as a social dyad. The explanation for this lies in language, which is said to be, for humans, species specific. Actually the explanation is to be found in the nature of meaning. Having spent a good many years in the investigation of theories of meaning, I have been able to come to no other than the unsettling conclusion that the meaning of an utterance is the response to that utterance and that the connection between the two is entirely conventional. That is, meaning is not immanent in utterance. If that is the case, as I believe it to be, it follows that any utterance is theoretically capable of eliciting all possible responses, and that all utterances are theoretically capable of eliciting but one single response. To put it this way gets out into the open both the phenomenon of variability of meaning responses, as in polysemy, and the phenomenon of channeling responses through time. Two kinds of what we call insanity can be understood from this point of view, the one characterized by an increasing randomness and unpredictability of response, the other by an increasing limitation of response, sometimes to the point that any utterance elicits one of only an increasingly smaller family of responses, or even but one response. It needs further to be pointed out that what is true of linguistic utterances is also true of nonverbal signs, of which linguistic utterances are a special case. Thus, to humans the world consists—except for reflex responses not fed through the brain—of signs, to each of which all possible responses are theoretically possible. There is, further, a good deal of evidence that this phenomenon, which we may call culture in the anthropological sense, is to be found in the pre-human level. Some animals certainly exhibit behavior which is transmitted, not genetically, but culturally or conventionally.

Social management may thus be more precisely defined as the limitation and channeling of semantic response to verbal and nonverbal signs and sign-constellations, or, in one aspect of language, the syntactical, sign structures. Against such channeling two forces are at work. The brain, such is its construction, constantly produces random variations of response—or at least at present the process is best understood as a random process, the nonrandom being obedience to the conventions and practices of a situation. Second, as situations change by the introduction of novel factors, semantic response becomes inappropriate. By this I mean that both these factors introduce incoherence into families of semantic response—a social role, for example. For interaction to continue, such incoherences need to be resolved, a matter Hegel built his *Phenomenology* upon. At this point, I must ask you to accompany me on a big leap to the proposition—not, I think, unacceptable—that in social systems, government is the court of final resort for the resolution of semantic incoherence.

The explanation for this lies in the fact that the biological individual is engaged only in manipulating the environment to his benefit. As Nietzsche put it, the only will is the will to power. Moreover, by "environment" must be understood the social as well as the natural environment, and the socially dyadic individual's relation to himself as well as to other social individuals. Of power over other social individuals there are two sorts, force and seduction. In any disagreement about semantic response, since such response is a matter of convention and not of immanence, the only possible way ultimately to resolve it is by the application of superior force. Should force fail, there is no other recourse. Hence seduction is a device for postponing as long as possible the application of force. For this reason, the ultimate foundation of any society is naked force, and the government is the repository of that force. Not freedom, but social stability comes out of the barrel of a gun. We are continually reminded of this by the omnipresence of civilian police, which has in the course of history taken the place of the omnipresence of military force. In verbal behavior, the most convenient term for seduction is, in the narrow sense, rhetoric. Thus, rhetoric is the verbal form of social management. But in view of what was said earlier, the concept of rhetoric can be extended to the nonverbal.

Power centers, whether governments or fathers of families, use rhetoric for explanation, justification, and validation of semantic response—that is, let me repeat, virtually all response—or of human behavior. For high power centers, such as governments or many-leveled religious hierarchies, rhetoric is called high culture—what Matthew Arnold meant by "culture." High culture may be thought of as the repository of the rhetorical resources of high power centers. When a sociocultural incoherence develops such that it can be resolved only by the application of force, governments turn to such repositories for the instruments of rhetoric, the only instruments which can postpone the application of force—for if force fails, all is lost. However, the relation of the rhetoric of high culture to power centers is complex. It is a symbiotic relationship, though economically parasitic. Thus the relation of high culture to governments is not only confirmatory but critical as well. Indeed, when a government attempts to control completely the activities of high culture, the government profoundly weakens its own position, just as a parent does who denies his child recourse to rhetoric. This can be understood by examining the activities of high culture. First, in its semi-independent position—or perhaps its quasi-independent position—it is constantly adding new resources to the rhetoric of a culture, as well as to the instruments of force of that culture. Its task in part is to discover sources of semantic incoherence before the government has to deal with such incoherence. This is the task of the scientist. The task of the humanist is somewhat different.

Any culture depends upon certain sacred texts as the ultimate court of rhetorical appeal for justification, validation, and explanation, and this is as true of science as it is of the rest of high culture. In highly developed sociocultural systems these sacred texts are exceedingly various and by no means coherent with each other. In our culture, for some purposes the Bible is the court of rhetorical appeal, for other purposes it is Darwin. It is an extremely important task of high culture to lead, as it were, the problems of an incoherence to the appropriate sacred text or texts—whether it be Einstein's or Dante's. It is the task of the artist to exemplify the systems of explanation, validation, and justification, the ultimate sanctions for which are the sacred texts. It is the threefold task of the humanist to preserve the sacred texts, to channel their interpretation, and especially to modify the received interpretation when an emergent incoherence can be resolved only by such modification—as St. Augustine modified the interpretation of pagan myths or Jan Kott modified the interpretation of Shakespeare. But to the three aspects of this task must be added another: by rhetorical manipulation to establish the sacredness of the sacred texts.

Thus the task of the English teacher, for example, is to implant in the young the sacredness of certain texts. Generally speaking, only those young in whom such implantation is effective can be recruited into high culture, though of course by no means all of them are. Obviously, to sustain the functions of high culture, the values of high culture—including the sacredness of sacred texts—must be widely diffused among the population. Arnold's famous "best that has been thought and said" is an excellent example of the rhetoric by which the sacredness of sacred texts is transmitted.

Several corollaries may be worth deriving. The functions of humanism are interdependent. Thus, an emergent sociocultural situation can drain a sacred text of its sacredness, as, for many people—perhaps for most contemporary humanists—the theologically justified sacredness of *Paradise Lost* is no longer operative. One mode of hermeneutic modification is to designate Satan as the true hero. Another mode has been to derive the poem's sacredness from its artistic or poetic quality. It is a peculiarity of the European culture of the last 170 years that Art has become an independent category of the sacred. The justification is that art is the primary revelation of the imagination, and for the most part Coleridge is the sacred text for that value, hermeneutically modified by I. A. Richards, among many others.

A second corollary is related to this mode of sacredness. The category of sacred text can be extended to sacred objects, particularly works of nonverbal art. The fundamental reason for this lies in what I have already suggested, the fact that art exemplifies systems of explanation, justification, and validation, which in turn are derived from sacred texts. It is one of the tasks of historical scholarship to trace down and recover the original sacred texts from which certain values of the rhetoric of high culture were initially derived. At the present time, it is sufficient for a work of art to be judged as successfully exemplifying the sacred category Art, a value for which every European language has its sacred text—products, for the most part, of the emergent high culture of nineteenth-century Romanticism.

I think it may be said, then, that the humanist values any political and governmental activity which facilitates his fourfold task of establishing and transmitting the sacredness of sacred texts and objects; of preserving, by textual criticism, the sacred texts and objects; of channeling their interpretation; and of modifying their interpretation. The nineteenth century, as I have suggested, was remarkable for the assumption by governments, with the aid of statesmen-politicians, of the responsibility for supporting the fourfold task of humanism. One has only to think of the immense sums poured into libraries, art museums, musical establishments of all kinds, archives, archaeological excavations, the preservation of ancient monuments—Prosper Mérimeé's lifelong task—and so on, to realize that a new social force had emerged, that an incoherence had developed. That new force, first recognized in all its power by, I believe, Walter Scott, was the emergence of the people on the stage of history. This emergent incoherence was met by extending the diffusion of high cultural rhetoric.

It is not necessary for an entire population to receive the implantation of the rhetoric of high culture, but it is necessary, for social stability, to have that rhetoric (what we call values) widely diffused with high intensity and much more widely diffused with low intensity, so that the majority of the population is directly susceptible to the social management of high culture by means of the rhetoric of seduction. In the nineteenth century, governments recognized that, in the task of social management—the limitation and channeling of semantic response—the humanists of a society are of prime importance. I would make one final point, lest we be too proud of our position and of our task in maintaining social stability. When the scientist inculcates at the higher levels of our educational system the value and sacredness of high science, he too is engaging in a humanistic activity. He too is a humanist, and he is as good at seduction as we are. Yet this factor in the scientist's role suggests that that role is ultimately under humanistic control.

20

THE CULTURAL CRISIS

OF THE 1970s

[1973*]

The topic to which I have been asked to address myself, modern and postmodern man, may profitably be considered as symptomatic of the 1970s. The 1960s, if not exactly over, are certainly fading away, but the *Village Voice*—nor is it alone— has pointed out that the 1970s have not received a name or a definition. It is not yet a period. The *Village Voice* was one of the more significant voices of the 1960s. It may be wondering if it any longer has a reason for existence. A couple of years ago one of the more conspicuous among the academic voices of the 1960s asserted that of all the movements of that decade only women's liberation was of truly lasting significance. Perhaps this merely means that as the last significant movement to emerge, it will be the last to fade away. Indeed, it already seems to be losing its centrality in contemporary problems. If the Equal Rights Amendment fails, the movement will probably retreat to increas-

* Delivered at the third annual Interdisciplinary Conference at Catawba College, Salisbury, North Carolina, on March 22, 1973.

ingly bizarre and resentful splinter groups; if the amendment succeeds, the movement will be dissipated by legal and economic incorporation into the inextricably complex and confused patterns of individual and institutional interaction which we call, too hopefully and too idly, a social system. Simultaneously, the current federal administration is dismantling what was once designated with an almost insane optimism "the Great Society." Is this an admission that the federal government cannot solve or even understand those problems which the Great Society thought it understood and set out to solve? We are told that they are better dealt with at the local level, but since the local level has already failed with them, does this not rather amount to an admission that they are in fact insolvable?

On the other hand, it may be an assertion that, in comparison with emerging international problems, our national problems must be considered as relatively unimportant, or as so dependent upon international problems that no treatment other than comparative neglect, benign or not, is even possible. The present inflation in food prices, particularly of meat, cannot, we are assured by the press, be separated from the massive sale of wheat to Russia or be considered as unrelated to the longstanding meat crisis in Europe. And is the current crisis in Britain a warning of what is in store for us? There the contest between the labor unions and the government suggests that the wage-price spiral— which no economist, I am informed by one of the best of them, pretends to understand—has run into an unbreakable ceiling. It is foolish of me to attempt to propose anything about the wage-price spiral, but it does seem that there is a connection between it and the steady improvement of the economic well-being of most of the population in the industrialized countries. It does seem to be part of that ill-understood mechanism which, for almost two centuries, beginning with England itself, has fed into the culture a continuous diet of rising expectations. In this country, labor's demands that if wages are to be controlled then corporate profits must be controlled does seem to me self-defeating, since it is a demand that capital available for reinvestment be limited, and hence that economic growth be halted. Such a demand seems to me a rhetorical strategy behind which is really the assumption that rising expectancies and economic growth, of which the wage-price spiral is a symptom, cannot be halted. It assumes that the rising expectancies are the consequences of a natural law of endless economic growth. The British crisis, our crisis, and similar crises in other countries suggest that the current administration may be right, or at least vaguely and confusedly moving in the only possible direction: the problems of nation-states are not within the area of national competence.

I am suggesting that labor, or rather the labor leaders, have not yet experienced, or at least will not yet act upon the admission that they have experienced, what a great many other people are already feeling with a slightly nauseating malaise—the era of rising expectancies may have come to an end. Let me admit at once that my social position as a member of the educational establishment may very well invalidate my suggestion. Education is the first to feel economic recession and the last to profit from economic growth, and in the category of education I would include such institutions as symphony orchestras and art museums, all of which are in severe financial difficulty. On the other hand, the built-in economic seismographs of academics may very well be excellent warnings of coming economic earthquakes. Four years ago I predicted that the higher educational establishment was getting into serious financial difficulties; my lecture engagements had gone down considerably, as had those of other lecturing academics. The importation of lecturers is marginal in a university's activities. It can easily be reduced or dispensed with entirely; and indeed, in the latter case, nobody is going to care very much, least of all the vast majority of students. My prediction was greeted with astonishment by several administrators, and yet events have certainly borne me out. In the same way, higher education itself is, to a considerable extent, a marginal activity in the society as a whole, and its activities can very possibly be enormously reduced without any immediate—or perhaps much long-term—damage. In short, academic sensitivity to economic difficulties may in fact be a highly reliable indicator. It may indicate a steady though gradual national and international impoverishment which will last for the rest of our lives.

The inflationary crisis, the ecological crisis, the energy crisis, the possibility that atomic energy has run into a dead end, the conflict over the dubious promise of geothermal energy, the indications that the automobile age is on the way to extreme restriction of the number and use of automobiles (a restriction which may very well extend to the use of airplanes for personal transportation)—all these crises may ultimately turn out not to be very real crises, or at least not terribly serious. It is quite possible that our scientific and engineering resources are sufficient to meet all of them, or at least can be developed to meet them. It may be that the crisis in Britain does not mean that the improvement of the lot of the British worker, and of the British people, is at an end. On the contrary, it may be that the perception of such crises is not the cause of the malaise of the 1970s but rather a symptom. It may be that these various crises are not the cause but the occasion, the trigger, for the current widespread disorientation which in fact has been present in our cultural tradition, though limited to a very small number of individuals at a high cultural level.

If, for example, the success of the Common Market has led to a current rise in expectations in Western Europe among the laboring and petit bourgeois classes, the explanation may be that the disorientation has not yet reached such classes. At a higher cultural level, however, the future may have already happened. The student uprising at the Sorbonne in the 1960s, occasioned by rising expectations for higher education for more individuals, has led to the abandonment of the intellectual tradition of the Sorbonne. At least so I am assured by friends who are members of the Sorbonne faculty. The government has apparently adopted a policy of neglect, concluding that it is confronted with a problem it cannot solve. One of the great scholars in art history, for example, has done nothing for years but write potboilers. He cannot afford to do anything else. The government attitude toward the Sorbonne seems to reflect that same loss of confidence in dealing with national problems which appears to be characteristic of our own government—a realization that the promises of social and individual fulfillment, supported by continuously rising expectations, cannot be met.

If this is the case, it seems worth considering that the disorientation has spread from a small intellectual elite to the centers of power, or at least to the centers of governmental power, and that the performance of governments (their abandonment of some problems, and their incoherent behavior in the face of other problems) is transmitting that malaise or disorientation to an increasingly wider public. The situation can be put rather neatly, I think, in the rhetoric of slang. It is the traditional boast and task of the ultimately regressive level of social hierarchies that "The buck stops here." The current malaise and disorientation amounts to the perception that the buck doesn't stop anywhere. Thus the 1970s have no name because there is no orientation from which emergent attributes can be perceived, no proposition which can subsume them. What is emergent is disorientation itself.

Now if the buck doesn't stop anywhere, there is no ultimate point at which power and responsibility are identical. Social problems emerge at what one might call the empirical frontier, the social area in which the instructions or directions emanating from the ultimate level of power are put into effect in the active management of individual and interactional behavior. Problems emerge when the directions for such management do not fulfill the purpose of the ultimate level and are in conflict with the validation and explanation of that purpose. Each level of social hierarchy above the empirical frontier attempts to resolve the problem emerging from the inadequacy of the directions, and if it cannot do so passes the problem, or buck, to the next higher level. The problem is supposed to be resolved at the highest level. If it cannot be resolved there, it is then the task of the intellectual elite to so manipulate the rhetoric of explanation and justification —sometimes by bringing in fresh empirical information—that the problem can be resolved. On the basis of this solution, new social managerial directions are issued from the ultimate level and are broken down into more specific levels until the empirical managerial frontier is once again reached. It is the task of the educational establishment, in the largest sense, to disseminate the explanation and justification or validation throughout the society, and in this task the arts are of great importance. Their task is to exemplify the explanatory ideology of problem resolution, and thus to justify or validate that explanation, since exemplification is the rhetoric of making comprehensible, and thus justifying and validating, an explanation. In literary criticism, for example—which is throughout the educational establishment an important aspect of social management—exemplification is regarded as the equivalent of proof, as it is, generally speaking, in ordinary linguistic behavior.

Now just as the the-buck-stops-here syndrome has traditionally obtained in governmental hierarchies, so it has obtained among the intellectual elite, the social task of which is the manipulation of explanation for the purposes of social management. This task, so far as we can tell from the dubious evidence of very ancient history, emerged at least in the Neolithic period, and indeed may have been the emergent social phenomenon of the Neolithic. In ancient Babylonia the grain was stored in temples, and the priests were its immediate guardians. The control of the storage and issuance of grain both for food and planting was thus under the protection of the god. The directions for the use of the grain were explained by the presence of the god and so justified and validated. Two considerations are of great importance in examining this practice: First is the fact that whatever else it may be, "god" is before everything else a word. And as a word, it terminates the explanation and validation of how the grain is to be used. Second, in performing their distributory and sanctifying or justifying rituals, the priests were naked. It would be hard to imagine a more effective way of indicating the distinction between the secular arm, the sanction of which is brute power or force, and the theological (that is the intellectual or explanatory) arm, the sanction of which is a word that terminates explanation, or, to use our valuable metaphor, stops the buck of explanation and the rhetoric of validation and justification.

If, in social management, directions are what manage behavior at the empirical frontier, then the directions from which the empirical directions are derived are meta-directions; and the movement from empirical directions to the ultimate directions issued by the centers of power is a regress of meta-directions. When, as I have suggested, the meta-directions of ultimate power fail, then it is the task of the intellectual establishment to manipulate them. Thus high culture may be defined as the manipulation—and in the high arts, as the exemplification—of the ultimate levels of the meta-directions of social management. However, a further interpretation of the naked Babylonian priests suggests that their nakedness not only separated them from secular power but also defended them from that power. It showed that they were under the protection of the god and thus they did not require the protection of their own wielding of force. That is, since the task of the intellectual establishment, in requiring manipulation of the explanatory-validational ideological language, necessarily requires innovation, its relation to the centers of power cannot be merely subordinate; it must be equal, even though economically parasitic, like the high arts. Its relation to the centers of power is a relation of symbiosis.

Nevertheless, it is an uneasy symbiosis. As I have suggested, the task of ultimate regressive levels of explanation is frequently innovation. The result is that power seeks to control the direction of innovation, and frequently to prevent it; while explanation needs independence to generate new explanations and relate them to ultimate explanations, i.e., to terminating meta-directions. Further, explanation frequently perceives the failures of the ultimate meta-directions of power when power itself resists that perception. The great Hohenstaufen emperor Frederick II, struggling with the papacy in order to make power independent of theological explanation and ultimately to desecularize the papacy, turned to the jurists of Bologna and elsewhere to provide the material for a new code of laws. Simultaneously he encouraged scholarship, poetry, and the various visual arts, as well as music and dancing, in order to establish a secular high culture and its exemplification independent of the explanatory system of the Church. Indeed, so full of the struggle between high culture and high power are histories of Europe and its various parts that one is inclined to conclude that one of the great tasks of European historians, as members themselves of high explanatory culture, has been continuously to exemplify the desirability of the independence of power and explanation. It is not surprising that they, as members of the high meta-directional establishment, seem to take every opportunity to underline the imposition of explanatory criticism upon high power, both in speculative treatises and in actual interaction and conflict between representatives of the two activities.

Now until about 170-odd years ago the regress of explanation was marked by the the-buck-stops-here syndrome, the termination of a high explanatory mode by an absolute truth. The term "god," of course, has been until recently the terminating word, and still is, except for a relatively small group. Much of the explanation provided by power still employs a deistic rhetoric—a continuation into the present time, especially during wars and other severe national crises, of a cultural condition in which the only explanatory mode available was theological. Since the eighteenth century, "nature" has been popular, as have such associated words as "instinct," the "unconscious," and "racial unconscious" (perhaps the most deliciously comic of all). "Science" too functions this way. In philosophy, particularly the philosophy of science, the terms "logical" and "logic" are frequently employed to terminate a regress of explanatory meta-directions. A curious and, to my mind, on the whole adequate direction of logic for this role is to be found in a recent statement by J. Bronowski, author of a book about Blake and of Science and Human Values; he is Associate Director of the Salk Institute, a man equally at home in the humanities, the arts, and the sciences.

The ideal of science is (in principle) to present a model of nature as a closed system of laws or axioms, from which the phenomena of the real world could all be shown to derive. However, it has now become clear that this ideal cannot be attained, either in practice or in principle. Modern theorems in logic make it evident that any system of axioms which seeks to describe nature will always be found to be incomplete.

Thus the system of science at any time is provisionally closed in the present, yet it necessarily remains open to the future. From time to time, a great scientific mind becomes convinced that a new phenomenon cannot be derived by any rearrangement within the accepted system of laws; and he then enlarges (and modifies) the system by proposing an additional law or axiom. Modern logic shows that this step cannot be supported by any logical procedure. It is an act of imagination, which takes the mind beyond the action of any logical machine; and it can in fact be taken as a definition of imagination, both in the sciences and in the arts.

The mind is forced to go beyond logic because a logical machine is circumscribed by the contradictions that arise when it uses its language to describe its own actions.

The notion of science which Bronowski presents in this opening sentence is one still widely accepted and is an excellent example of remote explanatory regress. But as the phrase "closed system of laws or axioms" makes clear, science itself is subsumed under the more explanatory validation of logic. But Bronowski, inspired I suppose by Gödel's law, rejects logic as an explanatory termination. Innovation, he asserts, transcends logic and is a still more regressive activity. Moreover, beyond innovation, in a further stage of regress from "the phenomena of the real world," he places the imagination.

I trust that there is not a humanist today who does not experience a shudder of delight at the appearance in such a context of the word "imagination," so sacred to him. Now I would not for a moment deny that there is no difference between the scientific imagination and the artistic imagination, but otherwise, to my mind, Bronowski—in appealing to the imagination—hasn't said a thing. Rather he has simply used the word as it is now currently used, to validate an innovation. Imagination was once not a particularly sacred word. By the end of the eighteenth century, it meant the exemplification in the arts of an already existent explanatory mode, in an innovative manner. When, however, reason achieved its independence from the theological control, the dangerously innovative powers of the imagination were termed the results of a disordered imagination. Coleridge, however, asserted that the exemplification of the categories of the understanding was a function, not of the imagination, but of the mere fancy; and the imagination was elevated, as with Bronowski, to a position above the reason, although Bronowski, more sophisticated and modern, places it above logic—that is, regressive beyond logic. Now I think we do indeed innovate regressive explanations that transcend logic, but I also think that such innovation is frequently in error. And by error I merely mean that it cannot be made coherent with the current remote explanatory mode, either by incorporation in that mode or by modification of it. Acceptance of it would involve too great a sacrifice of what is continuing to work as a fairly effective explanatory mode. An act of imagination in Bronowski's sense is to my mind neither more nor less than a validated innovation. Error and creativity (for Bronowski's use of "imagination" exploits the connection between "imagination" and "creativity") are both the result of the identical process of innovation. Whether it is dubbed creative or in error is a consequence of the social process, the process of social management. Bronowski has done no more than to validate his notion that logic is sometimes fruitfully transcended or violated by employing a word made sacred, principally in the arts, in the past 170 years. "Sacred" is indeed the proper adjective for words that terminate explanatory regresses, for it transfers an attribute of the original terminating term "God" to its heirs and rivals.

The passage I have been quoting goes on as follows:

The human brain, of course, cannot escape these problems of self-reference, which are implied from the beginning in *Cogito ergo sum*. Science is a procedure for circumventing these problems by pushing them (as it were) into the future; that is, by always treating the present system as provisionally closed. But the arts cannot make this separation, even provisionally; the writer, for example, sets out to share his state of mind with the reader, and literature owes its power to this self-reference. This is why science can be treated as a machine for turning information into (provisional) instructions for action, and the arts cannot: Through them we enter nature as a pure state of information.

I shall ignore what he says here about the arts, for I find it utterly untenable, and shall turn rather to what is of immediate use at this point: "science" as "a machine for turning information into (provisional) instructions for action." From what I have said about social hierarchies and their generation of directions for action at the empirical frontier, and about the necessity for regressive problem-solving when those directions turn out to be ineffective, I think that what Bronowski says about science applies equally well to such hierarchies. And I also think that the relation between such a hierarchy as a closed system and the high regressive explanation when the closed system is forced open by what I might as well call negative feedback is the same as Bronowski's relation between science as a closed system validated by logic and the imagination when the scientific closed system is forced open by negative feedback—by a "new phenomenon" which "cannot be derived by any rearrangement within the accepted system of laws."

A system of hierarchially regressive meta-directions in social institutions is a matter of linguistic behavior, and so is a hierarchially regressive explanation in a scientific system. When a closed social hierarchy is forced open by a new phenomenon, it has to change its laws; and worth noting is the metaphorical extension of social laws to scientific laws in the quotation from Bronowski. To change its laws a hierarchy must open itself to innovation; it is—by the demands of the situation and the revelation of its inadequacy—condemned to innovation. Thus it turns to the high or remote meta-directional establishment, as time after time the American government, in the past fifty years, has turned in times of national crisis to the universities. Frequently, however, it is not genuine innovation that is required or is forthcoming, but merely rhetorical manipulation. Thus, in appealing to the imagination to terminate his explanatory regress, Bronowski has innovated nothing. He has merely validated a certain kind of scientific innovation by employing a sacred rhetoric. If we consider "sacred" not statistically but dynamically, the word to use is "redemptive." Thus the the-buck-stops-here syndrome considered as a process is, I think, properly understood as a redemptive process. But since I mean by "redemptive" something a little different from what is usually meant, it is necessary to develop the term a bit.

I think it is no longer possible—at least it is no longer possible for me—to accept an immanent theory of meaning. Upon this rock I would build my heretical church, that the meaning of a term is the response to the term. One corollary of this is that the notion of immanent reference must likewise be abandoned.

It is idle to say that such-and-such an expression refers to so-and-so. When we make such statements, what we are doing is saying that it ought so to refer, and that if the other party in the discussion does not accept that normative assertion, then either discussion must cease or the normative assertor will use all the social forces under his control, including physical force if he controls that, to make the dissenting party accept that definition of the reference of the term in question. The explanation for this is that if the meaning of a term is the response to that term, then all possible terms are capable of eliciting but a single response, and every individual term is capable of eliciting all possible responses. Now this, of course, is precisely what does not happen, and the fact that it does not happen is responsible for the illusions of immanent meaning and immanent reference. However, if those guardians of remote meta-directions—such as philosophers—would observe what they are doing, instead of just doing it, they could scarcely fail to notice that what they are busy about is the limitation of response to remote explanatory terms: that epistemology, for example, is a normative linguistic undertaking. Social interaction, then, including interaction with oneself as a social dyad, can be defined as the limitation of response.

The explanation for this lies in the brain itself. It is not like a telephone exchange, but something infinitely more complex. However it works, the result is that it is impossible to learn anything precisely but the most simple sequence of behavior, and perhaps not even that. We may learn a sequence of seven digits exactly—and that is as much as most of us can remember—but even such a sequence is learned, like every sequence, by a process of perceptual reduction and simplification and abstraction. The consequence, as the anthropologist George Barnett pointed out a quarter of a century ago, is that innovation is the norm of human behavior. Thus, the transmittal of a validated pattern of behavioral response to a group of individuals, or to a single individual over time, always involves a spread of deviation from the norm. A sign, whether verbal or not, is a configuration to which a norm of response has been validated. Thus, interaction may be more adequately defined as the limitation of sign-response. To employ the metaphor of channel and delta, response is always threatened with a delta-like spread of deviation which must be countered by channeling. Channeling of patterns of response through time is social management. Now as I have suggested, innovation can be and usually is categorized as error or creativity. This in turn leads us to what I hope is a fairly precise notion of redemption. If the individual is returned from deviancy and error to the socially validated norm of that behavior, he is redeemed. On the other hand, when the inadequacy of the norm is revealed by negative feedback, and if a modified or emergent norm is the consequence of innovation, then that innovation is called redemptive. Whatever the explanations for the spread of Christianity, they all amount to the notion that for a large class of individuals in the Roman Empire the norms were perceived as ineffective and that Christianity offered redemption from that ineffectiveness. Why those norms were perceived as ineffective we cannot know; we can only offer verbal explanations at a fairly remote level of explanatory or meta-directional regress: that is, at the level of high culture.

The important, the central, attribute of redemption is that it terminates a kind of behavior. Either it terminates behavior that is deviant from the norm, or it terminates a social ineffectiveness, or it terminates a meta-directional, explanatory regress. It stops the buck. Something is settled, just as Bronowski seems to have imagined he had settled something when he dragged in the redemptive term "imagination." Either we go to heaven, a place where there is no innovation in sign response, and thus no need for social management (hell being a place where we are condemned to fruitless innovating attempts to escape from suffering, a place which redeems the nondeviant from the contaminating influence of the deviant); or a problem is terminated by the exercise of power, which is ultimately the only sanction for limiting response; or we terminate an explanation by finding a ground for the universe. Just as the illusion of meaning and reference is the consequence of the only partially successful, but continuous, effort to limit the response to words, so the illusion of redemptive finality is the consequence of the effort to limit response to all signs, to all instructions or directions, verbal or nonverbal. The effort focuses, even fixates, our attention; for the effort is to stabilize interaction, to make interaction predictable, without which social interaction is impossible. Since innovation is the norm of actual behavior, interaction is continuously threatened with nonpredictability. Redemptive modes of verbal and non-verbal behavior thus become our primary interest, and redemption becomes our primary goal.

Yet I believe that the task of post-modern man is to be anti-redemptive. Not that antiredemption is entirely novel. For one thing, as I have attempted to demonstrate in *Man's Rage for Chaos* (New York: Schocken, 1967), artistic behavior has always been antiredemptive, in the sense that it is, above all, the re-hearsal for the tolerance of tension; if nothing else, art makes the redemptive itch more endurable. The tradition of philosophi-cal scepticism is reasonably old. Plato himself can be interpreted as sceptical. Still scepticism itself always has redemption lurking in the background. If it questions the reliability of what purports to be knowledge, it does not question the reliability of its ques-tions. Scepticism is a useful dissolvent of redemptive explanations which are losing the power of rhetorical manipulation and inno-vation, but it is a verbal activity carried on at a level of meta-directions remote from the empirical frontier. It does not, in Bronowski's phrase, turn information into instructions for action. It is useful only for releasing remote explanatory innovation.

No, the antiredemptive tradition is to be found, not in scepti-cism, but in modern science as the most complete model of nega-tive feedback. I cannot agree with Bronowski's picture of the idea of science. Not only is it now "clear that this ideal cannot be attained, either in practice or in principle"; I do not think that rearrangements within the accepted system of the laws of a science are accomplished only from time to time by great scien-tific minds. On the contrary, modern science for the past seventy years has developed a heuristic conception of scientific models or theories. At least as long as fifty years ago George Herbert Mead recognized this, when he said that a scientist can be happy only when he finds his theory to be wrong. Instead of resisting the instability of theory—that is, of ultimate explanation—the modern scientist aims at exploiting that instability. That is why, I think, ever since the revolution in physics of seventy years ago, science has made such astonishing advances. Looked at from a sufficiently distant, historically sweeping, and comprehensive point of view, human behavior has proceeded by continuously modifying its ultimate levels of social management—the centers of power, and the explanatory systems which validate that power. However, that modification has always been resisted, and except for a tiny number of human beings even now is still resisted.

The scientific revolution of the seventeenth century amounted to a decision to interpret theory as a set of directions, the theoretical justifications for which were to be modified by nonverbal performance. That is the heart of the experimental method. Yet that interpretation was incoherent with the justification of scientific activity by ultimate explanatory truths, still dependent, even though remotely, upon the rhetoric of theology. Since then, the only philosophy worthy of the name has been the philosophy of science. Staggered by Hume, Kant saw the problem of knowledge as an irresolvable tension between subject and object. Now it is possible to see it as an irresolvable dialect between directions— or culture—and performance. This, it seems to me, is genuinely antiredemptive. Thus the post-Kantian tradition—nor was Kant alone in arriving at his position—which I identify with the Romantic tradition, has sought to escape from redemptive explanatory ideology. Romantic art steadily grew in its anti-explanatory character, steadily developed resources to exemplify, not redemptive explanation, but antiredemptive anti-explanation itself. It is not accidental that the revolutionary physicists of seventy years ago grew up in Romantic culture. By mastering the principles and techniques of social alienation, the Romantics discovered the path to cultural transcendence. Under the umbrella of the explanatory but nearly meaningless term "imagination," which they rendered meaningless by continuous redefinition, they built the validation of innovation into Romantic culture. That is, they justified in the most shameless manner whatever they wanted to do by a rhetorical but heuristic manipulation of the word "imagination." Bronowski's appeal to "imagination" indicates that he is still bemused by the sacredness of a word which the Romantics, scarcely knowing what they were doing, made sacred.

Until very recently, this conception of explanation as acceptable only if regarded as heuristic has been confined to an extremely small group. However, the movements and outbreaks of the 1960s were so evidently redemptive and so evidently failures, and the various crises of the 1970s—none of which yet offer any real hope for resolution—have been, I believe, the occasion for that spreading of the abandonment of the redemptive ideal, which is, I think, the disorientation of the present. Simultaneously, the antiredemptive concept of validation and explanation is spreading from an intellectual elite. A situation has arisen which improves its chances for reaching a segment of the population large enough to create a critical mass.

But this would not be the case were it not for another factor. Simultaneous with the development of the Romantic tradition and rooted in the same scientific revolution of the seventeenth century has grown up another institution, a nongovernmental institution, as increasingly free of the government of nation-states as the Romantic tradition has been increasingly free of reliance upon government-supported explanatory ideologies. Just as Romanticism protected itself with the doctrine of the imagination, so this institution protected itself with the equally empty dogma of the invisible hand: the belief that attention to economic self-interest is socially beneficial, and that profit, which is quantitatively measurable, is proof of social benefit. I refer, of course, to the American business corporation, which is the most complete institutional model of the scientific enterprise and therefore of the human enterprise. Its dangerous aspect, of course, is its confusion of institutional success with social benefit. Whether some other measure of institutional success than profit can be created I do not know, though there is reason to think that "profit" is becoming an increasingly meaningless word.

In terms of institutional effectiveness, the American business corporation has been the most extraordinary success in human history. I think, and I am not alone in thinking so, that the international corporation, which is the development of the national corporation, is going to transcend the nation-state. The abandonment by governments of what are supposed to be their problems is, I suspect, an indication of what is happening. It is perhaps the same kind of political development that occurred when the

nation-state transcended feudalism. Our malaise, our disorientation, arises in part, I believe, from the fact that we are vaguely
aware that this transcendence of the nation-state is the emergent
political situation. Moreover, the alliance between science and the
international corporation is now firmly sealed. They fit together
like hand and glove. Further, a heuristic conception of explanation cannot be socially effective unless it is in symbiosis with a
heuristic conception of power. The history of high corporate levels
suggests very strongly that such a conception of power is coming
to be part of corporate culture.

I would like to make two final points. One has to do with the
arts. Should the international corporations become the centers of
ultimate power regress, then the arts in the Romantic tradition—
that is, the high and avant-garde arts of today—will return to
their traditional task of exemplifying the explanatory mode which
validates power, only now it will be an anti-explanatory mode
which they exemplify, a heuristic mode. Often enough what goes
on in the arts is a hint of the future, and for more than ten years
the arts have been increasingly concerned, not with creating permanent works of art that will have an eternal redemptive value,
but with disposable art that has as almost its sole function the
creation of disorientation. What has been the covert task of art
may become, has become, its overt task.

The second point is that I by no means regard the transcendence of the nation-state as a necessarily progressive step. The
corporation's model is science, and the heuristic conception of
science, responsible for its great triumphs in the twentieth century, has been anything but an unmixed blessing. The social
damage it has done has been enormous, so enormous that one
wonders if it has done anything of real social value. But since
both the corporation and modern science are the model of human
history, then one wonders if the history of man has been beneficial to man. But this is something we cannot know. The human
mind is circumscribed by the contradictions that arise when it
tries to describe itself. Perhaps our growing awareness of this is
the real source of our malaise.

Nevertheless, Pollyanna that I am, I can see one bright spot.
In the past, the task of power has been to decrease the tension

between directions and performance. Otherwise, it was thought, no performance would be possible. But this may be a mistake. A heuristic use of power will increase that tension. The task of social management will not be to reduce problem awareness, but to increase it. Its purpose will not be to attempt to eliminate negative feedback, but to magnify it. If a problem-oriented and antiredemptive society replaces one oriented toward problem solution and redemption, then human history will lose, perhaps, some of its infinite stupidity.

Index

Acton, Lord John, 329
Adam, Robert, 46
Addison, Joseph, 42
Aggression, 23
Ainsworth, William Harrison, 41, 117
Alienation, 21, 37–39, 44, 88–89, 124, 137–38, 145, 157–58, 199, 306–9, 311, 312, 327, 346
Amateurism, 197, 322
American Revolution, 68
Analogy, 62–63, 65, 259
Anti-intellectualism, 322–24
Antirole, 57
Architecture, nineteenth-century, 46–48
Aristocracy, attributes of, 268–69, 277
Aristotle, 218–19
Arnold, Matthew, 76, 127, 358, 359
Art, 81, 213–14, 227, 294, 344–45, 359, 371, 375; Abstract Expressionism, 75, 348; addiction to, 307, 344, 345; avant-garde, 31, 75; concept, 220, 348; contemporary, 75; destruction of, 31; exemplification of, 75–76, 348, 359, 377–78; irresponsibility of, 218–19, 308–9; "kleenex," 221; mini, 348; museum, 211; Op, 348; and order, 310; Pop, 221, 348; and religion, 208–11, 220–21; semantic aspects of, 102; and value, 303, 311
Art Nouveau, 74, 91

Bach, Johann Sebastian, 5
Balzac, Honoré de, 50–52, 65–66, 73, 84
Baptists, Bible-Belt, 14
Barry, Sir Charles, 48
Baudelaire, Charles, 48
Beethoven, Ludwig van, 5, 78
Behavior, 140–42, 215, 271–72, 297; channeling, 86–88, 327, 357, 374; collecting as, 299; conventionalized, 9; deviant, 84–88, 205, 216–18, 219–20, 251, 373–74; drug use as, 300–301, 343–44; innovation as, 85–88, 243; and interaction rate, 88–89; interest as, 300, 343; limitation of, 373–74; and power, 275–76; randomization of, 25; scientific, 7, 8; stabilization of, 298–99, 336, 361, 375; theory of, 14–15; verbal, 9, 235
Bible, 344, 359
Blagden, Isa, 110, 117
Blake, William, 28
Boas, F. S., 118
Bourgeoisie, 269, 279
Bronowski, J., 369–72, 374, 375, 376
Browning, Elizabeth Barrett, 109–23
Browning, Robert, 38, 39, 50, 109–25, 132, 259; *Balaustion's Adventure*, 115; *Christmas-Eve and Easter-Day*, 114; and dramatic monologue, 110, 111–13, 120–23, 125, 132; *Dramatis Personae*, 115; "James Lee's Wife," 111; "My Last Duchess,"

ROMANTICISM AND BEHAVIOR

Composed in Linotype Palatino and printed letterpress by Heri-
tage Printers, Inc., Charlotte, North Carolina. The paper on which
the book is printed was supplied by the S. D. Warren Company
and is watermarked with the University of South Carolina Press
colophon. This paper was developed for an effective life of at
least three hundred years. The book was sewn and bound by
Delmar Companies, Inc., also of Charlotte.
The book was designed by Robert L. Nance.